THE
# Writer's
# *Essential*
# Desk
# Reference

## SECOND EDITION

THE
# Writer's
# *Essential*
# Desk
# Reference

## SECOND EDITION

**WRITER'S DIGEST BOOKS**
CINCINNATI, OHIO

00  99  98  97  96    5  4  3  2  1

**Library of Congress Cataloging-in-Publication Data**

　　The writer's essential desk reference — 2nd ed. / edited by Glenda Tennant Neff and Roseann S. Biederman.
　　　　p.　　cm.
　　Rev. ed. of the work under the same title, edited by Glenda Tennant Neff, c 1991.
　　Includes bibliographical references and indexes.
　　ISBN 0-89879-759-4 (hardcover: alk. paper)
　　1. Authorship. I. Neff, Glenda Tennant, 1961-  . II. Biederman, Roseann S. III. Writer's Digest Books (Firm)
　　PN151.W74　　1996
　　808'.02—dc20　　　　　　　　　　　　　　　　　　　　　　96-21730
　　　　　　　　　　　　　　　　　　　　　　　　　　　　　　　　CIP

Edited by Glenda Tennant Neff and Roseann S. Biederman
Cover designed by Angela Lennert Wilcox
Interior designed by Carol Buchanan

# Contents

# About the Authors

**Paula Deimling,** author of "Producing and Polishing It," is a writer and editor whose work has appeared in books, magazines and newspapers. She edited the 1985 and 1986 editions of *Writer's Market* and wrote "The Markets" column for *Writer's Digest* magazine. She works as a columnist for *The Cincinnati Enquirer*'s "Job Market" section and teaches writing and editing at the University of Cincinnati.

**Chris Dodd,** author of "Researching It," is a former markets editor for *Writer's Digest* magazine and has been a freelance writer and editor for the past twenty-six years. She currently writes speeches and provides other editorial support for the president of the Air Line Pilots Association in Washington, D.C.

**Bonnie Gordon,** original author of "Selling It," left Cincinnati in 1990 to return to her native East Coast. She has exchanged the freelance life for a full-time position as editor and video project manager for a national, nonprofit educational organization concerned with issues in legal education. In 1992, she completed an independent video documentary that won a regional award in Cincinnati for cable access productions and was shown at a Los Angeles Poetry & Film Festival. She continues to write fiction, which she has also published and read publicly in Philadelphia. **Robin Gee,** who did the revision of "Selling It," is former editor of *Novel and Short Story Writer's Market.* She is now a freelance writer and editor living in Madison, Wisconsin.

**Fred Kerner,** author of "Writing and Selling in Canada," is a prizewinning author as well as having garnered honors in both editing and publishing. In addition to a wide writing output, prior to his "retirement" he held executive positions with two international news agencies and a half-dozen multinational book publishers. He devotes his time away from the keyboard to assisting writers who have disagreements with publishers (especially in the area of contracts) and is a consultant to a variety of publishers in England, the United States and Canada.

**Glenda Tennant Neff,** author of "A Community of Writers," began her career as a newspaper reporter and editor at *The Clermont Sun* in Batavia, Ohio. She is a former editor of the 1988 to 1991 editions of *Writer's Market,* former assistant editor of *Fiction Writer's Market* and former assistant managing editor of the market books department at F&W Publications. She also holds a master's degree in education from Xavier University and is currently program coordinator for continuing education at the University of Cincinnati-Clermont College.

**Jack Neff,** author of "Living as a Writer," is a freelance writer based in Cincinnati who writes regularly on marketing, legal, financial and other business issues. He is a former newspaper reporter and editor whose work has appeared in *Advertising Age, The Atlanta Constitution* and other national consumer and business publications. He writes a "Business Tips" column for *How,* a magazine for graphic designers. And he is also author of small business books for woodworkers and graphic designers an coauthor of *The Insiders' Guide to Greater Cincinnati.*

# Foreword

The idea was simple enough: We wanted to pull together, in a single volume, the information and resources writers needed most.

Then we began the work, and we found out only the idea was simple.

From talking to a variety of writers we discovered they use—or need—a vast amount of information, ranging from advice on contracts to tips on finding out-of-print books. Writers sometimes find the sources they need, sometimes learn about them from other writers, and other times they simply do as well as they can without any help. They agreed, however, that putting background information and a list of these sources in one place would save them time and make their writing lives more efficient.

We organized this "most desired" information into five sections: Living as a Writer, A Community of Writers, Researching It, Producing and Polishing It, and Selling It. We designed the format with both text and listings to offer information and to guide writers to other books, directories, people and groups that could provide them with more specific information. For Canadian authors, whose needs are often overlooked in U.S.-published books, and those U.S. writers who want to know more about the specialties of the Canadian market, we included a chapter on Writing and Selling in Canada.

Although this is a reference book, we didn't want it to have a dry tone or textbook feel, so we asked six authors to gather and present information as though they were sharing tips from their experience with another writer. In distilling the information, we wanted to keep the writer's viewpoint in mind—and also the viewpoints of writers at different stages of their careers. Tax information is abundantly available, but if you want to know what is most likely to apply to you as a writer, this is the place to look first. It can save you hours paging through tax volumes of general information—whether you are making a little extra as a freelancer, planning to make it full-time or have been working that way for several years. And, depending on where you are in your career, you may want to take advantage of either the section on *choosing* a continuing education class or the section on *teaching* a continuing education class. We tried to look at each chapter this way to give you the information you need throughout your career.

You'll find, of course, that some information overlaps. Many resources can be used for both research and sales, for instance, and many groups offer services in more than one area covered in the book. For that reason, you'll want to make use of the extensive index and the references to other sections within the chapters.

*The Writer's Essential Desk Reference* isn't a substitute for your own research, bookkeeping or promotion efforts. But we hope it will be the *first* source you consult on writing-related matters, one that leads to other sources, provides you with tips you hadn't considered, and generally makes your searches less time-consuming. When valuable books, directories and other information sources are available, we've included the names of these sources. When a comprehensive directory is not available, we've included listings for those people who responded to our request for information. In most sections we also have a sampling of those sources for which we thought writers would be most likely to want information.

Both national and local resources are listed in the book, but you'll undoubtedly find many more on the local level. Be sure you explore these options; they often can provide you with the best value for your money, especially if most of your writing is on the local level.

As you use this book, and other reference books or directories, make it a habit to check information before acting on it. We've tried to include only those directories that are current, but all books with this type of information are subject to the constant changes of the publishing world. Book prices—as well as postage—increase, computer bulletin boards may no longer be available, computer software may be updated and contact people may change from the time we gathered this information until you use it.

Although we've tried to include as much information as possible, we'd also welcome your input about other sources you've found helpful in your writing life. Let us know about books, groups, directories and equipment you've found make your work more efficient and would make this book more useful to other writers.

# CHAPTER 1

# LIVING AS A WRITER

As you turn toward the path of freelance writing, you'll find the way strewn with the horror stories of those who gave up on it. They've scurried back to unpleasant jobs, begged for a place beneath the iron heels of the most imperious bosses. Anything but the poverty and insecurity of freelancing.

They probably didn't fail because they couldn't write well enough. They probably failed because they never grasped that writing is a business, too. The business side of freelancing may be as important to success as the creative side. But it's a lot less appealing. Tending to business seems greedy and pedestrian. It's certainly not what you became a writer for. So it's easy to shove business matters into the bottom drawer. There, they fester until one day they burst into your consciousness in a blaze of uncollected bills and overdue taxes.

Neglecting business can ruin even the most talented writer. But the chorus of moans from freelancers who've failed can drown out the fact that many freelancers make a decent living.

Nothing you've done to perfect your craft will prepare you to live as a freelance writer. The business side of writing is confusing. It takes time, hard work and talent. You don't have to consume yourself with business matters to keep them from eating away your livelihood. But you do need to adopt a businesslike approach and commit yourself to taking the time to handle the business chores.

## FINANCES FOR WRITERS

As you launch a freelance business, setting up a simple budget will make your life easier. Like any budget, it's only a representation of what's going to happen, not the real thing. But it's important to have some idea of what you're going to spend and earn in the coming year and months.

Once you've been freelancing awhile, budgeting gets easier. You have last year's expenses as a basis for this year's planning. You also have some established markets and clients to make your income a little more predictable. But as a beginner, you'll have to try some educated guesswork.

Start by estimating your costs, because you'll need to plan your income based on these. Monthly overhead, or what you must pay whether you have any work or not, should be the first category you calculate. Overhead includes any payments on your computer or other business equipment, rent on any office space or equipment for the business, publications, answering service, an estimate of your out-of-pocket auto expenses, etc.

Some things that you can deduct from your taxable income you don't need to include in your overhead calculation. For instance, you may be able to deduct some of the interest and value of your house. But since you'd be paying it anyway, you need not consider it business overhead for budgeting purposes.

Conversely, there are some nonbusiness expenses you should include in your overhead. These include the costs of your health and disability insurance. If you were an employee, they'd be part of your compensation. So as a freelancer, consider them part of your costs of doing business.

After figuring overhead, take a look at your household budget and calculate the minimum amount you'll need for living expenses. Include your rent, mortgage, car payments, other consumer debt, groceries and the like. Then, subtract from this amount any take-home pay from your spouse, or other sources of steady income.

Financial planners recommend freelancers or any entrepreneurs have two to six months of overhead and living expenses available when they start business. Even if you start with as much work as you can handle, you should still count on two to three months for the checks to appear in your mailbox. One survey by the Editorial Freelancers Association in New York City found that freelancers waited anywhere from a week to a year to get paid, with one or two months being typical. Nationwide surveys by the credit-reporting firm Dun & Bradstreet have found payments becoming slower through both good times and bad during the 1990s.

Ideally, your capital reserve will be in your savings account. If not, you may consider getting a personal line of credit from a bank. For a freelancer, one obvious obstacle to approval for such credit is not having any inventory or significant business assets as collateral. If you have a good credit record or other assets, such as a home with sufficient equity, you may get around this.

Realistically, the start-up costs for a freelance writing business are small enough that most freelancers can get by without borrowing. To finance a computer purchase or simply to have some reserves on hand, the most practical "line of credit" for many freelancers and other one-person start-up businesses is a credit card. If you go that route, it makes sense to apply for a separate credit card for business use (it can still be in your name). Any interest you pay for business purposes is tax deductible that way. And it's a lot easier to do your books with a separate business account. If your card has a grace period, as most do, and you pay your balance every month, your card works like a rolling line of credit with no interest cost whatsoever. If you are planning on carrying a balance, shop around for a card with the lowest rate you can find.

To get a bank loan, you may need to develop a business plan. It's probably not a bad idea to develop one anyway, even if you're not applying for a loan. Your plan should include:

- description of your business, including your background and why your services are unique and valuable to clients in the market
- analysis of the market, including the key characteristics of the publications and clients that will use your services and your competition
- your marketing or sales plan
- an outline of your finances, which will include a balance sheet, cash-flow statement and break-even analysis

If you're turned down for a loan—a distinct possibility—you may be eligible for a government-guaranteed loan through the Small Business Administration.

Even if the SBA doesn't give you a loan, it can give you something that may be more valuable. The Service Corps of Retired Executives (SCORE) is an SBA service that offers business advice to small businesses from retired executives who volunteer their services. They can help steer you through a business plan and other decisions you'll make in starting a business.

## HEALTH INSURANCE

Unless you're a Canadian writer covered by national health insurance or fall under the umbrella of a spouse's medical plan, health insurance will be one of the biggest expenses you'll face as a freelancer. Fortunately, premium increases have moderated in recent years, and options for small businesses and independent entrepreneurs are growing, as some states or insurers have created insurance pools for small businesses.

One option, if you're leaving a job with health benefits, is to continue coverage. Terms of the Consolidated Omnibus Budget Reconciliation Act (COBRA) of 1985 require employers to continue coverage for at least 18 months at their cost plus a 2% administration charge.

The advantage of COBRA is that you can continue a high-quality group plan. One disadvantage is that a year and a half later, you could still have to hunt for your own plan. And if your employer's plan is generous, you can expect to pay a generous premium.

Writers may also have access to group medical plans through writers' or business organizations. Many national and local groups of writers and affiliated professionals offer access to group health insurance. Some offer several choices, including major medical plans with a range of deductibles and health maintenance organizations (HMOs), in which a group of doctors and hospitals provide services.

For organizations that offer health insurance, check the listings in chapter two. Your local chamber of commerce may also have a group plan available to members.

Group plans may offer a discount over getting coverage on your own. But membership in one of the organizations may not guarantee you'll be accepted for coverage. And because states and some cities regulate insurance companies separately, not all group plans are available in all states. You should check with the organization and its insurance carrier for details of the plan, its cost and your eligibility.

Look closely at plans offered by these groups. Most are perfectly acceptable group plans. But some organizations target the self-employed with plans that provide only a fixed amount based on the number of days in the hospital and cover no expenses for outpatient care or physician treatment outside a hospital. If the deal sounds too good to be true, it probably is.

A third option is independent coverage. Such coverage isn't necessarily more expensive than a group plan, but an independent plan may offer lower benefits than an employer group plan. The annual deductible for an employer plan is often $100, with up to 100% of major medical costs covered above that. Most independent plans have deductibles of $500 and copayments of 20% for costs above that.

With independent coverage, your premiums are also based more on your individual risk factors. If you're young and healthy, your prices might be less than for comparable group health insurance. If you're older and have health problems, you're more likely to be charged a higher price or be denied coverage.

Most independent plans don't include frills like dental or optical coverage. And they may cover less than employer group plans for mental health and chemical dependency treatment. The reason for the no-frills approach in most independent plans is something the insurance industry calls "adverse selection." Dental and optical coverage are optional parts of such plans. So most of the people who opt for the coverages are those who need them. That drives the costs sky high and convinces others who don't use the coverages very much to drop them.

Check with local HMOs for independent coverage. HMOs may not be cheaper than standard indemnity insurance, but they may cover more of your expenses, including routine doctor visits and prescriptions with relatively small copayments.

One drawback to independent coverage is that, depending on your state's insurance regulations, you may be vulnerable to cancellation should you develop a lengthy, expensive-to-treat illness. Even if your policy isn't canceled, your premiums may rise precipitously.

Also, most independent coverage will have a waiting period of several months in which treatment for a pre-existing condition won't be covered. Whatever plan you choose, expect it to cost no less than $2,000 a year and possibly $8,000 or more, depending on whether it's an individual, two-person or family plan, and on your age and health.

A minor tax break may provide some consolation. If you're not eligible for coverage under a spouse's plan, you can deduct 25% of your self-employed health insurance costs from your taxable income. This deduction regularly expires and faces tough going for renewal each time, so don't count on it forever. If you don't qualify for this break, you may also be able to deduct insurance premiums and other medicals costs as an itemized deduction—but only when medical costs exceed 7.5% of your taxable income.

The tax treatment of health benefits for the self-employed is, simply put, a raw deal. Employees get health benefits tax free. The self-employed essentially pay tax on their benefits, because they can't deduct them fully. Depending on your circumstances, it may make sense to establish your business as a C corporation, which may allow you to have full deductibility for your health insurance. Of course, you need to balance whether the added accounting and administrative costs of incorporating are worth the tax savings. An accountant can help you evaluate the pros and cons of incorporating.

Your final option is one that many freelancers either choose or are forced to live with—going without coverage. Few people see this option as desirable, for obvious reasons. If you're young, healthy, have no dependents and few assets that creditors could attach, it may be worth the risk.

A less extreme approach is simply to opt for a plan with relatively high deductibles ($1,000 or more per year) and copayments. If you're relatively young and healthy, you'll probably save enough on premiums on such a plan to make up for the higher deductibles. A plan with a high deductible still does what insurance is supposed to do, which is keep you from getting wiped out by a huge medical bill. Most hospitals, physicians and other medical providers will let you pay off what you owe over time if you ask, since it's a lot cheaper than trying to collect it from you through other routes.

One of the best cheap-insurance options, if you can find it, is an HMO or preferred provider organization that will let you in with a high deductible and low premiums. This way, even what you pay the health care providers under your deductible should be charged at HMO or PPO rates rather than the higher rates charged to people who have conventional insurance coverage or who are uninsured.

## OTHER INSURANCE NEEDS

Leaving the ranks of employees also means leaving behind disability insurance in many cases. Unless you get coverage on your own, that could bring financial hardship on top of an extended illness or disabling injury.

"Disability insurance is really important for the self-employed, especially if they're supporting themselves and a family and no one else has an income coming in," says Elaine Bedel, an Indianapolis financial planner.

The self-employed should get a plan that covers the highest possible percentage of income for as long as possible. No insurance company will underwrite a policy that pays 100% of your income, because that would provide no incentive for you to go back to work once you become disabled. But policies may go as high as 80% and as long as 10 years or age 65.

Cost of a disability plan is determined by your age, health, how long you must be disabled before you collect and how long the payout is, Bedel says.

Many writers' organizations offer group disability coverage. Check with your group's membership director and insurance carrier for details of the plan and whether you're eligible. The groups may also offer relatively inexpensive group life insurance that can cover such items as your mortgage and other obligations.

It's important to look at disability plans closely. Some plans cover only a fixed period, so you'd be out of luck and money for a long-term disability. But plans that provide an indefinite-term benefit are costlier.

The difference is between a monthly cost in the single or double digits vs. a monthly premium in the triple digits.

If you work from your home, you should also check with your home or renter's insurance carrier to make sure your business equipment is covered against casualty and loss. If not, you may need to purchase a rider to cover them. Professional liability is another coverage to consider. Unless you operate some kind of storefront operation, your exposure to being sued for "slips-and-falls" and other common business liability suits is fairly minor. Your largest liability exposure is for libel. If your work seems likely to involve you in libel litigation somewhere down the road, you may want to try taking out a separate libel policy through a business insurance agent.

# PLANNING INCOME

The overhead calculation you did earlier is also important in figuring how much you should charge, or at least try to charge, for your services.

To calculate an hourly rate, figure the amount you hope to earn. That may be what you used to make at your old job, or what you'd dream of making at your new one. Then, add in your annual overhead expenses. Divide that figure by the number of "billable" hours you hope to work in a year. Even if you're a full-time freelancer, this won't be all the hours you work. Count on spending at least a quarter of your time doing your books, marketing your services and reading professional publications.

The hourly rate you arrive at is a starting point. Most magazines don't pay by the hour but by the word, inch or article. You can, however, analyze how long an assignment will take and multiply that by your hourly rate. That should be something resembling the fee you agree to for the article or project.

Remember to consider expenses, too. Try to estimate your costs for phone calls, mileage and other out-of-pocket expenses and add them to the fee you negotiate if you won't be reimbursed for them.

Freelance writers, like any independent businesspeople, are subject to market forces. And what the market will bear should be part of your calculations. Check with other freelance writers in your area to find out what they charge. In some cities, groups of freelance writers have done surveys to judge the going rate for various kinds of work. Usually, there's a range in hourly rates from entry-level to experienced writers. Try to judge where in that range your services fall and charge accordingly.

Don't charge more than you can get, but don't underestimate yourself either, even if you are just starting out. Lowball pricing may get you a few jobs. But it will hurt your image with clients and editors.

Once you've begun to establish yourself with some markets, try to estimate how much each one will pay you over the course of a year. You'll also want to take a shorter-term view. Keep a sheet or a computer file that lists your assignments or jobs for this month and two months down the road. Estimate how much each one will pay you and total your estimate. Though you can't do much now about this month, you can at least look at your projections for the following months and start marketing to meet your income goals.

# RECORDS AND ACCOUNTS

Nobody becomes a freelance writer to do bookkeeping. But freelancers quickly find it becomes an important part of their jobs.

Financial planners recommend you set up a separate checking account and credit for your business. That may help keep you from tapping business funds for personal needs. And it will provide clearer documentation of your self-employment income and deductible expenses. The Internal Revenue Service doesn't require separate accounts, but it does require you keep basic records of your income and expenses.

The basis of your recordkeeping system should be a daily log of income and expenses. All you really need is a simple, single-entry record-keeping system, as opposed to the more complicated double-entry acounting format used by larger businesses. In any business supply store, you can find a plain accountant's ledger or a bookkeeping record that will do a passable job.

If you're more comfortable keeping records on your personal computer, your local computer store should have a wide array of software that can do the job. Some more sophisticated programs will also help separate expenses according to client, track billable hours and bill clients. Depending on your level of computer know-how, you can also customize a recordkeeping system using a spreadsheet program.

If you do keep business records on a computer, that's one more reason to make backup copies of the data on your computer daily. That will prevent a bad floppy disk or a hard disk crash from destroying the records that can't be replaced.

You'll also need to develop a system for saving your receipts. It can be a series of shoe boxes, envelopes or tin boxes. Receipts can be organized by week or month or by their category. For instance, you may want to keep one envelope or box for auto expenses, another for office supplies, etc. Any system can work. Just keep in mind that you may have to show these receipts to an IRS auditor—so you'll want to be able to find them easily.

You need some kind of documentation for every transaction you hope to deduct. That can be a canceled check, a credit card slip or a cash receipt. Each receipt should also correspond to a dated entry in your records briefly describing what you bought and, if it's not obvious, the business purpose. You may also want to write the business purpose for the transaction on your receipt, check or credit card slip.

Since you'll probably deduct auto expenses on your tax form, you'll need a mileage log to substantiate them. The log must show the date of each trip, the beginning and ending mileage, and the business purpose for the trip. You should keep the log in your car and transfer information from it to your general records regularly.

Entertainment expenses require particularly stringent documentation. Each entertainment entry for these must show who was entertained and the business purpose for the meeting.

If you use a computer or a portable phone, you may need to keep an additional set of documentation on the business use of those items. These records should show the number of business and personal hours for each day. You'll also need additional documentation if you plan to deduct home-office expenses, such as a daily calendar that substantiates business use of the home and photos showing how the office is set up.

If you've got several clients, particularly national publications, long-distance phone calls can quickly become difficult to track come billing time. Even if you start marking up your phone bill as soon as it arrives, remembering why you called Pasadena five Mondays ago can be difficult.

Here are some ideas for making your job easier:

- If your phone company offers dial-one long-distance service, you can put different clients on different long-distance services. Calls you make for one client can be on your main long-distance company. You can make calls for other clients on competing long-distance lines by dialing an access code instead of 1 before the number. Dialing 10222 instead of 1, for instance, puts you through to MCI's lines. That gives you a way to divide your calls four ways, by AT&T, MCI, Sprint and Allnet.
- A slightly more expensive method is getting Call Accounting service for your business line. This allows you to dial a two-digit code that can separate your long-distance bill for up to 100 accounts.

- Keep a phone log, either on paper or on your computer, listing the number, person called, date, time and length of every call you make.

When calculating and billing your phone expenses, don't forget about taxes and directory assistance charges.

Federal, state and local excise taxes on long-distance phone service can increase your bill by as much as 10%, depending on where you live. To find out the tax rate in your area call your local phone company, or calculate it by dividing the tax line on your bill by the total long-distance charges.

Directory assistance charges, which are also taxed, can cost as much as $.75 each and add up quickly. They may not be itemized on your phone bill like long-distance calls, but you can keep a log of directory assistance calls if you need to itemize them when you bill publishers or other clients.

You'll have to find a safe place to keep all these records you've accumulated for at least two years. The IRS strongly recommends you keep all records for as long as the period of limitations for audits. In most cases, that's three years from the date the return was filed or two years from when the tax was paid, whichever is later.

Keep records documenting income for six years after the return was filed. That's the period of limitations the IRS has for going after unreported income that's greater than 25% of the amount shown on the return.

You'll need records for the cost of your home or improvements for as long as you own the home if you take the home-office deduction. Also, you must keep records of items for which you claim depreciation, such as cars, for as long as you depreciate them, plus the three years after you file your return. For more on depreciation and home-office expense, see the tax section of this chapter.

# TRACKING INCOME

Expenses are only half of what you'll be tracking. You'll also need to record income as you receive it and keep check stubs that support the income entries in your books.

Most publishers and other clients will report your earnings as an independent contractor to the IRS and send you a Form 1099 showing the amount. Your income records are important for comparing to the amounts reported on 1099s. And they will also document income not reported on a Form 1099 because you received too little from that source to qualify.

If you've been bartering with other businesses, receiving goods or services rather than cash in return for your services, you must also report what you receive in barter. The law requires you to report the fair market dollar value of what you receive. You can deduct from that amount any out-of-pocket expenses involved in your part of the transaction. But you can't deduct the cost of your labor.

Tax experts provide one additional word of caution. If you're self-employed and your bank account swells far beyond your reported income, that may pique the curiosity of an IRS auditor. So you should also document any nonbusiness income, such as gifts, savings or lottery winnings, that aren't part of your earnings. If you have cash or personal purchases that can't be accounted for from your earnings, and you don't have any record of legitimate sources for your windfall, you could end up paying additional taxes and penalties.

It's best to try to keep your bookkeeping system simple. As long as your system clearly documents your income and your expenses, you don't need much else for tax purposes. Ideally, recordkeeping should take you no more than an hour or two a week, even if you're a full-time freelancer.

# GOING WITH THE (CASH) FLOW

That first big check from your freelance efforts, or any check at all, will be a thrill. But don't get carried away. "We all have a tendency when that fat check comes in to think we're rich," Oberst says. "You're really not, because there's going to be a lean period."

Dealing with the choppy seas of cash flow takes a level head and a disciplined approach. Financial planners suggest putting yourself on a salary as one method that may help. If you incorporate your business, you'll have to start paying yourself a salary.

"It depends on the discipline of the individual," says Bedel. "Probably, a person should set a maximum that he or she will take out in any month. Of course, there should also be a minimum amount."

For tax purposes, it doesn't matter whether you hold the money in a personal account or a business account, unless you've incorporated. But it could have an important psychological effect.

"Some people, if they allow themselves free access to all that they bring in, end up spending it all," Bedel says.

# ESTIMATED TAXES

Living from check to check can be particularly dangerous because it can leave you in an immense hole on April 15. Freelancers don't have any taxes withheld from their income. As a result, they can be in for a big shock the first time they tally their taxes.

The self-employed are liable for paying estimated taxes quarterly once their net earnings exceed $500. If you owe the IRS more than $500 when you file your return, you may be subject to a penalty for underpayment of estimated tax. To avoid this, track your income and expenses so that you can document exactly when you began turning a profit. And get a copy of Form 1040-ES from your library or the IRS to calculate and make your estimated payments.

The IRS expects you to make a good faith effort to estimate your annual income, even though you're estimating it early in the year. And in most cases, the IRS expects you to pay the tax due on your income in four equal payments. The IRS assumes earnings came in an even flow, unless you can document otherwise.

You'll be safe from paying any penalties if you pay estimated taxes equal to at least 100% of your prior year's taxes or 90% of what you owe for this year. If you can't estimate this year's income accurately, a safe bet is to pay a sum equal to last year's tax liability in four installments.

Your state and city may also have rules requiring withholding. If your taxes exceed a certain amount when you file your return, you could also be forced to pay a penalty at this level, too. So you should also contact state and city tax officials to get appropriate tax forms.

To be safe, put aside 33% of your net earnings from self-employment each month. Those savings should cover your federal income and self-employment taxes plus state and local income taxes. Try to track when you reach the 28% federal income tax bracket and start putting aside 50% after that. Your tax return has a table near the back that shows the cutoff points.

While underpaying estimated taxes can bring an IRS penalty, overpaying brings another penalty. You lose interest on any money you pay the IRS before it's required. So pay the least allowed. For instance, if your income is up this year from last, just pay 100% of last year's tax liability and bank the rest until April 15. But if you're likely to spend any money you have, it's probably better to pay the IRS now. Otherwise, you may have to borrow later to pay your taxes.

# LEVELING OUT CASH FLOW

Systematically dealing with estimated taxes is one of the best ways freelancers can avoid cash-flow problems. A few other strategies may also help.

Marketing is a crucial element. There's nothing like regular work to provide regular cash. Developing a few key accounts, preferably large and reliable enough to cover your overhead and basic living expenses, is important. It's all the better if these accounts provide assignments as well as fielding queries from you, so it's not always your burden to come up with ideas.

Once you have such accounts, however, don't become complacent. Nothing lasts forever, so don't let any one account become more than a third of your business. If you want to avoid cash-flow problems down the road, keep working on developing new clients, large and small.

Incorporating a marketing strategy into your routine is also important. That means sending out queries or contacting potential clients even when you're busy. If you market only when things are slow, you may put yourself on a psychological and financial roller coaster—sending queries one month, getting assignments the next, and then waiting for the checks during another slow month. Try to set aside at least one day a month for marketing, even during the busiest times.

Once you're selling your work, you should meticulously track accounts receivable; that is, what publishers and other clients owe you. Unless you write a lot of low-paying articles or you've delved into a retail aspect of the business, such as résumé writing, this is a fairly easy task. You probably won't have more than 10 accounts at a time that owe you money. Find a way to record who owes you money, how much it is and when it's due on a weekly basis. To the extent possible, arrange payment on your terms. The norms vary widely depending on what you're doing. Book authors have the strong advantage of receiving advances, something article writers rarely enjoy. But you may be able to get some money up front for copywriting jobs, or even expense money up front from magazines.

For article writers, publications that pay on acceptance are obviously more desirable than those that pay on publication. If you're getting paid on publication, you could wait months for your article to be published, and at least a month after that to get paid. If paid on acceptance, you should get paid within a month of your final rewrite, no matter when the article is published.

Some writers refuse to work for pay on publication. While this is a principled stand for writerdom, it can crimp your marketing prospects. Payment on publication isn't so bad if you can develop a long-term relationship with a publication that will publish your work regularly and pay promptly. A publisher who pays promptly after publication is always better than one that allegedly pays on acceptance but strings you along for months with niggling rewrites and excuses.

Whatever payment cycle you ride, fast action is the key to good cash flow. "The quicker you move to collect, the greater the chance it will not become a lengthy account receivable," Oberst says.

Some other billing and business practices that should improve your cash flow:

- Incorporate billing into your weekly schedule.
- Bill as soon as payment is due, sending an invoice with your manuscript.
- Tabulate your phone and other expenses as soon as you can after the bill comes and send out expense bills to publishers.
- Send late notices or call when payment isn't received within 30 days.
- In most cases, you won't know how good a publisher's or client's payment practices are until they owe you money. So don't let a new, unproven account run up huge tabs before you get paid.

# CREDIT-CHECKING TIPS

Dun & Bradstreet, virtually the only source for comprehensive credit reports on businesses, is probably too expensive for most writers. But there are some informal ways to get a feel for how creditworthy a publication is.

First, look at a sample copy, and preferably several, before you do any work. Editors routinely advise writers to do this anyway. Their goal is to help you to mold your work to their format. But you also should do it to protect yourself.

Editorial quality is one sign of business integrity. If a publication shortchanges its readers, what makes you think it won't shortchange its writers, too? Some danger signs are headlines that promise what articles don't deliver and articles that are misleading, overhyped and underresearched. Look at the masthead, too. Who's the publisher? Does it list an address or just a post office box? Look also for contributing editors—freelancers who contribute regularly to the publication. Having contributing editors is one sign that a publication treats freelancers well enough to keep them coming back.

If still you have doubts, call and ask to be put in contact with one or more of the contributing editors. Ask them about the publication's payment practices.

Also look for bylines. Do writers seem to have bylines for several consecutive months and then drop out of sight? If so, it could be a sign they aren't getting paid. You may want to contact one of these writers to find out about the publication's payment practices.

Finally, count how many pages of advertising the publication has this month compared to preceding months and the same months the previous year. If the ad pages are slipping seriously, it could be a sign of a failing publication. Also check who advertises. Are the advertisers reputable companies?

These aren't scientific methods that will always keep you out of hock. But they are prudent steps that can steer you away from a few freelance sinkholes.

# SAVING FOR THE FUTURE

Once the cash starts flowing, it's time to start thinking about your future. As a freelance writer, you won't have an employer-sponsored pension plan. Social Security may, at best, pay a third of what you'll need to maintain your standard of living in retirement. Sure, you'll still be able to write in your retirement years. But you still will need some other savings if you hope to maintain your standard of living.

Self-employed writers have options that allow tax-free accumulation of retirement income and current deductions from taxable income. Your options include an ordinary Individual Retirement Account, a Simplified Employee Pension (SEP)-IRA, or a Keogh plan.

You may not qualify to deduct your contributions to regular IRAs if your spouse is covered by a pension plan or your earnings exceed certain limits. But a SEP-IRA isn't so restricted and provides the same benefits. Even if you have a pension from another job, you can set up a SEP-IRA for your earnings from self-employment and deduct your contribution to the plan from your current taxable income.

Each year, you can deduct up to 15% of your taxable self-employment income through SEP-IRA contributions, but only after you subtract the SEP-IRA contribution from that amount. The maximum actually comes down to about 13%. Also, your yearly contribution can't exceed $30,000 (a ceiling most freelancers won't have to worry about).

Under a Keogh plan, you have two options. A money-purchase plan requires you to contribute a fixed percentage of your income every year—up to 25%. With a profit-sharing Keogh you can put in as much or as little as you want each year. But you're limited to the same 13% of self-employment income as with a SEP-IRA. With either Keogh setup, you're also subject to the $30,000 annual limit.

The major advantages of these plans are that you can both deduct your contributions from current taxable income and accumulate interest tax free. At 8% interest, a $2,000 investment you make this year becomes more than $20,000 in 30 years.

But there are, of course, drawbacks:

- If you withdraw money from the plan before you reach age 59½, you're subject to a 10% penalty as well as the tax due on what you withdraw. You can withdraw the money in small amounts calculated to last the rest of your life and not pay the penalty, but still pay tax on your annual withdrawal.
- All this money is taxable when you take it out. But if you're in a lower tax bracket then, you've come out ahead. Plus, tax-free interest accumulation has left you with a lot more money than you'd have had saving the money without the plan.
- You must start to withdraw the money and pay taxes once you're 70½, whether you need it or not.
- If you hire employees someday, you'll have to cover them with whatever plan you've established for yourself.
- You can't reduce self-employment tax with these plans, only federal income tax. You may not get any deduction from state and local taxes for your contribution, either.
- You may have to pay somebody fees or commissions to administer your plan, such as a bank, brokerage, insurance company or mutual fund.

# SHOULD I INCORPORATE?

Once they're established, some freelance writers incorporate to protect their personal assets from creditors and litigants, or for tax purposes.

Generally, when professionals form corporations, only the assets of the corporation are liable for seizure by creditors or potential litigants. For freelance writers, however, that may not be the case.

Libel is one of the largest litigation traps a freelance writer faces. But because libel may be considered a personal statement, the legal doctrine of "piercing the corporate veil" could come into play. That means a court could make an incorporated writer's personal assets available to a successful plaintiff.

Incorporating can also subject a writer to double taxation. Since you become an employee of your corporation, you become responsible for such payroll taxes as employer Social Security, worker's compensation and unemployment insurance. Also, any profits of the corporation may be taxed, and then if you take a dividend from the corporation, that is taxed again.

If you opt for S Corporation status with the IRS, you can overcome this problem. For the most part, S Corporation profits are only taxed as income to the shareholders of the corporation.

Whether you have an S Corporation or a standard corporation, the salary you pay yourself is only taxed once. But if you use a high salary or a year-end bonus to avoid double taxation, the IRS may construe that as a "constructive dividend," which would subject you to double taxation all over again.

Traditional corporations do have a benefit in terms of deducting health insurance and other benefits. If you're incorporated, you can deduct 100% of your benefit costs from corporate income. If you're unincorporated or have an S Corporation, you can only write 25% of that cost off your taxes and nothing for such benefits as disability.

Whether to incorporate is a tough question best handled with advice from an accountant or lawyer who knows about your situation.

Should you opt for incorporation, the state office that oversees corporations, such as the Secretary of State, will send you a packet of information detailing the steps you need to take.

## FOR FURTHER INFORMATION

**Safeware**
*2929 High St., P.O. Box 02211*
*Columbus, OH 43202*
*(800) 848-3469*

Safeware sells insurance for computer equipment, and property and liability insurance for small businesses.

**Service Corps of Retired Executives (SCORE)**
*National Headquarters*
*409 Third St. SW, 4th Floor*
*Washington, DC 20024*
*(202) 205-6762*

### Support Services Alliance Inc.
*P.O. Box 130*
*Schoharie, NY 12157*
*(800) 322-3920*

This group administers health plans offered by many writers' and affiliated groups. For a small annual fee, SSA also offers the self-employed wellness programs, business newsletters, access to a credit union, discount pharmaceutical plan, group life insurance, etc.

### Volunteer Lawyers for the Arts
*1st E. Fifty-third St.*
*New York, NY 10022*
*(212) 319-2787*

This organization can make referrals to any Volunteer Lawyers for the Arts chapters in your area, some of which also offer accounting services or referrals to accountants. Fees may be free or based on a sliding scale depending on your income. You'll need to fill out an application and, in most cases, include your most recent tax return to qualify for free or reduced-fee services. Addresses and phone numbers of several local chapters can be found below.

### Boston Volunteer Laywers for the Arts
*City Hall Plaza*
*Boston, MA 02108*
*(617) 523-1764*

### California Lawyers for the Arts
*Fort Mason Center*
*Building C, Room 255*
*San Francisco, CA 94123*
*Oakland: (510) 444-6351*
*San Francisco: (415) 775-7200*

### Colorado Lawyers for the Arts
*100 Grant St.*
*Denver, CO 80203*
*(303) 722-7994*

### Maryland Lawyers for the Arts
*Maryland Art Place*
*Baltimore, MD 21201*
*(410) 752-1633*

**St. Louis Volunteer Lawyers for the Arts**
*3540 Washington*
*St. Louis, MO 63103*
*(314) 652-2410*

**Volunteer Lawyers and Accountants for the Arts**
*% Cleveland Bar Association*
*113 St. Clair Ave.*
*Cleveland, OH 44114-1253*
*(216) 696-3525*

**Volunteer Lawyers for the Arts**
*500 Sixteenth St. NW*
*Washington, DC 20006*
*(202) 429-0229*

# TAXING MATTERS FOR FREELANCERS

Becoming a freelancer means saying good-bye to the days you spent 30 minutes filling out your annual tax return on Form 1040 EZ. As soon as you make any money freelancing, you'll have to fill out the long form 1040 and Schedule C for business profit or loss. If you plan to deduct car or equipment expenses, you'll have another even more complex form to fill out. You'll also need to keep records of any expenses you hope to write off against your income.

If you don't want to bother about taxes and records, you could just refuse to take deductions. That will greatly simplify your recordkeeping. But it will also cost you hundreds or thousands in additional taxes each year. Or you could hire someone to do your taxes and keep your books. But even if you do, you'll have to be responsible for keeping your receipts and some records.

The best strategy is to spend a little time learning the tax rules that affect you and adopt a simple system of keeping records. Even if you do hire an accountant or tax preparer, keeping good records will save time and fees. Expect to pay more if you dump a shoe box full of unsorted receipts on your accountant's or tax preparer's desk.

## DEDUCTING EXPENSES

Freelancers can deduct from their taxable income virtually any legitimate expense they incur while doing business, provided they have a receipt or other documentation.

The IRS applies the "ordinary" and "necessary" rules in judging the validity of a business expense. That just means the expenses should be ordinary for your profession and necessary for carrying out your business.

Chances are one of your largest expense categories will be your car. If you work from your home, you can deduct mileage from home and back to any interview, trips to the library for research or travel for any business function. This is true even if you don't qualify for the home-office deduction, which will be discussed later. If you work from an office outside the home, however, you can't deduct mileage for commuting to the office.

You can calculate auto expenses using the standard mileage rate or the actual-cost method. Either way, you'll need to keep a mileage log. You'll also need to record your car's mileage at the beginning and end of the year.

To use the standard mileage rate, multiply your annual mileage by the current year's mileage rate. It's the easiest method in terms of record-keeping, but it may not yield the highest deduction.

As the name implies, the actual-cost method measures what it really costs you to operate your car, rather than using a rate that approximates the cost. For this method, you'll have to keep receipts for all automobile expenses, including gas, maintenance and repairs, insurance, taxes, loan interest and depreciation of the car's cost.

If you lease the car, you deduct the lease payments instead of the depreciation and interest. Don't count on leasing, however, as a way around annual limits on depreciation for expensive cars. IRS rules limit the annual deductions for lease payments for any car valued above $12,800.

If you use the car for both business and personal reasons, you calculate the percentage of business miles each year and deduct that percentage of your costs.

There are limits to how much of your car's value you may write off each year. For cars you placed in service for the first time after 1988, you can depreciate no more than $2,660 the first year, $4,200 the second year, $2,550 the third year and $1,475 in subsequent years. Those limits are reduced by the percentage of personal use. For details of the exact amount you can depreciate, you'll need a current copy of IRS Publication 917.

You may not have a choice of methods in some circumstances. If you lease your car, or you use more than one vehicle in your business, you must use the actual-cost method. But if you only use a second car occasionally for business, you can still use the mileage rate. If you deduct actual costs the first year you use your car for business, you will have to stay with that method as long as you use that car. If you use the mileage rate the first year, however, you can switch to the actual-cost method in later years.

Keep in mind that switching methods involves some complicated calculations. Given the difficulty of switching methods later, it makes sense to work through an estimate of what your annual deductions will be over several years under both methods before you first put the car into service. If you wait until tax time to decide, you'll probably be stuck with the standard mileage rate, because it's too late to collect receipts.

Which method is better for you depends on several factors:

- The first year you buy a car is usually the most lucrative time to use the actual-cost method.
- If you plan to use the car less than 50% for business it will restrict how quickly you can write the car off. So you're probably better off using the standard mileage rate.
- If you drive a new $25,000 car to your interviews and use the car more than 50% for business, you should probably deduct actual costs. If you're driving a 1976 Duster, the mileage rate will probably give you the biggest deduction.
- Living in an area with high auto insurance rates or steep automobile taxes may tip the scales in favor of the actual-cost method.

Starting in 1990, the IRS threw out limitations that made the standard mileage rate less attractive. Those limits sharply reduced the mileage rate after the first 15,000 business miles deducted annually or first 60,000 miles deducted over the life of the car. Now, one rate applies to all business miles.

## HOME-OFFICE EXPENSES

Qualifying for the home-office deduction means jumping through some regulatory hoops and increasing your risk of an audit. For these reasons, even freelancers who meet the requirements are reluctant to take the deductions. But the tax savings can be big and tempting. You may be able to deduct a percentage of your mortgage interest or rent, utilities, upkeep and value of your home each year.

To qualify for the deduction, you must use an area or room of your home regularly and exclusively for business.

"Regular use" is defined as use on a continuing basis. Occasional or incidental use of your home office won't cut it, even if you don't use the space for anything else.

"Exclusive use" means just that. If you use the office for any personal activity, it doesn't qualify. That means no games on your personal computer, no personal calls from the phone in your office, and no relatives rolling out sleeping bags there on the weekend. Some furnishings are off limits for your home office, too, like TVs and sofas. True, ordinary business offices may have these things. But in a home office, the IRS sees them as a sign of personal use.

Some confusing media reports of recent court and Internal Revenue Service regulations may give many writers the false impression that their home offices are no longer deductible. In fact, though the IRS has tightened rules, IRS Ruling 94-24 actually appears favorable to writers. The ruling says you can take a home-office deduction if:
• you regularly meet clients at your home office
• your office is used regularly and exclusively for your business
• you can document these things (through appointment books, photos, etc.)

If you don't meet clients at your home office, you can still qualify through one of two other tests:
• A relative importance test comparing work done at the home office with work at other sites (The IRS ruling provides an example that specifically addresses the case of a self-employed author who qualifies for the deduction because the essence of the work—writing—is done at the home office.)
• A time test comparing how much time you worked at home and elsewhere (Storing your old daily calendars from past years with your tax records isn't a bad idea, in case you ever need to substantiate your home-office or other deductions.)

If you're a freelancer who spends most of your time working at the offices of clients, you probably still won't be able to qualify for the home-office deduction. But this is a fairly rare situation. And if it describes your situation, you probably have more potential tax problems than the home-office deduction. If you're spending most of your time at the offices of clients—particularly a single client—you're probably an employee, not a contractor. And the client should be picking up the employer's share of Social Security and other federal, state and local payroll taxes.

The most accurate way to calculate the business portion of your home is to divide the square feet of the office by the total square feet of your home. If the rooms in your home are of roughly equal size, you can also divide one by the number of rooms in your home to arrive at the percentage.

Expenses you can deduct include the business percentage of:

- rent
- mortgage interest
- utilities and services, such as electricity, heat, trash removal and cleaning services
- depreciation of the value of your house
- home security systems
- repairs, maintenance and permanent improvement costs for your house

You can deduct 100% for repairs, painting or modifications of your home office. Beyond that, figuring out what you can deduct and when you can deduct it gets tougher.

Generally, if the work affects the whole house, such as a new coat of paint or a new roof, you can deduct the costs for the business percentage of your home. If the work only affects a nonbusiness part of the house, don't deduct it at all.

In one of its amazingly murky distinctions, the IRS makes you treat "repairs" differently than "permanent improvements." Repairs you can write off the first year. Permanent improvements are considered capital expenditures and subject to depreciation over several years. What's the difference between the two? IRS Publication 587 says that if repairs are part of a general plan to improve the house, they must be considered permanent improvements.

Keep in mind, if you itemize deductions on your tax return, you can still deduct the nonbusiness portion of your mortgage interest on Schedule A as you deduct the business portion on Schedule C.

Now for the disadvantages. The IRS believes the home-office deduction is widely abused, so it scrutinizes returns with home-office deductions more carefully.

Moreover, when you sell your home, you may have to pay income tax on the amount you depreciated through a home-office deduction. But you can get around this by officially converting your office to personal use at least 12 months before you sell your home. Just make a personal call, and that exclusive use disappears—along with the home-office deduction.

One other word of caution—you can't use home-office expenses if they put you in the red. They can't be used to help create a tax loss.

Before you take any home-office deductions, figure out what the tax savings will be. If the savings are minor, you may not want to bother. What you lose in taxes, you may gain in peace of mind.

## COMPUTERS

Computer equipment is another major expense for most freelance writers. Deducting the cost of computers may also involve some extra paperwork. That's because personal computers and peripheral equipment fall under the heading of "listed" property that commonly has both business and personal use, along with cellular telephones, automobiles and entertainment equipment.

If your computer is used in a regular business establishment, including a qualified home office, it doesn't fall under the listed property category. Otherwise, you'll have to calculate the percentage of business use for your computer in Part V of Form 4562. Even if your computer is in a home office, it might be a good idea to document your computer use in case the IRS denies your home-office deduction in an audit someday.

Documenting the percentage of business use means keeping a log much like an auto mileage log. You should record the date and hours each time you use your computer, and whether that use is personal or business. For business use, also briefly describe the business purpose. Your entry should read something like, "2/10, 2:30 P.M. to 5 P.M., wrote article for *Redbook*."

If you use your computer less than 50% for business, you'll have to depreciate the business percentage of its cost in equal installments over 10 years. If you use the computer more than 50% for business, you can deduct the business percentage of its cost over 5 years and up to 25% the first year. You may even be allowed to write off the entire cost the year you buy the computer system.

If you have a cellular phone you use in your business, you must keep a log similar to the log you use for a car or a computer—documenting every use of the equipment. The same listed-property rules apply to cellular phones as to computers.

## OFFICE EQUIPMENT

Desks, chairs, bookshelves, filing cabinets and other office furnishings are also deductible expenses if you use them in your business. They can be deducted even if you don't opt for the home-office deduction.

Like computers and other equipment with useful lives of more than a year, office equipment is subject to depreciation rules. You may deduct it over 7 to 10 years or, in some cases, deduct the full amount the year you buy it.

## DEPRECIATION AND SECTION 179

Though most business equipment and property must be depreciated over several years, freelancers and other small businesses can take advantage of Section 179, which allows up to $17,500 of business equipment costs to be fully deducted in the year of purchase.

Things you can't write off fully the first year under Section 179 include vehicles, computer equipment, cellular phones and entertainment equipment used less than 50% for business, and the business portion of your home.

But Section 179 can yield big tax savings in any year you make a capital expenditure, such as buying a computer system or car that you use more than 50% for business. Even if you don't use the equipment 100% for business, you can write off between 50% and 100% of the cost the first year rather than depreciating it over several years.

But if your business use of the car or computer equipment falls to less than 50% in later years, you may have to pay tax then on some of what you deduct now. Like the home-office deduction, Section 179 and other forms of depreciation can't be used to deduct more than you make from your business. But unlike home-office expenses, you can carry over Section 179 expenses to future years if you don't have income to deduct them from this year.

IRS Publication 534 provides more details on how to depreciate business property and use Section 179, including a full set of depreciation tables for various classes of property.

## CONVERSION FROM PERSONAL TO BUSINESS USE

You probably won't go out and buy all the equipment you use as a freelancer. Some of it you may already own. But you can still deduct the value of the office furnishings, computer equipment or car you've put in service for your business.

To deduct items converted from personal to business use, first determine the fair market value. Essentially, that's what the item would command if you were to sell it instead of using it for business. The fair market value can be depreciated over several years and deducted from your self-employment earnings. Property converted from personal to business use is not eligible for a Section 179 deduction.

## OTHER EXPENSES

Besides the big-ticket items above, there are several other expenses freelancers frequently deduct.

Among the largest noncapital costs for freelancers are phone expenses. Since 1989, the IRS has prohibited deduction of any percentage of your personal phone line, even if you use it for business part of the time. But you can still deduct business long-distance calls, even if they're from a personal line. You can also deduct the cost of a second line or other services used exclusively for business, such as a distinctive ring or voice mail.

If you entertain sources or clients, you can deduct 80% of that expense. You must keep a log of the date, location, person entertained and business purpose of the entertainment for every item you deduct.

If you travel in connection with your writing, you can deduct travel expenses. Those include transportation, lodging and meals.

Other deductible expenses freelancers often incur include:

- dues to professional organizations or unions
- costs of newspapers, magazines and other periodicals you use for your business (Note, most books are considered to have useful lives of more than a year, so they must be depreciated—probably not worth the trouble unless you're depreciating the value of an entire library you convert to business use.)
- research costs, such as copying services and the cost of online databases
- office supplies
- postage for business use
- cleaning supplies for your office
- legal, accounting and other professional services
- fees for business licenses, etc.

If publishers or clients reimburse you for some of your expenses, remember to keep records of those payments and either report them as income or subtract them from the expenses you report.

## SELF-EMPLOYMENT TAX

Besides ordinary income tax, freelancers must pay a self-employment tax for Social Security and Medicare. Employees pay Social Security tax too, as do their employers. But the self-employed pay roughly twice as much, because they're expected to cover both parts. When you look at your tax bill, you'll find that's one of the strongest motivations for taking every deduction you're allowed.

Keep in mind that the more you cut your self-employment tax, the lower your Social Security check will be once you retire. That considered, you'll still likely do better if you take some of your tax savings and put them in a tax-exempt retirement account.

To calculate self-employment tax, deduct 7.65% of your income, then multiply that number by 15.3%. Half of what you pay in self-employment tax also can be deducted from income subject to federal income tax, whether you itemize your deductions or not. The self-employment tax deduction also may provide a tax break in some states.

These new deductions were meant to soften the blow when the tax rate for self-employment increased in 1990. They reduce the effective self-employment tax rate to 13.07% for income in the 15% federal income tax bracket and 12.15% in the 28% bracket. The effective rate may be even lower, depending on how your state and city taxes work.

Instead, these changes made one of the nation's most regressive taxes even more so. That's because people who make more money are taxed at a lower rate than those who make less.

## CONTRACTOR OR EMPLOYEE?

A major reason publishers and other clients like using freelancers is that they don't have to pay the employer's share of Social Security taxes, not to mention unemployment, worker's compensation or benefits. These taxes are also a reason some companies treat freelancers as contractors even if they're really employees.

Here are some key points to consider in determining whether you're an employee or contractor:

- Contractors generally set their own hours, choose their work site as needed, use their own tools (such as computers and office supplies) and supervise their own work.
- Employees work during hours and at sites determined by and with tools supplied by the employer.
- Contractors generally submit bills or invoices for payment.

If you're being paid as a contractor but working as an employee, you're being cheated, and so is the government. That's because you're picking up the tab for the employer's Social Security taxes, and the employer is shirking some of its tax responsibility.

If the IRS finds out, the employer is more likely to get in trouble than you are—unless you haven't been reporting the income. But it's best to refuse to work under such conditions: Ask to rearrange circumstances so you actually qualify as a contractor.

## HOBBYIST OR BUSINESSPERSON?

Another tax distinction you may face is the one between hobby and business. Writing provides enjoyment as well as income. So the IRS is more likely to classify a self-employed writer as a hobbyist than it is, say, a plumber. Being classified as a hobbyist can have an important effect on your tax situation.

Income from a hobby is reported as miscellaneous income on Form 1040, not as business income on Schedule C. One plus is that you don't have to pay self-employment tax on hobby income. The down side is that you can't deduct as much of your expenses.

Hobby expenses, along with some other miscellaneous deductions, are only deductible to the extent they exceed 2% of your adjusted gross income. And you can't deduct losses from plying your hobby, though you can from a business. The IRS presumes you're in business if you make a profit in three of five consecutive years. The IRS also considers:
- whether you operate in a businesslike manner, such as maintaining complete and accurate records
- your professional expertise
- how much time you spend in the activity
- whether you've engaged in similar activity in the past for profit
- whether the activity is your sole source of income

If you're audited over the hobby-business question, the IRS will look at the complete picture rather than any single factor.

## SOME SCHEDULE C POINTERS
Schedule C is a catchall form for businesses ranging from widget makers to people who write about widget makers, and everyone in between. As such, much of it can be meaningless and mysterious for a freelancer. Here are a few things to note if you fill out the form yourself:
- You'll probably be checking the "cash" box for accounting method. That just means you record income when you get the check and expenses when you pay them. Few freelancers will use the more complicated accrual method or any more exotic variety.
- Check the "does not apply" box for method used to value closing inventory. You don't have any inventory. Unpublished manuscripts don't count.
- Under the income section, such items as returns and allowances and cost of goods sold probably will not apply to you.
- In the expenses section, you can't write off any bad debts unless you use accrual accounting.
- The office expense category is a catchall that includes office supplies, postage, etc.
- You only fill out the pension and profit-sharing portion if you have

employees participating in a plan. Your own plan contribution, if any, is reported on Form 1040.

- Tax and license expenses you can deduct include real estate and personal property taxes on business assets, employee Social Security and federal unemployment taxes and federal highway use tax, or any business-related state or local license.
- Long-distance charges fall in the utilities line. Since long distance can be a big expense for freelancers, it may be wise to itemize the components of your utility expenses on a separate sheet and attach it to your return.
- A big total in the "other expenses" column can make the IRS very suspicious. Break these items down as much as you can in categories in the space provided on Schedule C.
- Ignore the "Cost of Goods Sold" section, because you're not a retailer or manufacturer.
- Your "Principal Business or Professional Activity Code" will be 7880, "Other Business Services," unless your freelance writing is primarily public relations (7260) or advertising (7716).

## PROFESSIONAL HELP

As you've figured out by now, business tax forms are a lot more complicated than ordinary income tax forms, which aren't exactly easy. So you may want professional help with your taxes.

If so, your options include independent tax preparers and tax preparation services, accountants and enrolled agents. You may also get tax-preparer training offered by H&R Block or other services. That can save you money in the long run and even allow you to start a sideline preparing taxes for others.

If you're incorporated or face particularly complex business issues, you may need help from a Certified Public Accountant. CPAs are generally the most expensive option for tax preparation. Small or medium-size firms are most likely to be familiar with issues that concern you.

For strictly tax issues, don't overlook enrolled agents, who are required to pass a two-day exam given by the U.S. Treasury Department and then attend tax courses 24 to 30 hours a year. Many are former IRS employees. Though they aren't all accountants, EAs should know at least as much as accountants do about taxes. They can provide year-round tax planning. And they usually charge less than CPAs.

Franchise tax services are the fast-food operators of tax preparation— good at providing a consistent, mass-produced product. They're the cheapest option. But they may be less familiar with some of the unusual situations of freelancers than CPAs or EAs. And they usually aren't around for year-round tax advice.

Ask your prospective tax pro how many of his or her customers are freelance writers, or at least self-employed. If you plan to take the home-office deduction, ask how many of your preparer's customers have home offices. See listings at the end of the finance section for information about volunteer services that may help you, or may at least refer you to accountants versed in your area.

## THE DREADED AUDIT

People tend to fear something in inverse proportion to their chance of experiencing it. Such is the case with audits. Though costly and time-consuming, audits are relatively rare. The IRS audits fewer than 1% of tax returns each year, down from more than 2% in 1970.

Even if you're audited, you won't necessarily owe money. About a fifth of audit victims don't owe any additional taxes, and some even get refunds. Unless you're a celebrity or you committed fraud, you're unlikely to be sent to jail.

If you're self-employed and file Schedule C, however, your odds of being audited can quadruple. But, even among the most audited group of taxpayers—Schedule C filers with gross receipts of $100,000 or more—the audit rate is under 4%. If your gross self-employment income is under $25,000, your odds decline to under 1.5%.

Audits come in three forms. Mail audits are the least burdensome, requiring only an exchange of correspondence about specific points in your return. Office audits require you go to the nearest IRS outpost, receipts in hand, for that personal touch. The most intrusive form is a field audit, in which the IRS comes to you. The latter usually results in the biggest amounts of additional taxes, interest and penalties.

A properly calculated tax return with reasonable deductions is the best way to avoid an audit. The IRS analyzes returns according to average ranges of deductions for particular professions. The computer kicks out returns with deductions that are particularly high for taxpayers in particular professions. Then examiners can take a closer look. If you have an unusually large expense in relation to your income, such as $10,000 in travel expenses on $15,000 of income, you'd better have a good explanation. To avoid an audit, it's best to attach that explanation to your return.

## YEAR-END TAX STRATEGIES

The end of the year presents some opportunities to minimize your taxes. "A tax delayed is a tax saved," goes the old accountant's adage.

Well, at least it's a tax delayed for a year, during which you can earn interest on the money.

Among the things you can try:

- Bill late in December so checks won't arrive until after December 31 and you won't owe taxes until next year.
- Buy equipment you're planning to use next year before December 31, so you can take advantage of depreciation or a Section 179 deduction this year.
- Load up on office supplies and other essentials you'll need for the coming year before January 1.
- Pay for next year's subscriptions and professional dues in advance in December.

Publishers and other clients have their own year-end strategies. That means you'll see checks dated in December that end up in your mailbox in January. You aren't liable for taxes on money until you receive it, so you don't have to report those checks as income until the year you receive them. But since your 1099s may not agree with the income you report, be sure to document when you received the checks. You may even want to attach a note of explanation to your tax return and save the envelope, showing when the payment was postmarked.

## IRS PUBLICATIONS OF SPECIAL INTEREST TO WRITERS

  1 Your Rights as a Taxpayer
 17 Your Federal Income Tax (a digest of several key publications)
334 Tax Guide for Small Business
463 Travel, Entertainment and Gift Expenses
502 Medical and Dental Expenses
505 Tax Withholding and Estimated Tax
520 Scholarships and Fellowships
523 Tax Information on Selling Your Home
529 Miscellaneous Deductions (particularly important if your writing is a hobby rather than a business)
533 Self-Employment Tax
534 Depreciation
544 Sales and Other Dispositions of Assets
551 Basis of Assets
552 Recordkeeping for Individuals
560 Self-Employed Retirement Plans
587 Business Use of Your Home
589 Tax Information on Subchapter S Corporations

590 Individual Retirement Arrangements (including information on Simplified Employee Pension IRAs that the self-employed can set up)

910 Guide to Free Tax Services

917 Business Use of a Car

Copies of most of these publications are available at many public libraries. You also may order them by calling (800) TAX-FORM, (800) 829-3676, 8 A.M. to 5 P.M. weekdays and 9 A.M. to 3 P.M. Saturdays.

You can also get free help from the IRS in preparing returns. Look under "Telephone Assistance—Federal Tax Information" in the index of your tax form. The IRS listing in your phone book can give you more information about free tax preparation help available in your area.

# LAW AND THE WRITER

History offers few greater mismatches than that of publisher vs. writer. On one side, one of the world's largest and most profitable industries with armies of lawyers at its disposal. On the other, one of the world's most competitive, low-paying and unprotected professions. Many writers live in large part by trusting editors and publishers they've never met, without benefit of written contracts or anything else prudent souls would consider security.

As a writer, you probably can't afford to level the playing field by having a lawyer on retainer. But you can learn your way around the legal terrain and, with luck, bypass some of the quagmires and minefields.

## CONTRACTS: THE BEST AND WORST OF PROTECTION

Clearly the best security you can have as a writer is a written contract. For books, contracts are the norm. But understanding the contract's implications can be difficult. For articles, contracts are less common. Though many national consumer magazines and some trade journals offer them, many more don't.

While better than nothing, a contract sometimes isn't *much* better. A contract is only as good as your ability to enforce it. If the language is vague, or the cost of a lawsuit would far outweigh any return, the contract becomes fairly useless. If drafted the wrong way, a contract can become more like a chain than a bond. Clauses that give publishers dibs on unwritten, unconceived and quite unintended work have been inserted in book and periodical contracts.

Here are some pointers that could keep you from selling yourself into slavery or poverty.

## BOOK CONTRACTS

Book contracts fall within a fairly standard format. But writers have every right to negotiate the terms. The following are some of the major contract issues that may come up between author and publisher:

- Does the author have the right to review the copyedited manuscript? If so, how long is the review period?
- Are royalties based on a percentage of the list price or the publisher's net? In the latter case, getting a fair accounting becomes harder. Most writers' organizations recommend royalties be based on list prices.
- If arbitration of contract disputes is called for, the arbitration should be in accordance with the American Arbitration Association's rules. Also, does the contract state the place for the arbitration? If so, it should be a locale equally convenient to both parties.
- Does the contract have a noncompete clause prohibiting the author from writing, editing or publishing another competing book without written permission of the publisher? Some clauses are so vaguely worded that they seemingly would give the publisher control over virtually anything else the author produces. The Authors Guild in its model trade book contract recommends against any noncompete clause whatsoever. If you must have such a clause, make sure it's narrowly worded.
- Does the contract provide a time frame in which the manuscript is considered to be accepted even if the publisher does not expressly do so? A period of 60 days is reasonable for the publisher to accept or reject a manuscript or revision.
- Does the contract specify a time frame in which the author must complete any revisions? If so, is it enough time?
- Is there a provision for an audit of the publisher's records in accounting for royalties due the author?
- When is the advance to be paid? If payable in two or three stages, as is the norm, what are they? If some stages are beyond the author's control, is there a time limit to prevent foot dragging by the publisher?
- If the book is to be indexed, who is responsible for hiring and paying the indexer? Who is responsible for the cost of providing photographs and illustrations? If the author is responsible for such costs, are they to be withheld from the advance or royalties? The latter is in the writer's best interest.
- If an accepted manuscript is never published, does the contract

become void, allowing the author to sell it elsewhere? If so, does the author retain the advance?

- Does the contract provide for free copies to be furnished to the author and a discount for the author to purchase additional copies?
- Does the contract specify a dollar commitment for publisher's promotional expense? Does it obligate the author to make promotional appearances without provisions for payment or expenses?
- Does the contract give the publisher any options on future works by the author? The Authors Guild in its contract guide finds all such clauses unacceptable. Unless the publisher wants to pay you for this option, you should probably reject it.
- Does the author have veto power over the title of the book and the design of the book jacket?
- Do publication rights revert to the author when the book goes out of print?
- Does the author have the right of consent to any sales of subsidiary rights, such as motion picture, book club or anthology? Is there a provision for full subsidiary rights to revert to the author should the publisher fail to exercise such rights in a specified time?
- Does the publisher promise to pay for legal expenses arising from any libel action in connection with the book? If so, does the author have the right to choose his or her own lawyer?
- Is the author responsible for any of the publisher's legal costs?
- Does the publisher agree not to settle any claim without the author's consent?
- Can the publisher freeze royalty payments after a suit is filed? If so, what are provisions for resumption of payment following a settlement and assignment of claim among the publisher and author?

There are no "right" ways to handle these issues. But you should hold out for the best deal you can. Regardless of your excitement about getting a contract offer, take a cold, hard look at how you're treated under the contract or get a lawyer who can. It's the mark of a professional.

Some of the most common book contract problems involve subsidiary rights, says David Weinstein, a Denver attorney affiliated with the National Writers Association. In some cases, writers hand over potentially lucrative rights to negotiate motion picture deals, book club contracts, microfiche reproduction and more to publishers who have little interest in or ability to market those rights.

"Find out what the publisher's track record is in negotiating those deals," Weinstein advises. Publishers may recognize they have limited ability to negotiate subsidiary deals and be willing to license such rights for a nominal fee.

## DEALING WITH AGENTS

Similar situations arise with agents. "Authors should try to find out about the agent's ability and track record," Weinstein says, "before they sign a contract."

Some writers' organizations, such as the National Writers Union, maintain database lists of agents that could be of help in making your selection.

Agents customarily make at least nominal contact with all the appropriate publishers once a writer has contracted with them, Weinstein says. How vigorously and competently they handle those contacts is another issue. If the writer, entirely through his or her own efforts, later lands a deal with one of those publishers, the agent could still be entitled to a cut based on a perfunctory contact.

According to Weinstein, contracts with agents should spell out the agent's responsibilities clearly and prevent agents from claiming a share from contracts they didn't procure. That's one reason Weinstein prefers short-term agent contracts, such as 60 days, rather than long-term relationships.

Another issue to look out for is reading fees. Some agents charge less-experienced writers fees of several hundred dollars merely to review their manuscripts. The fees don't obligate the agent to make any other effort on your behalf.

## MAGAZINE AND OTHER PERIODICAL CONTRACTS

Compared to book negotiations, contracts and negotiations for periodicals seem simple. Yet the perils of taking insufficient precautions can be as great.

Getting written contracts for articles can be tough. Many publications operate on informal, verbal assignments without so much as a letter of confirmation, much less a contract. Listings in *Writer's Market* and other directories may be a useful guide to publications' practices, but they don't constitute a binding legal obligation. And many publications ask unproven writers to submit work entirely on speculation.

"I've worked a lot of times with editors who just told me to go ahead and do it, and it hasn't been a problem," says Steven Meyerowitz, a freelance writer and lawyer in East Norwich, New York. "Writers get paid poorly enough, and if you're going to start refusing work because you can't get anything in writing, you might as well give it up altogether."

Still, some kind of written agreement is preferable, if only an informal assignment letter from the editor. You can also try sending your own confirming letter to the editor. If nothing else, such a letter may clear up misunderstandings before it's too late to do anything about them. The American Society of Journalists and Authors offers members a suggested letter of agreement to be used when the publication doesn't offer written confirmation of an assignment.

"But if the letter isn't signed by the editor, the editor changes jobs or they decide they just don't like your work, that doesn't really offer you much protection," Meyerowitz says.

Among points to confirm on an article assignment are:
- the deadline
- the fee
- whether any of the fee will be paid in advance
- what kill fee the publisher will pay if the finished article is rejected
- under what circumstances a kill fee will be paid (To put it another way, will the author get a kill fee if the editor rejects the manuscript or only if the assignment is given and then terminated for some other reason?)
- what rights are conferred (First North American Serial Rights are a good starting point.)
- whether you will be paid on acceptance (If so, how long does the editor have to accept or reject the manuscript? And how soon after that will the publisher pay?)
- what expenses the publisher will pay—and when
- whether you will have the right to approve a final edited version of the article

The National Writers Union negotiated the following points in its contract with the *Columbia Journalism Review* that may serve as guidelines in your negotiations with publishers:
- a kill fee of 33% of the article fee
- a 66% kill fee on rejected assignments that involve rewrites
- full payment for accepted articles, even if not published
- payment for exploratory research or updating assigned articles
- automatic protection from libel suits
- right to approve edited versions
- acceptance or rejection within four weeks of submission
- payment within six weeks of acceptance
- exclusive rights that revert to the author after first publication

Some publications won't accept these terms. But you can use them as a point of departure and try to keep the journey as short as possible.

## ELECTRONIC RIGHTS

Electronic rights have become an increasingly controversial issue between freelance writers and their publishers. The American Society of Journalists and Authors and National Writers Union have been particularly adamant in fighting against contracts proffered by several major publishers stipulating that writers will receive no additional fees for use of their work in databases on the Internet or other electronic media. The union's position is that writers should be compensated for these additional uses, or should at least retain their rights for later negotiation.

As a practical matter, few publishers have actually begun to clear significant profit from the emerging multimedia use of magazine or other materials yet. And trying to account for additional payments to freelance writers in some uses, such as electronic databases, would be burdensome and of questionable value. After all, is putting an article in a database that much different than having the magazine on microfiche? By pressing the issue, writers could simply make it inconvenient and overly expensive for publishers to use freelance help.

On the other hand, some publications are developing pages on the Internet's World Wide Web that hold the potential of becoming quite profitable. Tracking user "hits" on particular articles is relatively easy on these Web pages. And that would seem to offer one solution for how to pay freelancers additional amounts for electronic use in this format.

At any rate, giving away your electronic rights without payment and without at least attempting to negotiate may not make sense. The ASJA reports several writers have had success negotiating at least nominal payment for electronic rights or in deleting onerous electronic rights clauses from contracts. As with everything else, look at the whole deal. You need not accept a publisher's first offer and should negotiate where you feel it's warranted.

Yet another emerging area is electronic book publishing—either through the Internet or via CD-ROM. The National Writers Union (see listing in chapter two) has suggestions and guidelines for authors to use in negotiating electronic book deals. The NWU argues that royalty rates generally should be higher for electronic books on discs than for print books to reflect the lower costs of production and because the full income potential is unknown.

The union believes proceeds should be fairly divided and accounted for so that authors may share in any long-term financial success of the product. Royalty rates should be even for network distribution of electronic books or "CD-ROM on demand" kiosks, in which production costs may be negligible, the union says. As with print books, the NWU recommends royalties be based on list prices rather than net. For some electronic publishers, a substantial portion of sales come from discs supplied to hardware manufacturers to bundle with multimedia kits. Publishers argue that they can't afford to pay list-price royalties on these copies, which are sold at huge discounts. But the NWU recommends this be addressed by adopting the print publishing practice of paying lower and/or net royalties on those specific copies that are sold outside of normal trade channels. In the case of electronic books, normal trade channels would include computer and software stores as well as book stores.

## PROTECTING YOUR RIGHTS

Understanding what rights you're selling a magazine is also important. The word "selling," in fact, is something of a misconception. Ideally, you should only lease your work to a magazine.

First North American Serial Rights, a standard deal for a magazine article, only give a publication the right to use your work first in North America. After that, rights revert to you. That means if the publisher wishes to reprint the article in another publication or another form, it must negotiate additional payment with you.

Many publications say they buy all rights, which essentially gives them ownership of the piece. That means they can reuse it in any form without paying you anything more. It also means you can't sell secondary rights to anyone else.

Even if a publication says it buys all rights, that is a negotiable issue. If you don't expect to sell the piece again, and you feel the payment you received is fair if the publisher wants to reuse the piece in another form, then selling all rights probably makes no difference. Otherwise, you may want to do some bargaining.

Keep in mind that a publisher has to get your signature on a contract in order to buy all rights. In absence of a written agreement otherwise, with some minor exceptions, the Copyright Law of 1978 states an author gives a publisher only one-time rights. These are much like first rights, only they don't guarantee the publisher first use.

Some writers feel so strongly about the issue that they refuse to sell all rights to any piece. In practical terms, many articles are so closely tailored to a magazine's format that no one else would want them anyway. In that case, you lose little by selling all rights.

Similar to selling all rights to a piece is a work-for-hire arrangement.

A work for hire becomes the property of the publisher. Generally, something is considered a work for hire if produced by an employee for an employer, such as a staff writer for a publication. Freelancers, however, have also been subjected to work-for-hire arrangements.

In 1989, the U.S. Supreme Court ruled that independent contractors own the rights to creative works unless they transfer those rights in written agreements.

Even if you do sign away all your rights, all is not lost. "You're just selling the rights to those 2,500 words in that particular order," Meyerowitz says. "The writer can still take the information, twist it, put another slant on it, and write it for another publication."

In some cases, you can sell your work to two or more publications at the same time if they don't have overlapping circulations. You should always inform the editor of simultaneous submissions—out of professional courtesy, if not legal obligation.

## COPYRIGHT

Technically, the only thing you must do to copyright work is put it down on paper. Since the United States accepted the Berne Convention in 1989, no formality such as a copyright notice is required. Some additional steps, however, can protect your copyright better:

- By adding a copyright notice to your work, you can defeat any claim by a publisher of "innocent infringement."
- By registering your copyright, you can bring suit against someone for infringing your copyright. Works created in foreign countries need not register their copyrights to have the right to sue. But you must register works created in the United States before you can file suit. You may still register your copyright after an infringement and then sue. But this means you can't recover attorney fees and some damages from the defendant. See listings at the end of this section for the address to write in order to register a copyright.

Even a registered copyright can't protect something writers often feel are most vulnerable—their ideas. Most articles are written on the basis of an idea proposal. That protects you from finishing a piece without having a market for it. But since you can't copyright an idea, you're left with little choice but trusting the editor who fields your query not to rip it off. Fortunately, the vast majority of editors are trustworthy. Sometimes editors may seemingly take your idea. But what appears to be piracy could be the result of a project that was already in the works before your query. An editor should, however, inform you of this when rejecting your query.

The American Society of Journalists and Authors Code of Ethics and Fair Practices defines a story idea as a "subject combined with an approach." It says a writer shall have a proprietary right to an idea suggested to an editor and have priority in developing it. Though not a legal right, this is an ethical standard that any editor with integrity should respect.

## GETTING PAID

Even if you've protected your rights throughout the process and turned in a manuscript that was accepted, you still have one big hurdle to pass—getting paid. Even having your rights spelled out doesn't put a check in your pocket.

During a recession, you may have to be a little more patient. It's likely your publisher is also getting paid slowly by advertisers and may not have any choice but to string its creditors along some. But don't be too patient. No matter how bad the publisher's cash flow, it's probably better than yours. In hard times, companies tend to put bills from freelancers and other independent professionals at the bottom of the stack. After all, you can't evict them, turn the lights off or repossess inventory like other creditors.

Even in good times, checks seem to travel through accounting departments and post offices at speeds in inverse proportion to their size. But even more aggravating is getting stiffed for a relatively paltry sum.

Whatever the size of the check, waiting for it is one of the most nerve-racking parts of being a freelancer. Even if you don't need the money right away, a doubtful proposition for the average shallow-pocket writer, you're still stuck with simmering resentment and the embarrassment of feeling like a sucker.

The resentment is called for, but useless. The embarrassment is uncalled for and potentially debilitating. After all, several bank executives in Manhattan have been sitting in their corner offices waiting for checks from Third World countries for years. So stop feeling bad and get to work. You may have to earn your money all over again, but at least you'll get it.

Here are some steps.

1. After payment is 30 days past due, call and/or write immediately. You need not be confrontational. Simply send a late notice or call to check on the status of payment or make sure your invoice wasn't lost. But do get a commitment from the editor or accounting office on when the payment will be sent.

2. Hold them to the promise. If payment isn't in your mailbox by the time promised, call to ask why. Be a little more persistent this time. If

you have a long-term relationship with the publication, this is a good time to let them know you won't be able to send any more work until payment is received. Your leverage is increased markedly if you're working on an assignment that's needed soon.

3. If payment isn't forthcoming the second time you call or write, the time for further action is nearing. Send a final notice informing the publisher that you will have to turn the account over for collection or legal action if payment isn't received by a specified date.

4. Take that "further action" promptly if the deadline passes. It could be a letter from a lawyer. Or you may want to hire a collection agency.

Some clubs, such as the National Writers Club, will write on behalf of members to publications that have not paid for published work. Several other organizations will note nonpayments in their newsletters as a warning to other members, and a few associations may even pursue legal action for members who have not been paid. If you learned about the publication in a directory, inform the directory's staff of your problem. They may also write on your behalf and consider deleting the publication from the next edition of the directory.

A letter from a third party is an attention-getter that will disgorge a check from many slow payers. But if you have reason to believe the publisher is failing and could be headed for bankruptcy, skip this rather time-consuming step, or at least start the next one immediately.

5. If all else has failed, it's time to consider serious legal options such as small claims court. In most cases, this is your only realistic option. Any higher court will require a lawyer, whose fees will likely outweigh anything you might be owed for an article. If it's a book, more-expensive options probably are warranted.

## SMALL CLAIMS COURT

When worse has come to worst, small claims court can be a writer's best friend. Filing fees are nominal. Lawyers aren't required. And novices are tolerated.

Expect to invest some time, though. You must wait in line to get papers to file, then wait in line to file them. In front of you will be lots of people who are as unfamiliar with the process as you are. So expect to take at least an hour. Later, you may have to press your case in a sort of cattle-call hearing that can take much of the day before your case comes up.

Unfortunately, small claims court won't handle every situation. Depending on the state, the court will have a claim limit of $1,000 to $5,000. Also, you may not be able to sue an out-of-state publisher in your local court.

"You can't sue anybody in your state if they don't do business in your state," Meyerowitz says. If the publisher has an office in your state or a significant percentage of its circulation there, you can probably sue locally. If not, you'll have to file suit out of state, which could increase your costs beyond the value of your claim.

With luck, your suit will convince the publisher to pay you. If not, be prepared to make your case in court. This is one situation in which a written agreement is a definite plus. You should also bring copies of any invoices you sent, a copy of your manuscript and, if the piece has been published, a copy of the publication with your article in it.

If you had an oral agreement, you may need to subpoena the editor to prove your case. This step will cost you more money, since you must pay a subpoena fee and the travel costs of any witnesses you call. If the editor is out of town, it may not be an affordable step. And the strategy will only work if you expect the editor to tell the truth. But in the right situation, a subpoena can be quite effective. Faced with the prospect of a day in court, the editor may become your staunchest advocate before the accounting department.

Even if you don't have a written contract and it seems unwise to subpoena anyone, you should still consider a suit. Possibly, the publisher won't send anyone and you'll win by default.

Sadly, winning your suit doesn't guarantee you'll be paid. You may need to follow up by filing for an attachment of the publisher's bank account. And if the bank is out of state, you may not succeed.

One reason to sue quickly if you suspect a publisher is failing is that bankruptcy could thwart you. A bankruptcy filing automatically stays all legal proceedings against the debtor. And, as you'll soon see, your chance of getting paid after a bankruptcy filing is razor thin.

## DEALING WITH BANKRUPTCY

If you're ever a creditor in a bankruptcy case, you'll wonder why debtors prisons were abolished. That's because bankruptcy puts creditors, particularly small fry like you, at a distinct disadvantage.

Bankruptcy lawyers, banks with loans backed by collateral and employees all have priority over you in getting paid. As an "unsecured creditor" you might get paid cents on the dollar if anything's left. If it eases your pain any, you do rank ahead of the owners, so they shouldn't get anything unless you do.

To protect your rights in a bankruptcy, you'll need to file a proof of claim. You can get the appropriate form by calling the U.S. Bankruptcy Court clerk where the debtor filed for bankruptcy. The clerk can also tell you the deadline for filing the proof of claim. You'll need to attach any supporting documents, such as your contract or invoice. If you don't have a written agreement, you can still file a proof of claim and hope the debtor accepts it anyway.

"You might as well file the proof of claim, because it doesn't cost you much," says Meyerowitz, who has had one magazine that owed him money go bankrupt. "But in most cases, you might as well write it off."

## LIBEL ISSUES FOR FREELANCERS

Besides deadbeat publishers, the next most likely thing to land you in court is a libel suit. A wide-ranging discussion of libel issues for writers is beyond our scope here. An AP Stylebook and Libel Guide should give you the basic background you need. And regular reading of a journalism trade magazine, the *Wall Street Journal* or the *New York Times* should keep you up-to-date on new developments.

Freelance writers do have some special issues of concern with libel. First, keep in mind that you aren't necessarily going to be defended by the publisher if your article or book prompts a libel suit. Conceivably, you could be sued and the publisher not, though it's hard to imagine a plaintiff not going after the deeper pockets of a publisher, too. Even if the publisher alone is sued, it could come after you for some of the damages if it loses.

You may have an agreement from a publisher indemnifying you in case of any libel suit. But make sure you don't sign an agreement indemnifying the publisher in case of a suit.

To protect yourself, it's good to have tapes to back up your notes of interviews. Keep in mind that taping phone conversations may be illegal in your state unless you tell the other party that the conversation is being taped. And an illegally obtained tape would never be admissible in court.

Not all libel suits may stem from anything you did. An overly aggressive headline writer or ham-handed editor could also provoke one. The best protection against this is getting to review a proof of the edited version, including headlines and photo captions. Since that's not always possible, keep a hard copy of manuscripts you send, particularly ones that seem like candidates for a libel action.

A manuscript need not be published in a magazine to be libelous. If you circulate it to editors, you've published it for the purpose of libel. Though rare, it could spark a suit without being published if, say, a fact checker or editor calls to verify points of the article and alerts a subject to libelous content. In that case, the publication is completely off the hook, while you're wiggling on it for all your life.

## RESOURCES

Several groups offer legal advice and help for writers, ranging from research reports to consultations with attorneys. For a listing of writers' associations and clubs along with the services they offer, see chapter two. In some cases, members can consult with an affiliated attorney for no charge and arrange fees if further work is needed.

Volunteer Lawyers for the Arts has chapters in 27 states, plus the District of Columbia, Puerto Rico and Canada. VLA also sells a variety of handbooks on such legal issues as small claims court, book contracts and taxes. VLA members can consult volunteer lawyers for free and then arrange further work if needed. Most VLA chapters have an income ceiling of $15,000 a year or less. But even if you don't meet the guidelines, a VLA chapter may be an excellent source for referral to a lawyer experienced with problems like yours.

Your local bar association can also refer you to an attorney in your area experienced in copyright law, collections, etc. You may be able to arrange a consultation with a lawyer for a relatively small fee before committing yourself to further work.

To register a copyright, request the proper form from the Register of Copyrights, Library of Congress, Washington, DC 20559. You'll need to send the completed form and a $20 registration fee.

# EMPLOYMENT AGENCIES, JOB BANKS AND CONTACTS FOR WRITERS

Writing can seem like a lonely profession when the mailbox brings a stream of rejection notices and nary a trickle of checks. Fortunately, you're not really alone. In many places, writers have banded together for mutual aid in getting work. National, regional and local groups offer help for writers seeking anything from freelance assignments to full-time jobs.

How the job programs work, however, varies significantly from group to group. The National Writers Club and its affiliated group, Associated Business Writers of America, offer information about freelance market opportunities through their monthly newsletter, *Flash Market News*.

The American Society of Journalists and Authors offers members listings in an annual directory that may be used by editors in search of writers. It also offers its Dial-A-Writer referral service, which allows editors to call with specific needs for freelance writers and be referred to writers who meet those needs.

The Society of Professional Journalists offers members a national job bank called Jobs for Journalists for an annual fee of $25. Journalists are entered in a pool of employment applicants nationwide. But jobs handled by the bank are mostly full-time positions.

Women in Communications, Inc., has a toll-free hotline listing national job opportunities for members. After listening to a recorded message about jobs, members can call for details about applying for them. Local chapters of WICI also have groups that list job seekers for potential employers and jobs submitted by employers. Most of WICI's job listings are for full-time employment, because local networks and agencies seem to get most of the traffic from freelancers and clients.

Local organizations or local chapters of national groups also offer job banks. The Editorial Freelancers Association offers a database of its members for potential clients in the New York City area through its Job Phone line. The National Writers Union has job banks with listings of opportunities for writers in New York, Boston and San Francisco. Freelance writer organizations in Florida and Texas also put members on a database available to potential clients through the Cassell Network of Writers.

See chapter two for individual group listings.

## WRITING-RELATED AGENCIES

Many areas also have for-profit agencies that provide work for freelance writers and editors. The agencies generally screen freelance writers to determine their interests, credentials and fee schedules. Then they put freelancers on databases available to their clients. The agencies mark up the fees charged by freelancers to cover their costs and profit.

Such agencies can provide a sort of business support system to you as a freelancer. They become your marketing department and your collection bureau. For a talented, experienced writer who's new in town, such an agency can plug him or her into instant work. The disadvantage is that you might make more by marketing your work directly to the end user, since you might be able to charge both your fee and at least part of the markup the agency gets.

Different agencies have different approaches and different specialties, such as technical writing, advertising copywriting or book editing.

For instance, Portfolio, a Cambridge, Massachusetts-based staffing agency, specializes in placing freelance copywriters and graphic designers in temporary or permanent jobs. According to general manager Nunzio Domicili, Portfolio differs from other temp agencies because its managers are creative and art directors. Writers and other creatives become employees of Portfolio, which in turn offers comprehensive health, dental, 401(k) retirement, disability and vacation benefits. Employees are free to continue accepting freelance assignments in addition to their work for Portfolio, which has operations in Atlanta, Detroit, Los Angeles, New York, San Francisco, Houston, San Diego and Washington, DC.

A slightly different twist is provided by Creative Consortium Inc., a full-service marketing communications agency based in Cincinnati, with associated professionals in cities around the United States. Creative Consortium handles writers, graphic artists and marketing specialists, says President Judith Hoyt Pettigrew.

"We're a brokerage firm for marketing communications talent," Pettigrew says. "We're really a marketing department for hire, though we provide talent for end users and advertising agencies as well."

Writing jobs handled by Creative Consortium include copywriting, employee and operations manuals, newsletters, scriptwriting for audiovisuals and press releases, to name a few.

"We've found a lot of people go through freelancing as a revolving door in and out of corporate jobs," says Pettigrew. "We look for professional independent writers who are prepared to stay out there living as freelancers."

Writers for Creative Consortium are independent contractors, which helps the company keep its rates competitive. Freelancers bid their fee for the job at the outset and are free to accept or reject any project.

## STANDARD EMPLOYMENT AGENCIES

More-traditional employment agencies and temporary services firms can also provide work for freelancers in some instances. Employment agencies may handle some full- or part-time jobs, with placement fees paid by you or the employer. Temporary agencies may also have calls for copyeditors, proofreaders or copywriters from time to time. You will be an employee of these agencies, which offer full- and part-time temporary assignments that sometimes lead to permanent positions. But most traditional agencies report they seldom handle jobs for freelance writers.

## OTHER FAST ROADS TO WORK

Besides agencies and writers' groups, most cities also have other opportunities for writers to find work relatively easily. These opportunities can also lodge your foot firmly in the door of better opportunities. Here are a few of your options.

## NEWSPAPER STRINGING

Community newspapers and metropolitan dailies never seem to have enough staff reporters to handle all the stories they need. They use stringers extensively to fill the gaps. Stringers cover everything from school board meetings to lower-interest sporting events to breaking spot news if they get there first. Catching on as a stringer is a lot easier than catching on as staffer. Even high school and college students are sometimes used.

Community newspapers are the easiest to break in with, whether they're the chains of suburban weeklies that ring most major cities or independent weeklies and small dailies. Pay for community newspaper stringers, however, is poor even by freelance-writing standards. They may pay as low as $15 to $25 per article. But they do provide a means of getting clips that can lead to better and higher-paying work.

While somewhat harder to break in with, metropolitan daily newspapers are by no means insurmountable markets for college graduates with some clips from college or community newspapers.

Community news coverage is by far the greatest need metropolitan dailies have for stringers. The explosion of suburban newspapers in the 1970s and 1980s sparked an equally explosive reaction by metropolitan dailies, which launched zoned suburban editions in hopes of recouping their advertising losses. This creates a news hole that many dailies can't afford to fill entirely with the work of staff writers. If you live in the territory covered by zoned editions, contact the editor for the edition. Chances are he or she is eager to add capable stringers to the pool.

Even if you don't live near or in a suburban area, or your daily doesn't have zoned editions, you may still find work covering community news for them. Metro dailies often need stringers in peripheral circulation areas that their reporters rarely visit. Contact the metro editor or managing editor to see if he or she needs a stringer in your area. It could result in a few bylines a year.

Metro dailies may also use stringers to cover high school sports, less-attended college sports like swimming and hockey, or even minor league professional sports. There's also a chance of selling your work to food and lifestyle sections or special sections on such issues as health care, home and garden, and automobiles.

Stringing for metropolitan dailies won't exactly make you rich, but it will pay better and generate better clips than community newspapers. Expect to make $35 to $250 per article, with most zoned news articles being in the $35 to $100 range and most articles that make the ROP sections in the $75 to $150 range. The paper may also pay an hourly rate for coverage of local government meetings or a lower rate for news briefs culled from a local government beat. Alternative weekly papers, free-circulation urban entertainment publications and local business newspapers can also be good markets for freelancers in many cities.

## WRITING A COLUMN

Columns are another way to get your byline, and possibly your face, into newspapers regularly.

Locally based humor columns are one avenue, though it can be a tough market to crack. Editors see a lot of such column proposals and have their pick of nationally syndicated humor columns, too. But a good column can still win editors over and lead to big returns, including national syndication. Erma Bombeck started writing her column for the *Kettering-Oakwood Times*, a suburban newspaper outside Dayton, Ohio.

If you have writing ability and expertise in a subject area, you could also develop a specialized column. Examples of locally produced columns that have run in community or daily papers include auto and home repair, real estate, education, tax preparation, antiques, nature, and stamp collecting. Community newspapers and zoned editions of metros also frequently use chatty columns that cover local events and personalities.

Of course, the best idea for a column is one that hasn't been done before. That way, the editor can't just rip something else like it off the wire service he or she is already paying for anyway. A copy of *Editor & Publisher's* annual syndicate issue, which may be available in a college or city library, is a good place to check what material is already abundantly available. A superior local column on a subject that's already got several syndicated columns can still sell. But you'll have the added responsibility of proving why yours is better than what's already out there.

The key to selling such columns is convincing the appropriate editor:
- You're an expert in the area.
- You can write.
- Readers will actually be interested.

The first is relatively straightforward. Your academic credentials, business experience or organizational accreditation should be sufficient to prove you're an expert, if you in fact are. If you're not, you may be able to collaborate with someone who is but who can't write.

You'll prove you can write the same way you would with any other market—by showing examples of your work. But with a column, have several installments ready. That will show you can produce it consistently.

The last area may be a little tougher. But if you can show statistics on club membership in your area or point to the universal appeal of your topic, you might succeed.

Pay for columnists is similar to pay for stories in community and metro newspapers listed earlier. No windfall, but it is steady work. And once you get the hang of putting the column out, it may be easy and fast. Bigger payoffs come if you establish a track record for your column and can start selling it to other publications or for national syndication. And even if you don't, a column could make a nice credit to list when sending queries for freelance assignments.

## *FREELANCE EDITING AND PROOFREADING*

Most cities and even small towns offer a wealth of opportunities for freelance copyeditors, content editors and proofreaders. But finding such work means sending out résumés, making calls and knocking on doors.

Even if you don't live in New York, many other cities have smaller book publishers that need freelance content editors, copyeditors and proofreaders for some of their projects. Book publishers also advertise needs for freelance editors in trade publications such as *Publishers Weekly*.

Printers, typesetters and graphic designers may need proofreaders and copyeditors. Even if they have such people on staff, they may need freelancers to fill in when work gets especially heavy. These same sources can also be good contacts for clients who need copywriting help for anything from brochures to annual reports. See chapter five for more information on selling your writing services in a variety of specialty areas.

## EMPLOYMENT AND OTHER AGENCIES THAT USE WRITERS

**Communicators Connection Inc.**
*7638 Holmes Run Dr.*
*Falls Church, VA 22042-3317*
*(703) 849-9191*

**Creative Consortium Inc.**
*4850 Marieview Ct.*
*Cincinnati, OH 45236*
*(513) 984-0614*

Specializes in marketing communications, with occasional needs for writers nationwide.

### CRS Contracting Inc.
*509 Madison Ave., Suite 1400*
*New York, NY 10022*
*(212) 302-3901*

Specializes in magazine and book publishing personnel.

### Editorial Experts Inc.
*66 Canal Center Plaza, Suite 200*
*Alexandria, VA 22314*
*(703) 683-0683*
*Fax: (703) 683-4915*

### Editorial Service of New England Inc.
*126 Prospect St.*
*Cambridge, MA 02139*
*(617) 354-2828*

Specializes in technical and general subject areas.

### Phone-A-Writer Inc.
*1 Fresenius Road*
*Westport, CT 06880*
*(203) 222-1425*

Specializes in providing copywriters and technical writers.

### Portfolio
This agency, which hires freelancers as employees, has offices at the following locations in the United States. You may also contact Portfolio through its site on the World Wide Web (http://www.portfolio.skill.com) or e-mail address (in-box@portfolio.skill.com).

*1409 N. Highland Ave., Suite 1*
*Atlanta, GA 30306*
*(404) 817-7000*

*30 Oak Hollow, Suite 340*
*Southfield, MI 48034*
*(810) 352-5552*

*3000 Wesleyan, Suite 110*
*Houston, TX 77027*
*(713) 871-1974*

*1501 Main St., Suite 201*
*Venice, CA 90291*
*(310) 581-1600*

*1133 Broadway, Suite 1301*
*New York, NY 10010*
*(212) 691-7800*

*633 Battery St., Suite 120*
*San Francisco, CA 94111*
*(415) 391-8100*

*1730 K St. NW, Suite 1350*
*Washington, DC 20006*
*(202) 293-5700*

**Remer-Ribolow Employment Agency**
*275 Madison Ave., Suite 1605*
*New York, NY 10016*
*(212) 808-0580*

Specializes in book and magazine publishing.

**The Write People**
*Three Corporate Square, Suite 340*
*Atlanta, GA 30329*
*(404) 321-5400*

**Writers Connection**
*San Jose, CA 95050*
*(408) 445-3600*

Specializes in technical writing.

# GRANTS, FELLOWSHIPS, AWARDS AND CONTESTS

As hard as it is to make a living as a writer, it's good to know some kind folks out there want to give you money. For many writers, grants are the only way to stay even marginally solvent through lengthy projects. Fellowships offer opportunities for career-enhancing education that freelance writers may not otherwise get, since they have no chance at paid leaves of absence, and financial aid is becoming scarcer all the time. Contests and awards can offer not only recognition for a job well done, but also money to do the next job well, too.

But as applicants know, these programs are anything but a free ride. It takes hard work and skill to get money. Much like selling an article or a book idea, getting a grant, fellowship or award means having a good idea, doing superior work and then searching for the appropriate market. You'll need to find catalogs and directories, then study the listings to find ones whose funding interests match your creative interests.

Many grants have strict eligibility requirements. Grants from state and local arts councils, for instance, require recipients to live in the state or locality. Some organizations allow you simply to apply. Others require nomination from a member of the organization.

The more money in question, the tougher the competition for it. Some of the biggest have rather high hurdles to face even before you apply, such as a number of years of professional experience, having a book previously published or having a set number of articles published in literary magazines.

Every organization approaches the application process differently. So one of your best sources of ways to work with that particular organization may be talking to someone who has received one of its grants in the past.

Generally, the process of applying for a grant or fellowship involves these steps.

1. Call or write to get details or any changes concerning the deadline, eligibility and application process. Be sure to follow exactly any details as far as manuscript preparation or display of published works. And find out if the deadline is when the application must be postmarked or when it must be in the door. You may need to send your application by overnight delivery to ensure on-time arrival.

2. Send in your application, which usually will include samples of your published work and may include an essay or letter of explanation about your plans for future work.

3. Wait for your application to be screened by a committee that chooses finalists.

4. If you've passed that stage, wait for the same committee, or possibly another one in some cases, to decide on winning entries.

5. In some cases, especially for higher-paying fellowships, finalists will be interviewed before the final decision.

Grant application is often framed as a mysterious art best left to experienced practitioners. But in many cases, all the bells and whistles you can muster in a grant application won't make much difference. The quality of your work as viewed by the judges is the primary criterion.

"Our panelists know absolutely nothing about who the writers are," says Bob Fox, literary program coordinator of the Ohio Arts Council. "They read the manuscripts anonymously. So their decision is based entirely on their subjective view of the writer's work."

His only suggestions are to follow the guidelines for submitting manuscripts and submit finished works instead of works in progress, because finished works tend to fare better with judges.

"The single most important thing we're looking for is commitment to the popularization of science and technology," says Victor K. McElheny, director of the Knight Science Journalism Fellowships. "We're looking for people who have tried this, proven themselves to be very competent at it and intend to go on."

In many cases, selection committees must wade through hundreds or thousands of applications for a handful of awards. Other, more specialized programs may only have a handful of applicants. For instance, the Knight Science Journalism Fellowships, a prestigious program that offers a stipend of $28,000 and relocation assistance of $2,000, only has about 25–30 applications for six fellowships each year.

Like submitting your work for publication, applying for foundation grants and fellowships means getting your share of rejections. Program administrators advise writers not to be discouraged by an initial rejection. Many writers go on from a rejection to find acceptance elsewhere or even from the same program in later years. Things change from year to year. The competition may not be as fierce next time. And you, with an extra year of experience, will have more accomplishments to show judges and more experience with the program.

To find your best prospects among the hundreds of grants, fellowships and awards available, the most comprehensive directory is *Grants and Awards Available to American Writers*, PEN American Center, 568 Broadway, New York, NY 10012. Writing and journalism publications discussed later in this chapter are also good sources for notices of grants and the like, and many directories noted later in this chapter have listings of contests.

The following are some other listings that may help. When sending for information from these organizations, include a SASE.

### Congressional Fellowship Program
*American Political Science Association*
*1527 New Hampshire Ave. NW*
*Washington, DC 20036*
*(202) 483-2512*

A nine-month fellowship for journalists with 2 to 10 years of experience in newspaper, magazine, radio or television work, preferably outside of Washington, to improve research and reporting on American politics.

### Kiplinger Reporting Program
*Ohio State University School of Journalism*
*242 W. Eighteenth Ave.*
*Columbus, OH 43210*
*(614) 292-2607*
*E-mail: neff.67@osu.edu*
*Director: James Neff*

A one-year program to develop enterprise reporting and complete a master's degree in journalism for journalists with B.A. degrees and five years of reporting experience.

### Knight-Bagehot Fellowship in Economics and Business Journalism
*Columbia University Graduate School of Journalism*
*New York, NY 10027*
*(212) 854-2711*

A nine-month fellowship to improve economic and business reporting through formal study for journalists with four years of experience in business or general reporting.

### John S. Knight Fellowships for Professional Journalists
*Building 120*
*Stanford University*
*Stanford, CA 94305-2050*
*(415) 723-4937*
*Fax: (415) 725-6154*

A nine-month program of nondegree study for journalists with seven years or more experience.

### Knight Science Journalism Fellowships
*MIT*
*77 Massachusetts Ave., Room 9-315*
*Cambridge, MA 02139-4307*
*(617) 253-3442*
*E-mail: mshenry@MIT.edu*

A nine-month fellowship for science, technical, environmental and medical writers with three years of professional experience, aimed at bringing them up-to-date on current developments in their fields.

### Nieman Fellowships for Journalists
*Harvard University*
*Walter Lippman House*
*1 Francis Ave.*
*Cambridge, MA 02138*

*(617) 495-2237*
*Contact: Program Officer*

A nine-month fellowship for full-time editorial employees or journalists with a minimum of three years experience.

### The Alicia Patterson Foundation
*1730 Pennsylvania Ave. NW, Suite 850*
*Washington, DC 20006*
*(301) 393-3995*

Offers journalists a grant to spend one year researching and reporting on a subject of their choice.

### Quarterly Review of Literature Awards
*26 Haslett Ave.*
*Princeton, NJ 08540*

Award and publication for previously unpublished book-length manuscripts of poetry, a poetic play, a long poem or poetry in translation.

### Wallace E. Stenger Fellowships
*Creative Writing Program*
*Stanford University*
*Stanford, CA 94305-2087*
*(415) 723-2637*
*Fax: (415) 725-0755*

CHAPTER 2

# A COMMUNITY OF WRITERS

Writing can be a solitary occupation, but it doesn't have to be. From writers' groups to conferences to continuing education programs, there are an endless number of ways for writers to learn from others, perfect their craft and share information about the writing life with other writers.

This section can help you connect with those opportunities. It won't provide you with all the organizations available, but it will let you know where they can be found, how to evaluate the best program for your development and how to get the best value for your money. If you'd like to start a workshop or be an instructor, we also include tips for entering this side of the writing business.

## PROFESSIONAL ASSOCIATIONS AND ORGANIZATIONS

Writers' groups and organizations are available across the United States, covering a wide range of interests and offering a variety of services. Some are small groups of writers who meet weekly over coffee around a member's kitchen table to exchange war stories, read each other's work and offer support. Others are massive nationwide organizations with 5,000 members and services that include medical and health benefits. Your involvement with a professional organization depends a great deal on your needs as a writer.

Professional associations and organizations typically have members nationwide. They frequently concentrate on a single area or target a specific group of people, such as American Medical Writers Association or Women in Communications, Inc. Some have very stringent guidelines for membership, including publishing credits or amount of time spent writing. Because many have a national membership base, they can offer national networking and job bank possibilities, along with workshops and professional discounts. The largest associations usually have chapters in large cities to accommodate members.

Many professional associations are formed with an emphasis on helping members tackle the business side of writing. The Authors Guild, for instance, includes members who write everything from textbooks to mysteries. The majority are not full-time writers. As with many associations, members are classified on more than one level. Authors with a book published in the past 7 years or 3 articles published in the past 18 months are regular members. Authors can join as associate members if a contract offer has been made for a book. The member-at-large category includes agents and other industry people.

Most guild members don't have agents and consider the services offered by the guild an alternative. Although The Authors Guild has a small staff, they have computer records, a full-time lawyer on staff and a quarterly bulletin. They also pride themselves on offering individual advice to members on all the business aspects of writing. One of the most prized possessions of membership is the guild's contract guide, a document that explains in detail the contract language used by most publishers and the meaning it has for authors. Because most members don't have agents, they feel this information helps them negotiate better contracts.

While organizations such as The Authors Guild work on the business side of writing, other associations concentrate on services for specialty writers. The Education Writers Association, for instance, offers referrals, ways of approaching topics, professional development seminars, fellowships, contests, newsletters, a guide for covering the education beat and national and regional meetings. According to Executive Director Lisa J. Walker, the group includes print and broadcast reporters and freelance writers whose concentration is "substantially" education oriented. This doesn't mean "just covering schools," Walker says, but overlaps youth and business interests, covering everything from early childhood education to adult education and training in the workplace for its 900 members.

Sometimes the specialty is not a particular beat as much as a particular constituency. Women in Communications, Inc., includes members in areas ranging from corporate communications to media to education. About 6% of its members are freelance writers, and 5% of the membership is men.

While a professional organization may offer many attractive options and services, these programs are not likely to be cheap. The cost of most memberships is $50 or more, with some ranging as high as $500.

# WRITERS' GROUPS

Writers' groups are more likely organized around a local or regional, rather than a national, base. Although they may have a specialized focus, they are much less likely to restrict themselves; most, however, concentrate on fiction and poetry. Local and regional groups usually are more open in membership requirements, and less expensive to join. They usually emphasize more feedback and interaction among members than professional associations. A medium-size city may support three or four writers' groups with a variety of meeting styles and focuses. Writers' groups can range in size from fewer than 10 members to a few thousand members, and their offerings also vary considerably, so it's up to you to determine which one suits you best.

If level of service is your desire with a writers' group, an organization such as the National Writers Association may be your choice. The club, with 3,000 members in 50 states and 20 countries, has both aspiring and professional writers with writing experience ranging from 3 to 30 years. The National Writers Association staff includes two full-time and one part-time member, as well as 12 people under contract to provide information and services. In addition to receiving 200 to 300 letters per week, the staff coordinates newsletter production, writing courses, medical plans and even a new literary agency service for members.

Service on a more regional basis is the aim of other large groups, such as the Florida Freelance Writers Association and the Austin Writers' League. Executive Director Dana Cassell says the Florida group, with 800 members, emphasizes a newsletter "with the very latest market information," medical plans, a critique service, a writer referral service and a state writers' conference. "The established writer wants in the group for information, writers' referral and more business information," Cassell says. "The part-time writer wants it for networking, conferences and a chance to be part of a group."

Although its name denotes a citywide group, Executive Director Angela Smith says the Austin Writers' League has about 900 members in the Austin area and 900 outside. An active job bank, professional business information, networking and several workshops attract members. According to Smith, "The reputation the organization has built up enables us to attract good people" for workshops and, in turn, increases growth.

A writers' group often will be free or fairly inexpensive to join. The highest rate is usually about $100 for a yearly membership to a large group, and local groups are frequently free.

## EVALUATING A GROUP

Before you join an association or writers' group, you should evaluate both your needs and goals as well as the group's services.

While joining a group may *help* your career, don't think of it as a magic potion. Joining a writers' organization won't turn you into a successful writer overnight.

Consider this information about each association or group before you join:

- Are your goals compatible with the group's? If your aim is to get critical feedback on your latest short story, you may be dissatisfied with a large association that emphasizes business services. If you are a specialty writer, you may not appreciate the far-flung interests of a local group. At least one group in California completely eschews writing technique; members gather to exchange business and marketing information only. You must look at the group as an extension of your business interests in writing; it must provide some payback to justify your time away from the keyboard.

- What programs and other benefits does the group offer? If you are a full-time freelance writer and need medical benefits, you'll want to look for an organization large enough to offer them. If you're a part-time writer and your main interest is in programs, look for a group strong in that area. If you are a specialty writer, you'll certainly want to check out related specialty groups as well as more general ones.

- What's the cost of joining? Annual fees vary widely—from free membership to several hundred dollars—so you want to be sure you'll get the most benefit for your membership fee. If you're paying for a high-service organization but are not using the services, perhaps you should look into a less-expensive, local group. If, on the other hand, your local or regional group isn't able to offer everything you'd like to have, perhaps you should weigh the benefits of a more expensive group.

- What's the size of the group? For some people, the most beneficial group is one that's small and allows them to participate in each session. Others value the resources of a large group. Some feel the best of both worlds is available through a local chapter of a large organization. You must determine which best fits your style.

- What kind of programs are offered? Try to visit a meeting before you join to determine whether or not you'll benefit from the group's programs. Some organizations offer small critique groups; others have large, formal meetings. In some, leaders of the group are there merely to facilitate discussion or introduce a speaker; in others they play a stronger role. If possible, talk to a few writers in the organization to determine what they like best about the group and its programs, workshops and other services.

- What's the experience level of writers in the group? Most writers' groups and organizations have a variety of members, ranging from aspiring or beginning writers to those with many years of experience. Beware of getting in a group with too many members at one end of the spectrum or the other. If you're experienced and the majority of members are not, most of the programs will be geared to beginners. You eventually may feel your time is being wasted. If, on the other hand, members are very experienced, they may be unwilling to help you develop in a specific area, or you may feel too intimidated to ask questions. Many organizations, especially large ones, have membership surveys that can let you know what the membership experience level is.

## FORMING A WRITERS' GROUP

Occasionally you'll find that a national organization doesn't suit your needs but a local group isn't available or doesn't have the programs you want. If you have the time and energy, you may want to form a writers' group of your own.

Remember, even the largest groups started small. Angela Smith says the Austin Writers' League started with 3 people in 1981 and now has 1,800. She advises organizers to gather as many aspiring writers together as possible. "When you get creative minds together, it's amazing what can happen," she says.

Dana Cassell of the Florida Freelance Writers Association says it's important to check out current groups that meet in the area through local newspapers, libraries and the Chamber of Commerce. To get the word out about a new group, she advises sending press releases to community newspapers and putting notices in adult education bulletins.

If your aim is to form a local chapter of a national organization, contact the parent group and find out what its requirements are. The National Writers Association, for instance, has a Chapter Development Guide it sends to interested writers, with everything from an outline of services to tips on running meetings.

Before you begin meeting, take time to consider these questions about the group you plan to form:
- What are your criteria for membership? Whether you plan to restrict it to published writers or to a particular genre—or keep it open to anyone interested—is something you should decide *before* you start meeting. Sometimes a genre focus can be helpful if there is no other similar group in the area. Mystery and romance writers, as well as poets, frequently benefit more from a group tailored to their needs. Most newly formed groups do not have stringent membership

requirements, however.

- What membership fees and services will the group have? When you start small, you usually must make membership free or low cost because prospective members have nothing on which to judge the value of a membership. Until you know what type of membership base you have, you also can't determine what services you'll be able to support. It's usually best to start slowly in this area and expand as your membership, and its needs, expands.
- What type of programs will you sponsor? Most groups try to set up a fixed time each month, so members can fit that time into their schedules. The format of meetings is less established. Some groups like to have members read from their work and obtain feedback. Others like structured meetings with outside speakers. Many groups try to provide a mixture to attract a variety of participants.

Many more questions will come up as you meet, form plans for a group and select leaders. With the formation of any group for creative people, keep in mind that flexibility and cooperation will allow you to provide the best service for writers.

## SOURCES FOR WRITERS' ORGANIZATIONS

Several sources of information about writers' groups and organizations are available, but there isn't one that's comprehensive. It's simply impossible to gather information about all the organizations, associations and individual groups.

The closest to a comprehensive directory is the *International Directory of Writers' Groups & Associations*, printed in 1988 by Inkling Publications, Inc. (824 Winnetka Ave. S., Minneapolis, MN 55426. (612) 546-0422). It contains 2,000 entries of clubs and organizations in the United States and internationally.

*Literary Market Place* and *International Literary Market Place* (both R.R. Bowker titles) have listings for writers' organizations, mostly the larger associations. National Writers Association, with more specific information in the following listings, also keeps lists of writers' organizations.

Although they probably won't have comprehensive lists, state arts councils sometimes have lists of writers' groups that have received grants. *Grants and Awards Available to American Writers* (PEN American Center, 568 Broadway, New York, NY 10012) has listings for state arts councils.

## *ASSOCIATION AND ORGANIZATION LISTINGS*

### American Medical Writers Association
*9650 Rockville Pike*
*Bethesda, MD 20814-3998*
*(301) 493-0003*

Members: 3,400
Individual and institutional memberships
Publications: quarterly journal, annual membership directory

### American Society of Journalists and Authors
*1501 Broadway, Suite 302*
*New York, NY 10036*
*(212) 997-0947*

### Associated Business Writers of America
*1450 S. Havana, Suite 424*
*Aurora, CO 80012*
*(303) 751-7844*

Members: 5,000
Executive Director: Sandy Whelchel
Professional memberships only
Services: electronic mail service, research reports, complaint service, medical plans
Publications: *Flash Market News* (monthly); *Authorship* (bimonthly)

### The Authors Guild Inc.
*330 W. Forty-second St.*
*New York, NY 10036*
*(212) 563-5904*

Members: 6,500
Executive Director: Paul Aiken
Full voting membership; associate/member-at-large
Services: contract guide, health and life insurance, surveys
Publications: *Authors Guild Bulletin* (quarterly)

### The Authors Resource Center, Inc. (TARC)
*4725 E. Sunrise Dr., #219*
*Tucson, AZ 85718*
*(602) 325-4733*

Members: 300
Director and Literary Agent: Martha R. Gore

Services: medical plan, reference library, answers to reference questions, critiques and editing for fee, workshops
Publications: *TARC Report* (bimonthly)

### Council of Writers Organizations
*One Auto Club Dr.*
*Dearborn, MI 48126*
*(313) 336-1211*

Members: 29,000
Contact: board chairman Len Barnes at address above. President Isolde Chapin is executive director of Washington Independent Writers, 220 Woodward Building, 733 Fifteenth St. NW, Washington, DC 20005.
Umbrella organization for 20 writing groups
Sponsors health insurance, no-cost or low-cost legal and IRS advice
Publications: newsletters by individual groups

### Education Writers Association
*1331 H St. NW, Suite 307*
*Washington, DC 20005*
*(202) 637-9700*
*Fax: (202) 637-9707*
*E-mail: ewaoffice@aol.com.*

Members: 900
Executive Director: Lisa J. Walker
Active and associate memberships
Sponsors annual writing awards, publications, seminars, regional workshops
Publications: bimonthly newsletter, guide to covering education beat, members directory (annual), occasional literacy newsletter, occasional issue briefings, urban education newsletter (5 times/year)

### Freelance Editorial Association
*P.O. Box 38035*
*Cambridge, MA 02238*
*(617) 643-8626*

Members: 500
One level of membership
Services: Members' Network, member-to-member phone connection, advice of Fair Practices Committee, free advertising in *Freelance Editorial Association Yellow Pages*, group insurance
Sponsors discussion groups, meetings and workshops
Publications: quarterly newsletter, *Code of Fair Practice*

### International Association of Crime Writers (North American branch)
*JAF Box 1500*
*New York, NY 10116*
*(212) 757-3915*

Members: 225
President: Roger L. Simon
Executive Director: Mary A. Frisque
Professional membership for authors, editors, booksellers, agents and translators
Sponsors reception for foreign authors and publishers; crime writing conferences abroad
Publications: *Border Patrol* (quarterly)

### The International Women's Writing Guild
*P.O. Box 810, Gracie Station*
*New York, NY 10028*
*(212) 737-7536*

Members: 2,000
Executive Director: Hannelore Hahn
Various levels of membership
Services: medical insurance, literary agents list, workshops, regional meetings
Sponsors 12 conferences per year; annual summer conference

### Mystery Writers of America
*17 E. Forty-seventh St., 6th Floor*
*New York, NY 10007*
*(212) 255-7005*

Members: 2,500
Executive Director: Priscilla Ridgway

### National Conference of Editorial Writers
*6223 Executive Blvd.*
*Rockville, MD 20852*
*(301) 984-3015*
*Fax: (310) 231-0026*

Members: 600
Executive Secretary: Cora B. Everett
Professional membership
Services: member services (critiques)
Sponsors 2 professional seminars, annual convention, foreign tours, awards
Publications: *The Masthead* (quarterly)

### National League of American Pen Women, Inc.
*1300 Seventeenth St. NW*
*Washington, DC 20036-1973*
*(202) 785-1997*

Members: 6,000
Contact: National President
Professional memberships in three classifications: letters, art, music composers
Services: 200 branches in the United States, biennial meetings
Publications: *The Pen Woman* (9 issues/year)

### Outdoor Writers Association of America, Inc.
*2017 Cato Ave., Suite 101*
*State College, PA 16801-2768*
*(814) 234-1011*

Members: 1,890
Executive Director: James Rainey
Individual professional, student and supporting (corporate) memberships
Services: insurance, discounted legal services, job file
Sponsors annual conference, member contests, annual international film/video awards, annual youth writing contest
Publications: *Outdoors Unlimited* (monthly); *OWAA Directory* (annual)

### Poetry Society of America
*15 Gramercy Park*
*New York, NY 10003*
*(212) 254-9628*

Members: 2,500
Assistant Director: Cynthia Atkins
Five levels of membership
Services: discounts on readings and lectures
Sponsors contests, workshops, readings and awards
Publications: newsletter (3 issues/year)

### Romance Writers of America
*13700 Veterans Memorial Dr., #315*
*Houston, TX 77014*
*(713) 440-6885*

### Science-Fiction and Fantasy Writers of America, Inc.
*5 Winding Brook Dr., #1B*
*Guilderland, NY 12084*
*(518) 869-5361*

Members: 1,200

Executive Secretary: Peter Dennis Pautz
Active, affiliate, associate, graphic illustrator, institutional and estate
memberships
Services: grievance committee, circulating book plan, insurance program
through Council of Writers Organizations
Sponsors SFWA Nebula Awards
Publications: *SFWA Bulletin* (quarterly); *SFWA Forum* (bimonthly); annual
membership directory; handbook; Nebula Awards Report (bimonthly)

### Society of American Travel Writers

*4101 Lake Boone Trail, Suite 201*
*Raleigh, NC 27607*
*(919) 787-5181*

### Society of Children's Book Writers and Illustrators

*22736 Vanowen St., #106*
*West Hills, CA 91307*
*(818) 888-8760*

Members: 10,100 +
Contact: Sue Alexander
Associate and full membership
Services: grants, insurance, regional meetings, members' manuscript
exchange
Sponsors annual conference, merit awards
Publications: *Bulletin* (bimonthly)

### Society of Professional Journalists

*P.O. Box 77*
*Greencastle, IN 46135*
*(317) 653-3333*
*Fax: (317) 653-4631*

Members: 14,000 (300 chapters)
Membership Coordinator: Lisa Mock
Professional and student memberships
Services: CareerNet job search
Sponsors annual convention and regional conferences, awards
Publications: *Quill* (monthly)

### Women in Communications, Inc.

*10605 Judicial Dr., Suite A-4*
*Fairfax, VA 22030*
*(703) 359-9000*

Members: 7,000
Professional and student memberships

Services: insurance programs, Member Card, national directory
Sponsors annual national professional conference
Publications: *The Professional Communicator* (4 times/year); *Leadership Bulletin* (4 times/year); *Career Connection* (monthly)

### Writers Guild of America
*7000 W. Third St.*
*Los Angeles, CA 90048-4329*
*(213) 951-4000*

*(East) 555 W. Fifty-seventh St., Suite 1230*
*New York, NY 10019-3402*
*(212) 767-7800*

Members: 7,500
Professional members only
Services for members only
Publications: *Journal* (11 times/year)

### Writers Information Network (W.I.N.)
*P.O. Box 11337*
*Bainbridge Island, WA 98110*
*(206) 842-9103.*

Members: 1,000
Director: Elaine Wright Colvin
Professional association for Christian writers
Services: 2 annual writers conferences and monthly workshops
Publications: bimonthly newsletter

## *UNION*

### National Writers Union
*873 Broadway, Room 203*
*New York, NY 10003*
*(212) 254-0279*

Members: 3,000
President: Jonathan Tasini
Associate Director: Anne Wyville
Services: contract advising, agent database, grievance handling, health care plans, New York and San Francisco job banks
Publications: *American Writer* (quarterly); local newsletters

# WRITERS' GROUPS

### Arizona Authors' Association
*3509 E. Shea Blvd., Suite 117*
*Phoenix, AZ 85028*
*(602) 867-9001*

Members: 500
President: Alexandra Owens
Services: information and referral service
Sponsors monthly meetings, workshops and seminars, contests
Publications: newsletter (bimonthly)

### Austin Writers' League
*1501 W. Fifth St., E-2*
*Austin, TX 78703*
*(512) 499-8914*

Members: 1,800
Executive Director: Angela Smith
Individual, student, senior citizen and family memberships
Services: discounts on books and audiotapes, job bank, study groups
Sponsors fall and spring series of workshops, informal classes, weekend
seminars, awards program, literary touring program

### California Writers' Club
*2214 Derby St.*
*Berkeley, CA 94705*
*(415) 883-6206*

Members: 900
Contact: Sylvia Landman
Sponsors biennial writers' conference, workshops and smaller conferences
by branches, monthly meetings, contest for nonmembers (with prize of
tuition to conference)
Publications: *California Writers' Club Bulletin* (monthly except July/
August); branch newsletters

### Florida Freelance Writers Association
*P.O. Box A*
*North Stratford, NH 03590*
*(603) 922-8338*

Members: 800
Executive Director: Dana K. Cassell
Services: medical plans, critique service, legal hotline, toll-free help
hotline, writer referral service
Sponsors seminars, contest, state conference

Similar regional associations for Georgia and Texas, based in New
Hampshire but have regional directories of writers and markets
Publications: *Freelance Writer's Report* (monthly); annual guide to Florida
writers; annual directory of Florida markets

### Georgia Freelance Writers Association
*(see Florida Freelance Writers Association)*

Members: 150

### Golden Triangle Writers Guild
*4245 Calder*
*Beaumont, TX 77706*
*(409) 898-4894*

Members: 900
President: Neal Morgan
Contacts: Kay and D.J. Resnick
Regular and associate memberships
Services: writer support group
Sponsors monthly meetings, annual conference (October)
Publications: *Scene & Sequel* (monthly)

### National Writers Association
*1450 S. Havana, Suite 424*
*Aurora, CO 80012*
*(303) 751-7844*

Members: 3,000
Executive Director: Sandy Whelchel
Associate and professional memberships
Services: research reports, critiques, marketing information, medical plans,
complaint service, small press, literary agent, agent referral, writing courses
Sponsors periodic workshops
Publications: *Authorship* (bimonthly); *Flash Market News* (monthly for
professional members)

### New England Poetry Club
*Two Farrar St.*
*Boston, MA 02138*

Members: 250
President: Diana Der-Hovanessian; Membership chair: Victor Howes
Student, honorary, friend, associate and full memberships
Sponsors regular meeting, prizes, annual workshop
Publications: *Writ* (semiannually)

### Ozark Writers League
*P.O. Box 1433*
*Branson, MO 65616*
*(417) 334-6016*

Members: 250
President: Dr. Robert K. Gilmore
Sponsors quarterly seminars
Publications: newsletter (quarterly)

### Philadelphia Writers Organization
*P.O. Box 42497*
*Philadelphia, PA 19101*
*(610) 649-8918*

Members: 300
President: William Wartman
Student, associate and full memberships (requires proof of publication)
Services: disability insurance, medical plan, small group discussions
Sponsors monthly meetings, workshop, writers' meeting and editors' marketplace
Publications: newsletter (11 issues/year)

### San Diego Writers/Editors Guild
*3841 Fourth Ave., #242*
*San Diego, CA 92103*
*(619) 223-5235*

Members: 100
Contact: Peggy Lipscomb
Professional and associate memberships
Services: meetings the third Monday of each month, discounts on conferences
Publications: newsletter (monthly)

### Texas Freelance Writers Association
*(see Florida Freelance Writers Association)*

Members: 200

### Washington Christian Writers Fellowship
*P.O. Box 11337*
*Seattle, WA 98110*
*(206) 842-9103*

Members: 300
Director: Elaine Wright Colvin
Various levels of membership

Services: critique, marketing, how-to, networking, press card, instruction
Publications: newsletter (bimonthly)

### Washington Independent Writers
*733 Fifteenth St. NW, #220*
*Washington, DC 20005*
*(202) 347-4973 or 347-4067*

Members: 2,500
Executive Director: Isolde Chapin
Full, associate, senior, student and dual memberships
Services: group health insurance, job bank, legal services plan
Sponsors monthly workshops, spring writers' conference, freelance basics
course
Publications: newsletter (monthly); directory of members (every 2 years)

### The Writers Alliance
*12 Skylark Lane*
*Stony Brook, NY 11790*
*(516) 751-7080*

Members: 125
Contact: Kiel Stuart
Individual and corporate/group memberships
Services: technological help for writers
Sponsors workshops
Publications: *Keystrokes* (quarterly)

### The Writer's Center
*4508 Walsh St.*
*Bethesda, MD 20815*
*(301) 654-8664*

Members: 2,200
Executive Director: Jane Fox
Student, regular, family and business associate memberships
Services: workshop and Book Gallery purchases, reference library, laser
printing and typesetting services
Sponsors four sessions of workshops each year in all genres; readings series
Publications: *Writer's Carousel* (bimonthly); *Poet Lore* (members receive
a subscription discount)

### Writers Connection
*P.O. Box 24770*
*San Jose, CA 95154-4770*
*(408) 445-3600*

Vice-President/Program Director: Meera Lester

Members: 2,500
Various levels of membership
Services: seminars, books, reference library, referral service, job shop,
grammar hotline
Sponsors "Selling to Hollywood" weekend conference (August)
Publications: newsletter (monthly)

*OTHER*

### Poets & Writers, Inc.
*72 Spring St.*
*New York, NY 10012*
*(212) 226-3586*

Nonmembership organization
Executive Director: Elliot Figman
Services: information center for the literary community
Co-sponsors readings throughout New York and California
Publications: *Poets & Writers* (bimonthly magazine); *A Directory of
American Poets & Fiction Writers* (biennially) with names, addresses and
telephone numbers of more than 7,000 poets and fiction writers organized
alphabetically by state, costs $24.95 (paperback) and $2.50 for postage
and handling; *California Resources List* (annually) with writing information
on magazines looking for work from California writers, services for writers
and literary landmarks, costs $2 plus a self-addressed, stamped envelope;
"Living Rooms for Literature: Literary Centers in the U.S.," a reprint of a
magazine article with 18 gathering places for writers, costs $2 and a self-
addressed, stamped envelope. Also offers *Writers' Resources*, a series of
eight regional editions that include listings of workshops, arts councils and
other organizations and resources for authors. Each regional edition costs
$6, plus $3.90 for postage and handling.

# THE ELECTRONIC COMMUNITY OF WRITERS

Increasingly these days, writers also can benefit from the advice and
companionship of other writers without leaving their homes or offices.
Along with the growth of the Internet and online services has come the
equally rapid growth of "virtual" writers' clubs, conferences and retreats
available through local bulletin boards, online services or the Internet.
Because so many writers work with computers, they've been among the
groups fastest to stake outposts in cyberspace. A quick search on Yahoo!
(http://www.yahoo.com), a sort of directory assistance service for the
Web, in late 1995 found more than 100 sites catering to writers in some

way. A similar search using Lycos (http://www.lycos.com. also accessible from Yahoo!), a Web search engine that casts a broader net, revealed more than 18,000 sites with some relevance to writers.

Communicating via modem is no substitute for the camaraderie and support a local or national writers' group can offer. But if you're a writer and you don't take advantage of the rapidly growing world of resources available online, you're missing out on a lot. The "misc.writing" news group on the Internet's Usenet, for example, averages 150 to 200 posts a day from or for writers. The messages include posts from publications seeking writers and advice on everything from researching to marketing—albeit interspersed with some more arcane or less useful chitchat.

One of the first places to check is your local "freenet." These are low-cost or no-cost local bulletin boards available in most major cities. Freenets often include local news groups for freelance writers or areas run by local writers' organizations. The major national online services, including America OnLine, CompuServe, Microsoft Network and Prodigy, also have special interest groups for writers. For example, the Journalism Forum, on CompuServe (go jforum), lists members by location and interests. Besides serving as a lively forum for debate on current issues confronting the trade, the forum frequently includes leads for freelance opportunities. Prodigy offers its Poetry Corner for poets to share ideas and work online.

Besides their own services and databases, the major online services also serve as jumping-off points for the Internet. If you use the Internet more than 9 or 10 hours a month, however, you're probably better off getting an Internet connection through a local Internet access provider. You can find local Internet access providers (probably under Internet Access or Computer Services in your local yellow pages) that provide unlimited hours for $20 a month or less.

You can reach the three national online services, who will be more than happy to send you free information and trial disks or CDs, at the following numbers:

- America OnLine—(800) 827-6364
- CompuServe—(800) 438-3690
- Prodigy—(800) PRODIGY, (800) 776-3449

Provided you have a Macintosh or Windows system, navigating the Web or anywhere on the Internet is fairly easy—mainly a matter of pointing and clicking your way to what you want. The hardest part is finding and correctly entering Web addresses into your Web browser software. But if you just start at Yahoo! (address above) and use the search box to find subjects that interest you, you can point and click your way out of that chore, too.

It makes sense to try a service for a month to get an idea of how good the service is before making any long-term commitment. The major services have their own World Wide Web browsers, but you may need to download a browser, such as the popular line of browsers available for free from Netscape (http://www.netscape.com). Your service provider should be able to provide you with the details you need to get up and running.

Trying to provide a listing of Internet sites of interest to freelance writers in a book is pointless. Though many sites have been around for years, the Internet and World Wide Web sites come, go and change addresses so rapidly that the best way to keep up with them is simply to get on the Internet and look around. Again, such search tools as Yahoo! and Lycos are by far the easiest ways to do this.

The Web gets its name because most sites contain hypertext (highlighted text) links to other sites, forming a giant and often tangled "web." So once you get on one site, you often can follow the links to many more. Here are a few of the interesting Web sites for writers that existed as of the writing of this book:

- Children's Writing Resource Center (http://www.mindspring/com/~cbi/): information and advice from the Children's Writing Resource Center
- Kidlit (http://mgfx.com/kidlit): information and resources for children's book writers
- National Writers Union Home Page (http://www.nwu.org/nwu/): News and advice from the National Writers Union
- Writer's (Stumbling) Block (http://alf2.tcd.ie/~mmchugh/writer/html): resources for writers of horror, fantasy and science fiction, including submission guidelines from several publishers
- Writers:Writers (http://tile.net/listserv/writers.html): a collection of numerous links to writers' groups and resources

# COLONIES, RESIDENCIES AND RETREATS

Some writers are happiest working in their own homes or offices and find they are very productive there. Others have a desire to get away from the regular routine at a colony or retreat. Among the colonies available, some are just for writers, while others are open to artists and performing artists. Few of the colonies could be considered tourist meccas, and some, such as Dorland, are extremely spartan.

The advantage of a colony is not in the accommodations, but the opportunities it provides. Colonies are not for every writer, but time at one can be extremely useful as a change of pace to get the most out of your creative powers in a short amount of time. A colony "is for people who don't have enough concentrated time," says Jill Charles of The Dorset Colony House for Writers.

Writers have a variety of reasons for attending colonies. Elizabeth Guheen, of Ucross Foundation in Wyoming, says writers want "the time— and for a lot of people, this is a region of the country they aren't familiar with. This is a really beautiful area, authentic West, with a lack of glitz." Other writers like the informal atmosphere of a place such as The Dorset Colony. "If they had the money to buy their own home in the country, this is what they'd have," Jill Charles says.

Characteristics of colonies vary widely. Some put a premium on unrestricted time and freedom from interaction with anyone. Others seek a balance of colonists so they can learn from each other. Very few have a regimented schedule, but a few require a plan from writers about what they will work on while they stay at the colony. You'll find that some are very competitive and others have a more open policy. Nearly all require that you bring any equipment you plan to use (typewriter, personal computer) while you're there.

Some colonies operate year-round, but others are open only in the fall and spring. Especially when applying for a highly competitive colony, consider going in the off-season to take advantage of fewer applicants. Many writers want to attend in the fall or spring, so you may want to consider applying for a summer or winter position if the colony will be open then.

At the Ucross Foundation, for instance, about 350 applications are received per year for 60 positions. A panel meets to choose "a good mix" of residents who will live in a home and eat dinner together but have separate studio space. Elizabeth Guheen says most residents have other employment but are on sabbatical or vacation and "find a way to make it work with their creative lives." The colony is expanding to accommodate eight residents at a time for an average stay of about six weeks.

Yaddo, one of the oldest and most well-known colonies, has about 1,500 applicants in writing and art, of which 220 are accepted. The focus is on poetry, fiction, film and playwriting. The colony, open year-round, has a recommended payment of $20 per day, and the average stay is one month, though longer stays are encouraged.

Flexibility is the key at The Dorset Colony. About 60 to 75 writers and performing artists make use of the space during the year, with some who have been there before calling ahead and getting approval for a weekend stay. In addition, writers cook their own food when they want. The average stay is about two weeks in a large house in a rural village.

Before applying at a colony, consider these points about each:

- What are the requirements for application? Colonies almost always require an application, some with accompanying writing samples, recommendations or references, and a deposit. At Yaddo, for instance, applicants are judged as if it's the first time they have applied even if they have been there before. The Dorset Colony, on the other hand, requires no formal application after the first time. After you've selected a colony for application, begin getting your material together about eight months or more before you would like to attend. This is necessary because applications are frequently considered about six months before attendance. Most colonies will let you know their requirements by phone; several have brochures or flyers they can send for a self-addressed, stamped envelope.

- What's the cost? Some colonies offer free accommodations to chosen applicants; many have a recommended daily fee of $10 to $40. A few charge weekly fees. The majority of colonies stress that payment is voluntary and no qualified applicant will be turned away simply because he or she cannot pay.

- How many other residents are there? Writers attending colonies frequently want the kind of freedom away from other people they can't get at home. If you're that type of person, consider a colony with few residents, and perhaps one in which the individual cooks his or her own meals. After concentrating on your work for several hours each day, you may enjoy some social time with other colonists, however.

- Does the colony fit your lifestyle? Some colonists think they'd like nothing better than a rural atmosphere, but later find they don't. Writers sometimes like to cook their own meals at their convenience, but others would rather have their meals prepared and ready at a regular time. These are all considerations you need to make before applying.

- How much time do you need? A few colonies offer residencies as short as a weekend, but the majority of colonies want you to stay two to eight weeks. Because most writers find they work more quickly and efficiently at a colony, you need to have a plan for what you'd like to accomplish while you're there—even if the colony doesn't require it for application.

If possible, talk to other writers who've been to colonies to find out how they used the experience. Most use it to finish up a project, start a new one or revise or reassess a "stalled" piece of writing.

## RESOURCES

Several reference books have information and listings of writers' colonies. Check *The Guide to Writers Conferences* (Shaw Associates). As a service to its members, The Authors Guild compiles a list of several colonies, and *Poets & Writers* frequently carries advertisements and notices of colonies. You may also want to check with your state arts council to see if officials there know of any colonies in the state.

*LISTINGS*

### Atlantic Center for the Arts
*1414 Art Center Ave.*
*New Smyrna Beach, FL 32168*
*(904) 427-6975*
*Program Director: James J. Murphy*
*Estab. 1978*

Offers 3-week interdisciplinary sessions 5 to 6 times/year. Cost is $200 for nonresident; $600 resident fee. Provisions include private room/bath, work space, meeting space, copy machine, limited access to typewriters. (Computers and word processors planned for future.) Accommodates 10 to 15/residency. Submission procedure varies with each Master Artist, but examples of writing are sent directly to that person, who then selects "associates." College credit may be available.

### Blue Mountain Center
*Blue Mountain Lake, NY 12812*
*(518) 352-7391*
*Director: Harriet Barlow*
*Estab. 1982*

Offers 4-week sessions during summer and fall at no cost other than transportation to center. Provisions include private room (bedroom and study), breakfast and dinner in dining room, serve-yourself lunch, laundry, copy machine, tennis court, lakes, boats, trails, recreation room. Accommodates 15 residents at one time. Submissions required by Feb. 1; decisions made by March 31. No college credit.

### Dorland Mountain Arts Colony
*P.O. Box 6*
*Temecula, CA 92593*

*(714) 676-5039*
*President: Mary Morton*
*Estab. 1979*

Offers 1- to 3-month residencies year-round. Cost is $150/month. Provisions include cabin with kitchen, bedroom, private working area. Meals are responsibility of resident. Accommodates 6 residents at a time. Request application with SASE; deadlines are Sept. 1 and March 1. No college credit.

### The Dorset Colony House for Writers
*Church Street, P.O. Box 519*
*Dorset, VT 05251*
*(802) 867-2223*
*Director: Dr. John Nassivera*
*Estab. 1982*

Offers sessions from 1 week to 2 months, Sept. 1 to Dec. 1 and March 15 to May 15. Cost is $95/week voluntary fee. Provisions include private room in 3-story house, kitchen, dining room, library/sitting room, phone room, porch area. Accommodates 8 residents at a time. Submit letter, résumé and brief statement of material/project to work on during stay. No college credit.

### Fine Arts Work Center in Provincetown
*24 Pearl St., P.O. Box 565*
*Provincetown, MA 02657*
*(508) 487-9960*
*Contact: writing coordinator*
*Estab. 1968*

Offers 7-month residencies from Oct. 1 to May 1. Fellows are provided with live-in studio and a monthly stipend of $375. Accommodates 8 first-year fellows and 2 returning fellows at a time. Application and information available ($35 application fee). Feb. 1 deadline. No college credit.

### William Flanagan Memorial Creative Persons Center
*("The Barn")*
*Edward F. Albee Foundation*
*14 Harrison St.*
*New York, NY 10013*
*(212) 226-2020*
*Foundation Secretary: David Briggs*

Offers 1-month residencies, June 1 to Oct. 1. Provisions include room for writers and composers; room and studio space for visual artists. Accommodates 2 to 3 artists per month. Application forms available. Résumé, 2 letters of recommendation, letter outlining proposed project,

2 mailing labels and SASE for return of material required. Applications accepted between Jan. 1 and April 1. No college credit.

### Green River Writers' Retreat
*11906 Locust Rd.*
*Middletown, KY 40243*
*(502) 245-4902*
*President: Mary E. O'Dell*
*Estab. 1986*

Offers 8-day residency in July. Cost is $50 ($15 of which is membership fee). Provisions include private and semi-private rooms (available in dorm housing at additional fee of $20 per night). Accommodates 36 residents at a time. Contact for application information. No college credit. Also holds a Novels Workshop each March.

### The Tyrone Guthrie Centre
*Annaghmakerrig, Newbliss*
*County Monaghon, Ireland*
*(353) 047-54003*
*Director: Bernard Loughlin*
*Estab. 1981*

Offers 3-week to 3-month residencies year-round. Cost is Ir 1,200/month. Provisions include private apartment, all meals. Accommodates up to 12 residents at a time. Requires samples of work for writers, slides of photographs for visual artists and tape recordings of work from musicians. No college credit.

### The Hambidge Center for Creative Arts & Sciences
*P.O. Box 339*
*Rabun Gap, GA 30568*
*(706) 746-5718*
*Executive Director: Judy Barber*
*Estab. 1934*

Offers 2-week to 2-month residencies from May to October. Cost is $100/week. Provisions include private housing, studios, dinner, laundry. Accommodates 7 residents at a time. Applications ($10 fee) are reviewed by committee. Deadline January 31. Application review begins in March. No college credit.

### Kalani Honua Conference Center and Retreat
*RR 2, Box 4500*
*Pahoa, HI 96778*
*(808) 965-7828*

*Director: Richard Koob*
*Estab. 1980*

Offers 2-week to 2-month residencies. Full-payment residencies year-round; stipended residencies as space is available, usually May to June and September to December. Cost is $40 to $100/day including meals; with stipend $30 to $60/day including meals. Provisions include option of private room with shared or private bath, work space/studio and meals. Accommodates 100 residents at a time. Write or call for application ($10 fee); documentation of work required. College credit must be applied for separately through University of Hawaii–Hilo.

### MacDowell Colony
*100 High St.*
*Peterborough, NH 03458*
*(603) 924-3886 or (212) 535-9690*
*Admissions Coordinator: Shirley Bewley*
*Estab. 1907*

Offers up to 2-month residencies year-round. Cost is "pay what you can." Provisions include studio space, room and board. Accommodates 10 to 20 residents at a time. Deadlines are Jan. 15 for May through August; April 15 for September through December; and Sept. 15 for January through April. Must apply about 8 months prior to desired residency. No college credit.

### Millay Colony for the Arts
*Steepletop, P.O. Box 3*
*Austerlitz, NY 12017-0003*
*(518) 392-3103*
*Assistant Director: Gail Giles*
*Estab. 1974*

Offers 1-month residencies year-round. Provisions include private room, studio space, all meals. Accommodates 5 residents/month. Application deadlines are Feb. 1 for June to September; May 1 for October to January; Sept. 1 for February to May. No college credit.

### O'Neill Theater Center
*234 W. Forty-fourth St., Suite 901*
*New York, NY 10036*
*(212) 382-2790*
*Artistic Director: Lloyd Richards*
*Estab. 1978*

Offers 3- to 4-week residency in August. No cost. Provisions include stipend, transportation from New York to Waterford, Connecticut, housing and meals. Minimally staged and unstaged readings. Accommodates 8 to 10 residents at a time. Send SASE for application form and guidelines, applications accepted between Nov. 1 and Feb. 1.

### Palenville Interarts Colony
*Two Bond St.*
*New York, NY 10012*
*(212) 254-4614*
*Artistic Director: Joanna Sherman*
*Estab. 1982*

Not currently accepting applications for residencies.

### Ragdale Foundation
*1260 N. Green Bay Rd.*
*Lake Forest, IL 60045*
*(708) 234-1063*
*Manager: Sylvia Brown*
*Estab. 1976*

Offers 2- to 8-week residencies year-round except for a period of 2 weeks in late spring and at Christmas. Suggested cost is $15/day, $84/week, financial aid and full or partial waivers are available. Accommodates 12 residents at a time. Provisions include separate studios; prepared evening meals. Deadlines are Jan. 15 for June through December; June 1 for January through May. $20 application fee. No college credit.

### Ucross Foundation
*2836 U.S. Highway 14-16 East*
*Clearmont, WY 82835*
*(307) 737-2291*
*Program Director: Elizabeth Guheen*
*Estab. 1981*

Offers 2- to 8-week sessions in February through June and August through December. No cost. Provisions include a private studio and room, meals. Accommodates 4 residents at a time—a mix of writers, visual artists and composers. Send SASE for brochure and application. Deadlines are March 1 and Oct. 1. No college credit.

### Virginia Center for the Creative Arts
*Mt. San Angelo*
*Sweet Briar, VA 24595*
*(804) 946-7236*
*Director: William Smart*
*Estab. 1971*

Offers 2-week to 2-month residencies available year-round. Cost is $30/day suggested fee. Provisions include a private room, studio and meals.

Accommodates 11 residents at a time. Send SASE for application. Deadlines are Jan. 25, May 25 and Sept. 25. No college credit.

### Helene Wurlitzer Foundation

*P.O. Box 545*
*Taos, NM 87571*
*(505) 758-2413*
*President, executive director: Kenneth Peterson*
*Estab. 1954*

Offers varying residencies from April 1 to Sept. 30. Rent-free and utility-free housing in the Taos, New Mexico, area available to persons involved in the creative, not the interpretive, fields in all media. Accommodates varying number of residents. Send SASE for application.

### Yaddo

*P.O. Box 395*
*Saratoga Springs, NY 12866*
*(518) 584-0746*
*President: Michael Sundell*
*Estab. 1900*

Offers year-round residencies of variable length. Provisions include room, board and studio space for writers, visual artists, composers and photographers. Accommodates about 220 residents/year. Send SASE for brochure and application. No college credit.

# CONFERENCES AND WORKSHOPS

With thousands of conferences and workshops available, writers can choose from a variety of subjects, lengths and locations to suit their writing needs and schedules.

Writers have many goals when they attend conferences and workshops. Some want to explore a new writing area or learn from a particular instructor. Others are interested in making publishing contacts with writers, editors and agents attending the conference. Still others like the inspiration and concentrated time with fellow writers.

Whatever your motivation for exploring conferences, you'll probably find that several sound interesting from written descriptions. Explore these further, obtaining any literature the conference has available and talking to previous attendees.

Many conferences attract mainly local participants in order to bring the national marketplace home to local writers. Others, however, attract writers from a wider area by featuring prominent authors. Generally, the cost of national or regional conferences is higher than the cost of conferences geared toward only local writers.

Registration at the Santa Barbara Writers' Conference is limited to 300 people and attracts participants from as far away as Australia. The conference features a number of best-selling writers and has classes for both beginners and advanced writers, including several genre classes. "The caliber of the workshops attracts people," says director, Mary Conrad.

A slightly smaller, week-long conference is the Cape Cod Writers' Conference, with about 150 participants. Nonfiction, fiction and poetry are always covered, along with a fourth rotating writing specialty. The conference attracts a large number of returning participants who credit it with providing them with ideas and industry contacts.

Consider these aspects of the conference, too:

- Who is on the faculty? For some writers, this is the most important of all criteria. They want a well-respected, published writer from whom they can learn for a day, a weekend or a week. Look for writers who have credits in the particular area they will teach *and* can communicate with other writers without simply lecturing. Marion Vuilleumier of the Cape Cod Writers' Conference says she looks for "teachers who are teachers *and* published. We don't want a college class." The New Orleans Writers' Conference is one of a few that offers one-on-one consultation and free manuscript evaluation. Director Beverly Gianna says, "We try to select faculty that are good and have a sharing, approachable attitude."

- How many people attend the conference? There is very little one-on-one instruction in large conferences, but some offer individual conferences with editors, agents and other instructors—usually for an additional fee. Obviously, your chances of individual meetings or instruction are greater if the conference is smaller, but smaller conferences frequently attract less-prominent speakers, too. Instead of focusing on the total number attending the conference, ask about the number in each session. If you find this number is 30 or less, you'll probably have more of a chance to ask questions or discuss your work with the instructor.

- What type of sessions does the conference offer? Is the format set up in a lecture style, or does it involve some give-and-take with instructors and speakers? Are there panels with writers, editors and agents who may offer their opinions on subjects of interest to the group? Are the programs geared to beginning, intermediate or professional writers?

These are questions you will want to evaluate against your own preferences.

- What kind of personal feedback can you expect? As stated before, most individual conferences, manuscript evaluations and other personal feedback must be arranged ahead of time and paid for separately. That doesn't mean you can't make contact with people in the business, but you usually can't count on it. If you are paying or making an appointment, however, you have every right to know what to expect from the meeting. Don't go in expecting to find an editor who will want to publish your work or an agent who will want to represent it. Certainly, this kind of serendipitous meeting has happened before. Just don't be disappointed if it doesn't.

- What's the average level of other writers at the conference? Most conferences attract a variety of writers, ranging from beginners to professionals. A quick look at the program offerings can give you a clue to whether most sessions are geared to beginners or professionals, and you may want to avoid a conference, or at least those sessions, that seems too far below or above your level of experience.

- How much does the conference cost? Last, but certainly not least for any writer, is the value for the dollar. Many writers save money by attending regional conferences where they can stay at home and commute each day. Others combine vacation and work and attend a conference in Cape Cod or Santa Barbara, for instance. The average cost for a one- or two-day workshop ranges from $15 to $50, although some run as high as $200. Conferences that last from four days to a week usually will cost from $100 to $800 and most often include lodging and meals.

## STARTING A CONFERENCE

A great deal of work has to go on behind the scenes to pull off a conference for 300 people, so it's typical for organizers to wonder, after the conference ends, how they accomplished it.

Mary Conrad's husband, Barnaby, taught at a prep school and set up the first writers' conference for 35 students from the school. It's no longer affiliated with the school or restricted to students and has become one of the largest and most well-respected conferences in the United States. "It just steadily increased," she says. "We never dreamed it would be this big."

Likewise, Marion Vuilleumier says a group of writers on Cape Cod wanted to start its own conference "because we couldn't go away in the summer because we were taking care of guests." She consulted with

editors at *The Writer* magazine who advised her on ways to attract participants and teachers. The programs offered now include a young writers'
section, a literacy program, a TV book show and a workshop arts
program.

If you'd like to start your own conference, follow these tips from
current conference directors:

- Start small, perhaps with a weekend workshop, to work out
  scheduling.
- Offer a mixture of programs to appeal to beginners and advanced
  writers.
- Look for ways the conference can provide individual feedback and
  personal attention to participants.
- Take advantage of contacts you may have made in the publishing
  business through magazine and book publishers or writers you've met
  at other workshops.
- Most important to the success of the venture: Organize the type of
  conference you'd like to attend.

## SOURCES

The best source for writers' conferences is probably *The Guide to
Writers Conferences*. The fifth edition is currently available from Shaw
Guides, P.O. Box 1295, New York, NY 10023. Darlene Kaplan says they
do a "massive mailing" to obtain listings from more than 400 sponsors
of writers' conferences, workshops, seminars, residencies, retreats and
organizations. The guide has an index by month, a geographic index and
a subspecialty index, as well as information on conferences that provide
continuing education or college credit, award scholarships and sponsor
contests. *The Official Guide to AWP Writing Programs* (Associated Writing
Programs) has information on writers' conferences, colonies and centers;
and the May issue of *Writer's Digest* also has conference listings.

Other sources include *Writers Conferences*, with dates, addresses,
fees, deadlines and workshop leaders for 200 conferences, available
March 1 each year from Poets & Writers, Inc., 72 Spring St., New York,
NY 10012. (212) 226-3586; fax: (212) 226-3963. Cost is $8 with $3.90 for
postage and handling. Also available is *Author & Audience: A Readings
and Workshops Guide*, which covers 400 organizations that present readings or workshops, arranged alphabetically by state. It also has information on running successful programs. Cost is $10 and $3.90 for postage
and handling.

## *LISTINGS*

### Alabama Writers' Conclave
*P.O. Box 230787*
*Montgomery, AL 36123-0787*
*(205) 822-3086*
*President: Donna Tennis*
*Contact: Ann Moon Rabb*
*Estab. 1923*
*Held first week of August*

Three-day workshop covering fiction and poetry, scriptwriting when possible. Send SASE after Feb. 1 for details about workshop and cost.

### American Christian Writers Conference
*P.O. Box 5168*
*Phoenix, AZ 85010*
*(800) 21-WRITE*
*Director: Reg A. Forder*
*Estab. 1981*

Three-day conference to promote all forms of Christian writing. Cost: $199 plus meals and accommodations.

### American Society of Journalists and Authors
*Sheraton New York Towers and Hotel*
*53rd between 6th and 7th*
*New York, NY 10019*
*(212) 997-0947*
*Executive Director: Alexandra Cantor*
*Estab. 1971*

Two-day workshops with various panels concentrating on topics of interest to journalists. Cost: $125.

### Antioch Writers' Workshop
*P.O. Box 494*
*Yellow Springs, OH 45387*
*(513) 767-7068*
*Director: Susan Carpenter*
*Estab. 1985*

One-week workshop covering novels, poetry, short stories, screenwriting and nonfiction. Includes daily classes, mini-workshops. Cost: $450 tuition plus room and board.

### Appalachian Writers Workshop

*P.O. Box 844*
*Hindman, KY 41822*
*(606) 785-5475*
*Director: Mike Mullins*
*Estab. 1977*
*Usually held end of July or beginning of August*

Five-day workshop covering fiction, nonfiction, poetry, children's writing and playwriting. Cost: $350.

### Arkansas Writers' Conference

*1115 Gillette Dr.*
*Little Rock, AR 72207*
*(501) 225-0166*
*Director: Clovita Rice*
*Estab. 1944*
*Held first weekend in June*

Two-day conference on various types of writing and marketing. Cost: $10 both days; $5 for one day. Program includes $2,000 in contest awards. Information available by Feb. 1.

### Biola University Writers Institute

*13800 Biola Ave.*
*La Mirada, CA 90639*
*(800) 75-WORDS*
*Associate Director: Susan Titus*
*Estab. 1984*

Four-day conference is the largest Christian writers' conference in the nation, covering beginning writing, article writing, fiction, nonfiction and writing for children. Six major morning workshops and 36 afternoon electives are offered. Includes a video correspondence course, spring article writing contest and manuscript critique service. Cost: $280 plus room.

### California Writers' Conference

*2214 Derby St.*
*Berkeley, CA 94705*
*(510) 841-1217*
*Contact: Dorothy Benson*

Weekend (Friday noon through Sunday lunch) conference covering all genres. Cost: $295 resident; $195 commuter.

### Cape Cod Writers' Conference
*% Cape Cod Conservatory, Rt. 132*
*W. Barnstable, MA 02668*
*(508) 375-0516*
*Executive Director: Marion Vuilleumier*
*Estab. 1963*
*Usually held third week of August*

One-week conference covering fiction, nonfiction, poetry, juvenile writing and a fifth course that rotates. Cost: $80 registration, $90 per course (full time); $25 registration, $25 per course (one day); $60 for manuscript critique, $30 for personal interview with staff (plus housing and meals). Average cost is $200 to $300. Group also sponsors Cape Literary Arts Workshops on a variety of topics.

### Chisolm Trail Writer's Workshop
*P.O. Box 297026*
*Fort Worth, TX 76129*
*(817) 921-7822*
*Director of TCU Press: Judy Alter*

One-day conference, generally on fiction with a Western flair. Cost: $30 (tentative).

### Christopher Newport University Annual Writers Conference
*50 Shoe Lane*
*Newport News, VA 23606-2998*
*(804) 594-7158*
*Coordinator: Terry Cox-Joseph*
*Estab. 1981*

One-day workshop covering nonfiction, poetry, fiction and juvenile fiction. Includes writing contest. Cost: $69.

### Colorado Mountain Writers' Workshop
*Colorado Mountain College*
*Spring Valley Center, 3000 County Rd. 114*
*Glenwood Springs, CO 81601*
*(303) 945-7481*
*Director: Doug Evans*

One-week conference covering novels, poetry, short fiction, nonfiction and scriptwriting.

### Desert Writers Workshop—Canyonlands Field Institute
*P.O. Box 68*
*Moab, UT 84532*
*(801) 259-7750 or (800) 860-5262*

*Program Coordinator: Karla Vanderzanden*
*Estab. 1984*

Three-day conference covering creative nonfiction, fiction and poetry (all with emphasis on landscape). Cost: $385 (members of CFI); $400 (nonmenbers).

### Fiction from the Heartland
*P.O. Box 32186*
*Kansas City, MO 64111*
*(816) 254-4901*
*Conference Chair: Judy Johnson*
*Estab. 1988*

Two-day conference covering commercial fiction—romance, mystery/suspense, fantasy/science fiction, horror. Cost: $50.

### Flight of the Mind
*622 SE Twenty-ninth Ave.*
*Portland, OR 97214*
*(503) 236-9862*
*Director: Judith Barrington*
*Estab. 1984*
*Usually held end of June, beginning of July. Two workshops in summer for*
*   7 days each*

One-week, all women's conference covering fiction, poetry, screenwriting and nonfiction. Other offerings vary. Cost: about $700, including tuition, room and board. Brochure for 1 first-class stamp, no SASE.

### Great Lakes Writers' Workshop
*3401 S. Thirty-ninth St.*
*P.O. Box 343922*
*Milwaukee, WI 53234-3922*
*(414) 382-6176*
*Director, Telesis Institute: Debra Pass*
*Estab. 1985*
*Held during second week of July*

One-week conference covering a variety of subjects. Cost: less than $100.

### Green Lake Christian Writers Conference
*American Baptist Assembly*
*Green Lake, WI 54941-9300*
*(800) 558-8898*
*Director of program: Dr. Arlo R. Reichter*
*Estab. 1948*

One-week conference covering nonfiction, devotional, poetry and fiction. Cost: $80 tuition; room and meals additional.

### Hofstra University Children's Literature Conference
*Hofstra University, UCCE*
*205 Davison Hall*
*Hempstead, NY 11550-1090*
*(516) 463-5016*
*Director, Liberal Arts: Lewis Shena*
*Estab. 1983*

One-day conference covering children's writing: fiction, nonfiction, picture books and submission procedures. Cost: approximately $47.

### Hofstra University Summer Writers' Conference
*Hofstra University, UCCE*
*205 Davison Hall*
*Hempstead, NY 11550-1090*
*(516) 560-5016 or 463-5016*
*Director, Liberal Arts: Lewis Shena*
*Estab. 1971*
*Usually begins the Monday after July 4*

Ten-day conference covering fiction, nonfiction, poetry, children's books and stage/screenwriting. Cost: $625.

### Iowa Summer Writing Festival
*116 International Center*
*The University of Iowa*
*Iowa City, IA 52242-1802*
*(319) 335-2534*
*Director: Peggy Houston*
*Estab. 1987*
*Held each summer in June and July*

One-week conferences offering 60 different classes. Cost: $335–360 per week.

### Maple Woods Community College Writers Conference
*2601 NE Barry Rd.*
*Kansas City, MO 64156*
*(816) 437-3042*
*Coordinator: Paula Schumacker*
*Estab. 1983*

One-day workshop covering a variety of writing and publishing topics. Cost: $45.

### Midland Writers Conference
*Grace A. Dow Memorial Library*
*1710 W. St. Andrews*
*Midland, MI 48640*
*(517) 835-7151*
*Conference Chair: Katherine Redwine*
*Estab. 1979*
*Usually held second weekend in June*

One-day conference covering poetry, writing for children, and fiction. Cost: $45 until May 17; $55 after. Senior citizens and student discounts.

### Midwest Writers Workshop
*Department of Journalism*
*Ball State University*
*Muncie, IN 47306*
*(317) 285-2080*
*Director: Earl L. Conn*
*Estab. 1972*

Four-day conference covering fiction, nonfiction and poetry, plus one or more specialized areas. Cost: $175.

### Mount Holyoke Writers' Conference
*P.O. Box 3213-B*
*Mount Holyoke College*
*South Hadley, MA 01075*
*(413) 538-2308*
*Director: Michael Pettit*
*Estab. 1988*

One-week conference covering fiction, nonfiction and poetry, including agents' and editors' panels. Cost: $700 tuition, room and board; $400 tuition only. Scholarships are available.

### Napa Valley Writers' Conference
*Napa Valley College*
*1088 College Ave.*
*St. Helena, CA 94574*
*(707) 967-2900*
*Program Director: Sherri Hallgren*
*Estab. 1981*
*Usually held last week of July or first week in August*

One-week conference covering fiction and poetry. Cost: $450.

### The New Orleans Writers' Conference
*Office of Conference Services*
*Metropolitan College*
*ED Room 122*
*University of New Orleans*
*New Orleans, LA 70148*
*(504) 286-6680*
*Conference Director: Anne O'Heren Jakob*
*Estab. 1989*

Three-day conference covering fiction, nonfiction, poetry, play/ screenwriting, juvenile writing, romance, mystery.

### Ozark Creative Writers Inc. Conference
*6817 Gingerbread Lane*
*Little Rock, AR 72204*
*(501) 565-8889*
*Director: Peggy Vining*
*Estab. 1973*

Two-day conference covering fiction, nonfiction, writing for children and poetry. Cost: $35 registration, additional charge for lodging and food. Held at The Inn of the Ozarks in Eureka Springs.

### Port Townsend Writers' Conference
*Centrum, P.O. Box 1158*
*Port Townsend, WA 98368*
*(206) 385-3102*
*Director: Carol Jane Bangs*
*Estab. 1974*
*Usually held second week of July*

Ten-day conference covering mainstream and experimental fiction, poetry, nature writing, essay writing and writing for children. Cost: $400 for tuition; approximately $315 for room and board.

### Professionalism in Writing School
*4308 S. Peoria, Suite 701*
*Tulsa, OK 74105*
*(918) PIW-5588*
*Coordinator: Norma Jean Lutz*
*Estab. 1983*

Two-day conference for Christians who write broad spectrum (includes all genres, Christian and secular). Cost: $145 advance; $165 at door.

### St. Davids Christian Writers Conference
*Eastern College*
*St. Davids, PA 19087*
*Mail should be addressed to:*
*1775 Eden Rd.*
*Lancaster, PA 17601-3523*
*(717) 394-6758*
*Registrar: Shirley Eaby*
*Estab. 1957*
*Usually held end of June*

Five-day conference with rotating workshops, including adult and children's fiction, journalism, articles, feature and devotional writing, poetry, serious and humorous writing and scriptwriting. Cost: $400 to $500, including classes, room and board.

### San Diego State University Writers' Conference
*8465 Jane St.*
*San Diego, CA 92129*
*(619) 484-8575*
*Director: Diane Dunaway*
*Estab. 1986*

Two-day conference covering fiction, nonfiction, children's books, screenwriting, consultations with editors and agents, and critiques. Usually held third week in January. Cost: $194.

### San Diego State University Writers' Conference
*The College of Extended Studies*
*5630 Hardy Ave.*
*San Diego, CA 92182-0723*
*(619) 594-2517*
*Extension Director: Jan Wahl*
*Estab. 1984*

Two-day conference covering fiction, nonfiction and screenwriting. Cost: approximately $225.

### Santa Barbara Writers' Conference
*P.O. Box 304*
*Carpinteria, CA 93014*
*(805) 684-2250*
*Directors: Mary and Barnaby Conrad*
*Estab. 1973*
*Held the last Friday-to-Friday in June*

One-week conferences covering all genres of writing. Cost for 1995 conference (all workshops and lectures, 2 al fresco dinners and room) was $1,010 single, $740 double, $350 day students.

### Society of Children's Book Writers and Illustrators Conference
*22736 Vanowen St., Suite 106*
*West Hills, CA 91307*
*Director: Lin Oliver*

### Space Coast Writers Guild, Inc.
*P.O. Box 804*
*Melbourne, FL 32902*
*(407) 727-0051*
*President: Dr. Edwin J. Kirschner*
*Estab. 1981*

Two-day conference covering a variety of writer's subjects. Cost: $50 for members, $70 for nonmembers.

### Steamboat Springs Writers Conference
*P.O. Box 774284*
*Steamboat Springs, CO 80477*
*(970) 879-8079*
*Director: Harriet Freiberger*
*Estab. 1981*

One-day conference covering fiction, nonfiction, general creativity and/or poetry. Cost: $25 for members; $35 for nonmembers.

### Stonecoast Writers' Conference
*University of Southern Maine*
*96 Falmouth St.*
*Portland, ME 04103*
*(207) 280-4076*
*Director: Barbara Hope*
*Estab. 1977*

Ten-day conference covering fiction, poetry, scriptwriting and nonfiction. Cost: $399 plus room and board.

### Trenton State College Writers' Conferences
*Department of English*
*Hillwood Lakes CN 4700*
*Trenton, NJ 08650-4700*
*(609) 771-3254*
*Director: Jean Hollander*
*Estab. 1981*

One-day conference covering fiction, poetry, newspaper and magazine journalism, playwriting, scriptwriting, literature for young people and nonfiction. Cost varies.

### UCLA Extension Screenwriting Workshops
*The Writers' Program*
*10995 Le Conte Ave., #440*
*Los Angeles, CA 90024*
*(800) 388-UCLA or (310) 825-9416*
*E-mail: writers@unex.UCLA.edu.*

One-, two- and four-day formats for beginners and advanced writers.

### University of Wisconsin School of the Arts at Rhinelander
*726 Lowell Hall*
*610 Langdon St.*
*Madison, WI 53703*
*(608) 263-3494*
*Administrative Coordinator: Kathy Berigan*
*Estab. 1964*
*Held third or fourth week of July*

Five-day conference covering fiction, nonfiction, poetry, creativity; also classes in visual arts, folk arts, dance, photography, drama. Cost: $125 to $205, not including food and lodging.

### Vassar College Institute of Publishing and Writing: Children's Books in the Marketplace
*P.O. Box 300*
*Poughkeepsie, NY 12601*
*(914) 437-5903*
*Associate Director of College Relations: Maryann Bruno*
*Estab. 1983*
*Conference held second week in June or July*

One-week conference covering children's books (fiction and nonfiction), illustrating, and understanding the market. Cost: $800, includes room and board.

### Wesleyan Writers Conference
*Wesleyan University*
*Middletown, CT 06457*
*(203) 685-3604*
*Director: Anne Greene*
*Estab. 1956*
*Held last week of June*

Five-day conference covering fiction, poetry, literary journalism and nonfiction. Scholarships available. Cost: $620 (tuition) (plus $105 for room and board, includes meals).

### Western Reserve Writers and Freelance Conference
*34200 Ridge Rd., #110*
*Willoughby, OH 44094*
*(216) 943-3047*
*Coordinator: Lea Leever Oldham*
*Estab. 1984*
*Usually held second Saturday in September*

One-day conference covering fiction (romance, science fiction, short stories), nonfiction (books, articles, humor), poetry, photography, cartooning. Cost: $49, including lunch.

   (Also sponsors Western Reserve Writers Weekend at Cedar Hills Conference Center. Covers fiction, nonfiction and general writing, editing and marketing information. Cost: $175, including sessions, room and board.)

### Wildacres Writers Workshop
*233 South Elm St.*
*Greensboro, NC 27401*
*(910) 273-4044*
*Director: Judith Hill*
*Estab. 1984*
*Usually held second week of July*

One-week conference covers fiction, poetry and playwriting. Cost: approximately $360, including double room, all meals and manuscript critique.

### Woodstock Guild's Byrdcliffe Arts Colony
*34 Tinker St.*
*Woodstock, NY 12498*
*(914) 679-2079*
*Program Director: Sondra Howell*
*Estab. 1902*

One to four 1-month sessions for writers, playwrights and visual artists. Cost: June and September $400; July and August $500. Scholarships are available.

### World-Wide Writers Conference
*186 N. Coleman Rd.*
*Centereach, NY 11720-3072*
*(516) 736-6439*
*Director: Dr. David Axelrod*

Two-day conference covering all genres. Cost varies.

### Write On The Sound

*700 Main St.*
*Edmonds, WA 98020*
*(206) 771-0228*
*Arts Coordinator: Christine Sidwell*
*Estab. 1986*
*Conference held second weekend in October*

Two-day conference covering various fiction and nonfiction writing. Cost: $75 for 2 days; $40 for 1 day.

### Writers in the Rockies: TV and Film Screenwriting Conference

*1980 Glenwood Dr.*
*Boulder, CO 80304*
*(303) 443-4636*
*Director: Carolyn Hodges*
*Estab. 1984*

Weekend conference covering screenwriting topics. Cost: $200, includes scripts and large packet of screenwriting materials, 2 meals (accommodations are extra).

### Write-to-Publish Conference

*9731 Fox Glen Dr., #6F*
*Niles, IL 60714*
*(847) 296-3964*
*Director: Lin Johnson*
*Estab. 1971*

Five-day conference with a variety of levels and classes. Conference includes visit to publishing house. Cost: $325.

### Writing for Money

*34200 Ridge Rd., #110*
*Willoughby, OH 44094*
*(216) 943-3047*
*Contact: Lea Leever Oldham*
*E-mail: fa837@cleveland.freenet.edu.*

One-day workshops held in educational institutions in northeastern Ohio, covering business and submission topics as well as general writing tips. Cost: $39/day.

### Yellow Bay Writers' Workshop

*Center for Continuing Education*
*University of Montana*
*Missoula, MT 59812*
*(406) 243-6486*

*Program Officer: Nancy J. Harte*
*Estab. 1988*
*Usually held mid-August*

One-week conference covering poetry, nonfiction or personal essay, and fiction. Cost for 1995 was $425 commuter fee; $725, tuition and single-occupancy cabin/meals, $695, tuition and double-occupancy cabin/meals.

# WRITING INSTRUCTION

If you're looking for writing instruction, or you'd like to supplement your income as an instructor, you have choices ranging from university degree programs to correspondence schools. In addition, several professional writers' groups offer regular classes and workshops for members. See the listings under Professional Associations and Organizations and Writers' Groups for more information, and check out individual offerings from other groups in your area.

Choosing a writing program or course means evaluating what benefits you want, how much you can spend, how much time you have to write and what type of instruction you find best suits you.

## UNIVERSITY PROGRAMS

Writing programs offered through universities typically demand at least part-time attendance at group classes and workshops. Some universities offer independent study; inquire about this if it is your only option and you'd like to work on a degree. There are a few drawbacks to degree-granting programs. The application process can be confusing, and you may be unsure what degree you want to pursue. In addition, university writing programs are fairly expensive and time-consuming. If you are writing part time and have a full-time job, or you're earning a fairly good living writing full time, the pursuit of a degree may cost more than you can comfortably afford to spend.

On the other hand, writing programs have proliferated on college campuses for good reason. Michael Bugeja, in a *Writer's Digest* article, says the programs are considered "the minor league for writers." Writers enroll for many reasons, most having little to do with the actual degree. More often they look for the opportunity to study with a particular writer, concentrate more fully on techniques of the craft, hone their writing skills and establish industry contacts.

A good writing program may provide you with an entrance to the world of publishing. Not only do agents scout the major programs for talent, some students have their work recommended to editors and agents by writing program faculty members. Universities also support more experimental writing and have literary magazines that will publish noncommercial writing.

Tips on choosing programs:

- Have a few choices available. Don't bank on acceptance from one program and only apply there. The competition is quite daunting in some programs. The Iowa Writers Workshop, for instance, receives about 560 applications in fiction and 300 in poetry, and it only accepts 25 students in each category.
- Weigh the benefits of a local program versus an out-of-state one, both in terms of what's offered and what you can afford.
- Make sure your writing samples are ready to go. Now's the time to polish them and select the best ones for the program to which you're applying. A sample poetry submission will have 10 to 20 poems, and a fiction or nonfiction sample includes three stories.
- Register to take any tests required for entrance or be sure your test scores are available.
- Decide what approach you want in a program. Some writers prefer a small program where they'll receive individual attention; others want a large program with a prestigious faculty. If you can, talk to other graduates of the program. A master's degree usually requires more reading, while a master of fine arts program requires more writing but fewer literature classes. (At least one program, Stanford, doesn't even confer a degree.) Some programs are conducted in a straight classroom setup, but a typical workshop approach has about 12 students and a teacher. During a class session, one student will bring in work to be critiqued by the teacher and students.
- Evaluate the "extras." The community of writers around the program may be very helpful in your development as a writer. Look for the caliber of visiting writers in addition to faculty and the literary magazines, readings and festivals that also may be offered.
- Cost of programs is nearly always a consideration for writers, so find out what kind of financial aid is available and what teaching assistantships are available. In addition, you'll want to look at the cost of living in the area.

Here are some other tips offered by graduates of writing programs:

"Look for track records—where writers are going who are coming out of the program."

"You're going to be there two years or more, so choose a place you'll like to be."

"Financial aid is fairly available, but you should look into this early."

"Know who's teaching. Read their work. It will help you select the best submissions to make from your own work."

"Line up your references early. Start a reference file, so professors won't have to write several times."

"Know the little things about the programs. If you choose someplace like Columbia, it'll be easier to make connections with other writers and editors since you'll be in New York. At Iowa, you know there'll be editors and agents scouting, so you can be in touch with the publishing industry. If you just want to write, though, you may not want some place that's so competitive and distracting."

## *LISTINGS*

The best source of information on writing programs is *The Official Guide to AWP Writing Programs*, edited by D.W. Fenza and Beth Jarock. The book includes information about 350 writing programs in the United States and Canada, both at the undergraduate and graduate level, and has indexes by state and degree offered. Write to Associated Writing Programs, George Mason University, Fairfax, VA 22030. (703) 993-4301. Following are some of the more well-known writing programs.

### *Boston University*
*236 Bay State Rd.*
*Boston, MA 02215*
*(617) 353-2510*

Offers a bachelor's degree in English; master's in creative writing. Contact: Leslie Epstein, Creative Writing Program.

### *Brown University*
*P.O. Box 1852*
*Providence, RI 02912*
*(401) 863-3260*

Offers a master's degree in writing; associate's degree in English with honors in Creative Writing. Contact: Graduate Writing Program.

### *Columbia University*
*School of the Arts*
*Writing Division*
*404 Dodge Hall*

*New York, NY 10027*
*(212) 854-4391*

Offers a 2-year MFA in creative writing; also offers undergraduate writing classes through School of General Studies. Contact: Writing Division, School of the Arts.

### Cornell University
*Goldwin Smith Hall*
*Ithaca, NY 14853*
*(607) 255-6802*

Offers a bachelor's degree in English with creative writing component; MFA in creative writing, and MFA/Ph.D. program. Contact: Director of the Creative Writing Program, English Department.

### Indiana University
*Bloomington, IN 47405*
*(812) 855-8224*

Offers an MFA in creative writing; master's in English with a concentration in creative writing. Contact: Director, Creative Writing Program, Department of English.

### Johns Hopkins University
*Baltimore, MD 21218-2690*
*(410) 516-7562*
*Fax: (410) 516-6828*

Offers a bachelor's degree in the writing seminars; master's in the writing seminars. Contact: Margaret Zawadzki, admissions secretary, the Writing Seminars.

### Louisiana State University
*Baton Rouge, LA 70803-5001*
*(504) 388-2236*

Offers bachelor's and MFA degrees. Contact: Director of Creative Writing, % the English Department.

### Ohio University
*Athens, OH 45701-2979*
*(614) 593-2838*

Offers a bachelor's in English with concentration in creative writing; master's in English with creative thesis and Ph.D. in English with creative dissertation. Contact: Program in Creative Writing, Department of English, Ellis Hall.

### San Francisco State University
*1600 Holloway Ave.*
*San Francisco, CA 94132*
*(415) 338-1891*

Offers bachelor's and master's degrees in English with concentration in creative writing; MFA in Creative Writing. Contact: Secretary, Creative Writing Department.

### Stanford University
*Stanford, CA 94305*
*(415) 723-2637*

Stanford Writing Program confers no degree; fellows in creative writing attend a weekly workshop. Contact: Gay Pierce, Program Coordinator, Creative Writing Program.

### Syracuse University
*Syracuse, NY 13244-1170*
*(315) 443-2173*

Offers an MFA in Creative Writing. Contact: Stephen Dobyns, Director, Creative Writing Program, Department of English.

### The University of Alabama
*Tuscaloosa, AL 35487-0244*
*(205) 348-5526*

Offers a bachelor's degree in English with minor in creative writing; MFA in creative writing. Contact: Director, Program in Creative Writing, Department of English, P.O. Box 870244.

### University of Arizona
*Tucson, AZ 85721*
*(602) 621-3880*

Offers bachelor's degree and MFA with major in creative writing. Contact: Steve Orlen, Director of Creative Writing, Department of English.

### University of California, Irvine
*Irvine, CA 92717*
*(714) 856-6712*

Offers a bachelor's degree in English with creative writing emphasis; MFA in writing. Contact: Administrator, The Program in Writing, Department of English and Comparative Literature.

### University of Houston
*Houston, TX 77204-3012*
*(713) 743-3004 for BA*
*(713) 743-3015 for MA, MFA, Ph.D.*
*Fax: (713) 743-3029*

Offers a bachelor's degree in English with concentration in creative writing; master's in English and creative writing with creative thesis; PhD in English and creative writing with creative dissertation. Contact: Creative Writing Program, Department of English.

### University of Iowa
*Iowa City, IA 52242*
*(319) 335-0416*

Offers a bachelor's degree in English and an MFA in creative writing. Known informally as the Iowa Writers' Workshop. Contact: The Writers' Workshop.

### University of Massachusetts
*Amherst, MA 01003*
*(413) 545-0643*
*Fax: (413) 545-3880*

Offers an MFA in English. Contact: Director, MFA Program in English, 452 Bartlett Hall.

### University of Michigan
*Ann Arbor, MI 48109-1045*
*(313) 763-4139*
*E-mail: graduate_English_Admission@om.cc.umich.edu*

Offers a bachelor's degree; MFA in creative writing. Contact: MFA Admissions, Department of English, 7617 Haven Hall.

### University of Montana
*Missoula, MT 59812-1013*
*(406) 243-5231*

Offers a bachelor's in English with creative writing emphasis; MFA in creative writing. Contact: Director of the Creative Writing Program, Department of English.

### University of North Carolina at Greensboro
*Greensboro, NC 27412-5001*
*(910) 334-5459*
*Fax: (910) 334-3281*

Offers a bachelor's in English with concentration in creative writing; MFA in creative writing; Ph.D. in English with creative writing dissertation. Contact: Mary Ellis Gibson, Director of Graduate Studies in English, Department of English, (910) 334-5221.

### University of Oregon
*Eugene, OR 97403-5243*
*(503) 346-3944*
*Fax: (503) 346-0537*
*E-mail: catelay@oregon.uoregon.edu*

Offers bachelor's, master's and MFA in creative writing. Contact: T.R. Hummer, Director, Program in Creative Writing, 114 Columbia Hall.

### University of Southern Mississippi
*P.O. Box 5144*
*Hattiesburg, MS 39406-5144*
*(601) 266-4321*

Offers a bachelor's in English; master's and Ph.D. in English with creative writing emphasis. Contact: Rie Fortenberry.

### University of Utah
*Salt Lake City, UT 84322-3200*
*(801) 750-2733*

Offers bachelor's with creative writing emphasis, master's degree, MFA and Ph.D. Contact: Director of Creative Writing, Department of English.

### University of Virginia
*115 Wilson Hall*
*Charlottesville, VA 22903*
*(804) 924-7105*

Offers bachelor's in English and MFA in creative writing. Contact: Creative Writing Program, English Department, (804) 924-6675.

### Washington University
*Campus Box 1122*
*St. Louis, MO 63130*
*(314) 889-5190*

Offers a 2-year MFA in writing. Contact: Eric Pankey, Department of English.

## CORRESPONDENCE SCHOOLS

Correspondence schools have some advantages over traditional university programs. If you live in a rural area without easy access to a university writing program, or if your schedule prevents you from meeting at a regular classroom time, you may want to explore a correspondence course. In addition to the advantage of scheduling and access, most courses offer you one-on-one instruction with the same teacher throughout the course. You also have the advantage of being able to work at your own pace.

Correspondence work has its disadvantages, too. Usually the course is set up with the average student in mind, and you may be unable to adapt the course to your needs. If you are the type of person who finds it difficult to meet deadlines, a correspondence course is not for you. Correspondence allows you to set your own pace up to a point, but most courses have a deadline and getting an extension may cost you. Many writers also enjoy the "community" feeling and feedback that come with interaction among students and teachers.

When you see advertisements or brochures for correspondence schools, don't let that information be your only guide. Evaluate courses with these things in mind:

- Does the course suit your needs? Some courses offer a smorgasbord of topics, and you'll study everything from newswriting to fiction in a single course. Others concentrate on a single subject such as the romance novel or the short story. You need to decide what you want to study and whether or not the course fits that need. It's also nice to be able to inspect the course for a week to 10 days and be able to return it if it's not suitable. Look for this feature and/or ask if it's available.
- What's the length of the course? Most correspondence or home study courses can be finished in a year or less. That may be more time than you want to invest, or perhaps you'll see the course and think it's not *enough* time to learn everything you need to know about the particular type of writing.
- What's the cost? Costs of correspondence courses vary widely, from as low as $200 to as high as $2,000. Not only should you compare the course against other comparable courses, but compare it against other writing instruction available in your area. Also ask what kinds of payment plans are available and if refunds are offered within a certain amount of time if you decide to withdraw from the course.
- What's the experience level of the instructor? A correspondence school should be willing to give you information about the caliber of its instructors, and it also should be willing to reassign you to another instructor if things don't work out. In a correspondence course, feedback from the instructor can make or break your learning experience, so it's important to get a good match. Look for instructors who not only know the subject but have recent sales in the area.

- What amount of feedback can you expect? Will your instructor provide you with a detailed critique of your work, pencil in grammar and style corrections, or just give you an overall evaluation? How often—and how soon after you return an assignment—can you expect feedback? This is an important part of correspondence school learning, so you need to be sure you'll get the type of feedback you can use to improve your writing.

Finally, be wary about amazing claims, or business practices that seem out of the ordinary. As the saying goes, if it sounds too good to be true, it probably is.

## TEACHING IN CORRESPONDENCE SCHOOLS

If you think you'd like to be on the other side of the mailbox, you can do several things to enhance your chances.

Some correspondence schools ask professional organizations for references or place notices in association newsletters. A scan of these will usually tell you whom to call and what credentials are required. Most school directors will ask for a résumé and writing samples, along with your credentials to teach. (If you haven't seen an advertisement or notice but are interested, write to the director of the school and ask if instructors are being sought.)

You should ask for information about the course, including your role in shaping the course, the feedback expected and the general level of students enrolled. You'll also want to know the pay rate, of course, and the number of students typically assigned to an individual instructor.

## LISTINGS

One book with listings of correspondence instruction opportunities is *Correspondence Educational Directory* (Racz Publishing). Check with your local university to see if it offers correspondence or independent study courses. Some groups, such as the National Writers Association, also offer correspondence instruction.

Selected writing correspondence programs:

**Hollywood Scriptwriting Institute**
*1605 North Cahuenga Blvd., Suite 216*
*Hollywood, CA 90028*
*(800) SCRIPTS*

Offers courses in professional screenwriting.

**National Writers School**
*(see National Writers Association in Writers' Groups section)*

**Writer's Digest School**
*1507 Dana Ave.*
*Cincinnati, OH 45207*
*(800) 759-0963. Outside U.S., (513) 531-2690.*

Variety of writing courses in fiction and nonfiction.

## CONTINUING EDUCATION PROGRAMS

Continuing education programs are offered by a variety of groups ranging from professional associations to local high schools. Check professional magazines such as *Publishers Weekly* for notices of professional classes and workshops, too. Local classes are usually publicized through writers' groups, library bulletin board notices and free distribution catalogs. Call your local university's continuing education department to ask about offerings. Often classes are also available through community-based programs at high schools or "free university" workshops.

Although few continuing education programs offer credit, they can provide you with a fairly inexpensive way to explore new types of writing. Most courses of this type cost $50 to $100, and the average length is six to nine weeks. It may not be long enough for you to learn everything you want to know, but it should give you an indication of whether or not you want to pursue the subject more seriously. With the exception of professional continuing education programs, which usually focus on a narrow topic such as indexing, most continuing education programs offer information for the beginner.

The caliber of instruction is an important consideration here. Although you won't be investing a considerable amount of time and money, you certainly don't want to waste it. Tom Clark, *Writer's Digest* editor and a frequent workshop instructor, counsels writers to look for an instructor with experience as an editor, publisher or writer. "It's important to look for relevant credits too," he says. "Don't go to someone who's only written nonfiction for a fiction class or to a novelist for newspaper writing."

Because continuing education programs usually have open enrollment, you may or may not find fellow students helpful in your development as a writer, and your instruction will rarely involve any individual attention from the teacher. On the other hand, a local program can help you determine what direction you want to go with your writing without a major investment of time and money. It can also provide you with local contacts, a valuable resource for any writer.

## TEACHING IN CONTINUING EDUCATION PROGRAMS

If you have the credits and interest in sharing with other writers, you may want to explore continuing education programs as a supplemental source of income.

First, find out what's offered in your area. It's always helpful to sit in on an existing class to find out more about the students and what works and doesn't work for you. Sometimes it also can give you ideas about a new class you'd like to propose.

Contact the director of the continuing education program about your idea for a class; most are very flexible and eager to offer new courses of potential interest. Follow up that contact with a formal outline proposal for the course, and include a statement of your qualifications to teach the class.

From there, be prepared to back up your proposal with a solid class that will continue to interest students. The majority of continuing education programs have minimum student enrollments necessary to justify holding a class.

# CHAPTER 3

# RESEARCHING IT

Research. The very word brings sweaty palms to most writers, no doubt a throwback to the days of pawing through a dusty card catalog only to find that, with your first real deadline looming, all the available books on Beowulf had been checked out by your fellow student/writers.

But we've grown up, and research has grown up, and new technologies have streamlined the process and made it far less sweaty.

Volumes have been written about how to conduct research, whether it be for a short nonfiction article, a historical novel, a family genealogy or any other purpose for which you have to look something up. This chapter is by no means a short course in library science, just a primer to some of the most used (and some relatively unused, but nevertheless valuable) resources available to writers.

A more comprehensive guide to finding information is *The Writer's Ultimate Research Guide*, written by Ellen Metter (Writer's Digest Books). Metter is a professional studies bibliographer at the University of Colorado at Denver who has worked as a reference librarian there and at several university libraries.

Overall, the advice offered time and again by professionals interviewed for this chapter was "Put yourself in the hands of a good research librarian." Some writers, perhaps not wanting to appear as rank amateurs, eschew the services of a librarian—rather like the traveler who, preferring to make all his or her own reservations, avoids the services of a travel agent.

Both are missing a good bet.

A good travel agent can save you money, time and headaches, lead you to some exotic, sometimes unexpected, locales, and generally ensure a pleasurable, sometimes profitable, trip.

Speaking of travel, Michael Wallis, author of *Route 66: The Mother Road*, helped jumpstart his 17 years of research on that highway in a unique way. Wallis was working with a research librarian in Tulsa, Oklahoma, and a search of conventional sources had turned up little when the two had a sudden inspiration. Wallis sang the lyrics to the "Route 66" theme song, which lists many of the cities along the route, and the librarian compiled a list of other agencies—newspaper libraries, state highway departments and tourism boards—in those cities. The writer, who probably would have hit a dead end in his research otherwise, now had a whole new road map to follow, one that provided a lot of useful information.

A postscript: A busy public library may not be the best source if you'll need to spend a significant amount of time with a reference librarian. A university library reference staff might be less rushed, and they are generally very willing to help if you clearly explain the type of project that you're working on. It's best to call in advance to see if the reference librarian is available and let him know what you're interested in researching so perhaps he can get a head start on pulling out the sources you need.

# LIBRARIES

The first word that writers generally speak in the same breath as "research" is "library," but, thanks to interlibrary loan and new technology, the modern library's scope extends far beyond the walls of your neighborhood branch. Interlibrary loan allows writers far removed from large metropolitan libraries access to a staggering number of sources in far-flung locales.

Lonnie Wheeler, a freelance sportswriter and author, for example, enlisted the services of a research librarian at the University of Cincinnati to help him prepare a biography of Hank Aaron. The librarian was able to send for microfilm copies of the *Indianapolis Recorder*, a black newspaper, old photographs and other resources that added richness to Wheeler's account of Aaron's career.

For those unacquainted with interlibrary loan (ILL), it's the cooperative lending of materials between libraries. Generally governed by lending rules established by the American Library Association (ALA), it takes only a valid card from the library system that will be making the ILL request for you and the title of the work or works you're looking for.

Suppose, for example, you're researching a major piece on global warming, and a book that is the definitive work on the subject is not available anywhere in your library's system. The librarian may check the request against the Online Computer Library Center (OCLC), a catalog network of more than 19,000 college, government, law, medial, public, school, specialized and university libraries in the United States, Canada and around the world. The OCLC database contains information on and locations for books, serials, records, audiovisual material, maps, manuscripts and computer files. The search will turn up which library or libraries hold the particular book or other material for which you're searching.

Armed with this information, the librarian can process the request. The library from which you are requesting materials sets the rules on whether it will loan particular materials or not. Reference materials, rare books, audiovisual materials and recordings, microfilms and fiches are frequently not circulated through ILL, but most libraries will comply with requests for photocopies of these materials. They also set the rules on how long you can keep things—generally three or four weeks. Overdue charges usually are based on those of your home library.

The cost of ILL to you will primarily be postage, copying charges and sometimes a processing charge. (Check with the library originating the ILL request for you to find out the approximate charge and the form of payment it requires for these materials. Some library systems require a check or money order made out to the library system sending you the materials, *not* your home library.)

Other tips for using interlibrary loan:

- Allow enough time for processing requests and for requesting renewals on materials. Receipt of materials through ILL can take two to four weeks—or longer—depending on the availability of the material you're requesting and the work load of the libraries on each end of the request. To renew the materials in your possession, give your local library at least a week's notice to process a renewal.
- Give the librarian all the available information you have—author, title, publisher and year published, if available—and be sure it's accurate. If you request the wrong issue of a magazine, for instance, you'll more than likely have to pay for the mistake nonetheless.
- If processing a large number of ILL requests (for example, for book research) through a large public library, it might be wise to file your requests a few at a time. That way, all your research materials won't arrive at the same time.
- ILL materials must be picked up and dropped off at the library branch initiating the request.

## PHONE AND FAX

For library research that needs a quick answer, most libraries will answer questions by phone. Some larger libraries have also instituted fax service—i.e., transmittal of information by telefacsimile (fax machine). If you don't have a fax machine, some libraries will, for a fee, fax the information to a branch library near your home.

## LIBRARY CO-OPS

Most writers, unless they have very specialized research needs and/or unlimited travel budgets (or a computer, as we'll see later), will patronize libraries within a comfortable driving distance from home, and then network through these to obtain the necessary materials through interlibrary loan. It pays, then, to know the locations and policies of these institutions, some of which may be off the beaten path. If your local library belongs to a regional consortium or cooperative, you may discover local libraries you had not been aware of and be entitled to borrow materials directly from any of its member institutions, return materials to a more convenient location and benefit from other perks such as free parking and reduced photocopying charges. The Greater Cincinnati Library Consortium, for example, represents 144 academic, public, school and special libraries that will honor a valid college, university, public library or company ID card to grant lending privileges.

The *American Library Directory*, published by R.R. Bowker, lists public, academic, government and special libraries throughout the United States and Canada. Arranged geographically, the notations include subject interests and whether the library is open to the general public. The *Library and Book Trade Almanac* (also known as the "Bowker Annual") is available in most libraries and lists these networks, consortia and other cooperative arrangements by state. Phone numbers are included. The *Encyclopedia of Information Systems and Services*, published by Gale Research Inc., also carries a section listing these cooperative library groups.

## SPECIAL LIBRARIES

If your research runs to the exotic, or if you're seeking materials outside the ken of public or academic libraries, you might investigate special libraries. More than 10,000 special libraries exist across the United States, representing information sources vital to any number of entities, from banks to businesses, museums to media relations experts, nonprofit groups to news organizations. The Special Libraries Association, 1700 18th St. NW, Washington, DC 20009, maintains a list of 12,500 members but does not generally provide information about locations and subject matter of member libraries, according to Kathryn Dorko, manager of information resources for SLA.

When a writer calls the SLA seeking a special library, whether it deals with the art of tattooing or the collected works of Mark Twain, the association refers the caller to the *Directory of Special Libraries and Information Centers*, Gale Research Inc. The book describes more than

21,000 libraries and information centers in the United States, Canada and abroad. A *Subject Directory of Special Libraries*, also by Gale, reorganizes the subject into three volumes: business, government and law libraries; computer, engineering and science libraries; and health science libraries. Both resources are available at larger libraries.

Other special-interest library associations:

Music Library Association, P.O. Box 487, Canton, MA 02021. (617) 828-8450.

Art Libraries Society of North America, 3900 E. Timrod St., Tucson, AZ 85711. (602) 881-8479.

## NEWSPAPER LIBRARIES

For background on a prominent citizen, a natural disaster, a crime in the headlines or other localized topic, don't overlook the library (or "morgue") of the local newspaper office. Two caveats here, however: Due to staff shortages and the disinclination to handle a lot of requests, many larger newspapers have closed their libraries to the general public. A letter outlining your legitimate research request may get you around that problem. The second warning: Also due to lack of staff, the quality of newspaper libraries is spotty. Some "libraries," especially at small town papers, are nothing more than two or three file cabinets stuffed full of poorly filed clippings.

Also, many of these facilities can't—or don't—correct errors that may have appeared in the file materials, perpetuating the errors through the researchers who use them.

Despite all this, newspaper libraries can provide exciting "on the scene" looks at events and people who have shaped that region. The SLA publishes a bibliography of *Newspaper Libraries in the U.S. and Canada*. It's available for $9 in paperback. (202) 234-4700.

## LIBRARY OF CONGRESS

The "nation's library" holds more than 100 million items, including books, music, pamphlets, disks, tapes, maps, microforms, photographs, prints, drawings and personal papers from some of America's most distinguished citizens. It publishes the *National Union Catalog*, a record of publications held by more than 2,500 libraries in the United States and Canada, and also serves as headquarters of the federal Copyright Office.

Housed in three buildings within walking distance of the Capitol (it maintains its original purpose as a research facility for members of Congress to the present day), it's a fascinating place to browse and, obviously, a first-rate reference site for researchers in the Washington, DC, area. Those writers working on projects needing extensive use of the general collections may want to contact the Research Facilities Office (Library of Congress, Washington, DC 20540) to inquire about assigned desk space or study shelves. A valid photo ID is required.

For researchers outside the Washington area, the Library of Congress does participate in interlibrary loan service to academic, public or special libraries making requests on behalf of persons doing serious research, provided the materials can't be procured elsewhere. This is an important proviso—the Library of Congress staff reports, in all seriousness, that it is the "library of last resort." Photoreproductions of many materials in the collections are available from the library's Photoduplication Service. A price list is available on request.

The Library of Congress doesn't ordinarily provide large numbers of items for a single project, nor will it lend out certain materials—those frequently used by Congress, for example, or certain rare books and other items. ILL requests should be made through your librarian. For single reference questions, a note or phone call may suffice. Direct written inquiries to the General Reference Division or, in the case of photoreproductions, to Photoduplication Service, Library of Congress, Washington, DC 20540, (202) 707-5640. The phone number for reference questions is (202) 707-5522; for general information, (202) 707-6400. A helpful brochure, *Public Services in the Library of Congress*, is available for free by writing Public Services in the LOC, National Reference Service, Library of Congress, Washington, DC 20540-5570.

## NATIONAL ARCHIVES

Anyone who's visited Washington is usually acquainted with the National Archives, 7th Street and Pennsylvania Avenue NW, where researchers over 16 with a valid photo ID card can browse. But a lesser-known fact is that the archives also maintains 11 field branches throughout the United States where copies of many of the same documents (usually chosen on the basis of regional interest) are housed. For a list of field branches, a description of archives policies, or to pose a specific question in a research area, call or write National Archives and Records Administration, Washington, DC 20408. (202) 501-5402. The Research Consultation office is open weekdays from 8:45 A.M. to 5:00 P.M. EST.

## OTHER NATIONAL LIBRARIES

Information on almost any facet of medicine and the health sciences is available at The National Library of Medicine, 8600 Rockville Pike, Bethesda, MD 20894.

Materials are available on the premises, and the library participates in interlibrary loan. The National Library of Medicine maintains MEDLARS, a group of over 30 databases indexing more than 3,000 medical journals from around the world. MEDLARS is adding databases regularly—several on AIDS, for example—and is considered *the* database for serious medical research. NLM even developed its own special software for searching the library's collections—called "Grateful Med." (Who said academics have no sense of humor?) Order forms for the software and pricing information are available by calling the reference number below.

Out-of-town researchers who contact NLM by phone will generally be referred to one or two medical libraries in their area, or else to relevant organizations and/or associations. The reference number is (301) 496-6095. An automated menu walks you through available services.

The National Agricultural Library of the United States Department of Agriculture, NAL Building, Beltsville, MD 20705, contains 2 million volumes and 27,000 periodical titles received annually from throughout the world. NAL participates in interlibrary loan. Brief questions can be answered by phone through the reference branch, (301) 504-5479, or by mail (address queries to USDA, National Agricultural Library, Public Services Division, Reference Branch, Room 111, Beltsville, MD 20705).

Its collections can be searched online through the AGRICOLA database by a number of the commercial vendors (see section entitled "Researching Online").

## FINDING SPECIAL COLLECTIONS

Libraries have strengths in specialized areas, much as writers do. If you're seeking in-depth information on a particular topic, you might want to determine what library or libraries have specialized collections that may lend an added fillip to your research. (This is particularly helpful in researching fiction.)

*Subject Collections: A Guide to Special Book Collections and Subject Emphases*, by R.R. Bowker, catalogs 20,000 special collections housed in more than 5,800 university and college libraries, public libraries and special libraries and museums in the United States and Canada. The listing for the Santa Barbara Botanic Garden library, for example, reports that it's "especially strong on California native plants."

*Special Collections in College and University Libraries*, published by MODOC Press Inc. (Macmillan Publishing Co.), catalogs these collections in academic libraries. The general index here is helpful for subject browsing. Entries are arranged geographically, which gives you a clue to the treasure troves that might be available in your own backyard.

## SERENDIPITOUS SEARCHES

Rather than drudgery, library research can be intriguing, challenging and sometimes even serendipitous. The key things to remember are to be flexible, use the technology and keep an eye out for other avenues to explore through cross-references and other clues.

Suppose you're looking for background on television violence and its effect on adolescent behavior. The old method might have been to head first for the *Reader's Guide to Periodical Literature*. But the General Periodicals Index, and several other helpful indexes, are available in CD-ROM format, which means you can not only type in a general description of your topic and see what turns up, but also possibly have a printer make a copy of the relevant citations, rather than, as in the past, laboriously copying them by hand.

The General Periodicals Index, for example, has you type in "Television" followed by "Psychological Aspects." Out of two dozen citations, you turn up seven that are most promising.

A research librarian might head for the Wilson Indexes, the set of indexes covering journals in the social sciences, education, art and a wide range of topics, to find out what type of research has been done on the subject.

In the Social Sciences Index, for example, a check of "Television—Psychological Aspects" turns up an article on "Adolescents and death on television: a follow-up study" in *Death Studies* journal. If you scan further, under "Violence in Motion Pictures," an article titled "Does a single exposure to filmed violence affect aggressive tendencies?" in *Psychological Reports* might be of interest.

Education Index also turns up a listing under "Television broadcasting and children" of "Why Children's Television Should Be Regulated," an article in *Education Digest* that might provide an insight for your article, or maybe even the name of an expert to interview.

Speaking of experts—and we'll treat that at greater length later—if you scan *Subject Guide to Books in Print* or *Forthcoming Books in Print*, you'll no doubt find one or more authors of books on the subject as live interview subjects. And the writer's old standby, the *Encyclopedia of Associations*, lists dozens of associations dealing with television and/or violence. The National Coalition on TV Violence might provide you with other interview possibilities.

You get the idea. There are, of course, even more avenues to pursue—computer searches to find additional information on the topic, searches of statistical sources, probably even government studies dealing with television and its sociological effects. All of these possibilities will be touched on in the sections that follow.

*ADDITIONAL RESOURCES*

*Map Collections in the United States and Canada: A Directory*, 4th ed., David K. Carrington, ed., and Richard W. Stephenson (Special Libraries Association).

*Archives, Libraries, Museums and Information Centers with Index Archivum*, Michael Duchein, ed. (K.G. Saur).

*Guide to the Use of Libraries and Information Sources*, 6th ed., by Jean Key Gates (McGraw-Hill Book Co.).

*World Guide to Special Libraries*, by Helga Lengenfelder (K.G. Saur).

*Archives: A Guide to the National Archives Field Branches*, by Loretto Szucs and Sandra Luebking (EIG Publishing).

*Finding Facts Fast*, by Alden Todd (Ten Speed Press).

# RESEARCHING ONLINE

To this point, we've talked about conventional research methods, i.e., browsing through the resources at a local library. But in the last decade, the research opportunities that have been presented along what has come to be known as the "Information Superhighway" have exploded. It seems that almost everyone—from individuals to universities, to businesses, to even the U.S. government—has gone online to provide information and dazzling graphics. And even conventional libraries themselves are offering high-tech resources such as Internet access to patrons.

If you use a computer for writing and don't avail yourself of the research opportunities that it and a modem can afford you, it's a little like investing in a fine racehorse and tethering it in the backyard to give the neighborhood kids pony rides. Of course it will do the job, but it could be doing so much more for you on the track at Santa Anita!

By computer, a writer can, with racehorse speed, access any number of library indexes, statistical resources, encyclopedias or other fascinating data sources at any time of day or night, all without leaving the comfort of home.

Gathering information from these sources need not be expensive— though it certainly *can* be. The trick is to become adept at defining the parameters of your research, learning the best sources for finding that particular information and even finding some free or low-cost sources offering the information.

If you're a computer novice, the idea of online research might be intimidating. It doesn't need to be.

This section is not designed to be a comprehensive how-to manual. Volumes have been written—and continue to be written—on computer basics and advanced applications. For beginners, or even nonbeginners, who are looking for crystal-clear explanations of terminology, troubleshooting and the like, the IDG Books "Dummies" series (e.g., *PCs for Dummies*, *Internet for Dummies*, etc.) can't be beat.

But once you get familiar with pointing and clicking, with pull-down menus, with hypertext and the wonderful places it can lead you, you may get hooked. The speed and ease of online research can be addictive. So we'll add a piece of advice from professional researchers: Don't become so enamored of the technology that you begin to think database searching is the only way to research. Since many of the services came on line only in the 1970s, online searching is not always comprehensive and may not include older materials. It is unparalleled, though, for specific current research topics with definite parameters; e.g., what's been written of late on AIDS education and its effect on interest in blood donations?

So where do you access these wonderful fonts of information? Some of them are available at a cost, while others can be had for little or no money, if you know where to find them.

## COMMERCIAL VENDORS

Think of commercial vendors as somewhat like department stores. Most of them offer access to a wide range of research materials, some of them duplicated by other vendors and others offered as exclusives. The research sources offered by the commercial vendors are truly staggering, from *Books in Print* and *Magazine Index*, familiar to most writers, to more esoteric offerings such as Coffeeline, summarizing articles and data from more than 5,000 publications relating to that industry, to releases from the Xinhua News Agency, the English language news service originating in Beijing.

In addition, commercial vendors also offer other services—online shopping, electronic mail (or e-mail) and financial information—that can be useful to nonwriting endeavors. Some offer custom clipping services that let you type in a subject of particular interest, monitor the bases for new information on that subject while you're off-line and then deliver the full text next time you sign on. This is a real time-saver if you're looking for up-to-the-minute information on a particular topic as you're writing.

The special-interest groups and forums on these services allow you to chat in real time with persons who share interests in, say, writing, or Star Trek, or tai chi. Forums may be arranged into libraries, message centers and live-conversation areas. Libraries house files on particular subject areas. Message centers, as the name suggests, represent a place where a writer can post a missive to another participant. The live conversations can be one-on-one or group chats about a topic related to the forum's subject matter. In the latter, a moderator frequently "directs" the discussion so that chaos doesn't result. A popular feature now is for celebrities to join in these discussions at a preappointed hour.

Of course, you pay for the dazzling array and the convenience. Most charge a flat monthly rate for a set number of hours (usually 5 or 10) and a per-hour charge thereafter.

Like department stores, commercial vendors advertise heavily and are only too happy to send potential customers descriptions of what they offer and how much they charge and, frequently, unsolicited software to entice you to sign up. Call them for an information packet and rate sheet, and carefully compare costs, services, etc.

Here are three of the better-known commercial vendors:

1. America OnLine offically wrested the title of largest online service from CompuServe in September 1995, reporting 4 million subscribers. Call (800) 262-6600 for a free start-up kit, free software and trial membership (10 free hours). After that, membership costs $9.95 per month for five free hours, $2.95 per connect hour after that. AOL's address is 8619 Westwood Center Dr., Vienna, VA 22182-2220.

2. CompuServe boasts the most online services (3,000). Call (800) 862-1272 for a free membership kit and software, which entitles you to a free month's membership. Thereafter, your $9.95 per month gives you five hours free each month; each additional hour will cost you $2.95. The address is 5000 Arlington Center Blvd., Columbus, OH 43220-9910.

3. Prodigy offers free software and 10 free hours the first month. Call (800) PRODIGY, ext. 691. Thereafter, you'll pay $9.95 a month for five hours connect time, $2.95 per hour thereafter. Prodigy's mailing address is P.O. Box 8667, Granville, TN 37615-9967.

How to use these to best advantage:

- Use your free month to explore and find valuable reference areas, forums with compatible interests to yours, etc. You'll quickly learn which sources are more sizzle than steak.
- Learn to compose messages off-line, and also to download files for reading off-line (i.e., when the fee meter isn't running).
- Keep careful track of how much time you've spent, or you may be surprised by your monthly credit card bill. Some services have a built-in clock to show you just how many minutes you've spent in an online session.

How would you use a commercial service in a writing project? To add authentic touches to a story about the Southwest, for example, you might sign on to the Travel section of America OnLine, for example, to access Frommer's City Guides. Check out the guide to Taos, New Mexico, and scroll to the section on Art and Architecture, or perhaps Religion and Myth. Or, perhaps, you need to examine a picture of an Indian church in the Southwest to add a few descriptive details. Again in AOL's Travel section, turn to Pictures of the World. Within a few minutes, you've downloaded a photograph of an adobe church. Of course, in the Writer's Club area, you can also post a message requesting information from fellow writers living in the Southwest who are willing to share information. The fact is, there are any number of ways to experiment in using these online services to enhance your writing.

## MAGAZINES AND NEWSPAPERS ONLINE

Magazines and newspapers are offering their own online services, some with access to the Internet (see next section) too. The *Washington Post* introduced Digital Ink this year as an interactive online service geared to computerphiles in the DC area. Besides access to back issues of the *Post* to 1986, the service, priced at this writing at $9.95 per month, offers the Associated Press wire service, Reuter News Service, Academic American Encyclopedia, Kiplinger's Personal Finance magazine and other resources. Access to the Internet live chat, games and other services are expected to be added as the service expands.

As with any service, it's wise to read the fine print on fees beforehand. Digital Ink, for example, offers access to researchers who want to browse the *Post*'s archives, but it charges $.50 *each* to read or download an article. To their credit, you're notified in advance that such a charge will be levied.

## DO I NEED THE INTERNET?

In terms of an "Information Superhighway," the Internet would be tantamount to the autobahn. The Internet is the global "network of networks" that provides access to information located in hundreds of thousands of computers around the world. Many of the resources mentioned in the conventional research section of this chapter—library catalogs, government publications, statistical records, ad infinitum—can be found in various places on the Net, as it's popularly called. You'll need to know the Internet "address" of the information source—a string of letters, symbols and periods that will direct your computer to the destination.

Because of the recent development of "browsers" and other tools that permit relatively easy access to finding information, the Internet has become user friendly to even nontechnical researchers.

## WORLD WIDE WEB

The World Wide Web (or WWW) is one of the most popular services on the Internet. Developed in Switzerland by the European Laboratory for Particle Physics, the Web offers access to certain sites on the Internet in a multimedia format. The appealing part of browsing the Web is the use of hypertext, specially formatted text that allows you to jump to related information by clicking on the formatted text. Users of the Web frequently speak of Web "sites" or "home pages," areas established by individuals, businesses, universities, etc. that offer access to their particular information. The U.S. government currently has more than 1,000 Web sites.

Some home pages provide a launching pad for further exploration of the Net. Yahoo! (address http://www.yahoo.com) is one of the most popular of these sites. Originally developed by two Stanford University students, it provides a category menu for areas of exploration. Under the Reference: Telephone Numbers heading, for example, you click to call up Health Information Resources, a collection of toll-free numbers offering health information, as well as the Swiss telephone book and Telephone Directories on the Web, a link to U.S. and international phone number resources.

For someone just getting started in online research, the important thing is to get comfortable with the technology, advises Kathy Rutkowski, a publisher and consultant in applications of networking technology.

Rutkowski believes that electronic mail (e-mail) is the most important tool that researchers have. "It helps them network, it helps them find people who will ultimately help them fine-tune their research."

She recommends that researchers spend some time going to list servers (programs that automatically send e-mail to and from a particular group of subscribers) "because that will give them contact with people who are already out there networking in their particular field." Other computerphiles recommend Usenet, which is a collection of "newsgroups," or discussion groups, devoted to particular topics, for smoking out specific information.

She also suggests that those writers new to the Net access newsgroups through one of the commercial vendors, most of whom offer at least some Net capabilities at this writing. It's a simpler, more user-friendly way to get started than by dealing with "shell accounts," or SLIP connections, which call for some technical expertise.

The exciting thing about researching online that sets it apart from more traditional methods of research, Rutkowski points out, is this "interact-ability.... It gives us a broader reach. We can contact more experts and more people who can help us, even review our work, add to our work. In a way, you can become your own intelligence agency because you have access to global resources that you didn't before."

One tip from Rutkowski on searching efficiently—and more economically—online: Get acquainted with Gopher. Gopher is a "search engine," named for the mascot at the University of Minnesota, where the program was developed, that helps look for information on the Internet. Gophers have been likened to present-day librarians in that they narrow down and "suggest" sources of information and then help researchers track them down.

If you want to speed up your research and keep your bills down, there is often the capability of "shutting off" the graphics and reading text only, Rutkowski counsels. This is a particularly good tip "if you're easily distracted," she laughs.

What about experts online? With the relative anonymity of online research, what's the risk of encountering "experts" who are not what they seem? As with any type of research, Rutkowski counsels, it's best, first of all, to go to established sources. But even interaction with non-established sources can be valuable. "If you contact someone in Prague who isn't a recognized 'expert,' that person may still be a valuable source of information." If you come across an "expert" involved in an online chat, she advises that you simply follow the conversation for a while to get a fix on whether that person may be legitimate or may simply have an ax to grind, and also network with other individuals to determine an authority's credentials.

As a guide on using the services on the Internet, Rutkowski recommends Susan Estrada's *Connecting to the Internet.* Another helpful volume is *The Internet Complete Reference* (Osborne/McGraw-Hill), which contains an appendix listing over 750 Internet addresses.

We won't leave this discussion about researching online without one other editorial comment, which is, admittedly, highly personal.

Unless what you're writing is a business report, a scholarly paper or some other endeavor that does not require something besides "just the facts, ma'am," there's another downside to confining your research only to those things you can find online—as wondrous and far-flung as they may be: Researching on a computer screen is two-dimensional. You can call up a famous painting or the recipe for profiteroles, but when you've finished, do you know anything about the texture of either? To a writer of fiction, especially, but also a writer of nonfiction who turns out work with any soul, using the rest of the senses to gather information—touching and tasting, hearing and speaking to real people, experiencing real events—enriches the writing process, not to mention your life, far more than squinting day and night at a computer screen. Writing is a solitary enough profession as it is. Sometimes it's essential to get out into the real world.

## PAYING FOR A SEARCH

If you'd prefer not to invest in one of these services (though those writers who get involved with them invariably get hooked), or if you have a onetime project and/or a looming deadline, it's possible to contract for database searching by any number of sources. Most major public libraries offer data retrieval services. Check with yours for rate scale and available databases.

One of the largest is the Cleveland Public Library's Research Center (formerly Facts for a Fee). The center has worked with reporters all over the world on searches and other research assistance. Rates for online searching vary with the database used. For information, write or call Cleveland Research Center, 325 Superior Ave., Cleveland, OH 44114-1271. (216) 623-2999.

With the explosion of computer technology, in fact, a growing number of individuals have set up their own database search services as a cottage industry of sorts. The benefit of dealing with one of these services, if you're a neophyte in computing, is that you won't be frustrated by the sometimes confusing, frequently expensive trial-and-error process of learning your way around online services. In addition, many of these individuals and companies have access to a broader range of vendors/ databases than the average writer could afford.

For more information on finding search services, these directories are available at most larger libraries:

*Directory of Fee-Based Information Services*, by Helen P. Burwell (Burwell Enterprises, Inc.). Divided by states, indexed by company name and subject areas.

*Encyclopedia of Information Systems and Services*, Amy Lucas, ed. (Gale Research Inc.). The Information on Demand section lists firms that conduct customized research, provide bibliographies and do other legwork for writers willing to pay for someone else to do it.

## FREE INFORMATION ONLINE

As advances in telecommunications knit the world closer together, a great deal of useful information can be accessed by modem at little or no charge. Government, business and educational institutions—historically collectors of massive quantities of data—have established data banks and bulletin board systems (BBSs).

Like commercial services, BBSs can provide access to database information, provide libraries of files for browsing or allow "conversations" in real time or via message areas. But they are limited in that they usually focus on one topic. They also differ from the commercial services in that you must call the area where the BBS is located, rather than a local number, for access.

Not all BBSs are accessible to the general public. Many were created by businesses for the use of their employees or customers.

Mark Leff, a reporter for CNN in Atlanta and a member of the Society of Professional Journalists' Technology Committee, eschews services of the commercial vendors, as there is so much valuable information on the BBSs. One of his favorites, for instance, is ALF, the BBS run by the National Agricultural Library in Berwyn, Maryland, (301) 504-6510.

Many colleges and universities run BBSs on a number of specialized topics. Your best bet for uncovering this information source is through membership in a local BBS.

Unfortunately, there's not a definitive listing of the free and low-cost BBSs available, primarily because the boards seem to come into and go out of existence frequently, the numbers change without notice, "and most book listings of BBSs are outdated almost as soon as they're published," Leff notes.

He's managed to collect a good variety of numbers, which he publishes monthly on the Rock & Roll Atlanta BBS, (404) 982-0960, through networking with other computerphiles, reading the popular computer magazines and newsletters and even finding lists of other BBSs on BBSs he's accessed. (ALF, for instance, has a list of other agricultural BBSs available.)

Users of BBSs are generous about sharing information—most ask that you leave any corrections about the information listed or new information you have on the board. Once you're plugged into the network, you should have all the information you'll possibly need.

Mathew Lesko (see the "Resources" section) publishes *The Federal Database Finder: A Directory of Free and Fee-Based Databases and Files Available From the Federal Government*, 2nd ed., edited by Sharon Zarozny; and *The State Database Finder*. These helpful volumes identify government-generated databases plus sources for tapes and diskettes sold by agencies and departments. The information runs the gamut from the Fossil Energy Information Center's Acid Rain database in Oak Ridge,

Tennessee, to the World Fertilizer Market Information Service, headquartered in Muscle Shoals, Alabama.

Some of the bases listed in the latter are not directly accessible by outside users, but some will have staff run searches for you. Some are free, while others charge fees to cover the cost of computer and staff time and office services.

## REPORTING IN THE ELECTRONIC AGE

Beyond accessing traditional research sources, computers are beginning to be recognized as invaluable tools for processing and analyzing other electronic data as well, and that power is giving rise to a new form of journalism.

Computer-assisted reporting is taking nonfiction writers beyond the shoe-leather approach to newsgathering. For example, the *Providence Journal-Bulletin* won a Pulitzer Prize after it analyzed 30,000 mortgage records to uncover evidence of fraud in a state housing agency.

Techniques for using computers in newsgathering and analysis are beginning to be taught through seminars and workshops. Two programs providing information on such training are the National Institute for Advanced Reporting, Indiana University School of Journalism, IUPUI, ES 4106, 902 W. New York St., Indianapolis, IN 46202, (317) 274-5555, and the National Institute for Computer Assisted Reporting, % University of Missouri School of Journalism, 120 Neff Hall, Columbia, MO 65211, (314) 882-0684.

*ADDITIONAL RESOURCES*

*Directory of Online Databases* (Cuadra/Elsevier). Published quarterly, lists 4,200 databases available through one or more of the 622 online services. (It also indicates whether CD-ROM versions of the data are available.) An index grouping the services by subject is especially helpful.

*Data Bases: A Primer for Retrieving Information by Computer*, by Susanne Humphrey (Prentice-Hall).

*Encyclopedia of Business Information Sources* (Gale Research Inc.). Lists online sources as well as other sources for business data. Includes phone numbers and 800 numbers for contact.

# GOVERNMENT DOCUMENTS

A word about the amount of information produced by and for the federal government: The volume is so huge and the means of searching, sorting through and selecting any of it for use by the average citizen so mystifying that nearly an entire industry has grown up around how and where to get government information.

## TITLES FOR SALE

The Government Printing Office (GPO), while not the largest printer of government materials, is nonetheless a prolific one. GPO publishes about 30,000 new titles a year from a variety of federal agencies, ranging in subject from consumer-oriented pamphlets like *Eating Better When Eating Out* to esoteric training manuals for federal employees. If you're seeking information on nearly any subject, from care of the aging to NASA exploration of the planet Neptune, more than likely some publication on the topic has rolled off the GPO presses on it.

More than fourteen thousand titles are available for direct sale from the Superintendent of Documents, U.S. Government Printing Office, Washington, DC 20402-9325. For ordering new publications and getting a periodic update of new offerings, you can dial the office directly, (202) 512-1800. The department's FaxWatch line is available 24 hours a day, 7 days a week at (202) 512-1716.

GPO documents can also be ordered online by subscribers to Dialog, and selected titles may be purchased directly at any of the following two dozen U.S. government bookstores across the country.

*Alabama*
*O'Neill Bldg.*
*2021 Third Ave. N.*
*Birmingham, AL 35203*
*(205) 731-1056*

*California*
*ARCO Plaza, C-Level*
*505 S. Flower St.*
*Los Angeles, CA 90071*
*(213) 239-9844*

*Room 1023, Federal Bldg.*
*450 Golden Gate Ave.*
*San Francisco, CA 94102*
*(415) 252-6334*

*Colorado*
*Room 117, Federal Bldg.*
*1961 Stout St.*

*Denver, CO 80294*
*(303) 844-3964*

*Norwest Banks Bldg.*
*201 W. Eighth St.*
*Pueblo, CO 81003*
*(719) 544-3142*

### District of Columbia
*U.S. Government Printing Office*
*710 N. Capitol St. NW*
*Washington, DC 20401*
*(202) 512-0132*

*1510 H St. NW*
*Washington, DC 20005*
*(202) 653-5075*

### Florida
*100 W. Bay St., Suite 100*
*Jacksonville, FL 32202*
*(904) 353-0569*

### Georgia
*First Union Plaza*
*999 Peachtree St. NE, Suite 120*
*Atlanta, GA 30309*
*(404) 347-1900*

### Illinois
*One Congress Center*
*401 S. State St., Suite 124*
*Chicago, IL 60605*
*(312) 353-5133*

### Maryland
*Warehouse Sales Outlet*
*8660 Cherry Lane*
*Laurel, MD 20707*
*(301) 953-7974; (301) 792-0262*

### Massachusetts
*Thomas P. O'Neill Bldg.*
*10 Causeway St., Room 169*
*Boston, MA 02222*
*(617) 720-4180*

### Michigan
*477 Michigan Ave., Suite 160, Federal Bldg.*
*Detroit, MI 48226*
*(313) 226-7816*

### Missouri
*120 Bannister Mall*
*5600 E. Bannister Rd.*
*Kansas City, MO 64137*
*(816) 765-2256*

### New York
*26 Federal Plaza, Room 110*
*New York, NY 10278*
*(212) 264-3825*

### Ohio
*1240 E. Ninth St., Room 1653, Federal Bldg.*
*Cleveland, OH 44199*
*(216) 522-4922*

*200 N. High St., Room 207, Federal Bldg.*
*Columbus, OH 43215*
*(614) 469-6956*

### Oregon
*1305 S.W. First Ave.*
*Portland, OR 97201-5801*
*(503) 221-6217*

### Pennsylvania
*Robert Morris Bldg.*
*100 N. 17th St.*
*Philadelphia, PA 19103*
*(215) 636-1900*

*1000 Liberty Ave., Room 118, Federal Bldg.*
*Pittsburgh, PA 15222*
*(412) 644-2721*

### Texas
*1100 Commerce St., Room 1C50, Federal Bldg.*
*Dallas, TX 75242*
*(214) 767-0076*

*Texas Crude Bldg., Suite 120*
*801 Travis St.*

*Houston, TX 77002*
*(713) 228-1187*

**Washington**
*915 Second Ave., Room 194, Federal Bldg.*
*Seattle, WA 98174*
*(206) 553-4270*

**Wisconsin**
*310 W. Wisconsin Ave., Room 150, Reuss Federal Plaza*
*Milwaukee, WI 53203*
*(414) 297-1304*

A GPO title you might want to add to your reference shelf is *The United States Government Manual*—$33 at this writing, stock number 069-000-00063-1.

The Consumer Information Center, an arm of the General Services Administration, also processes requests for certain GPO titles, but don't order from this source if you're on a tight deadline. It's painfully slow.

A good, basic, free reference from CIC, familiar to many freelancers, is the *Consumer's Resource Handbook*. It's available, along with a catalog of other publications, by writing CIC, Pueblo, CO 81009. Expect to wait four to six weeks by mail.

## TITLES AS REFERENCE

To access government publications as reference materials, you have to understand something of how and where government documents are stored, and also something of the myriad indexes used to catalog them.

To serve as a collection point for many of the government's publications—those issued by the GPO, but also many other agencies—a depository library system was created. This designated some 1,400 public and academic libraries around the country to receive, free of charge, those publications considered of informational value to the general public. Fifty have been designated as regional depositories, which means they retain a permanent collection of material and provide interlibrary loan service for the other depository libraries in the area. A list of the addresses of these depository libraries is available free from the U.S. Government Printing Office, Superintendent of Documents, Stop: SM, Washington, DC 20402. Ask for publication 570W, "Directory of U.S. Government Depository Libraries."

Especially in researching through government documents, consulting with a reference librarian who specializes in this area is valuable for several reasons:

Most libraries that house government documents shelve them in a manner that parallels their regular collection, using the Superintendent of Documents (SuDocs) numbering system rather than Library of Congress numbering. SuDocs numbering is according to issuing agency, rather than subject matter, which makes for a somewhat illogical arrangement of documents to the uninitiated.

Few government documents are listed in most libraries' conventional card catalogs. And unless the library has a specific Documents department, the information on a particular agency you're looking for just might turn up in an unexpected location. The Uniform Crime Reports at our local library, for example, are included in the Education Department, rather than the Government Department you might expect.

Another reason for seeking out a librarian well versed in this area, which can be especially daunting to the novice, is that all government documents are not created equal. A librarian experienced in dealing with government publications should be able to tell you, for instance, which statistics (for example, those provided by the Census Bureau) are rock solid and which were compiled by part-timers hired to do a "quick and dirty" government report. A librarian trained in dealing with government documents can help you sort out the best sources of information. Poorly chosen information sources reflect poorly on your writing.

Another tip: If you're after a particular document, be sure you have the complete and official name of the document, not the popular title, or as much information about it (subject matter, issuing agency, year, etc.) as possible. Presidential commission reports, librarians complain, pose particular headaches. If you come in asking for the "Red Book," for example, most librarians will point you to the Standard Directory of Advertising Agencies, but there's a Hotel/Motel Redbook and other references commonly known by that title.

If you expect to do an extensive amount of work with government documents and can't find someone to help, an excellent reference—one recommended by documents librarians—is *Tapping the Government Grapevine: The User-Friendly Guide to U.S. Government Information Sources*, by Judith Schiek Robinson (Oryx Press).

Also by Oryx, the two-volume *Using Government Publications*, by Jean L. Sears and Marilyn K. Moody, breaks the hunt down according to your quarry. Search by subjects and agencies, statistics or, for more esoteric information, patents and trademarks, standards and specifications, etc.

Another nifty little volume is titled *Easy Access to Information in U.S. Government Documents*, by Julia Schwartz. Published by the American Library Association, Schwartz's guide leads you very gently through two dozen of the major indexes to government documents. It's available at many libraries.

Armed with the above advice, we can proceed with a short course on some of the most frequently used indexes of government documents.

The best reference for the latest offerings of the Government Printing Office is the *Monthly Catalog of U.S. Government Publications*, available at most libraries. It is indexed semiannually, and many libraries have a computer version that lists publications issued back to 1976. The monthly catalog indicates which publications are available for sale and which are available through depository libraries.

Publications Reference File (PRF) is a microfiche version of the monthly catalog.

A note from some librarians regarding catalog browsing versus screen browsing to find government documents: Though computer technology might seem the quickest way to plow through government-related (or any) research, there's still much to be said for old-fashioned browsing through paper copies of listings. Because the *Monthly Catalog* is divided by departments, you might uncover unexpected listings by paging. (Anyone who's scrolled back and forth on a computer knows how screen myopia can set in.) And because most of these computer catalogs didn't come online until 1976, they're useless for finding older documents.

Not everything the government prints, though, ends up in the monthly catalog. Reams of reports, documents, findings, etc., are produced annually by the federal bureaucracy, and it would be a perfect world for researchers if the government also had the mechanisms in place for finding them.

Unfortunately, it's not a perfect world, and it's fallen to "civilian" publishers to sort out much of Uncle Sam's paperwork. Below are listed several of the most commonly used indexes of government information. Keep in mind, though, that even if your local public library has an impressive array of these indexes in its reference section, it may or may not have the actual documents on hand (they're expensive). But the document you're looking for, if not in-house, can more than likely be borrowed through interlibrary loan.

Congressional Information Service Inc., based in Bethesda, Maryland, publishes several indexes that are excellent sources regarding legislative matters. *Index to Publications of the U.S. Congress* catalogs the reports, prints (i.e., background data) and important press releases issued by that body since 1970. It also publishes a *U.S. Congressional Committee Hearings Index*, an index to the *Federal Register*, where rules of the regulatory agencies, presidential documents and other information are published, and other indexes that can help you wade through the bombast and bureaucratic baggage to find what you need.

*Congress in Print*, issued weekly by Congressional Quarterly Inc. and available in larger libraries, lists reports of congressional committees and subcommittees and how to order them. There is no charge for ordering copies of bills, reports and public laws, but there's a limit on the number of requests that will be filled per day. CQ's *Weekly Reports* analyze specific happenings in Congress during the week, but also carry in-depth special reports—e.g., the "new frontier" expected as a result of the telecommunications bill.

For current U.S. legislation, consult *The Digest of Public Bills*, which includes a summary of the text, or *CCH Congressional Index*.

*Index to U.S. Government Periodicals* is issued quarterly by Infordata International Inc. of Chicago. This indexes 175 major periodicals produced by the government, from *Agricultural Outlook* to *Woman and Work*.

*Government Reference Books, A Biennial Guide to U.S. Government Publications*, catalogs the most important directories, indexes, handbooks, statistical works and almanacs produced during the previous two years, by subject. Libraries Unlimited, Englewood, CO 80155-3988.

*PAIS International*, published by Public Affairs Information Service, indexes more than 1,200 periodicals, books, pamphlets and reports of federal, state and city governments and public and private agencies "related to business, economic and social conditions throughout the world." It's also available on CD-ROM.

## SCIENTIFIC DOCUMENTS

Another government agency and a higher volume printer by far than GPO (80,000 titles annually) is the National Technical Information Service. NTIS collects, reprints and catalogs the thousands of technical reports produced by government contractors on various subjects, as well as many nontechnical documents. (A story on Olestra, for example, could be researched through NTIS documents.) NTIS indexes are very specialized and very expensive: They may not be in your public library, but may be available from a specialized library in your area.

They are indexed through *Government Report Announcement and Index* (GRA&I), which is updated biweekly and available online or via CD-ROM.

## THE NUMBERS GAME

If you're looking for statistics, some of the commonly available resources librarians will steer you to are listed below. Note that all three indexes cover not only government-generated statistics, but also those compiled by business, industry and other sources:

*American Statistical Index (ASI)* covers federal statistics from 1972 to date. Also available online.

*Statistical Reference Index (SRI)* covers nonfederal statistics from state and industrial sources.

*Index to International Statistics.*

A two-volume "road map" to finding other sources of statistics from business and industry, financial and educational institutions and elsewhere is *Statistics Sources* (Gale Research Inc.).

Speaking of statistics, the U.S. Census Bureau is a rich resource for materials, available through state and regional offices and data centers, as well as through its Customer Services office in Washington, DC. (301) 457-4100.

## GOING TO THE SOURCE

If it's a specific fact or statistic you're after, of course, it may be quicker—and more fruitful—to try to get it firsthand from the proper governmental office or agency. If, for example, you're looking for information on the surgeon general's latest recommendations on diet, you might contact that office directly. Notice we said "may be quicker." Anyone who's ever gotten the runaround from a government bureaucrat may feel differently. But try the Public Affairs or Public Information office of the department you're contacting, identify yourself as a writer and explain the type of project for which you need information. Most information officers, if they can't help you, can point you in the direction of someone who will. That's their job.

For finding phone numbers of these agencies, and—always a good idea—specific names of key personnel there, there are a number of popularly priced directories available. One is

*FEDFind: Your Key to Finding Federal Government Information*, by Richard J. D'Aleo (ICUC Press).

The *Washington Information Directory*, published by Congressional Quarterly Inc., is a thick almanac published annually and covering the federal government as well as the private nonprofit sector in Washington. The book is well indexed by agency name and personnel listed, and also is divided into 18 subject areas in case you don't have a clue what agency might provide the information you need. A "Ready Reference List" provides names, addresses and phone numbers for nearly any Washington bigwig you may need to locate.

The problem with buying such directories, of course, is that the information quickly becomes outdated.

Larger libraries may have copies of the *Federal Yellow Book*, published quarterly. (Congressional and State Yellow Books may also be available. See the "Resources" section later in this chapter for more information on these.) And in addition, the *Information Report* published monthly by Washington Researchers, P.O. Box 19005, Washington, DC 20036, (202) 333-3533, lists information available for free from the government. An annual subscription is $160.

If you don't have a clue as to which federal agency is the correct one to address, you might try calling a Federal Information Center (FIC) office, listed in most major city phone books under U.S. Government. FIC offices are designed to direct citizens' questions to the proper agency.

*ADDITIONAL RESOURCES*

*Directory of Federal Libraries* describes more than 2,400 libraries serving the U.S. government here and overseas, their collections, whether they are open to the public, etc., William R. Evinger, ed. (Oryx Press).

*Congressional Publications & Proceedings: Research on Legislation, Budgets and Treaties*, by Jerrold Zwirn (Libraries Unlimited).

# BIBLIOGRAPHERS

The idea of compiling a bibliography *before* starting a writing project might seem like putting the cart before the horse. When writing that college paper on Beowulf, for instance, most of us probably stumbled along collecting books in our research, used some portion of them in the actual writing, and gratefully included the whole lot of them in a bibliography at the end as a means of turning in the required 10 or 25 pages.

A bibliography compiled at the beginning of a project can save time by doing some of the legwork for you, eliminating some of the dead ends and time-wasters.

Don't overlook some of the subject bibliographies already prepared at your local library—many on current topics—e.g., substance abuse, divorce and children, nutrition and health, teen suicide. While not exhaustive treatments of the subjects, and not necessarily geared toward your particular project, they can sometimes provide a starting point—or a clue to what's been covered, or not covered, on the subject.

Subject bibliographies are available from other sources as well. The Government Printing Office publishes a Subject Bibliography Index listing nearly 240 bibliographies on a wide variety of topics. (Some of its historical bibliographies may also be of help to fiction writers.) The Index (021-599-00501-0) is free, as are the bibliographies listed in it. These are available through the Superintendent of Documents, U.S. Government Printing Office, Washington, DC 20402.

The Library of Congress, described elsewhere in this chapter, also provides interesting subject bibliographies, especially on current topics—e.g., the presidential election process. Unfortunately, as these are prepared by individual Library of Congress departments, there's no centralized and printed listing of them. A few are mentioned in the Library of Congress's *Publications in Print*, available from the Library of Congress Central Services Division, Washington, DC 20540. Otherwise, write or call the LOC department dealing with your subject area to find out what resource list may already have been pulled together.

## COMMERCIAL BIBLIOGRAPHIES

Some editorial services also help writers in the preparation of bibliographies. Though most often the customers are scholars carrying out in-depth research, some writers, too, call on professional bibliographers for help.

"Researching is like following a tree that may have many branches," observes Karen Pangallo, a freelance bibliographer and indexer based in Salem, Massachusetts. A skilled bibliographer will know which branches bear fruit and which are barren. Because they know the terminology to pursue research topics, have access to more databases and other sources than the average writer might, and may specialize in a field—natural history, for instance, or French literature or American poets—the services of a bibliographer can be worth pursuing.

Most charge an hourly rate from about $12 an hour at the low end of the spectrum to $50 per hour and up at the high end. They ask that, above all, the writer/client knows what he or she wants—i.e., defines the parameters of the writing project as well as the parameters of the sources to use. (Note: Some bibliographers are trained to provide foreign-language sources as well as English.)

*LISTINGS*

*Literary Market Place* provides a list of bibliographers under the Editorial Services heading. In addition, the *Directory of Fee-Based Information*

*Services*, published by Burwell Enterprises Inc., also lists some of these firms.

Following are some of the firms that provide bibliography services:

**Book Builders Inc.**
*762 Madison Ave., 4th Floor*
*New York, NY 10021*
*(212) 737-8210*

**Barry R. Koffler**
*Featherside*
*High Falls, NY 12440*
*(914) 687-9851*

**Karen L. Pangallo**
*27 Buffum St.*
*Salem, MA 01970*
*(508) 744-8796*

**Wordworks**
*85 Eastern Ave.*
*Gloucester, MA 01930*
*(508) 281-8655*

# PERMISSIONS

Sooner or later in doing research, every writer runs across the perfect quote, the succinct and absolutely on-target description, the clear-as-a-bell explanation that will add the right fillip to the project at hand. The problem: The quote, or the passage of description, or the paragraphs of explanation are under another writer's byline.

Gaining permission to use another's material—and knowing when and where such permission is even necessary—is a mysterious and muddied area to many writers, especially in light of recent revisions in the copyright law. This section will go somewhat beyond the scope of research. While offering help on how to avoid infringing on another's work, it will include a basic description of the procedures you'll use to protect your own. Let's start with the second part first.

Revisions to the federal Copyright Law over the years have been refinements to the original constitutional provision protecting "authors and inventors" from having their "writings and discoveries" ripped off— to use a distinctly twentieth-century expression.

Under the law, your magazine article, short story, novel or essay, whether published or unpublished, is protected from the moment it exists in "fixed form"—i.e., typewritten, in longhand, shorthand, on a tape recording or however you choose to write. Not eligible for copyright protection are works *not* in fixed form (e.g., a speech delivered but not written or recorded), works made up of information that is "common property" (e.g., tables of weights and measures), ideas, concepts and principles, and titles, slogans and short phrases (although, as we'll see later, these may have their own protection as registered trademarks).

Copyright Law revisions during the last century represent changes in the duration of copyright protection and also in the requirements for formal registration.

The Copyright Act of 1909, for example, differentiated between unpublished works (protected only through state copyright protection) and published ones (which required a system of formal registration with the Copyright Office to protect a work for a renewable period of 28 years).

The Copyright Act of 1976, which took effect January 1, 1978, remedied some of the weaknesses in the 1909 act concerning protection for writers who had failed to formally register their works. It also revised the period of copyright protection to the "life of the author plus 50 years" or, in the case of anonymous or pseudonymous works, to a single term of 75 years.

In 1989, the United States joined the Berne Convention, which, as John H. Baker wrote in *Publishers Weekly*, helped "weave the United States more firmly into the pattern of international copyright agreements."

Joining the Berne, among other things, meant the elimination of the requirement for copyright notice and copyright registration—which many writers had ignored anyway. So is it still important for writers to register their works?

Attorney Ellen M. Kozak, in her excellent book, *Every Writer's Guide to Copyright and Publishing Law* (Henry Holt and Co.), notes that if your work is infringed upon and is registered, you may recover statutory damages and have your attorney's fees reimbursed by the infringer. If you've not protected your work ahead of time, you will be entitled only to compensation for your actual losses—and you'll bear your own legal costs.

Though you may still register your work after it's been infringed upon, delays in processing your application through the Copyright Office can delay your action against the infringer—who all the while may be making money at your expense. Better to be safe than sorry, Kozak cautions.

Registering the copyright on a piece of work is a simple procedure.

Call the Copyright Office and request the proper form (TX for non-dramatic literary works; PA for works of the performing arts, including musical and dramatic works; SE for serial works intended to continue indefinitely—e.g., if you're publishing your own newsletter, magazine, newspaper or journal). The fee (nonrefundable) for registering a copyright is $20.

A number of helpful circulars are available by calling or writing the Copyright Office, Library of Congress, Washington, DC 20559. Those you might want to add to your library include R1, "Copyright Basics," R1c, "Registration Procedures," and R22, "How to Investigate the Copyright Status of a Work."

The Copyright Office Forms Hotline number is available 24 hours a day at (202) 707-9100. If you want to speak to an information specialist in the Copyright Office, call (202) 707-3000.

For a further discussion of copyright and other legal matters of interest to writers, another useful book is the *Writer's Encyclopedia*, published by Writer's Digest Books. This book covers copyright, libel, contracts, taxes and many other matters dealing with the business side of writing.

## USING OTHERS' MATERIAL

The Copyright Law that protects your creative works, of course, extends similar protection to the works of countless other creative individuals. This section deals with the procedures for securing permission to use portions of others' copyrighted works, and those instances when no permission is required.

To take the latter case first, works that fall into what is referred to as the "public domain" require no permission to reprint. These include works created before the institution of the Copyright Laws, works on which copyright permission has expired and works that by their nature cannot by copyrighted—e.g., the exemptions discussed at the beginning of this section and publications of the U.S. government.

The Copyright Law also contains a "fair use" provision that covers those situations in which you can quote from another's work without first seeking permission. But fair use is a gray area, and perhaps the best advice to follow is: "If you want to use a portion of someone else's material, no matter how small, it's safest if you ask."

The fair use provision holds that the work to be quoted must be used in a "reasonable manner." But what is "fair" and what is "reasonable" are open to discussion. Some writers and publishers use a rough rule of thumb to determine what constitutes fair use (say, for example, 5% of the total of a novel, or up to 100 words of a short story or article).

But copyright experts such as Kozak will tell you in no uncertain terms that nowhere is a numerical formula for fair use written down and, in an increasingly litigious society, this yardstick may afford you no protection.

The courts consider these four criteria in copyright infringement cases:

- the purpose and character of the use, including whether such use is of a commercial nature or is for nonprofit educational purposes
- the nature of the copyrighted work—i.e., is it largely factual, with information that is readily obtainable, or interpretative
- the amount and substantiality of the portion used in relation to the whole (that is, how much of the work are you borrowing?)
- the effect of the use upon the potential market for or value of the copyrighted work

Another mistaken notion is that simply paraphrasing a passage or section can absolve you from needing permission. Detailed summaries of books, articles, studies, etc., would probably put you on thin ice with the courts; better get permission before undertaking anything of this nature.

How to begin? If you're preparing a book manuscript and have contracted with a publisher, the publisher may have its own permissions department that handles the necessary requests or can advise you how to proceed. It's best early on to make clear in your contract who will pay the fees that some permissions grantors require. Some publishers will agree to bear all or some of these costs; some may grant a special advance just for this purpose; some will stipulate that these fees will be paid out of the author's royalties; and some will place all of the responsibility for securing/paying for permissions on the writer himself.

If you're working on your own to secure permissions for a book, article or other project, the process, while time-consuming and sometimes frustrating, need not be a mystery. It simply takes common sense, thoroughness and a bit of advance planning.

Barbara Bartolotta, former manager of the Copyrights and Permissions Department of Scott, Foresman, Inc., a textbook publisher, says many writers simply "do not understand what information a [permissions] grantor needs," which is as complete a description as you can provide of the material to help the grantor identify the passage and know what use you plan to make of it.

To know who to contact, look for the copyright notice on the title page of the book or magazine from which you're quoting (or the page following it) to see who holds copyright on the work. It's wise, too, to check the acknowledgments page of a book to make sure that the passage you're interested in quoting hasn't been reprinted from another work. (You must contact the original copyright holder then.)

Write to the Permissions Department of the book or article's publisher. If no address is supplied, check *Literary Market Place* or the *Gale Directory of Publications* and give the following information: title of the work, name of author or editor, edition (if relevant), year of publication (for a magazine article, complete date and year), page the passage appeared on and a copy of the original selection. If you plan to alter the original (e.g., use ellipsis, use the material as the basis of a parody, etc.), you should mention that as well. The copyright holder may not agree to the proposed alterations.

The writer should be very explicit in detailing how the material will be used, Bartolotta notes, as that will be used by the grantor to determine if permission will be forthcoming and whether—and how much of—a fee will be charged. The information should include the number of copies to be made—or how large a press run is planned—what form the copied material will appear in (a softcover or hardcover book, photocopied newsletter, magazine article, etc.) and how and when it is to be distributed. In the case of a book, you can obtain this information from your publisher.

A sample letter used by authors for Writer's Digest Books appears below, and will give you an idea of how to frame your request:

Dear _____ :

I am writing a book, tentatively titled _____,
which Writer's Digest Books plans to publish in the _____
of _____ . The book, which will be a _____
edition of approximately _____ pages, will retail for about $_____ .
An initial printing of _____ for the trade market is planned.

I would like your permission to include the following excerpt(s) (photocopies attached):

I'm seeking nonexclusive world publishing rights in all languages, including subsequent editions and special nonprofit editions for use by the handicapped.

I am looking forward to receiving your permission. Please indicate the acknowledgment you wish to have printed in the book.

Thank you very much for your help.

Sincerely,

William Righter

Bartolotta, who has amassed "two shelves full" of books on the subject of copyright law, says the simplest and most helpful resource for writers to understand the basics of the permissions process is the annual *A Writer's Guide to Copyrights*, published by Poets & Writers Inc. The guide includes sample forms and glossary for $6.95 plus $3.90 postage and handling (New York and California residents must add appropriate sales tax). Ordering address is 72 Spring St., New York, NY 10012-4013.

If a publisher charges you a fee for using copyrighted material, how much can you (or your publisher) expect to pay? *Publishers Weekly* reports the going rate for permissions can be anywhere from $15 to $100 per page of prose and $5 to $25 per line of poetry. Music lyrics (whose copyrights are jealously guarded) often command *very* high fees—if you can determine who holds the copyright—and some publishers encourage writers to simply rewrite a passage *sans* lyrics rather than put up with the headaches.

## PERMISSIONS SERVICES

For projects in which an author needs to seek a number of permissions or is too busy or unable to do the job personally, the help of an editorial service that specializes in this area may be secured. (Many of these firms, of course, offer other services as well—researching, indexing, editing of manuscripts, etc.).

To work effectively and efficiently with one of these services, it's imperative to:

- Notify them far enough ahead of time to get the job done—three to six months ahead of the date your manuscript is due was mentioned most often. Allow more time if permission from works published abroad needs to be secured.
- Call in advance to discuss the project.
- Provide complete copies of material requiring permissions adequate source data—i.e., where it came from and description of where and how you intend to use it.

Randall E. Greene, who heads an editorial service for book and newspaper publishers in Cynthiana, Kentucky, encourages authors to be scrupulous during the writing process about keeping full and accurate notes on material they plan to quote: "An incorrect listing for a publisher, a missed page number, an incomplete title anywhere along the way can make the permissions process expensive and sometimes unworkable."

Many of these services charge an hourly rate (generally from $15 to $50 per hour and up), though some charge per permission. Phone, mail and fax expenses are usually added on top of these.

*LISTINGS*

*Literary Market Place* runs listings of permissions services under Editorial Services. A few are listed below:

**BZ/Rights & Permissions Inc.**
*125 W. 72nd St.*
*New York, NY 10023*
*(212) 580-0615*

**Catalyst Communications Arts**
*2241 Boulevard Del Campo*
*San Luis Obispo, CA 93401*
*(805) 543-7250*

**GREENECommunications®**
*P.O. Box 8003*
*Cynthiana, KY 41031*
*(606) 234-3266*

**Silberfeld Communications**
*2336-B NW Pettygrove*
*Portland, OR 97210*

## TRADEMARKS

We'll add a note here about registered trademarks because their improper use by writers routinely raises the blood pressure of trademark holders.

Many trademark holders—the makers of Styrofoam, for example—prefer that you use a generic term (e.g., "expanded foam") in referring to their products. If you insist on having your protagonist use a Weedeater on his front lawn, however, you'd better be certain to refer to it as a "Weedeater® brand trimmer." The fact that it doesn't have the same flow is of no concern to the holder of that (or any other) trademark. Their concern is to protect and preserve their good name.

An incorrect use of a trademark will frequently bring you a nasty letter from the owner—and it's amazing how they keep track of even obscure publications. But if it's thought the use was malicious, or casts the trademark holder in a poor light (a play on the name Coke with drug connotations, for example), you might well find yourself the target of a lawsuit.

For proper spellings of trademarks and their descriptive terms, consult *Trade Names Directory*, published by Gale Research, or the *Standard Directory of Advertisers*, both available in larger libraries.

In addition, the International Trademark Association provides information and maintains a library open to writers on the subject of trademark usage. "Trademark Checklist" and "Trademarks: The Official Media Guide" are available through the International Trademark Association, 1133 Avenue of the Americas, New York, NY 10036. A Trademark Hotline, (212) 768-9886, is staffed from 2 to 5 P.M. EST, Monday through Friday, to answer questions.

# RESEARCHING FICTION

Fiction writers, as well as nonfiction writers, dig for facts—the facts necessary to set a mood, to move the reader into a unique time or place or even, as Truman Capote and others have shown, to be the basis of the story's action itself. Sometimes it's not possible to try out an experience firsthand. John Gardner, who's continued the James Bond series since the death of Ian Fleming, relied on book descriptions of how to fly a particular aircraft when he couldn't find access to a simulator or the genuine aircraft.

And until time travel becomes a reality, writers in historical genres will have to rely on book research. Author Rosemary Rogers confesses to relying on *Timetables of History* to find out what was happening in other parts of the world at the time her characters were "doing their thing."

Obviously, many of the same resources used by nonfiction writers will be helpful to fiction writers as well. Some of these resources may even trigger ideas for stories.

Even for nongenre fiction, adequate research, well used, "gives a texture to your story, a ring of authenticity," says Jack Heffron, editor at Story Press.

The fiction writer's research must be every bit as careful as that of his nonfiction-writing brother or sister: One false note can jar the reader out of that fragile landscape of words the fiction writer has crafted.

If your story is set in a service station, for instance, the story is strengthened and enriched if the sounds and sights and smells are included—and, above all, accurately portrayed. Editors are scrupulous about details that might detract if they're carelessly or wrongly used.

Occasionally a writer may have to do research to know what to leave out of a story as well. Heffron says he once had to determine whether a certain popular fast food chain had a branch in Gary, Indiana. The restaurant was a key locale for a story Heffron was writing about cocaine running in the Midwest. He wanted to make sure the setting was realistic—but not too realistic—on the outside chance the restaurant might sue.

Beware of "overresearching" your story, Heffron adds. "Some authors writing about the fifties or sixties seem to want to drop in every pop culture cliché there is." He advises having someone else read your work before sending it out to make sure the background touches add to your story but don't overpower it.

So how do you accumulate the information for these "background strokes"? We've all read about "name" authors globe-trotting to gather information on exotic locales for their latest novels, but few of the rest of us have the travel budget for such a luxury.

Careful research is the answer, and even veteran writers acknowledge that "doing the homework" is necessary whether it's your first novel or short story or your fortieth.

Jory Sherman, author of nearly 150 books over a 25-year career, has amassed more than twice that number of reference books on life in the Old West and knows writers who have as many as 1,000 in their collection. To write his westerns and novels of the West, Sherman uses many sources, including interlibrary loan through The School of the Ozarks in Point Lookout, Missouri. (For a description of how ILL works, see the "Libraries" section.)

Sherman also advises calling, writing or visiting the historical society in the area in which you're interested. These groups have access to obscure books, maps and other artifacts that can add detail and color to your writing, and they frequently publish scholarly monographs. Sometimes their members are experts on rare and interesting subjects and are willing to share information. (Historical societies' libraries are valuable resources as well. To locate these, check out the *Directory of Historical Societies and Agencies in the United States and Canada*, published by the American Association for State and Local History, available at most larger libraries.)

Even globe-trotting authors frequently don't set foot into a new book's setting until they've laid out a groundwork of book research. James Michener, for example, reportedly reads 300 to 400 books on an area before starting a new blockbuster. (For *Texas* he reportedly read 500 books on that state.)

Patricia and Clayton Matthews, a husband-and-wife writing team who between them have written nearly 100 novels, dozens of short stories and countless other pieces in a wide range of genres, have logged many miles in their on-site research. But they still frequently sketch out the setting for a story line in advance from their Prescott, Arizona, home. The Matthewses consult travel magazines (*National Geographic* and *Smithsonian* are particularly helpful) and sometimes travel films (larger public libraries frequently have good selections) to scout out the topography, climate and landmarks beforehand.

Fiction writers who have computers and modems can check out some of these details electronically, but veteran fiction writers recommend that nothing beats an on-site visit to check the accuracy of your yarn.

Jory Sherman actually walked in the ruts left in the ground by wagons traveling the Santa Fe trail. Patricia Matthews rewrote the opening to *Love, Forever More* after a visit to Virginia City showed that the initial description she'd written of that locale was off the mark.

There's another reason these travels are invaluable. Visiting old bookstores, the local newspaper office and even tourist attractions can turn up privately published booklets, pamphlets and other source materials not available through conventional research methods. Jory Sherman and Patricia and Clayton Matthews also scour local bookstores and say owners frequently know who—or where—the best "repositories of information" are.

Many fiction researchers take conventional notes on these scouting trips, but others find a small, unobtrusive tape recorder (or, in some instances, a video camera) useful for recording information on landmarks, customs and, especially, interviews with locals. The latter can provide "earwitness" accounts of speech patterns, colloquialisms, etc., that can give your dialogue—as well as your plot—the ring of truth. (Remember to keep records and receipts from all such trips—they're legitimate business expenses and are tax deductible.)

Rather than drudgery, research can be a serendipitous event for the fiction writer, turning up unexpected legends, little-known colorful characters or folklore that can give writing a new twist or spark ideas for further stories, the Matthewses point out. "I've never understood why anyone would want to have a stranger do their research," says Patricia Matthews. "A lot of the story comes from assimilating the culture yourself."

When they're not traveling or at the typewriter, the Matthewses are researching. Patricia suggests keeping clip files of magazine and newspaper articles containing news items in your area of expertise (e.g., police procedurals). Even if you're not working on a project that can use that information at the time, a clipping about a new method in crime detection, for instance, might prove useful at a later date.

## FIRSTHAND EXPERIENCE

Some writers like to tell how they've worn many "hats," even for short periods, to soak up atmosphere as further seasoning for their stories. Mary Higgins Clark sits through "a lot of trials" to get close looks at psychopathic killers. ("They look perfectly normal.") Marion Zimmer Bradley worked as a fortune-teller at a circus for one of her novels. The announcement that you're a writer and the offer to work free for a couple of days or even a couple of hours are a combination that many gatekeepers find irresistible.

## EXPERT ADVICE

Short of verifying details of your stories personally, you can call on experts on travel, history, technology, etc., to answer questions related to your story. Most people are flattered and willing to expound on their field of expertise, provided you identify yourself as a writer with a legitimate project, do the obvious homework first and arrange for a mutually agreeable time and way to conduct the mini-interview. Some writers find that a letter with a self-addressed stamped envelope for a reply works just fine, while others swear by the telephone interview. (For hints on how and where to find experts, consult the "Resources" section.)

But don't overlook friends, relatives and co-workers who may be untapped sources of information. For just the right poisonous plant to describe in one of her novels, for instance, Patricia Matthews called on former co-workers at California State in Los Angeles for help. (She made it clear that the plant was intended for her fictional—not her real-life—spouse!)

## NETWORKING

Belonging to writers' groups that specialize in your area of interest also helps, most fiction writers point out. Members of groups such as Romance Writers of America, Mystery Writers of America, Science Fiction and Fantasy Writers of America, and others are generous about sharing information and frequently sponsor seminars, workshops, etc., that touch on special research needs. Their addresses are in the "Community of Writers" chapter.

## FICTION RESEARCH RESOURCES

A number of other books deal exclusively with providing accurate details for fictional works. For mystery and crime writers, Writer's Digest Books' "Howdunit Writing Series" offers eight titles covering subjects ranging from forensic medicine to how private investigators *really* work. Writer's Digest Books' "Everyday Life" series, including *The Writer's Guide to Everyday Life in the Middle Ages*, *The Writer's Guide to Everyday Life in the 1800s* and *The Writer's Guide to Everyday Life: Prohibition to World War II*, provides "background strokes" for historical settings.

*What People Wore: A Visual History of Dress from Ancient Times to Twentieth Century America*, by Douglas Gorsline (Bonanza Books), remains one of the bibles in the fiction research field, though many writers have scouted out their own guides to various historical periods. Clayton Matthews recommends the various series published by Time-Life Books (on the Old West, on United States history, on seafarers, etc.). Patricia Matthews also favors *Historical Dress in America*, by Elisabeth McClellan (Tudor Publishing), who wrote several versions covering various periods in early American life. She also enjoys *A Browser's Book of Beginnings*, by Charles Panati (Houghton Mifflin), which describes the "who and when" behind a number of common objects, and uses Avenel Books' *Seven-Language Dictionary* to provide a foreign word or expression on occasion.

### ADDITIONAL RESOURCES

*The Facts on File Visual Dictionary Series* (Facts on File) gives the correct terminology for the component parts of more than 3,000 objects.

*Characters in 20th Century Literature* (Gale Research Inc.) summarizes major works by twentieth-century authors. It's indexed by author, character and title.

*Timelines of the Arts & Literature*, by David M. Brownstone and Irene M. Franck (HarperCollins).

*The New York Public Library Desk Reference* contains charts, lists and other compendia representing some of the most-asked questions of the reference desk at that venerable institution. Fun for both research and pleasure reading.

*The Regency Companion*, by Sharon Laudermilk and Theresa Hamlin (Garland Publishing).

*Romance Reader's Handbook*, by Melinda Helfer, Kathryn Falk, Kathe Robin (Romantic Times).

*What's What: A Visual Glossary of the Physical World*, by Reginald Bragonier Jr. and David Fisher (Hammond).

# INFORMATION ACCESS

Those used to dealing with government bureaucracies on a regular basis know that the information controlled by the various agencies is, for a variety of reasons, not always made readily available through conventional indexes, published reports or other channels. And civil servants of a government supposedly of, by and for the people are sometimes reluctant to share public information with the press or even with interested citizens.

For that reason, a quarter of a century ago, the government took steps to ease access to information.

The federal Freedom of Information Act (FOIA), enacted in 1966, was designed to allow public access to records in the possession of any federal agency. The act allowed for nine exemptions of material from FOIA requests: classified material that might jeopardize national security; agency rules that are "predominantly internal in nature"; information exempted by another federal statute; "trade secrets"; internal memoranda; documents that would invade personal privacy; investigatory records; and two other specialized categories of exemptions involving banking and oil.

The government, in the Sunshine Act (generally referred to simply as the "sunshine law") passed 10 years after FOIA, provides for the right, again with certain exceptions, to attend meetings and gain access to the records of specific federal agencies' governing boards.

Since FOIA, most states have enacted their own access laws involving records and meetings that pertain to the operations of local governments. So the mechanisms are in place to provide for a free flow of information between government agencies and the people to whom they're answerable, right?

Well, right and wrong. Despite amendments to FOIA in 1974, there still remain some serious bugs to be ironed out in the machinery—delays in processing requests and, more seriously, questions on just what constitutes a record under FOIA jurisdiction.

When the original laws were passed, of course, the computer had not yet become the record gatekeeper of the office as it is now and records were most always paper documents or microfilmed copies. The battle is currently on as to whether FOIA covers access to computer files, and the law probably will have to be rewritten to govern the computer age. Until that time, writers will have to cope with the hazy areas of the law and also with delays in processing FOIA requests—a frequent complaint from applicants.

Under the law, an agency is supposed to respond to a properly filed FOIA request within 10 working days, and some do. But many extend the deadlines, and delays of months—and years—are not uncommon.

Some of the delays are the result of poorly prepared request letters—vague descriptions of the materials sought, addressed to the improper person or agency, etc.

Kathleen Edwards, manager of the Freedom of Information Center at the University of Missouri, says many of the calls to the center's FOIA "hotline" at (314) 882-4856 (staffed 8 A.M. to 5 P.M., Monday through Friday) are seeking "elementary advice" on what's available through FOIA—and how.

The center, which handles approximately 3,000 calls annually, dispenses information and counsel from very basic FOIA matters to more complex queries—e.g., citing case law to bolster the arguments of writers appealing the denial of an FOIA request. The center also has its own Web site (http:\\www.missouri.edu\~foiwww).

"The nation's most comprehensive files on freedom of the press and free speech" are housed at the center, Edwards says, and can be used on-site or accessed for a nominal research fee and photocopying charge. The thousands of topics covered in the files are far-reaching, from illiteracy on the international front to obscenity rulings on the domestic front.

The way to expedite your request, Edwards advises, is to be as specific as you can in what you request and to whom you direct that request. Check with the agency you've determined has the information you seek, and find out the name of the person who processes FOIA requests.

Find out, too, the fee schedule for processing such requests. Under the law, the agency may charge for searching for and copying documents. You may be entitled to a reduction or waiver of the search fee if you will be using the information for a noncommercial scientific, educational or journalistic purpose, or if you can prove that disclosure of the information is in the public interest.

The letter you write should state clearly all of these things:
- that it is an FOIA request for [include the specific name of or specific description of document or documents]
- whether you are requesting a waiver or reduction of fees—and why—

or the maximum amount of fee you are willing to pay
- complete addresses on both ends—yours (including a phone number, if possible) and the agency to whom you're sending the request

Writers used to filing FOIA requests admit that persistence and patience are the most effective tools in prying out information from bureaucrats.

Journalists and others are constantly testing the limits of the FOIA, and the courts are constantly issuing rulings relating to access. Consequently, if you will be using this process frequently, it's wise to keep abreast of current developments on the FOI front. The National Freedom of Information Committee of the Society of Professional Journalists (formerly Sigma Delta Chi) and Gannett News Service annually produce a Freedom of Information Report that includes a roundup of FOI-generated stories and how their reporters got them, hotlines to obtain FOI help and a state-by-state description of open meetings and records (sunshine) laws. Formerly a tabloid on newsprint, the report is now a special fall issue of *Quill* magazine, the official publication of SPJ-SDX. A copy of the report can be ordered from the Society of Professional Journalists for $3 (plus $2 shipping and handling) by writing 16 S. Jackson St., Greencastle, IN 46135, or calling (317) 653-3333.

If you're still confused about FOI requests, a number of other agencies, associations and organizations publish helpful materials.

The Government Printing Office (see the "Government Documents" section) offers *A Citizen's Guide on How to Use the Freedom of Information Act and the Privacy Act* ($3, order stock number 052-071-00129-3). *FOIA Subscription*, an update containing news articles on FOIA interpretations, etc., is also available from GPO. Price is $5 per year and order number is 727-002-00000-6.

The Consumer Information Center, P.O. Box 100, Pueblo, CO 81002, has released "Your Right to Federal Records," a 25-page booklet (order booklet 462W) for $.50.

The American Civil Liberties Union (ACLU) and Bantam Books publishes *Your Right to Government Information, A Basic Guide to Exercising Your Right to Government Information Under Today's Laws*, by Christine M. Marwick, $4.95

The Reporters Committee for Freedom of the Press, 1101 Wilson Blvd., Suite 1910, Arlington, VA 22209, publishes *How to Use the Federal Freedom of Information Act* ($3 plus $1.50 shipping) and *Tapping Officials' Secrets* on state open meetings and records statutes ($8 plus $2.50 shipping and handling). Other publications include a quarterly magazine, *The News Media and the Law* ($25), and *Access to Electronic*

*Records* ($5 plus $1 shipping and handling). The RCFP also staffs a hotline to field FOIA questions: (800) FFOI-AID.

## DIGGING OUT FACTS WITHOUT FOI

Filing an FOI request is not always necessary for obtaining information. James Derk, an editor at the *Evansville* (Indiana) *Courier*, has trained reporters in investigative techniques and says that a helpful exercise is to send a new reporter to city hall, county court or some other agency "and simply to introduce himself or herself to each person in the offices there for a rundown on the types of records they keep."

Derk, a former investigative reporter whose stories have won numerous awards and have been followed up by *60 Minutes* and other news organizations, says that the county recorder's office, board of elections and other agencies can be gold mines of information for all types of stories.

"You'd be surprised at the kinds of documents that are kept on individuals, and the broad range of places that they're kept." He once tracked a subject down from a softball roster kept by the city's Parks and Recreation Department.

His tips for a successful "paper chase":

- If you're looking for information on a person, a company or an organization, put yourself in their shoes to determine the best source of information: Have they bought or sold property? Filed bankruptcy? Paid (or not paid) taxes? Any (or all) of these can lead to information sources.
- If you're dealing with government documents, try asking directly without making an FOIA request, but make it clear that you'll file one if necessary. "Sometimes an agency would just as soon not bother with the paperwork required in an FOIA request."
- Again in dealing with the government, try requesting the same information from a number of related agencies (or a congressman on a particular committee involved with the subject). Since delays are common in dealing with government bureaucracy, if you're facing a deadline, you'll improve your chances if you aim at more than one target.
- Another, somewhat unorthodox, tip that not every writer would agree with: "From time to time, I've asked for a lot more material than I was really after so that the bureaucrat would call me up and say, 'Look what is it that you *really* want?' and then he'd ship it to me," Derk laughs. "Sometimes it helps to ask for the moon when all you want is a little piece of cheese."

A resource Derk recommends for writers who plan to do a number of in-depth investigations is Investigative Reporters and Editors, a nonprofit organization of approximately 4,000 investigative journalists and editors from around the country. IRE, headquartered at the University of Missouri School of Journalism, offers, besides a network of writers skilled in investigative techniques, these resources:

- *IRE Journal*, a "how-to" for members, published six times per year. (A subscription is included in the annual membership fee: $40 U.S., $55 outside U.S., $25 student.)
- Access to the Paul Williams Memorial Resource Center, a collection of several thousand investigative pieces done by newspapers, magazines, TV and radio (searches of this collection are conducted free for members).
- *The Reporter's Handbook*, a 500-plus page guide covering where and how to find personal records (birth and death certificates, marriage and divorce papers), tax records, credit records and court records. The third edition is a short course in investigative techniques, as well as a fascinating read, as it's liberally laced with true-life investigations. The price, at this writing, is $21 for members, $26 for nonmembers. Add $4 for first-class postage and handling or $2 for book rate.

Stories from the IRE's morgue can also be searched through its Web page (http:\\www.ire.org). Mailing address for IRE is 100 Neff Hall, School of Journalism, University of Missouri, Columbia, MO 65211. (314) 882-2042.

# RESOURCES

Despite the importance of doing background research in preparing an article, the live interview remains the heart of most writing projects. Unless you have an editor who'll give you a specific lead on who to contact ("Go out and talk to Mrs. Gottrocks about the dog show on Saturday"), finding live interview subjects—good interview subjects, not just live bodies—is up to you.

The *Encyclopedia of Associations* is the first place a lot of writers look to find national experts on a variety of topics. But there's one drawback to it, as far as writers are concerned: Many of the associations listed simply don't have the staff—or the resources—to act as information clearinghouses for writers.

Matthew Lesko considers himself the guru of low-cost and free information from the government and other sources. (A frequent guest on talk shows, the hyperkinetic Lesko resembles Ralph Nader played on fast forward.) His phone book-sized *Lesko's Info-Power II* lists 45,000 sources that provide "answers to . . . questions at home, at school, on the job, at play." The book is available for $39.95, plus $4.50 postage and handling, by calling (800) 54-LESKO. The information in the book is also updated continuously online for subscribers to CompuServe (see the "Databases" section).

Not as much fun as Lesko's books, but still helpful, is the *National Directory of Addresses and Telephone Numbers*, published by General Information Inc., 401 Parkplace, Kirkland, WA 98033, (800) 722-3244; in Washington, (206) 828-4777.

*Find It Fast: How to Uncover Expert Information on Any Subject*, by Robert I. Berkman (Harper & Row), identifies government departments and other agencies that are "rich resources" and tells how to mine them most effectively.

*The Yearbook of Experts, Authorities and Spokespersons*, published by Broadcast Interview Source, 2233 Wisconsin Ave. NW, Washington, DC 20007, (202) 333-4904, is an indexed encyclopedia of over 3,500 persons willing to be interviewed on topics ranging from attention deficit disorder to zoos and phobias. Broadcast Interview also publishes *Power Media Selects* and *Talk Show Selects*, by Alan Caruba, both references full of experts.

Writers looking to keep their long-distance bills down might want to invest in AT&T's *Toll-Free 800 Directories*, available by calling—what else—an 800 number: (800) 426-8686. Updated each fall, the volumes come in both a business edition with 120,000 entries and a consumer edition with 60,000 entries.

Speaking of phone numbers, phonefiche, which represents the listings in more than 300 phone books, is available at many larger libraries. It's valuable for finding addresses or for bypassing directory assistance charges.

Monitor Publishing Company produces a library of "leadership directories"—that is, phone books targeted to provide information on reaching the movers and shakers in government, industry, etc. *Federal Yellow Book* covers federal departments and agencies, while the *Congressional Yellow Book* and *State Yellow Book* provide information in those areas. The firm also publishes *The Corporate 1000*, *The Financial 1000*, *Over the Counter 1000* and other yellow books. (These are sometimes available in larger libraries.) For a catalog, or ordering information, contact them at 104 Fifth Ave., 2nd Floor, New York, NY 10011, (212) 627-4140.

To smoke out resource people to contact you, some writers have successfully tried *Partyline, the Public Relations Media Newsletter*, which circulates to public relations persons in universities, hospitals, professional associations, public relations agencies and businesses large and small. *Partyline* contact Betty Yarmon says the weekly newsletter handles requests from writers for "verified publications." They'll run a brief description of your research needs free of charge and many get good response. Lead time for the newsletter is 10 days to two weeks. Write 35 Sutton Place, New York, NY 10022; call (212) 755-3487 or fax (212) 755-3488.

An online message posted to a computer BBS or special-interest group can also provide an interview source.

If you're looking for resource people in your own backyard, veteran writers know of a ready source in most large and medium-size cities—the faculty of local colleges and universities. If you have a question on or need an interview with someone on anything from child rearing to Chinese artifacts, there's generally someone in local academic circles to provide answers—or leads. The public information office of many colleges and universities can generally give you a line on faculty members' particular expertise, and many regularly publish directories spelling out the subject areas in which professors are willing to speak/be interviewed, etc. Don't be shy about calling, writing or e-mailing an academic public relations office with your request. Most are only too happy to help their faculty members get into print.

## ADDITIONAL DIRECTORIES

*Celebrity Register*, with listings on entertainment, sports, arts and politics, 1780 Broadway, Suite 300, New York, NY 10019. (212) 245-1460 or (212) 757-7979.

*Current Biography*, a monthly magazine with background information on people in the news, celebrities and politicians. Bound copies are available at the library.

*The Sports Address Book: How to Contact Anyone in the Sports World*, by Scott Callis (Pocket Books). Covers all the usual sports and even some of the unusual—horseshoes, martial arts, aerobics, etc.

*The Capital Source: The Who's Who, What, Where in Washington* (National Journal, Inc.), 1501 M St. NW, Washington, DC 20005. (800) 356-4838 or (202) 739-8543.

American Federation of Television and Radio Artists, (213) 461-7145, or the Screen Actors Guild, (213) 856-6741. Most actors are registered with one or the other, and they can provide you with a manager or representative's name to contact.

## CLEARINGHOUSES/NONPROFIT INSTITUTIONS, ETC.

Organizations, interest groups, etc., whose activities are detailed or described in popular media have an interest in ensuring that those descriptions are accurate and complete. Therefore, many have established clearinghouses and other avenues for answering questions, providing expert input and the like for writers, and they can be valuable research aids. Remember, though, that some sources, especially those underwritten by commercial enterprises, strive to present their topic only in a favorable light, and therefore may present material that is somewhat biased.

Some helpful sources whose titles are fairly self-explanatory:

*Media Resource Service*
*355 Lexington Ave.*
*New York, NY 10017*
*(800) 223-1730, or (212) 661-9110 in New York State*

*National Health Information Center*
*P.O. Box 1133*
*Washington, DC 20013-1133*
*(800) 336-4797*

Menu choices offer information on a variety of health topics.

## OUT-OF-PRINT/RARE BOOKS

Writers are sometimes frustrated when they learn that a title they're after is out of print. R.R. Bowker's *Books in Print* carries an "Out of Print/ Out of Stock Indefinitely" supplement that carries listings of out-of-print retailers and wholesalers (by state), wholesale remainder dealers ("remainders" are those books that make it to the bargain table) and search services—firms that, sometimes for free, will help you find which source around the country still carries your rare or out-of-print title. Bowker's *American Book Trade Directory*, available at larger libraries, also includes a listing under Antiquarian Book Dealers for tracking down old or rare books.

The Antiquarian Booksellers' Association of America (ABAA) maintains a directory of about 450 sellers and buyers of old books, some of whom provide search services for locating old titles. The directory provides addresses and phone numbers for these specialized stores, while indexing them geographically and by specialty (50 Rockefeller Plaza, New York, NY 10020, (212) 757-9395).

For dealers in your city, check the yellow pages under Book

Dealers—Used and Rare. Some of the larger ones (Pomander Books in New York City is one) will help writers track down out-of-print titles.

## OTHER WRITERS

We've made reference before to the benefit of joining writers' groups as a source of quick answers to questions on writing fiction, etc. And, as any satisfied group member will attest, the benefit of having fellow toilers around to celebrate/commiserate with is perhaps the best attribute of membership.

Writers' groups are treated at length in the chapter of this book entitled "A Community of Writers," but, in terms of research benefits, it should be mentioned that a number of writers' groups maintain reference libraries of varying sizes for use by their members. (Some carry only references that can already be found in any good public library, but many writers like to browse the specialized selection.) A few with reference resources are:

**The Authors Resource Center Inc. (TARC)**
*4725 E. Sunrise, #219*
*Tucson, AZ 85718*
*(602) 325-4733*

**Community Writers' Library**
*McKinley Foundation*
*809 S. Fifth St.*
*Champaign, IL 61820*
*(217) 344-0297*

**Literary Center**
*1716 N. Forty-fifth St.*
*Seattle, WA 98103*

**The Loft**
*Pratt Community Center*
*66 Malcolm Ave. SE*
*Minneapolis, MN 55414*
*(612) 379-0754*

**Poets House**
*772 Spring St.*
*New York, NY 10012*
*(212) 731-7920*

**Van Voorhis Poetry Library**
*Poetry Society of America*
*15 Gramercy Park*
*New York, NY 10003*
*(212) 254-9628*

**Woodland Pattern Book Center**
*720 E. Locust*
*Milwaukee, WI 53212*
*(414) 263-5001*

**The Writer's Center**
*4508 Walsh St.*
*Bethesda, MD 20815*
*(301) 654-8664*

**The Writers Room**
*153 Waverly Place*
*New York, NY 10014*
*(212) 807-9519*

In addition, a collection of books and periodicals about the book industry, The American Booksellers Association Information Center, is open by appointment at 137 W. 25th St., New York City. Brief reference questions may be answered by phoning (800) 637-0037; and The Council of Literary Magazines and Presses (CLMP) has donated a library of 1,600 different literary magazines to the New York Public Library.

# CHAPTER 4

# PRODUCING AND POLISHING IT

Irene Prokop, editor in chief at Jeremy P. Tarcher, has a favorite expression: "Anyone who aspires to be a writer should work in publishing for a year."

She's right, but for many reasons most writers don't and can't opt for this education. What you would see on the job are the mechanics of the business—and the overwhelming demands on editors' time.

Book and magazine publishing has always been a busy venture, but especially today—with publishing houses merging and costs being cut—editors have less time to devote to the actual editing of manuscripts. If you're an experienced writer/editor who has found your writing niche, this industry-wide trend won't affect you as much. But if you're a new writer or an experienced author venturing into a new style or genre, it's difficult to get in-depth advice on your manuscripts from editors.

Consider the history of books, and you'll encounter anecdotes of how author and editor working together significantly enhanced the final version of a book. (Of course, there are also horror stories where personality clashes overshadowed the book.)

Today, some writers and agents are opting to have a book manuscript professionally edited before sending it to publishers. This approach enables the book "to be a better book . . . to meet its full potential," says Renni Browne, founder and owner of The Editorial Department, 119 E. Depot St., Greeneville, TN 37743, (423) 639-2025. Her company of 21 experienced editors provides this service in addition to putting authors in touch with agents.

To give your project luster and more clout in the marketplace, you can employ a freelance editor who will help you rewrite and polish your work. Or, if you have a track record in editing and publishing, you can offer your services as a freelance editor or coauthor to persons needing such help.

As a writer committed to your craft, you should refine your editing skills so you can send your work directly to publishers without the help of a freelance editor. Freelance help, though, speeds up this learning process and enables the editor to earn extra dollars that sometimes are recycled into the freelancer's writing career.

Whether your goal is to find a freelancer or find clients to help, this section will explore the many opportunities. From freelance editing to collaborating, from graphic designing to desktop publishing, you'll learn what to expect from these freelancers and how to offer these services.

# HELPING HANDS

As a writer/client or freelance editor, you'll be making a short-term or long-term commitment to someone you've never worked with before. Such partnerships can affect your professional life and goals, as well as your partner's—for better or worse.

If you're coauthoring a book or editing an unpublished writer's first book, you need to promote a positive working relationship: thoughtful, helpful and timely responses, and terms and rates that do not take advantage of the writer.

If you're a writer hiring a freelance editor, you need to promptly pay the editor, give her carefully prepared material and responses and trust her judgment. "Some people want an editor but don't want anything touched in the manuscript," points out Dorothy Beach, director of the American Society of Journalists and Authors' Dial-a-Writer Referral Service. Study the critiques and suggested editorial changes provided by your editor, and use this opportunity to learn more about your writing style.

The physical interaction between writer and freelance specialist— either editor, proofreader, translator or indexer—has become easier, thanks to the electronic/online media. (*The Online Journalist: Using the Internet and Other Electronic Resources* [Harcourt Brace] is a good primer for showing you how.) Today, you and your freelance partner can exchange manuscripts and correspond via computer terminal and fax machine, or you can correspond by mail.

As wordsmiths, we work with words (and usually computers), but ultimately we're working with people. It's the old-fashioned relationship of trust and respect for one another's expertise that fosters a productive exchange of ideas.

Best-selling author Samm Sinclair Baker, who has written 32 books (16 as coauthor), stresses that partners must work together as a team without trying to cheat one another. "My basic rule for a successful and profitable coauthorship is the writer should care more and do more for the well-being of the partner than for one's self."

This advice applies to any editorial partnership.

Your first step as writer or freelancer is to carefully investigate the possibilities rather than jump into a relationship you or your wallet can't live with. Ideally, look for a person whom you like, respect or want to help or work with, especially if the project will demand a long-term partnership.

Also, it's important to have a signed letter of agreement before you invest time in a project. That protects both you as a writer, freelance editor or collaborator *and* protects your editorial partner. "Writing out the terms of agreement fixes more clearly the expectations of both parties and also focuses their attention on issues they might otherwise fail to notice," recommends the Freelance Editorial Association's Code of Fair Practice. "Up-front discussions help each party comprehend the other's expectations and avoid disputes."

Letters of agreement ensure that crucial commitments have been discussed and agreed upon: What will be provided, by when, in what form, at what price and/or percentage and with what exceptions? Who will provide the expenses like postage, long-distance calls and photocopying? Get these business considerations out of the way so you can focus on the reason for the partnership.

## FINDING A FREELANCE PARTNER

Writers and editors live in big cities and small towns, but where can you find that freelancer who can enhance your writing? And where are the writers who need help?

Consider looking first in your hometown or a nearby city. Even in small cities, you can sometimes find editors who edit national magazines or professional writers who freelance frequently with New York magazines.

The cost will vary depending upon the credentials of the freelance editor and whether your freelancer works from his home or in an agency office. In addition, the amount of work your manuscript needs and the amount an editor charges per hour or per project will affect the final bill.

Most freelancers have a set price for various editing jobs, but will negotiate or vary the price depending on the project. There are no industry-wide pay standards. In fact, associations are prohibited, by law, from recommending standard rates, but some editorial associations publish a range of rates charged by their members. Freelancers subscribing to the same referral services or organizations may charge more or less than their colleagues. Where the freelancer lives—and the amount of local competition—can affect the rates she charges, and likewise, where you live can affect the rates you charge your clients.

One of the most cost-efficient ways to receive feedback on an article, story or book chapter—and to get ongoing writing advice—is to take a writing course at a nearby college or community center. Even if the instructor does not edit your work line by line, he can advise you on what a manuscript needs so you will know what type of editor to contact.

The typical college student, directly out of high school, rarely thinks to inquire about a professor's writing/editing credentials, but it's best to inquire before you enroll in a course. If you're a mystery writer, for instance, you'll probably want an instructor who understands the conventions of the genre. If the instructor has not worked in a particular style or genre, a course can be a waste of time and money.

During the course, don't hesitate to ask the instructor for more feedback on your manuscript, especially if the instructor assigns letter grades and few comments.

It's important, however, not to abuse a teacher's willingness to help you. Don't expect a teacher to edit your book or additional stories. If you benefited from the teacher's critiques, consider negotiating an agreement with the teacher for additional editing—*after* the course has concluded.

Another way to find people locally who can edit your work is through editors' and writers' associations. Watch for notices in your local newspaper about upcoming meetings, or call the editor of a nearby publication to inquire about editors' groups in your hometown. Also consult the yellow pages' Business-to-Business Directory under Editorial Services and any freelance specialty you need.

On the local level, many organizations publish a directory with members' names, media affiliations, addresses and phone numbers, and a monthly or quarterly newsletter—which can provide you with names of area people to contact. (See "A Community of Writers" chapter for more information.)

To be listed in some organizations' directories, you'll need to first join the organization. (This membership can also be a springboard to networking and learning more about writing and editing.) Some organizations, such as the Cincinnati Editors Association, publish a freelance directory (in addition to a membership directory). Both members and nonmembers pay a nominal fee to be included in the freelance directory.

Some organizations, such as the Austin (Texas) Writers' League, will match members with local persons and companies needing freelance work, but will also respond to calls from anywhere in the United States. Regional groups with limited funding and the goal of helping local professionals and companies will limit their referrals to a particular geographic area.

Another way to contact writers or freelance specialists is to run an ad in an editorial organization's newsletter. For some groups, running an ad is a membership privilege, and there is no charge; sometimes there is a nominal charge. In the monthly *Austin Writer* newsletter, for instance, the classified ad rate for 30 words is $10 for members and $15 for non-members. This newsletter is circulated to the league's 1,600 members. The monthly *Writers Connection* newsletter, published by the Writers Connection in San Jose, California, charges $.75 per word with a 10-word minimum and 20% discount for six consecutive ads.

## CONTACTS ACROSS THE COUNTRY

You can find a freelance editor, indexer, translator or coauthor by contacting any of a number of organizations. Among them is the American Society of Journalists and Authors, which offers a Dial-a-Writer Referral Service at (212) 398-1934. ASJA's service will match writers in the United States and overseas with publishers, corporations, universities and individuals who need the assistance of a professional writer or editor.

Clients then negotiate the fee directly with the ASJA member, and there is no charge for a quick referral. Persons requesting an extensive search for a book collaborator, or corporations seeking referrals, pay a search fee.

To get freelance jobs through the Dial-a-Writer service, you'll have to join the 1,000-member organization, but not all writers are eligible. ASJA requires substantial freelancing credentials of its members. Most ASJA members are active freelance writers, many of whom have published numerous books, which makes Dial-a-Writer an excellent source for finding competent freelance assistance.

Cassell Network of Writers Publishing, Editing and Promotion Inc., based in North Stratford, New Hampshire, provides an International Writer Data Bank that helps writers and editorial specialists find one another. Copyediting, ghostwriting/collaboration, indexing, manuscript editing/revision, proofreading and translating are among the writing/editing skills under which persons' names are filed. Approximately 170 skill areas and subject specialties, such as travel, parenting and business, are included in the data bank. The phone number is (603) 922-8338.

For freelancers wanting to broaden their knowledge and client base, and for writers wanting a freelancer with big-city publishing credentials, the Editorial Freelancers Association and the Freelance Editorial Association are valuable resources.

The Freelance Editorial Association (P.O. Box 380835, Cambridge, MA 02238-0835, (617) 643-8626) publishes a *Yellow Pages* of freelancers as a service to members in the Boston area and across the country. (This is not the same *Writer's Yellow Pages* published in the 1980s by Steve Davis Publishing.)

The *Yellow Pages* includes a detailed Code of Fair Practice, in addition to listings for editors (copy, developmental and substantive), desktop publishers, illustrators, indexers, researchers, project managers, proofreaders, translators and writers interested in freelance projects. The 20-page Fair Practice Code covers freelance responsibilities and tasks, guidelines for fees and project terms, and contracts and disputes with a sample contract and letter of agreement.

The Editorial Freelancers Association (71 W. 23rd St., Suite 1504, New York, NY 10010, (212) 929-5400) provides referrals for freelance editorial services and also publishes a nationally circulated directory with a geographic index. EFA's more than 1,000 members are editors, writers, indexers, proofreaders and translators.

The EFA Job Phone, (212) 929-5411, narrates a list of available full-time and freelance editorial jobs. Anyone may call the Job Phone tape, but only EFA members who subscribe to the service (for $20) can get further details on the jobs from EFA's 24-hour answering service.

Helpful services provided by both EFA and FEA include newsletters, members' disclosures on good and beware-of clients, and guidelines on pay rates. FEA's guidelines include various types of work, estimated pace of work and recommended fees. For instance, a person doing basic copyediting generally would complete an estimated three to eight double-spaced pages per hour for $20 to $30 per hour. *Editorial Freelancers Association Professional Practices Survey* booklet includes detailed breakdowns and percentages of hourly fees received by its members for numerous editorial specialties.

The National Writers Union (873 Broadway, Suite 203, New York, NY 10003, (212) 254-0279) publishes a *Guide to Freelance Rates & Standard Practice* with the going rates for six major freelance markets.

Payment from some clients can be a problem for freelancers, but this is less likely to happen with referral services. Organizations like ASJA and FEA have Fair Practice Committees which help resolve disputes between freelancer and client.

To find additional writers' organizations that might direct you toward editorial freelancers or clients, consult the *Encyclopedia of Associations*, the *Book Publishing Resource Guide* and *Literary Market Place*.

As an editorial freelancer with book publishing references, you can request to be listed in the annual *Literary Market Place*. This comprehensive directory of the American book publishing industry, available in most city libraries, includes an Editorial Services activity index of persons and agencies that offer copyediting, fact checking, ghostwriting, indexing, line editing, manuscript analysis, proofreading and translating.

*Literary Market Place* lists editorial freelancers free of charge, but it by no means gives free advertising to just anyone. Potential nominees for the next edition must fill out a detailed questionnaire, give references (for first-year listees) and meet the March 31 deadline. References are then checked by *LMP*.

*LMP* listings give each person's or agency's name, address, phone number and brief description of the services and specialties.

Weekly magazines such as *Publishers Weekly* and *Editor & Publisher* include classified advertising sections in which writers can advertise for assistance and editors can advertise for clients.

*Writer's Digest*, *The Writer* and other writers' and editors' magazines also run ads for people looking for or willing to be collaborators, editors or proofreaders. This enables you to contact freelance editors eager to edit and/or proofread your manuscripts.

Another source of freelance help is the Writer's Digest Criticism Service. You can receive detailed advice for improving and selling books, novels, articles, short stories, scripts, poetry and query letters. Professional writers, freelancing for the service, write a detailed critique about the manuscript's strengths, what needs to be changed and how to make those changes. If your manuscript is marketable "as is" or with slight revisions, you'll receive specific marketing suggestions with the names of publications and editors who buy that type of writing.

Some literary agents (and other individuals) provide a critique of manuscripts for a fee, but this is no guarantee the agent will represent you or your book. The ideal agent is not in business to give literary critiques but rather to get authors' books published at commercial or small-press publishing houses and to negotiate a fair contract. *Literary Agents of North America* (Author Aid Associates), *LMP* and the annual *Guide to Literary Agents* (Writer's Digest Books) list agents who, in addition to representing books, critique writers' work.

## WHAT TO EXPECT FROM EDITORS AND CLIENTS

You can receive a "polish" on your manuscript from a freelance editor in many ways: rewriting, content editing, copyediting and proofreading. Some freelancers provide a critique or manuscript analysis. Knowing the differences between the concepts helps you hire a freelancer suitable to your needs.

"Make it clear to the freelance editor what you expect and acknowledge the editor's expertise," recommends Kirk Polking, coeditor of the *Beginning Writer's Answer Book* and author of *Writing Family Histories and Memoirs*.

David Hall, publisher of the Editorial Freelancers Association's directory, recommends the freelancer—in response—be candid about what she can and can't provide on a given project.

## HOW TO CONTACT A FREELANCE PARTNER

To contact an editorial freelancer, send a brief letter of inquiry and a self-addressed stamped envelope (SASE) to the person. In your letter, request information on the services offered and the costs.

Don't hesitate to ask for the credentials of the person who will be editing or evaluating your work. Kirk Polking suggests that you ask a potential freelance editor about his past clients. Would a publishing company hire this particular person? Any freelancer worth his blue ink will have a bio sheet to send to potential clients. If not, go elsewhere.

Look for a freelancer whose work experience and credentials reflect a commitment to the type of material you write. For instance, if you need a children's book edited, the ideal freelance editor will have worked for a children's magazine or have published several children's books. The best editors provide specific ways to improve the manuscript so that it is not only grammatically correct but also marketable. To make a manuscript salable, the editor must know the markets to which the manuscript would be submitted.

"What is it exactly that editors do?" queried one writer on the Internet's "miscellaneous writing" newsgroup. In summary: anything from developing the concept of a book to writing the jacket copy.

Most people don't understand what editors do and don't understand the various stages of editing," says Renni Browne. "Editing is not [only] about fixing mistakes and catching contradictions."

The first stage, evaluative or conceptual editing, demands that the editor see and understand the architecture of a book. The editor must see not only the book's overall structure, but also the balance of one element against another, say, plot and characterization. Unlike the writer, a competent editor will see the book's problems and provide solutions the author hasn't thought of.

The second stage, line editing, involves sentence and word "line" changes. "Line editing has to sound like the author," says Browne.

The final step is copyediting, where language-related elements such as grammar, punctuation and spelling are evaluated and corrected. The ideal copyeditor knows one or more of the frequently used guides, such as *The Associated Press Stylebook* or *The Chicago Manual of Style*. A copyeditor needs a thorough knowledge of the language and a sharp eye for inconsistencies.

It's important to realize that an editor, like a physician or attorney, will generally be stronger in one specialty to the exclusion of others.

Contact several editors before entrusting your project to a freelancer. This will enable you to survey the variety of services, prices and qualifications of freelance editors. Browne cautions writers about hiring an editor who offers to read and edit any manuscript sight-unseen. She will return a book to a writer—without charging editing fees—if she doesn't believe the book will ever get published.

If you need assistance on a book project, hire a freelancer first to edit a magazine article or short story you've written. This is a good way for you to evaluate this editor's helpfulness—before making an expensive long-term commitment.

Analyze the person's ability to communicate the strengths and weaknesses and to show you how to improve your manuscript. A good editor will not only point out what needs to be improved, but will show you how—*on* the manuscript—depending, of course, on whether you've requested editing or an analysis.

As a freelancer marketing your services, you'll be in competition with other editorial freelancers. Writers—the smart ones—will shop around. That's OK. For you, the benefit of this search is that potential clients who have selected you will be convinced that they have made a good choice and will be eager to receive your comments.

Some freelancers prepare a brochure that lists their services, prices and credentials. A brochure or carefully designed information sheet can *illustrate* your professionalism. State your policies in writing. Under what conditions will you agree to take on a manuscript? (Some freelancers prefer to work with beginners; others prefer to work with experienced writers whose books are likely to land on publishers' forthcoming lists.) Define for potential clients what constitutes a critique—or any term you'll use in working with them.

## FREELANCE FEES

An editor with a national track record generally charges more than that "friend-of-a-friend who was an English major in college," but from the professional you should receive advice to make the manuscript complete and grammatically correct, interesting to read and marketable. Here's a case where that worn cliché applies—you get what you pay for—unless that acquaintance is also an accomplished editor.

Book content editors charge $15 to $50 per hour and more, or $600 to $5,000 per manuscript, depending on the size and complexity of the project. If you need someone to rewrite your book, the charge is about $18 to $50 per hour, or sometimes $5 per page. Services for a book copy-editor can range from $10 to $35 per hour or more, or $2 per page.

Ninety-five EFA members who edit books for publishers reported hourly rates ranging from $12 to $100 per hour; the most frequent rate (23.2% of respondents) was $25 per hour.

Textbook copyediting can earn $15 to $20 per hour, depending on whether the book is a technical or nontechnical elementary, high school or college text. Freelance editors of medical texts charge $25 to $65 per hour.

You can expect to pay about $160 for a critique of a book outline with the first 20,000 words. A critique for an article or short story of up to 3,000 words costs $20 to $25 per hour, or an estimated flat rate of $40 to $60.

*Writer's Market* lists a range of payment rates for numerous freelance specialties. Use these guidelines and those from freelance associations to set your freelance rates or to compare the rates you've received from freelancers.

If you don't have extra money to spend for freelance editing, consider bartering for this service. In return, you would provide an equally valuable service for your partner. Writers and designers sometimes do this; so do pairs of writers. But bartering generally won't work if one person would receive substantially less than the other person, or when the payoff (for the freelance editor), say, is a percentage of an as-yet-uncontracted book. Here, you'd be asking the freelancer to assume an author's financial risk with no guarantee of this person being paid.

Ideally, you should engage a freelance editor to hone your skills so that you no longer need this "middle man" to get your work ready for publication. Any freelance editor who convinces you that you can't write a marketable manuscript without this outside editorial help is creating a dependency that will cost you money, time and self-esteem.

You need to master the rules and variations of the language and to spot where you can improve a manuscript, or else you'll be turning over one of the most satisfying parts of writing—the polish—to another person.

The ideal freelance editor will encourage you to become your own editor—even when it costs that editor a client.

## PROOFREADERS

In precomputer times, all published material had to be proofread as a separate stage of the publishing process. Now most editors edit and proofread simultaneously—and they actually proofread the version that appears in the publication—without having to employ a proofreader. Type compositors/printers and publishing houses, though, still employ proofreaders, some of whom are freelancers.

If, as a writer, you want someone to proofread your work, you can hire a proofreader. But with the hourly rate for proofreaders and copyeditors so similar, you can get more for your money by employing a copyeditor who will also correct poor word choices.

Another option would be joining or starting a proofreading co-op. When members of the Cincinnati Editors Association and the Greater Cincinnati Women's Network started a "Coffee, Tea, and Fees" group in 1995, one of the discussion topics became "proofreading." They formed a proofreading co-op to give one another a second eye on important documents. Members have agreed to charge one another $5 per hour for proofreading and to respect the confidentiality of what they might read.

As a proofreader for a printer, you would compare the printer's proofs or galleys against the edited manuscript to identify and correct errors in the typeset copy, in addition to making sure that the type and headings conform to the specifications.

Before soliciting proofreading assignments, consider working in-house as a proofreader to learn the expectations of clients and to gain speed and accuracy. Contact area publishers and printers first. Consider running a small ad in your hometown newspaper.

To develop a clientele, send a cover letter, résumé and (optional) proofread page proof with your marks to publishers and printers. Most companies will not respond, but from those that do, you can begin to find proofreading work. When a company is pleased with your work, you'll continue to get calls.

As a freelance proofreader, you can set your own hours, but sometimes to meet publishers' and printers' schedules, you will encounter long hours and short deadlines. Some companies may want you to work exclusively for them, which you can't do as a freelancer—unless the price is right.

Before you accept a proofreading assignment, ask for an estimate of how long the job will take or how much work is expected within a specific time.

Most proofreading jobs offer a set hourly rate. Freelance proofreaders of books earn $6 to $25 per hour and sometimes $1.50 to $3 per page. If you proofread corporate publications, you can earn $15 to $30 per hour. Medical proofreading assignments earn $12 to $30 per hour.

Publishers will usually tell you what they pay. If you have significant credentials, payment may be negotiable. Some publishers pay a per-book rate, which will vary from book to book, depending on how complicated the book is.

## TRANSLATORS

As a translator, you can specialize in commercial, literary or technical translations, or you can accept assignments in all three specialties. Today, the immediate demand in this field is for translators of technical material.

Depending on the language(s) you know and the type of material you prefer to translate, you need to get your name into the hands of publishers, companies and individuals who need translations. "There is more demand than ever for translators," says ATA executive director Walter Bacak.

If you are a translator looking for work, contact the 5,900-member American Translators Association, 1800 Diagonal Rd., Suite 220, Alexandria, VA 22314, (703) 683-6100, fax (703) 683-6122. The association publishes a monthly newsletter, *ATA Chronicle*, in which members and nonmembers advertise translating services (15 words or less for $10) or place a more costly display ad. The newsletter also provides leads from companies and individuals who need translators.

ATA's *Translation Services Directory*, published every two years, lists translators, their languages and specialties, but to be included in the directory, you must be an active ATA member and pay the annual $95 membership fee.

To find a translator, consult ATA's directory or the *Literary Market Place* directory that lists translators, their languages and specialties. Translators and interpreters are indexed by source and target language.

Payment for translating projects will vary greatly, depending on the languages to be translated, the translator's credentials and sometimes the publisher's availability of funds. Translators who know languages of lesser diffusion—such as Portuguese, Vietnamese or Finnish—can earn a higher rate of pay than translators of languages such as French or Spanish.

On book translating projects, the division of the royalty between author and translator is a negotiable matter, but the author's royalty is almost always higher, points out Clifford Landers, administrator of ATA's Literary Division.

He recommends translators and their clients use the Translator's Model Contract of the PEN American Center's Translation Committee. This contract and a translators' packet from PEN include guidelines and provisions on translation terms and rights. Peter Newmark's *A Textbook of Translation* (Prentice-Hall) is also a good source for translators.

Commercial translators charge $80 to $140 per 1,000 words. If you receive a translating project through an agency, you might owe a commission to the agency, an estimated 33⅓%. Government agencies pay up to $125 per 1,000 foreign words into English. Technical translations pay about $125 for 1,000 words. Translators of magazine articles can earn $17 per hour, and sometimes more.

Literary translators charge a per-project fee, or one calculated by increments of 1,000 words ($95 to $125 per 1,000 English words).

If you want to be a literary translator, prepare a translation of a work you feel strongly about. Send this translation sample (a maximum of 10 pages) with a letter stating your credentials. "Enthusiasm and concern for a text are what will attract a publisher rather than being there on a list and being competent," says Pulitzer Prize-winning poet Richard Howard, who has translated 150 books.

One way to add to your list of credentials is to write reviews of book translations for periodicals. Your critique of the translation shows your ability to understand language and translation.

## INDEXING

Indexers read books and manuals—as do all editorial freelancers—but in a much different way. "When indexing, you are reading to pick out what are the concepts and ideas that someone will need to find and what are the relationships between them," says full-time indexer Alexandra Nickerson, who works for numerous book publishers and producers/packagers.

An index can take a few hours to hundreds of hours to create. Whether you work with index cards and a typewriter or with a computer and commercial indexing software, this freelance specialty demands long hours, adherence to details and deadlines and a commitment to clients. Because of the constant decisions on entries and cross-references, it's a skill that takes practice and indexing know-how. "There are two major components in the indexing task, one intellectual, the other mechanical," points out David Billick in the American Society of Indexers' pamphlet, *How to Get Started Indexing*. Book production editors prefer to work with professional indexers.

As more and more information is being transmitted electronically, the field of indexing is in a transition period. "The question is, What is going to happen with all this electronic stuff and what role will indexers play?" points out Nancy Mulvany, author of *Indexing Books* (University of Chicago Press).

Indexers who take the time to learn more about technology will probably have a wider choice of opportunities. "Indexers who are able to move their skills over to other [computer-related] environments will find work," says Mulvany. At the same time, she is optimistic about publishers' continuing needs for well-written indexes.

To market your skills as an indexer and to stay abreast of new indexing opportunities, consider joining the American Society of Indexers. This national association publishes numerous books to help the indexer, including four 1995 resources: *A Guide to Indexing Software*, *Starting an Indexing Business*, *Running Your Indexing Business* and *Marketing Your Indexing Services*.

If you need to hire an indexer, consult ASI's *The Indexer Locator* ($10 for ASI members and $15 for nonmembers). This directory lists indexers and their specialties. For publications, contact ASI:

*P.O. Box 48267*
*Seattle, WA 98148-0267*
*(206) 241-9196*
*Fax: (206) 727-6430*
*E-mail: asi@well.com*
*World Wide Web: http://www.well.com/user/asi*

Another source for finding indexers or indexing jobs is through colleges that offer library science degrees. Consult also the directories mentioned earlier in this chapter.

Many trade publishing houses delegate the responsibility of writing the index to a freelance indexer, according to self-publishing experts Marilyn and Tom Ross. The author may also choose to prepare it or ask the publisher to find an in-house or freelance editor to do it. Often an indexer's fee will come out of the author's royalty.

Authors tend to overindex. "It's hard to be objective about one's own work and to analyze it from a potential reader's point of view, both essential for creating an index that is a useful tool," points out Nickerson, chairman of ASI's Education Committee and an indexing instructor for the U.S. Department of Agriculture's Graduate School. "People not experienced in indexing often index details but overlook central topics and themes."

Indexers occasionally are employed to edit indexes provided by authors—to refine the style. "The author may refer to a topic by one term, and it's the indexer's job to think about the audience and come up with any alternative terms they might be likely to look under," she says.

When you receive an indexing assignment, you'll use page proofs to compile the index. A few publishers are now shipping page proofs to indexers on disk, and some publishers will allow the completed index to be submitted via modem or e-mail, with the hard copy of the index to follow by express courier.

Payment is negotiable. It depends on the level of difficulty of the book, the comprehensiveness desired in the index, and the size of the book, the page and the typeface. More experienced indexers can command a higher rate of pay. Indexers get paid more for medical books, legal texts and highly technical materials.

You can be paid by the page (proof page, not manuscript page), hour, entry, line or project. Today most indexers prefer to be paid by the hour or by the page. There are advantages and disadvantages to each method of payment.

You can earn $15 to $45 per hour, or an estimated $1.50 to $6 per indexable page (excluding front and back matter). The fees vary widely, depending on the complexity of the project and the geographic location of the freelancer.

As a freelance indexer, insist upon a letter of agreement with authors. If the author submits the page proofs late to the indexer or delays sending the index to the publisher, the indexer can get blamed.

The American Society of Indexers has compiled a sample letter of agreement—on paper and on disk—to help members avoid potential problems. Indexers' agreements should specify the rights acquired (if any), author of the index, credit and editorial approval, subcontracting (whether the publisher will allow the indexer to subcontract the work), payment, delivery of work and a termination clause.

One potential problem with hiring indexers or compiling indexes is timeliness. Your indexer must be able to meet deadlines. Of course, as the writer, you need to be timely with the promised materials. "Inability to meet the planned schedule for delivery of the material to be indexed must be communicated to the indexer promptly, since busy indexers need to adjust their schedules in order to make time for a project that is late or has been revised after indexing has begun," Nickerson points out. "Failure to maintain communication with your indexer may leave you without an index when you wanted it or with a job that suffers from being rushed."

When employing a freelance indexer, ask for references and a sample of his or her work. When you have chosen your freelancer, it's important to discuss with the indexer what you want in an index. Assuming that you were impressed with the credentials of the person you hired, trust your indexer as you should any freelancer you hire to enhance your work.

## COLLABORATION

Whether you dream of producing romance novels, textbooks or lavish coffee-table books, a collaborative writing arrangement can help you achieve that goal. Today, in nearly every genre, writers are sharing the work load, profits and sometimes bylines that in some cases would not be possible without a two-person team.

Of the 52,000 to 53,000 books that are published each year, it is impossible to estimate how many result from collaborations, but industry sources cite a steadily increasing number.

Glance at the book covers in your bookstore, and you will quickly see examples of collaborations. A telltale sign is the celebrity's or sports hero's name in large type with a small, less prominently placed byline that says *With the-name-of-the-collaborator.*

"Today with the interest in celebrity books, there is a growing need for more people who can talk well to subjects and draw them out and, most importantly, organize their thoughts well into a book," says John F. Baker, editorial director of *Publishers Weekly.* "Part of being a successful collaborator is to shape a book out of somebody's random reminiscences, thoughts and opinions."

The O.J. Simpson trial has spawned more than 40 books, and that number will probably increase (as more writer-collaborator deals are signed). In other arenas, Luciano Pavarotti (and coauthor William Wright) and Colin Powell (with collaborator Joseph E. Persico) have written recent books, as have many sports figures and hero-pilot Scott O'Grady.

With high-profile court cases and extraordinary news events, the major players have a marketable story to tell, but usually they're not writers. To produce a timely, highly readable book, publishers and agents pair a person-with-a-story-to-tell and a writer. The celebrity brings to the collaboration unique life experiences—experiences that bookbuyers will pay money to read about—while the writer brings writing and story-telling skills to the collaboration.

Baker notes that books about "true crime" are a lucrative area for writers and publishers. Today's bookbuyers also have an enormous appetite for books on popular musicians, and television and radio stars. The political memoir has recently been superseded by political books where individual politicians talk about their lives and what they intend to do.

There are various approaches you can use to initiate a collaborative writing agreement, and different roles you can play as a collaborator—with these varying amounts of credit:

coauthor (By Leslie Jones *and* Your Name)
collaborator (By Leslie Jones *with* or *as-told-to* Your Name)
ghostwriter (By Leslie Jones—and no byline for you)

You'll encounter varying amounts of work with each project and, of course, need to carefully explore each collaborative option—the benefits and drawbacks—before agreeing to work on a project.

Collaboration can mean that you'll write the entire manuscript based on your partner's tape recorded dictation and several face-to-face meetings, or that you'll provide extensive or light revision to a manuscript that your partner has written. With a 50/50 coauthorship, you and another author would each write, say, eight chapters in accordance with the outline that both have drawn up. As a ghostwriter with a nonwriting partner, you'll assume—while writing—the "voice" of the celebrity, the sports hero, the business leader or politician.

What is important is that you first consider your time, personality, writing goals, interests and financial needs, and then reach a written agreement that will satisfy you, your partner and your publisher.

With publishing houses and agents eager to work with collaborating writers, you have the opportunity to carve a niche for yourself in a specialty that writers, working alone, have overlooked.

If the thought of working with another person or writer scares you, consider the benefits. In some cases, your partner's life experiences or knowledge will be the research that might take you years to collect. An expert in a field—be that person a physician, lawyer, psychologist or teacher—can provide the content of the book while you produce and polish the material and collect additional anecdotes, quotes and facts. In some cases, the collaborating writer becomes a translator, translating highly technical research and ideas into lay terms, points out Irene Prokop, editor in chief for Jeremy P. Tarcher.

Collaboration can also be an alternative if you write fiction. For instance, one person might be an expert story plotter and creator of dialogue; the other partner might have a knack for fresh characters and page-turning narratives.

Some publishers will resist publishing fiction by two authors (it takes twice the effort to promote the book), and yet sometimes, especially with romance novels, the name on the novel is a pseudonym for a two-person team: for instance, Leslie Holden is the pen name for collaborators Holly G. Miller and Dennis E. Hensley. (They recently coauthored *Write on Target: A Five-Phase Program for Nonfiction Writers*, a nonfiction book bearing their real names.)

If you're considering collaboration, also consider the drawbacks: sharing the profits, receiving a fair share (if you're a writer without a track record, you may only get 10%), deciding who has the final word (when both collaborators disagree) and venturing into a long-term arrangement where it's impossible to predict potential problems.

## THE IDEAL PARTNER

The ideal partnership means that both parties bring something unique to the book—a unique story to tell, research and writing ability, knowledge of a topic, access to sources or a combination of these qualities—in addition to a sincere commitment to complete the book.

Choosing the right partner is the most important step in collaborative writing, points out Miller, who has written 13 books (11 of which were collaborations).

If two writers are collaborating on a book, it's especially important that each writer bring a power source to the project. This power source is a combination of expertise, insight and skills that will complement the other collaborator's expertise and skills, points out Hensley. Avoid choosing someone whose attributes and perspectives are too close to your own.

Collaboration adds more layers of editing to a book and sometimes takes more time even though the work load may be shared. Select a partner who will conscientiously tackle the expected and unexpected demands of the book.

Today, at least one partner should be comfortable with online research, especially if you're planning to do informational nonfiction. With a modem and communications package, you and your partner can find and interview experts around the world. "It enables the writer to become a national writer," says Miller, travel editor for *The Saturday Evening Post*. The ability to research electronically would be one power source that a collaborator would bring to a project.

Designating one of the collaborators as the leader also helps you resolve potential problems. When a writer and expert-in-a-field collaborate, the expert in writing the book—the writer—makes the best leader. When two writers collaborate, decide which person will play this role.

To decide if collaboration is a good option for your writing talents, consider ghostwriting a magazine article. You can earn $300 to $4,000 for the article and at the same time evaluate your client's suitability for a long-term project. Also, you might decide to expand the topic of that article into a book. That's what happened to author Samm Sinclair Baker. "I sent an article on skin cancer to a leading health magazine, and the editor said he wanted the article, but it would be much more valuable to him and they would pay a lot more if the article were coauthored with a dermatologist," says Baker. "That first gave me the idea to coauthor." That project later became a book.

When selecting book topics, choose a subject that excites you exceptionally and has the potential for a big sale, Baker recommends. Otherwise, the collaborators will be working more for their own satisfaction than income *or* may not even get the book into print. Self-satisfaction can be a valid reason for writing a book, but discuss this prospect in advance with your partner: Can we afford to write this book if it doesn't earn any money?

## FINDING A COLLABORATOR

The search for a collaborator begins with deciding what type of collaborator your book project demands. Do you need (and want) an expert-in-a-field/collaborator or a writer/collaborator or an expert/writer/collaborator?

If you have an agent and are interested in actively pursuing a collaboration, tell your agent. Most agents, though, will suggest this possibility to the writer/client if and when there is a suitable collaborator. Today, agents often initiate a publishing "package" that includes a writer and an expert or celebrity.

To find a collaborating writing partner, begin exploring many of the leads that you would in finding a freelance editor. Consult writers' and editors' publications and directories, and contact college English or journalism departments. Watch for ads in *Writer's Digest*, *Publishers Weekly* and other trade and association newsletters.

By attending meetings and joining editors' and writers' associations, you can meet potential coauthors (writer/collaborators). That approach will also work if you are looking for someone to write your life story. But don't "pop the question" of collaboration until you know that person and his or her abilities. Realize that building mutual rapport and respect takes time, sometimes many months. If your topic demands immediate action, a newspaper reporter or magazine writer could be a potential collaborator. An ideal a writing collaborator should be your equal in talent and skill, says Hensley.

If you want to collaborate on a book in a particular field or specialty, you'll need to look where these experts work, publish and gather. Consult the local yellow pages where professionals are indexed by category. Attend conferences where you can meet specialists in the field that you'd like to write about.

To find contacts in a specialized field, also consult the *Encyclopedia of Associations* and the trade journals of that field. Persons quoted in articles may be willing sources for collaborations. And bionotes at the end of articles sometimes tell you that the article writer specializes in this or that topic.

For additional contacts, consider running a small ad in a field's most respected trade journal: "Published author with M.A. in music willing to ghostwrite or collaborate on book projects. Send details with SASE for response to. . . ." Some journals may allow you to run a brief notice at no charge.

To market yourself as a collaborator, contact by letter the person whose story you'd like to write. Say that you would like to discuss *the possibility of* writing an article or book together. If you don't receive an answer within a month, follow up with a phone inquiry. Unless your book idea revolves around a recent now-or-never news topic or trend, don't demand an immediate answer. A potential client may be a decisive leader in his or her field, but extremely careful and hesitant in selecting a collaborator.

In providing information to a potential partner, give your publication credentials and education in a succinct one-page biography accompanied by a cover letter. Any evidence that shows you've collaborated with other writers or experts is helpful. You might have to convince a potential collaborator to select you over several other contacts.

When you meet this person face to face, you'll again need to decide if you want to proceed. Perhaps you won't like one another's personalities, demands or expectations for the book.

For some people, the ideal collaborator will live in or near your city, but today, with e-mail and fax machines, location is not necessarily the most important consideration. More importantly, your collaborator must share an eagerness to proceed with the project. He or she must also have the attributes that fit you and the project.

### CONTRACTS AND INCOME

As a collaborator, insist on two signed agreements—a contract with a publisher and a letter of agreement with your collaborator—before you invest considerable time and effort in the project.

While there are few guarantees in any writing project, a contract and advance with a publisher tell you that you're pursuing a marketable project. Whether the book sells 10,000 or 500,000 copies depends on many factors, but with a contract, the book has a better chance of reaching readers.

Agent and author Richard Curtis recommends that writers have a separate collaboration agreement in addition to a publisher's contract. "Publishing agreements define the collaborators' joint obligation to their publisher, but they don't define their obligations to each other," says Curtis in his book *How to Be Your Own Literary Agent* (Houghton Mifflin).

In a collaborative agreement or a letter of agreement that some authors use, the collaborators define who specifically will do what, for what royalty, hourly rate or per-project fee, within what time frame and with what deadlines, and who will pay for what expenses. Partners should agree in writing and in advance who has the final approval on the finished manuscript, and select a person who would serve as arbitrator—editor, agent or attorney—if a dispute arises.

Decide in advance if one or both collaborators' names will appear on the book and in whose name the copyright will appear. Sometimes experts-in-a-field or celebrity collaborators will pay a larger portion to the writer who is willing to forgo the byline. Consider how important that byline is to your publishing goals, and then decide whether you prefer to be a coauthor or ghost.

Before agreeing to "ghost" a book and to forgo the byline, consider the best and worst case scenarios. What if the book becomes a megaseller? Would you be content with only the up-front fee you'd received? Or, on the other hand, if the book is not successful—and if you've received a substantial fee for the ghostwriting project—you might actually end up earning more than the author whose name appears on the cover.

Ghostwriters, who forgo as-told-to credit on the book, charge from $5,000 to $35,000 (plus expenses), paid at the completion of each chapter or at four intervals: down payment, half-finished, three-quarters finished and completion. Six months' ghostwriting work on a corporate book can earn you anywhere from $20,000 to $40,000. The hourly rate for a ghostwriter can vary from $25 to $100.

Generally in a collaborative arrangement, one of the collaborators will have contributed more to the book, points out literary agent Michael Larsen who, with writing collaborator Hal Zina Bennett, wrote *How to Write with a Collaborator*. Ideally, the breakdown of what each collaborator receives should be equal, but that won't always be the case.

How much each collaborator will receive from a collaborative arrangement often depends on each person's track record and perceived value in the marketplace.

Today, a writer-collaborator will sometimes receive 10% to 25% of the book's royalty, while the celebrity-collaborator receives the larger remaining amount. "The publisher is really paying for the name of the celebrity, and that's where most of the money has to go," says *Publishers Weekly* editorial director. "I'm afraid for all too many collaborators it is a rather unsung and not particularly well-paid job."

Sometimes, though, an unsung job will give you more clout in negotiating later collaborations and books. Here, you'll have to weigh the short-term and long-term benefits of a proposed contract. Will the collaboration be a springboard to establishing your own audience and your own market value?

For noncelebrity books, experienced collaborators recommend that the profits from the royalty and expenses be divided evenly. "An equal partnership means equal respect," says Samm Baker.

## GRAMMAR SERVICES

*Parents Magazine* and television news programs *48 Hours* and *60 Minutes* have phoned the Writers' Hotline in Emporia, Kansas. So has a speechwriter at the White House. They're among the thousands of callers each year who seek grammar and writing advice from dozens of grammar hotlines across the country. Beginning and long-time writers, and anyone too smart to guess about the English language, can try this alternative.

The lifeline of most hotlines is the telephone (and a conscientious person to answer it), but today some hotlines are beginning to offer online answers. Purdue University's On-line Writing Lab (OWL), for instance, is accessible via the Internet through Gopher, World Wide Web and electronic mail. No matter how far you live from West Lafayette, Indiana, you can access and download more than 100 handouts on various grammar subjects and writing skills.

Grammar and writing hotlines provide free, fast answers to questions on writing, grammar, punctuation, diction and syntax. You might also call a hotline when you've looked for but couldn't find a word or preferred usage. Raymond Walters College's Grammar Hotline, for instance, received a call from someone inquiring about the plural form of a computer mouse. After a quick consultation with computerphiles, writing lab director Bonnie Johnston recommended the word *mice*.

Questions about publishing might also be suitable. How do you solicitize your poetry, asked one caller to the Purdue hotline. The caller was puzzled over a letter from a publisher saying he accepted only solicited poetry.

Most hotlines are operated by colleges or former teachers as a public service to writers (and the language). "There is no organization of grammar hotlines," says Donna Reiss, associate professor of English at Tidewater Community College. Many of the country's hotlines are a service of university writing centers.

If you plan to phone a hotline, it's more cost-effective to call one in your city. Most hotlines won't pay the long-distance telephone charges. *The Grammar Hotline Directory*, published by Tidewater Community College, includes 69 hotlines across the country and in Canada.

Grammar hotlines have varying policies. Follow the guidelines of the one you have contacted. For instance, the Emporia Writers' Hotline will accept mail, phone and in-person inquiries. ESU has an answering machine in operation when the office is closed and asks that writers pay the long-distance costs.

Tidewater College—which underwrites the cost of the grammar directory—cannot answer grammar questions by mail and asks that callers pay the long-distance charges.

Hotline hours throughout the country vary. Some are open during school hours and closed during summer and term breaks. Few hotlines are open in the evenings, but if you live on the East Coast, you can call a West Coast hotline for an answer later in the day. Some hotlines have 24-hour answering machines and will return your call as soon as possible. Johnston recommends that callers speak slowly and clearly when leaving a message.

To get the most from a hotline, have the question or manuscript in front of you when you call. (Asking one or two brief questions is the best—and most fair—approach.) Faculty members, graduate students and former teachers who staff phones generally will answer technical, mechanical and grammatical questions, or refer you to reference librarians or appropriate sources when they can't answer your question.

With an online hotline, you can send the sentence or paragraph in question to the writing lab, but it's important not to abuse the person's willingness to help. "You cannot expect someone at the other end to edit the manuscript," points out Ann Woolford-Singh, director of Tidewater's Writing Center and Grammar Hotline.

Most hotline assistants, says Woolford-Singh, attempt to document answers to help the caller understand the rules behind the answer rather than just giving the answer to the question. Some programs require that staffers look up the answer in two sources before giving the answer.

Some callers will contact several hotlines about a difficult question. Hotline veterans applaud this approach. "Calling for corroboration is another sign of the professionalism of the writer, not a sign of ignorance or weakness," says Reiss, a former writing-lab and hotline director.

Be patient when you call a hotline. Sometimes, at college writing centers, the hotline assistant will be helping someone in the office and you might have to call back. Don't get angry if this happens. The first obligation of a college writing center is to its students. "It's extra help if we're available and if time and resources permit," points out Purdue OWL director Muriel Harris.

Here are a few grammar hotlines. To get a complete list of hotlines, send a self-addressed envelope with one first-class stamp to Tidewater Community College. Sending an SASE is also the best approach if you are soliciting information from a hotline that accepts mail inquiries.

## HOTLINE LISTINGS

### Grammar Crisis Line
*Ball State University*
*The Writing Center*
*Muncie, IN 47306*
*(317) 285-8387*
*E-mail: writingctr@bsuvc.bsu.edu*

Open Monday through Wednesday, 10 A.M. to 7 P.M.; Thursday and Friday from 10 A.M. to 5 P.M., August through April; Monday through Friday, 10 A.M. to 2 P.M., April through August.

### Grammar Hotline
*Emporia State University*
*Emporia, KS 66801-5087*
*(316) 343-5380*

Open Monday through Thursday, noon to 4 P.M.; Wednesday, 7 to 10 P.M.; Tuesday and Thursday, 8 to 10 A.M.; Thursday night, 7 to 10 P.M.; Sunday, 4 to 6 P.M.; summer hours vary.

### Grammar Hotline
*Northeastern University*
*English Department*
*Boston, MA 02115*
*(617) 373-2512*

Open Monday through Friday from 8:30 A.M. to 4:30 P.M.; summer hours vary.

**Grammar Hotline**
*Tidewater Community College*
*% Grammar Hotline Directory Request*
*1700 College Crescent*
*Virginia Beach, VA 23456*
*(804) 427-7170*

Open Monday through Friday, 10 A.M. to noon; additional day and evening hours vary.

**Grammarphone**
*Amarillo College*
*Amarillo, TX 79178-0001*
*(806) 374-4726*

Open Monday through Thursday, 8 A.M. to 9 P.M.; Friday, 8 A.M. to 3 P.M.; Sunday, 2 P.M. to 6 P.M.

**National Grammar Hotline**
*Moorpark College*
*Moorpark, CA 93021-1695*
*(805) 378-1494*

Open from August through June, Monday through Friday from 8 A.M. to noon; 24-hour answering machine.

## WORKING WITH ARTISTS, DESIGNERS AND ILLUSTRATORS

Let's forget about the words of your manuscript for a minute. Picture your manuscript's message. What images would best illustrate and enhance what you're writing?

That's how artists, designers, illustrators and photographers approach their work. While you focus on the words, the visually oriented person sees the images, their placement and other design aspects. Thank goodness, because while we struggle to find the best words to convey a message, the artist is working to visually enhance that message or, in the case of a novel, to capture the atmosphere.

If you are self-publishing a book or newsletter, you can act as your own art director or hire one. Of course, much of the advice we discussed about editorial freelancers applies to working with illustrators and designers: Respect and understand their talents, use good common sense and communicate.

The type of artist you hire depends on what you want to visually depict, and in what medium. Do you want a fine art painting with carefully placed titles or a bold words-only cover for your book? Do you want pen-and-ink line drawings or photos to illustrate a how-to process in chapter three? Or maybe your newsletter needs a distinctive nameplate or logo. These are just some of the decisions that an artist/designer can help you make.

Before you hire a specialist in one type of artwork, though, research the vast variety of graphics that will complement your work. Illustrators, for instance, tend to have a distinct style, and so you would hire a particular illustrator to get a particular style of illustration. Designers, on the other hand, will have either a distinct style *or* have developed a reputation for creating an individual style to suit the demands of each project.

A careful scan of *Artist's & Graphic Designer's Market* (Writer's Digest Books), especially listings in the Book Publishers and Magazines sections, will show you the artistic skills that art directors look for. Some of these techniques—say, calligraphy or charcoal pencil drawing—you might prefer for your publication or book. In graphic design books, look for various techniques, styles and effects. The *Art Directors Annual* (Art Directors Club, 250 Park Ave. S., New York, NY 10003), for instance, showcases outstanding work in one volume. Photocopy and collect favorite examples and styles, but be careful not to infringe on the original designer's work.

Next, talk with several graphic designers who can show you a wide choice of art/design possibilities within your budget. Most designers won't charge you for the initial consultation. Usually, at first meetings, designers will show you their portfolios, ask you about your prospective project and discuss some general approaches and prices. Show examples of the designs you like so the designer won't have to guess, but also be open-minded to the expert's suggestions.

Cincinnati graphic designer Deborah Dent recommends that you involve the designer at the "concepting" stage rather than at production time. "Ideas are better when shared as teams," she points out.

To find a designer who specializes in the type of publication(s) you wish to produce, consult local as well as national directories of artists, designers and illustrators. Some source books focus on artists and design agencies in geographical areas: *Chicago Creative Directory* (Chicago illustrators and designers), *Madison Avenue Handbook* (New York City area agencies) and *The Work Book* (California designers and artists). Some directories include artists, designers and illustrators throughout the United States: *American Showcase*, *Creative Black Book* and *RSVP*. *Literary Market Place* lists artists and art services.

If the visual design of a publication is a new venture for you, explore local sources first, especially in small cities. That enables you to meet face to face with potential designers/artists.

However, with electronic mail, fax machines, overnight delivery services and the advantage of putting what you want/expect in writing, you can still work effectively with an out-of-town designer. This is particularly advantageous if you live in a large city but can't afford the cost markup of metropolitan design firms.

The best designers—for self-publishers on a budget—will suggest cost-effective ways to add variety and "color" to your pages without using the expensive four-color process, unless your book's topic demands color.

Design specialists charge various rates, depending on the complexity of the project. "Most designers will work in one of two ways: fixed bid or hourly rate plus expenses," says Dent, also owner of Willow Design.

The hourly rate for designers ranges from $30 to $150 plus expenses. Expenses can include anything from overnight shipping to a markup on services that the designer may have subcontracted on your behalf, for example, camera-ready resin-coated pages.

If the project takes less time than the designer had imagined, the hourly rate option will be best for your budget. If the project takes more time, you might wind up spending more than you or the designer estimated. Up front, it's nearly impossible to guess the final cost unless you've opted for a fixed-price bid. Having received a bid, you know exactly how much to budget for design work, but then the designer has had to build in additional costs. "The fixed-bid price will reflect the worst case scenario so it could appear high," says Dent.

Whether you opt for a fixed bid or hourly rate, make sure the number of concepts (to be presented by the designer) and the rounds of allowed revisions are spelled out in the contract.

You could spend between $300 and $5,000 for your book's interior design and between $500 and $3,500 for the cover, but most covers will cost between $800 and $2,000. The design of a masthead and cover for a magazine can cost between $500 and $3,000.

If your publication doesn't demand one-of-a-kind artwork, consider clip art. This black-and-white representational line art (and sometimes color reproductions) is available on disk, CD-ROM or in booklet format and can be published without infringing on artists' copyrights.

Desktop design programs, like Corel Ventura and Aldus PageMaker, enable you to decrease long-term design costs but do not guarantee that you'll produce graphically dynamic results.

If you'll be wearing the designer/art director's hat and don't have extensive graphics training, consider hiring a designer as a part-time consultant. For $45 to $90 per hour, a designer will review the prototype or sample pages you've prepared and provide suggestions on how to enhance your graphic approach.

As you determine the design format for your publication, begin looking for artists who specialize in the type of artwork you want. Local galleries and sidewalk and library art shows enable you to browse until you find a technique or style you really like. Attend art shows at nearby colleges. Young artists are eager to establish a reputation, and most would work hard for the opportunity to have their work in a book, newsletter or magazine.

Working with artists-in-training can benefit your first-time publishing efforts and the artists if you can provide additional guidance and be patient about small mistakes that might occur because of inexperience. And if you're willing to provide a learning experience for a college artist, the graphics side of your book or publication could become a two- to three-month nonpaying internship for the student assigned to your project. You would have to follow the guidelines required by the specific art school, but in most cases your willingness to work with a student will provide you with valuable and inexpensive graphics assistance.

When you have selected an artist/designer/illustrator, you need to provide specific "guidelines" so that person can best enhance your writing: the manuscript(s) to accompany the graphics, samples or rough sketches of what you want and a letter of agreement or contract outlining the terms and what needs to be done. New York attorney and author Tad Crawford has written a series of books to help creative people negotiate contracts: *Legal Guide for the Visual Artist, Business and Legal Forms for Fine Artists* and *Business and Legal Forms for Illustrators* (North Light Books).

The terms will vary depending on whether you're contracting for several illustrations or whether you and the illustrator will be collaborating on a book. If you and the illustrator will be collaborating on, say, a children's book, you will probably share the work load. In such a case, then, you wouldn't be assigning illustrations; as partners, you and your artist would discuss the needs of the book and responsibilities to one another.

Artists, designers and illustrators will be especially concerned about retaining the copyright and ownership to their work and appreciate receiving credit for illustrations. *The Artist's Friendly Legal Guide* (North Light Books) and *Make It Legal* (Allworth Press) will help you understand this complicated subject. Business and copyright articles in *Artist's & Graphic Designer's Market* also provide guidelines.

When you negotiate a price and the rights for artwork, you'll suddenly understand why magazine editors—whom you've encountered while freelance writing—want to purchase all rights. It's easier for you to commission an artist on a work-for-hire basis and own all rights to the artwork, but that's the same thing publishers say when they buy all rights to your writing. You'll have to resolve this ethical dilemma for yourself. Be sure, whatever you decide, that you specify—in your letter of agreement—the rights purchased and the price in addition to terms that will make your relationship mutually beneficial.

Experienced artists/designers/illustrators will also want the following areas addressed in the contract or letter of agreement: method and timing of payment, copyright and reproduction rights, termination and cancellations, artistic control, insurance and delivery charges and expenses.

The money-motivated self-publisher can draft one-sided agreements, especially with new artists or photographers who don't understand the consequences, but then the cycle of abusing creative people continues; the self-publisher perpetuates what she is trying to escape from.

If you are assuming the role of the art director, assigning the artwork and illustrations as soon as possible is the best approach to ensure a careful job. Allow extra time for unforeseen delays and revisions. Some design firms have a traffic manager who directs the flow of work to various specialists to meet all deadlines, but most freelance artists, working alone, juggle their own projects. Most freelancers encounter the "feast or famine" problem of having too much work or not enough at a given time. As you interview prospective artists, inquire about their turnaround times. Does the artist use a computer or drawing board to create and change images? How long does it generally take for the artist to redraw or redesign a project? Is there an extra charge for immediate turnaround?

An important guideline in working with artists or any vendor is to build extra time into your publishing schedule for each step, but be firm in expecting deadlines to be met.

Computers have revolutionized the design field—giving designers, illustrators and publishers more options and flexibility than ever before—but the efficiency of computers has also led to misconceptions. Software sales materials suggest that users can instantly create a document with graphics. True, but ideas and concepts, expressed in words and art, take time to develop and refine.

In some cases, computers have reduced the time and graphics costs, but just because a designer uses a computer does not mean designs will cost less. Flexibility is the big advantage of desktop design equipment. A designer can change the typeface or move an illustration from column one to column two with a touch of the mouse. To cut down on phone calls, layers of changes and billable expenses, request revisions and alterations at one time, rather than in several sessions.

Keep in mind that all graphics work, illustrations and photos have a market value, regardless of the time it took to create them. If an experienced book designer is able to create and output a jacket design in two hours, he or she will most likely charge the going rate for a cover in the specific market.

"It's unfair to just estimate how long the execution will take because they're going to have to set aside time to plan and to conceptualize the piece. Also their talent is worth something, too," points out writer Susan Conner, a former editor of *Artist's & Graphic Designer's Market.* "Time isn't the only element."

The complexity of a project, the skill and experience of the artist/designer, the turnaround time and rights will affect the prices you'll have to pay. One drawback for you as a small publisher or self-publisher is that you'll be competing with commercial publishers for the services of artists and designers. Some designers, however, will accept a lower profit margin when the project has a limited market value, such as a small town's history or a church's recipe book. That won't be the case if your book, magazine or newsletter has national or international potential.

"Cash isn't the only currency available to you," points out Mary Cox, current editor of *Artist's & Graphic Designer's Market.* "There are all kinds of opportunities to barter for the services you need. Initiate innovative ways to collaborate with vendors and other creative talent on mutually beneficial projects." Cox uses this example: "You and a designer friend could approach a paper company and printer with an idea for a beautiful promotional brochure all three of you could then mail to clients. Offer your writing and design services in exchange for printing costs. People are more open to bartering than you might think."

Professional designers often use the Graphic Artists Guild's most recent *Handbook of Pricing & Ethical Guidelines* to determine the costs for specific projects. To get another range of prices, study the publishers' entries in *Artist's & Graphic Designer's Market*—you'll see what publishers are paying artists, designers and illustrators. For instance, Grosset & Dunlap pays by the hour for book design, $15 to $22 for mechanicals, and pays $1,500 to $2,500 for book jackets/covers. The Modern Language Association pays $750 to $1,500 per jacket/cover project. *National Geographic* magazine pays $3,500 for inside color illustrations and $750 for black-and-white illustrations. On the regional level, *Orlando Magazine* pays $400 for a color cover; $200 to $250 for inside color.

When you've hired an illustrator for your project, arrange to review the early drawings and then allow the person to work in his or her own way. "If you know that artist's style, then you're going to have to have a certain element of trust, but then you also need proof that they understand what the concept is," says Conner.

Allow artists the freedom to do what they do best, and your words—on well-designed pages with evocative graphics—will look as they never have before.

Following is a list of organizations to contact for more information about artists, designers and illustrators.

*LISTINGS*

**American Center for Design**
*233 E. Ontario, Suite 500*
*Chicago, IL 60611*
*(312) 787-2018*

**American Institute of Graphic Arts**
*164 Fifth Ave.*
*New York, NY 10010*
*(212) 807-1990*

**Graphic Artists Guild**
*11 W. Twentieth St.*
*New York, NY 10011-3704*
*(212) 463-7730*

## WORKING WITH PHOTOGRAPHERS AND STOCK PHOTO AGENCIES

Whether you're a self-publisher, a magazine journalist or a technical writer, you may need the services of a photographer.

When photos will accompany a manuscript you're writing or publishing, you have three choices: hire a photographer to shoot the photos, lease photos from a stock photo agency or shoot photos yourself. All three demand careful scrutiny because obtaining photos is not as simple as offering, say, $25 per photo.

When setting fees, most photographers consider their time, expenses, how you will use the photo and for how long. That person is like you when selling a manuscript—the photographer offers specific rights for a particular price. Most photo buyers prefer exclusive rights to a photo, but with this exclusivity comes a much higher price.

To understand the photo market from the photographer's perspective, read *Sell & Re-Sell Your Photos* and *How to Sell Your Photographs and Illustrations* (Writer's Digest Books). You'll see why photographers are reluctant to immediately quote a set price.

Three economical ways to obtain photos are to shoot the photos yourself, acquire the services of a friend with competent photographic skills or contract with a stock photo agency. With each of these options, the cost, responsibility to the photographer and the professionalism can vary.

If your writing projects constantly demand photos, consider developing your own photography skills. With a photo course and practice, you can produce competent photos. This approach works especially well when magazines offer no additional payment for photos or when you want exclusive rights to the photos without having to pay the high cost. *Photographer's Market* (Writer's Digest Books) provides a list of photography workshops across the country. On the local level, colleges and community education programs offer classes and workshops.

You can develop a better eye for design and photography by studying magazines such as *Communication Arts*, *HOW*, *Photo District News* and *Step-by-Step Graphics*.

If you're designing pages and shooting photos for a book or newsletter, you can ensure a more professional end product by seeking a graphic design consultant. "There are certain visual trends happening in the marketplace," points out former *Photographer's Market* editor Sam Marshall. "There's nothing worse for a book, especially a self-published book, than to look like it's 10 or 20 years behind the times." Ideally, a book should look contemporary today and in the immediate future.

With an hour or two of intensive advice, you can learn current design trends, avoid amateurish mistakes and get tips on how to add variety and composition to your pages and photos. You can pass along this advice to your photographers—whether that photographer is a friend or professional.

The ask-a-friend option to acquiring photos has both benefits and drawbacks. If you're getting amateur photos for an affordable price, you're getting exactly what you pay for. A stock photo agency then becomes your best option.

"What is making stock photography so important to many buyers is that it is less expensive and time-consuming than hiring a photographer or trying to find a photographer who has the exact image, because the stock agency acts as a clearinghouse," says Marshall, a Cincinnati-based journalist covering the photography and design fields.

The stock agency provides one-stop shopping for you as the newsletter publisher or book self-publisher who might need a variety of photos. The agencies can range from a one-person operation to firms that represent 50 to 150 photographers. At small agencies, you might get more personal attention, quicker service and a lower price. But you might not have the more comprehensive selection of a large agency to draw upon.

*Photographer's Market* lists an estimated 200 stock agencies—from the perspective of the agency that acquires images from photographers, but it will show you the variety of stock agencies.

The Picture Agency Council of America (P.O. Box 308, Northfield, MN 55057, (800) 457-7222, fax (507) 645-7066, e-mail: pacaoffice@aol.com) is an excellent way to locate stock agencies and be assured of their reliability. The council's member agencies have signed a Code of Ethics to ensure fair business practices for the stock agency in dealing with photographers, clients and other agencies. PACA members agree to keep adequate records of each image's sales history, to avoid bribery and deceptive advertising, to honor all client confidentiality requests and to protect photographers' copyrights.

Photo researchers will ask numerous questions when you call a stock agency. Your answers will help them determine what types of photos you need and how you will use them. Consider and decide what you want before inquiring about a stock agency's images: Horizontal or vertical? Color or black and white? People in the photos (and of what age, gender and ethnic background)? Do you need space in the photo where you will superimpose words? Be open to suggestions and remember that a stock agency is a partner in the creative process.

All stock agencies want to know whether an image will be used on a cover or on inside pages, whether it will be quarter, half or full page, and whether you're using it in advertising or editorial space. The press run and circulation of your newsletter or book are other crucial questions upon which agencies determine their fees.

A photo can cost $110 to $165 or more for a quarter page depending on how many you buy. A full-page photo can cost $225 to $300 or several times that amount. The photographer will usually get 40% to 50% of the amount (before taxes, marketing and other fees), with the other half going to the agency.

Some agencies will charge you a research fee (around $100) or waive that fee when images are leased. There might also be a holding fee if you keep the images from 30 to 90 days without leasing or buying them. Find out specifically the policies of the agency you plan to work with. Also inquire about an agency's specialties, and select one that has a substantial collection of images in your field. For instance, Glacier Bay

Photography (P.O. Box 97, Gustavus, AK 99826-0097, (907) 697-2416) specializes in Alaska scenics, people in nature, and wildlife. Stock Montage,
Inc. (104 N. Halsted, Suite 200, Chicago, IL 60661, (312) 733-3239) offers
an estimated 1 million contemporary, vintage, mystery and myth images.

"Know what you want or have a good idea before you call, and don't
go on a fishing expedition," recommends stock specialist John Patsch.
"And allow some time."

Involving a stock agency at the outset of the project gives researchers
more time to locate specific images you need. Some agencies will also
arrange for photos to be shot if none fit your project. With extra time,
you can use both approaches, acquiring some photos from a stock
agency and assigning others to a photographer of your choice.

Photos already shot and in stock provide "a certain convenience,
but there's sometimes a trade-off in creativity and composition," Marshall
points out. Commissioning a photographer to shoot a particular image
in a particular way gives you more flexibility.

When hiring a photographer, look first in your city. Scan the yellow
pages' section on photographers and check area publications for photo
bylines. Local editors', photographers' and art directors' clubs will usually
recommend photographers. Directories published by photography organizations are excellent sources, although the self-publisher on a budget
might not be able to afford the services of higher-priced professionals.

The American Society of Picture Professionals (Woodfin Camp, 2025
Pennsylvania Ave. NW, Suite 226, Washington, DC 20006), for instance,
issues a membership directory every two years that provides information
about each member and is cross-referenced by region and company
names.

When you call a photographer, one of his first concerns is to establish
the terms of copyright and usage with you. He will want to know some
of the same information that a stock agency does: How will the photos
be used? What is the press run and circulation?

To arrive at a price for photos, most photographers will use a three-
point formula that includes a basic shooting fee, expenses and usage. A
photo for a nationally distributed book with long-term shelf life will cost
you more than one for a local newsletter. Overall, photographers are
selling a product and a service in addition to a one-of-a-kind image that
can be marketed over and over again.

"Most photographers will want to avoid surrendering the copyright
to their image, and people who don't work in the industry on a daily
basis assume that when they pay a photographer, they own the picture,"
Marshall says.

Unless you have purchased exclusive or all rights to a photo (and can prove this in writing), you will owe the photographer for any second printing or subsequent use.

Major magazines will generally go to the extra expense of offering assignments to photographers because they want unique photos precisely tailored to articles. But newsletter publishers and book self-publishers can usually save money by buying onetime rights.

As the publisher of your own magazine, newsletter or book, weigh the advantages and disadvantages of each approach. And if you need photos for a manuscript/photo package to submit to a magazine, you have the additional option of collaborating with the photographer in a 50/50 partnership. Then you'll follow many of the guidelines of a writing collaboration and can hammer out an agreement to fit both partners' creative and financial needs.

If you need historic photos for histories or biographies, contact organizations or even families with unique photos in their files. Historical societies, archives, churches, schools and private foundations have varying policies and prices for photos. Your best approach here is to call or write for this information. If you encounter reluctance to share these photos, offer to credit the photographer or organization *and* emphasize how important it is that readers have the chance to see the photos.

Some other affordable sources of photographs are government agencies and public affairs/information offices. Sometimes, in return for a photo byline, you'll be allowed to publish the image in your newsletter.

The professional photographers' organizations below can provide valuable insight and leads. Some of these groups have local or regional chapters and can provide details on local photographers, workshops and price ranges.

## LISTINGS

**Advertising Photographers of America (APA)**
*27 W. Twentieth St., Suite 601*
*New York, NY 10011*
*(212) 807-0399*

**American Society of Media Photographers (ASMP)**
*14 Washington Rd., Suite 502*
*Princeton Junction, NJ 08550-1033*
*(909) 799-8300*

**National Press Photographers Association (NPPA)**
*3200 Croasdaile Dr., Suite 306*
*Durham, NC 27705*
*(800) 289-6772*

**Professional Photographers of America**
*57 Forsyth St. NW, Suite 1600*
*Atlanta, GA 30303*
*(404) 522-8600*

# THE BUSINESS OF PUBLISHING

## DESKTOP PUBLISHING

For centuries, writers have turned over their manuscripts to somebody else who decided how the words would be arranged on pages and how the pages would be bound. Writers wrote. Typesetters set type. Publishers published. The book's creator had little choice or control.

Today, technology has merged these roles, and you have more choices: You can control how your words appear in print. You can now be the writer, typesetter, page designer and publisher, depending on the time and funds you are willing to invest. You can use desktop publishing as a final prepress step in producing newsletters *or* as a stepping stone to becoming a self-publisher or small-press publisher.

This potential capability, however, can cause more problems than it attempts to solve, especially if you rush out to buy the needed equipment and don't have a graphics or publishing background.

Robert Runck, executive director of the National Association of Desktop Publishers, urges writers to proceed carefully when considering desktop publishing as an option. "Don't get involved with desktop stuff unless you're serious," he says. "Desktop publishing is not for dabblers."

Desktop publishing—actually techniques for electronic creation of a document—has become "an area of special skill and expertise," points out Runck, also editor in chief of *Desktop Publishers Journal*.

The technology in the past several years has advanced to the point where users need expertise to use this "highly technical realm to produce professional results." Runck compares desktop expertise to that of a Linotype operator or graphic designer, who spends many years learning the necessary skills.

If you're seriously considering buying desktop publishing equipment, talk with several people in the desktop business, network, and join desktop organizations. The National Association of Desktop Publishers

(NADTP) publishes the monthly *Desktop Publishers Journal* on the industry's latest technology and trends, in addition to offering collective buying power on products and desktop books. One of NADTP's best benefits is the Member HelpLine Network. This HelpLine gives you free technical support for desktop hardware and software problems.

Runck, who also has more than 20 years experience as a trade book and textbook publisher, advises writers who want to self-publish a book to hire a desktop specialist to format and create the book. This way, the self-publisher will have more time to focus on the book's marketing.

The other option is to invest in equipment and training, but then be willing to make the commitment to learn the craft of desktop publishing—not only what keys to press, but how to effectively design a newsletter or book.

If you don't want to spend your writing time as an art director or book designer, then desktop publishing won't be a good option.

Desktop equipment gives you the tools of a publisher in your own work space. With a computer and a variety of accessories that we'll be discussing here, you can design the pages of a book, magazine or newsletter, and design charts, brochures and calendars. With word processing software, you no longer have to pay a printer to typeset your manuscript because you do the typing.

With desktop publishing software—and here's where your training as a writer can't provide all the answers—you lay out what text and art will appear on each page. "Art" in this case means any visual element that a publisher uses to enhance the text: titles and chapter headings, charts, drawings, photos and lines that add a unified look to each page.

With these professional capabilities in your office or home, you also have the option of renting desktop time to small companies and writers at a cost that is affordable for them and money-making for you. Robert C. Brenner's Brenner Information Group publishes a *Pricing Guide for Desktop Publishing Services* with guidelines on what to charge for desktop services. The 372-page book can also help you calculate what it will cost to hire desktop and design services.

Hourly rates for various desktop services—graphic design, layout, flier design and newsletter design—ranged from $36 to $50 in Brenner's 1994–95 survey of North American businesses. The Freelance Editorial Association lists pay ranges of $25 to $30 per printed newsletter page, or $35 to $60 per hour for desktop services for books.

But before hiring out your desktop equipment, you'll have to assume the initial costs—which brings us back to the issue of how and if a desktop system will benefit you as a writer.

It's like buying a car. No one but you can decide what's best for you. Study computer catalogs first, but realize that photos and brief descriptions are only the beginning of your research. Books on desktop publishing, such as David Browne's *Welcome to . . . Desktop Publishing/From Mystery to Mastery* (MIS Press), enable you to explore desktop options. Computer magazines frequently discuss the pros and cons of various desktop approaches. Ask writers and self-publishers what works and what doesn't work for them, and why.

One misconception about desktop publishing comes from its name. Desktop software gives you the technical power of a publisher, but to actually publish your manuscripts, you have to develop the reputation, know-how and savvy of a publisher.

*Desktop publishing* provides the prepress steps of typesetting and layout, and then the role of *self-publishing* begins: The desktop-produced pages need to be printed and bound, marketed and distributed.

To start at the ground floor of desktop publishing, you need a computer, a word processing software program, a page layout software program, a printer and training on how to use them.

Consider the degree of proficiency and professionalism you hope to achieve, and then the products and prices. Price, of course, will depend on the decisions you make in the previous areas.

The single biggest mistake that a writer can make in venturing into desktop self-publishing is "not to understand how time-consuming and complex the process will be," points out Norman Paddock, executive director of the Association of Desk-Top Publishers.

## PROFICIENCY

Imagine, for a moment, tubes of paint and the artist's canvas. From them, the artist can produce an ineffective muddle or a museum masterpiece, depending on how proficient the artist is in using the materials. The same is true for the computer and TV-like monitor that becomes the desktop publisher's "canvas."

Used effectively, a desktop system can produce a book or newsletter that looks like one from a top New York publishing house. But the system doesn't have a mind, like you, so it needs to be told what to do. That's why proficiency and training are so important.

Unlike writing, graphics training is not a requirement of most high school or college programs; most writers (and this is changing today) never imagined that they could do their own graphics work or could own typesetting equipment like a publisher.

A proficiency in knowing what goes where in a book and on a page—

based upon the accepted conventions of commercially published books—is crucial. Unfortunately, the ability to choose what you want on each page does not guarantee that you will make the best choices.

Betty Wright, publisher of Rainbow Books and former director of the National Association of Independent Publishers, sees 400 to 500 books that small-press publishers and self-publishers submit to the group's annual contest. Sometimes a book topic will be a good idea, but the book will be poorly planned or poorly printed—for instance, no index or bibliography.

To produce a professional product, you must learn how to use the sophisticated computer software and how to design an effective publication. Courses on these topics aren't as plentiful as writing classes, but today we're seeing more of them at the college level as well as one-day workshops on desktop publishing. The costs of training vary greatly depending on the sponsor and format of the classes.

Workshops can cost as much as $100 to $200 per day or as little as $40 when a nonprofit group offers a workshop for its members. You can also opt for video training programs on VHS tapes.

If you already have desktop expertise and credentials to prove it, consider approaching writers' groups and community education programs about teaching such a course. Writers will be grateful, and you can earn $10 to $60 an hour or as much as $350 per day plus a percentage of the tuition fee, depending on the sponsoring group's budget. Some desktop publishers will conduct a workshop for a nonprofit group—at little or no stipend—to establish contacts in the city.

Step-by-step guides to desktop publishing—both from the computer perspective and from the graphics perspective—provide an inexpensive way to learn desktop publishing: *Looking Good in Print/A Guide to Basic Design for Desktop Publishing* and *Newsletters from the Desktop* (Ventana Communications, Inc.) and *Dynamic Computer Design* (North Light Books). If earning lots of money is also your goal, see *How to Make $100,000 a Year in Desktop Publishing* (Betterway Books).

As you'll see, the commitment and cost of desktop publishing equipment make it feasible only for people who will use the equipment on a continuing basis.

*PROFESSIONALISM*

How proficient you are in using the software and in making effective design choices will determine the "professionalism" of your book, magazine or newsletter. No one likes amateur productions. Readers don't know how to design books, but they can spot flaws that mark it as amateur: too many typefaces, no consistent visual "look," or borders around pages of text.

As the cost of desktop equipment has decreased, more individuals and small groups can afford it. Desktop users who understand how to use the equipment to the fullest, however, get the best return on this investment.

## THE PRODUCTS

Apple Computer, in 1984, made the publishers' domain more accessible to writers by pairing a Macintosh personal computer with the Aldus PageMaker page layout program. Other computer firms have joined the race to attract computer users to their word processing, page design and graphics software.

Most computer specialists recommend that you find the software features you need and then find the computer that will accommodate them. If you have a computer, however, then your primary concern is finding desktop software that is compatible with your hardware.

"There's really nothing magical going on in this whole process—it's understanding how the software works and what kind of hardware you need to make it work," says MacMillan Graphics owner Gregg MacMillan.

If you're trading your typewriter for a new computer with desktop capabilities, consider an IBM-compatible PC or an Apple Macintosh computer with at least a 500-megabyte (MB) hard disk drive. A minimum 8MB of memory is also needed when you combine word and graphics processing. There are numerous microcomputer brands, and less expensive clones of the name brands, but with a lower price come little technical support and no warranty. Some computer companies offer the option of purchasing a service contract that enables you to make a specified number of calls for step-by-step instruction and troubleshooting. If you have no computer experience, track down the store in your area with a reputation for answering questions and following up on requests. Ask local writers where they buy their computers and desktop equipment.

The most crucial decision will be what software to purchase. If you're interested in publishing newsletters rather than books, consider more simple text-oriented software packages, such as Microsoft Publisher. Complex desktop publishing packages, like Demeba Software's Canvas, Frame Technology's FrameMaker, Aldus PageMaker, QuarkXPress and Corel Systems' Corel Ventura, offer the experienced desktop publisher and book self-publisher a wider variety of choices.

The Association of Desk-Top Publishers publishes a review of hardware and software, and NADTP's *Desktop Publishers Journal* reviews hardware and software on a monthly basis.

Another important decision is what type of printer to buy. You can use an inexpensive dot matrix printer to proofread your work, but for the final output, you generally need a printing resolution of 300 dots per inch (dpi). A bottom-of-the-line laser printer (able to print 300 dpi) is a good investment for a writer because you can print camera-ready copy as a self-publisher and also produce attractive query letters.

Laser printers range in price from $500 to $4,000. A $500 to $700 printer will still give your document a 300- or 600-dpi resolution. The major differences between a top- and bottom-of-the-line laser printer are the print speed, volume and memory. What you'll use the printer for will dictate what features you'll need.

Self-publishers wanting higher quality camera-ready pages (from 1,000 to 2470 dpi) will generally contract with a professional service bureau for these services. This subcontracting saves you from purchasing the $20,000 to $70,000 phototypesetting equipment that publishers can afford.

"The quality of the original prototype that you create will have a large impact on the ability of the printer to create a quality product," says Clifford Weiss, former director of publications for the Printing Industries of America.

### PRICES

What desktop publishing will cost you depends on what equipment you want and what you plan to produce. With each capability that you add to your desktop repertoire, you'll incur additional costs. For instance, if you want to turn your black-and-white newsletter into a color magazine, you'll need software designed for color and a color monitor. For some computers, that can be an expensive change; for others, the conversion is not possible.

A desktop publishing system can range in price from $2,000 to $4,000 or more. That would include an IBM-compatible computer or Macintosh computer, word processing and page design software and a printer. It is often difficult to compare prices because sometimes a Microsoft Windows program will be included in the price of the computer and sometimes not. In comparison shopping, you might also find that the monitor and keyboard are not included in the computer's basic price.

If you don't want to invest in desktop equipment now, you can continue to watch for new developments in the field and more affordable prices.

## ASSOCIATIONS

### Association of Desk-Top Publishers
*3401-A800 Adams Ave.*
*San Diego, CA 92116-2429*
*(619) 563-9714*

### National Association of Desktop Publishers
*462 Boston St.*
*Topsfield, MA 01983*
*(800) 492-1014 (for membership inquiries) and (800) 874-4113*
*Fax: (508) 887-6117*
*E-mail: NADTP@aol.com*

## SELF-PUBLISHING

Writers have always been able to self-publish by hiring a printer or operating a small printing press in the basement, but the finished product usually lacked the polish of a commercially published book. Today you can control many of the prepress steps and ensure a professional product—whether you do the work yourself or contract for desktop services.

Estimates of what it costs to self-publish a book vary greatly because so many factors and choices are involved. The overall minimum cost of publishing a professional-looking book (not including desktop publishing equipment or professional consultations) can range from $8,000 to $15,000. However, some self-publishers will spend much less, and others will spend much more than these amounts.

The most difficult part of self-publishing is the *publishing* not the printing of the book. Printers are accustomed to following specifications, and your book will have the qualities—dimensions, paper, ink, binding—that you specified in the contract. But it's knowing what to specify that becomes the difficult part. "By nature, writers focus on a manuscript," says publisher Mary Bold, of Bold Productions.

When you take your book into the marketplace, there will be little predictability. Advertising, marketing, distribution (through bookstores and/or direct mail) and travel expenses for you can yield good or disappointing results, but in either case will cost you time and money.

Despite the drawbacks of self-publishing (which we'll discuss in a few minutes), most writers venture into this hands-on approach because established publishing routes have said "no" or didn't offer enough flexibility. *Huckleberry Finn, What Color Is Your Parachute?, Ulysses* (James Joyce's version) and *The Elements of Style* began their literary lives as self-published books.

You might have an excellent book that caters to a narrow market, causing a commercial publisher to doubt its salability. Or you might want to earn more than the standard 6% to 15% royalty and retain more control over the editorial or visual content of the book. Some writers self-publish a book in order to fulfill the dream of being an author; some people self-publish for professional advancement.

The economics of publishing and self-publishing can be discouraging, though, no matter which avenue you choose and how much money you have.

A New York publishing house invests thousands of dollars per book and thus carefully selects books, usually with a focus on each book's marketing potential. Commercial publishers generally want a book to retail for about eight or nine times the first-run production costs.

"The reason that the publisher gets to make all of those decisions and be nasty about what the title is going to be and what the cover looks like and even the rewrites is because he's footing the bill," says Bold. "It boils down to who's putting out the money."

Bold, also the author of *The Decision to Publish*, turned her interest in producing newsletters into a small press that bears her name and uses desktop publishing to produce books and newsletters. Unlike major New York publishers, she budgets $5,000 to $15,000 per book and has a nine-title book list.

While she has survived many of the self-publishing hurdles, she sees writers who aren't so lucky. Conducting seminars on self-publishing and desktop publishing, Bold sometimes sees participants' poorly printed books that do not conform to book buyers' standards. Another major stumbling block is approaching distributors.

Author and former Writer's Digest Books editor Nan Dibble says, "The bottom line is always distribution; that is the hard part. If you cannot reach your potential readers with even the news that your publication exists, then you have to have a large basement and be prepared to have it filled for a long time."

Today, via the Internet and World Wide Web, some writers are sharing book chapters and stories. "If profit is not your immediate goal and dissemination is, the online option is a very viable and important communication alternative to printing," says communications director Clifford Weiss of the National Association of Enrolled Agents.

However, for most writers, text on a screen will never replace the emotional "feel" of a book or will never satisfy the dream of being a published book author.

"The key to successful self-publishing is to do it right," points out Florida self-publisher and book packager Jim Salisbury.

To give you an overview of self-publishing, we've divided the process into eight stages, from "The Decision to Self-Publish" to "Writing and Acquiring Other Books." Of course, each stage demands a series of carefully researched steps.

### THE DECISION TO SELF-PUBLISH

Unless you have definite reasons for wanting to avoid commercial publishers, consider sending your book manuscript to publishers. With this approach, your book gets published without you having to invest thousands of dollars. *Writer's Market, The Writer's Handbook* and *Literary Market Place* list publishers; *Writer's Market* and *The Writer's Handbook* detail the submission policies and the types of books each publisher specializes in.

A commercial publisher assumes all steps of the publishing process for the right to collect 85% to 94% of the revenues. You can continue doing what you do best: writing.

When you decide to self-publish, you assume not only the writing/editing responsibilities but also the business concerns. You are responsible for the bills, no matter how few books you sell.

Give your manuscript and your writing the benefit of one to two years of circulation among publishers. Attend writers' conferences where book editors are speaking, and investigate small and regional presses, and even self-publishing cooperatives.

If these contacts don't lead to a book contract, ask yourself: How is my book different from and better than those already on the market? How does my book contribute to the vast knowledge of readers? (You wouldn't want to invest thousands of dollars in a book with a flooded market or in a treatise that demands extensive revisions to make it marketable.) Finally, is the book worth publishing?

If your answer is yes, then self-publishing could be your best alternative. Self-publishing works best when you've written a nonfiction book geared to a distinct audience. (That's exactly what commercial publishers do: invest book dollars in topics and authors with built-in and acquired audiences. Consider a recent gamut of examples: angels and O.J., Martha Stewart and Howard Stern.)

Small-press publishers and self-publishers, likewise, can sell more books by gearing them toward specific audiences looking for answers to particular questions. "Smart small publishers have a niche, and they work that niche," says Betty Wright.

A distinct audience provides an opportunity for targeted mailing lists and specialized outlets (conferences and newsletters, for instance) for your book. A mainstream novel or book of poetry, on the other hand, would be bought by a general audience; mass-market mailings would not be affordable. Not all books are good candidates for self-publishing.

Talk with commercially published and self-published authors and associations devoted to small-press publishing. What works and doesn't work for them? What would they do differently next time? What are the latest trends and tricks? The International Association of Independent Publishers (COSMEP) publishes a monthly newsletter with this kind of information. "What COSMEP really does best is train publishers to be high-quality publishers," says acting executive director Terri Boekhoff.

The worst mistake that a self-publishing writer can make is to work in isolation, reiterates Open Horizons publisher John Kremer.

*YOUR BOOK PROPOSAL AND MARKETING PLAN*

When you've decided to self-publish a book, you need a detailed book proposal and marketing plan to steer your efforts. It's easy in the busyness of producing a book to delay the more distant steps, such as applying for an ISBN (International Standard Book Number) code and a Bookland EAN bar code, and contacting book distributors, which will be vital to the sales of your book.

You'll need to work simultaneously at several self-publishing stages and to tackle the marketing and distribution while still making editorial decisions. Most of the promotional work for a book must be done before the book is printed.

Marilyn and Tom Ross's *The Complete Guide to Self-Publishing* (Writer's Digest Books) includes an excellent "Publishing Timetable" to show you what to do and when. Likewise, publisher and author Dan Poynter provides "Your Book's Calendar" in *The Self-Publishing Manual* (Para Publishing).

*EDITING YOUR BOOK*

No matter how well you write, your book will benefit from the careful reading by an editor—both content editing and copyediting. This person can bring an objectivity to your manuscript that you can't. A good editor can spot inconsistencies, inaccuracies and grammatical problems. For instance, author Jim DeBrosse, in his novel *The Serpentine Wall*, implied that Dave Parker was a Cincinnati Reds player; the copyeditor at St. Martin's Press recalled that Parker was a Pittsburgh Pirate at the time in the novel. You need this kind of editorial watchdog that self-publishing does not provide.

As we mentioned earlier in this section, you can hire an editor on a per-project basis. This will increase the cost of your book, but it will also ensure that the contents within your expensive covers maintain a consistently professional quality.

As more and more writers self-publish their books, it is easier to find another writer who also needs an editor. By joining writers' groups and associations devoted to desktop publishing and self-publishing, you increase your chances of meeting someone who might serve as your editor, and you could serve as his editor. Of course, such an arrangement should be carefully approached. Does the person have a knowledge of your book's topic—to be able to spot inaccuracies? Will the person be able to assess the book's organizational and grammatical problems? Will your partner be available to edit your book to fit your publishing schedule, and vice versa?

If you choose this more cost-effective reciprocal approach, though, be sure you and your partner thoroughly discuss the demands of editing one another's books. One book could be 160 pages; another could be 600 pages. Prepare and sign a letter of agreement, stating what services you will receive and provide, to ensure that you and your partner will be compensated by one another's editing services.

Some writers will hire a book packager/producer to assist them with the major steps of getting a book into print. Such services will add another layer of cost but can provide expertise in areas from editing to PPB (printing, paper and binding) if you don't want to make unassisted decisions in these specialized areas. One drawback to packagers is that a company might be strong in one specialty, such as book design, and not as knowledgeable in other areas. "People aren't good at all things," says Kremer, who cautions writers against thinking they can get all the answers for a self-published book at a one-stop shop.

## PAGE AND COVER DESIGN

One of the best tools for selling a book is a great cover. It becomes your book's silent salesman and also a protector of the pages inside. Experts and booksellers agree that this is one area you don't want to skimp on.

A graphic designer could charge up to $5,000 for a cover design, but the average range for a cover design is $800 to $2,000. The cover's artwork can also be used in your book's promotional materials and catalog, assuming that you have negotiated this use with your illustrator/designer.

Page and cover design, if used effectively, can enhance your book in several ways: providing visual clues to each page's content, directing the reader's attention to important elements and creating a tone or atmosphere compatible with the words. That process is crucial on each cover and page.

Book covers may use a photograph or an illustration, coupled with the title typography, or may include only title typography. A trained designer can advise you on which approach will produce the effect you want. For instance, how-to and business books look fine with type-dominated covers, but a coffee-table book, cookbook or visually oriented topic would be best packaged with artwork and type on the front cover.

Your book's page layout can be done entirely on the computer or done with a combination of computer typeset copy and paste-up. But first (and preferably before the editing stage), you need to select your book's design. What typeface will you use for chapter headings and the text? Will you use up style (all words of a heading using capital letters) or down style (only the first word and proper nouns being capitalized in a heading)? Will headings be centered or flush left (aligned with the left margin)? Will you justify the right margin or have a ragged right margin? A quick scan of the books on your shelves will show you a variety of approaches.

Most importantly, follow a standard book format rather than guessing what belongs on what page, especially for the introductory material. Books such as *The Self-Publishing Manual* and *The Complete Guide to Self-Publishing* give you step-by-step advice on format.

## MANUFACTURING AND PRINTING

Another important decision you'll make as a self-publisher is who will print your book. For some self-publishers, the choice is easy—they are adamant about a book manufacturer rather than a printer. Other self-publishers of chapbooks, short-run books or academic manuals take them to quick printers in their neighborhoods. And another option is the commercial printer who uses metal plates to print large print runs and has the capability to produce books with spines (the flat narrow strip between the front and back covers).

Marilyn and Tom Ross recommend that self-publishers work with a book manufacturer. Because book manufacturers specialize in books, they have the know-how and equipment to best accommodate a book print run. For instance, a manufacturer with a Cameron Belt Press or Compu-prep can save you about 20% on a large-quantity printing bill.

No matter who your printer is, though, you won't escape the steadily increasing price of paper. Paper prices have increased the printing costs of a book by 10% to 20%, estimates publisher Mary Bold.

Marie Kiefer's *Directory of Printers* (Ad-Lib Publications), will help you in your search for a printer, as will *Getting It Printed* (North Light Books) and *Graphically Speaking* (Elk Ridge), both by Mark Beach. *Literary Market Place* lists book manufacturers and finishers.

To get printing bids and quotes, you'll need to develop a specifications sheet for your book. Sending spec sheets is the self-publisher's way of shopping around. Sometimes a printer 1,000 miles away can offer a better price, even when you add several hundred dollars' worth of shipping charges. Ask printers and book manufacturers for a list of recent customers and books they have produced. And before signing a contract with an out-of-town firm, check with the Better Business Bureau in that area.

One of the most difficult questions at this stage is how many books to print. You can get significant volume discounts for larger print runs, which will lower your per-unit cost, but don't let this "bargain" prompt you to order more books than you can distribute. Unless you've received prepress orders on books or have a ready market for your books, order from 1,000 to 2,000 books. "Nine times out of 10, you've got the wrong title, the wrong cover or the book is missing something," says Kremer. "If you've only printed a few copies, you can make a change more quickly. You don't have to live with your mistake for 10,000 copies."

Kremer, founder of the Mid-America Publishers Association, especially recommends a 1,000- to 2,000-book print run for first-time publishers. That will leave you with a smaller printing bill and more money for marketing.

A typical PPB (printing, paper and binding) for a book would be $1,500 to $5,000 for a 1,000-book print run, and $3,000 to $7,000 for 2,000 books, says Kremer. As your sales and publishing savvy increase, you can usually schedule a second printing in three to five weeks.

## PAMPERING YOUR BOOK
## (PROMOTION/ADVERTISING/MARKETING/PUBLICITY)

"Promotion is more important than content," points out author and literary agent Michael Larsen. Commenting on book industry priorities, he sees marketing as the key element—an estimated 80% of a book's entire process. "The content is only 10% of the book," he estimates, with the other 10% of effort needed to get the book into the hands of the best editor."

Think about the time you'll spend on your book's content. Now, consider how much time (and energy) you need to spend on its promotion. Your estimate here is probably an astounding amount of time, but otherwise, how will readers know your book is in the marketplace?

You'll want to use a combination of strategies to best promote your book. Most self-publishers weigh the anticipated results of each strategy against the costs and develop an affordable marketing plan.

Advertising in *Publishers Weekly* and book trade magazines is the most efficient way to reach reviewers and book buyers, but also the most expensive and not practical for the first-time self-publisher. A full-page black-and-white ad in *Publishers Weekly* costs an estimated $5,015. The price for a full-page ad goes down to $4,960 if you run the ad in three issues, but of course that would cost you nearly $15,000. A sixth-of-a-page ad costs about $1,255.

There are cost-effective ways, though, to get attention for your book— if you're willing to research your book's specific market and actively promote the book. For instance, three-line classified ad rates in trade journals and newsletters can cost as little as $10 per insertion.

News releases alert print and broadcast editors to your book. They might not use your 400-word release word for word, but it can provide background information upon which the medium will prepare its story. Kay Borden's *Bulletproof News Releases* provides advice from 135 newspaper editors on how to write effective news releases.

If you can find an angle, or reason, that makes the release of your book extremely important for the audience of a publication or station, you'll be on your way to this free form of advertising. For instance, the human interest story of 88-year-old Helen Hooven Santmyer and her novel, *And Ladies of the Club*, got nationwide media attention; print and broadcast editors were touched when the Book-of-the-Month Club unanimously voted to include this unknown author's book as a main selection.

Numerous marketing/advertising outlets exist. One thousand and one, if you ask John Kremer, author of *1001 Ways to Market Your Books* (Open Horizons Publishing Co.). Books like this and *Sure-Fire Strategies for Selling Your Books*, by Marilyn and Tom Ross, show you step by step how to do your own marketing.

You also have the more expensive option of hiring a marketing consultant with book publishing credentials. Marilyn and Tom Ross's book consulting firm, About Books, charges a onetime launch fee of $3,200 to $4,500 for developing a custom marketing plan and promotional materials for the book's specific audience, and for contacting distributors and wholesalers.

You can locate marketing professionals in *Literary Market Place* and the *Book Publishing Resource Guide*. A specialist with a track record in your type of publication is your best investment if you don't want to do your own marketing.

Because promotion and distribution are ongoing problems for publishers, numerous books have been written on the subject, and publishers' trade associations frequently address these problems in their newsletters and conferences.

Membership in trade associations places you in the company (and pipeline) of publishers. COSMEP, for instance, exhibits members' publications at the annual conventions of the American Booksellers Association and the American Library Association, in addition to holding its own conference on publishing topics and offering members discounted ad rates for *Publishers Weekly*.

The American Booksellers Association, the National Association of Independent Publishers and the Mid-America Publishers Association likewise give members publishing leads and benefits slanted toward the organization's membership.

Regional bookseller and publishers' associations provide additional outlets. The *Book Publishing Resource Guide* can help you find associations in your state, such as the Book Publicists of Southern California or the Mid-America Publishers Association.

Marketing approaches can range from interviews on radio talk shows to point-of-purchase sales displays in bookstores. You can even start your own small advertising agency to receive advertising discounts. Before trying any of these approaches, however, learn more about them from books, seminars and industry professionals. Some have disadvantages such as printing a Christmas catalog for a specific year (the unused material could not be merged with other sales promotions).

Not starting to market a book early enough can be a major problem for self-publishers. Marketing review copies need to be sent four to five months before a book's publication date.

### DISTRIBUTION

The distribution stage is where most self-publishers fail. A book, magazine or newsletter might be excellent in content and form, but if you can't get it into readers' hands, your efforts in the preceding steps will have been wasted. Also, the momentum and scope of your promotions will lay the groundwork for the type of distribution you will use.

You can approach major bookstore chains, but do so with prepared sales materials, and plan frequent mail and phone follow-ups.

Some of the large bookstore chains include Barnes and Noble, Bookland, Books-a-Million, Borders, Crown Books, B. Dalton Bookseller, Doubleday Book Shops, Follett College Stores and Waldenbooks Company, Inc.

"It's harder to get your books into the stores as a self-published author," says *Publishers Weekly* editorial director John F. Baker.

If you are fortunate enough to sell most of your print run to a major chain, though, remember that the stores can return the books if they aren't selling and request a refund. For this reason, don't immediately consider those books sold and order a second printing. You can generally get a book manufactured in three to five weeks, so don't risk having unsold first- *and* second-run books.

Independent non-chain stores provide an excellent outlet for self-publishers. Their buyers don't have to abide by corporate rules, and they can be more receptive to local authors and the reading habits of their customers.

One of the most efficient ways to get your books into stores and libraries is through distributors and wholesalers. But you have to contact wholesalers and distributors at least six months before the publication date.

With a distributor, you would sell your books on its consignment basis and receive payment 90 days after the sale. Wholesalers will buy your books outright. Realizing that you can't call on every book buyer in person, most self-publishers must use these approaches. Distributors that cater to various markets—bookstores, libraries, schools, religious market, etc.—increase your chance of getting books into readers' hands.

One surprise to new self-publishers is that distributors and wholesalers will not pay the cover price for books. "They expect discounts of 55% to 65%," points out Marilyn Ross.

Today, book distribution is in the hands of fewer people and companies, and thus it's crucial to deal professionally with these contacts. Most how-to books on self-publishing provide advice on how to approach distributors and wholesalers.

Direct mail is another approach to marketing self-published books. Readers, in response to ads or publicity, send a check and fee for postage and handling, and you ship the book. To help you figure every cost and what percentage of response you need based on your selling price, consult John Kremer's book, *Mail Order Selling Made Easier* and *Mail Order Spreadsheet Kit* (on computer disk).

Your best approach is to use a combination of distribution methods to reach professional and consumer book buyers.

Another cost-effective way of self-publishing your book is to produce and distribute copies as you receive the orders. By photocopying the laser-printed page prototypes and then binding the printed pages in response to several orders, you can avoid printing too many copies. This option, though, will only work with mail-order distribution or periodic demands, say, when you address an audience that might afterward want to purchase your chapbook or manual. The practice of producing one copy at a time (when ordered by a customer) will work with fanzines, poetry chapbooks, scholarly monographs, cookbooks or any type of book that does not demand a factory-bound cover.

## WRITING AND ACQUIRING OTHER BOOKS

When you have found your readers and niche in the marketplace, there is no reason to stop with one book. And if you've been publishing a magazine or newsletter, it might be time to spin off a book on the same nonfiction topic. If your books have inspired readers to refine their art or archery skills, or their awareness of people or the stock market, they will want *more*. You can then write similar books or find authors whose books will enhance your list.

At some point, though, decide if you wish to work mainly as a publisher or author. You can do both, but writing another book when you should be writing news releases can water down your talents for both crafts. Decide which areas you are best at, and consider hiring part-time employees to handle day-to-day tasks, such as shipping book orders and answering the phone.

Self-publishing a book gives that book a better chance of being sold to a commercial publisher, thus enabling you to turn over your publishing responsibilities to a publisher while you continue writing.

If you want to turn your self-published book into the cornerstone for a small press, you'll need to acquire additional books (written by you or other authors). By compiling a book catalog, you can simultaneously "sell" all of the titles when readers inquire about one book. Small-press experts estimate that a small publisher needs a minimum list of four books to maximize the costs of operation.

Distributors and wholesalers will be more receptive to a self-published book if you have a line of books. That way, if they must return a book that isn't selling, you can offer them a credit toward another book from your list. They are often afraid that the self-publisher won't have the available cash to make the refund.

As you progress from one stage to another, you'll be learning new tricks for future publications—whether you continue self-publishing, writing or combining both crafts.

## PRINTERS AND TYPESETTERS

Unless you're accustomed to working with printers and typesetters (the human kind), you'll be sailing into uncharted waters and into the printer's triangle. Quality, service and price constitute the triangle.

Printers attempt to offer quality, service and a good price to customers, but when you want, say, high quality and fast turnaround time, then the price will increase. If you want to decrease the price part of the triangle, quality and service will suffer. "You can usually get two of these three things," says MacMillan Graphics owner Gregg MacMillan. "Which two of these three are most important?"

Only you can answer that question, but in the competitive marketplace, you'll want to carefully weigh the quality of the printing that you're buying. Paper texture, weight and durability will affect the life and appearance of your book, magazine or newsletter. Printing costs vary from company to company and from market to market and depend on the specifications you request.

Thumb through several books on your shelves. Compare the feel of each book's pages. When you find several paper types you like, use these samples to show a printer what you want. She can then advise you on the advantages and disadvantages of various paper stocks, and the prices.

"Make sure when you come in for your initial meeting that you have a good idea of how you want the concept in your mind translated to paper," says Minuteman Press vice-president Edward Breyer Ryder IV. "That saves your time and saves the printer's time."

Also, you need to decide whether a quick printer or commercial printer, or combination, will best cater to your publication. That will generally depend on the type of book you plan to produce. For example, many quick printers can print and bind a softcover spiral-bound manual but do not have the facilities to produce a clothbound book with a spine, even though they could print the pages. You would need to ask the print shop if such a service were available or could be subcontracted.

One of the major differences between quick printers and commercial printers is the equipment they use. Commercial printers produce a metal plate that makes possible large print runs, whereas quick printers usually use nonimpact printing. You can find both quick printers and commercial printers listed under Printers in the yellow pages; bookbinders are listed under the heading Bookbinders.

There are several nationwide chains of quick printers that provide easy access to the printing process. Minuteman Press, (800) 645-9840, with numerous independently owned franchised locations across the United States and Canada, offers black-and-white and color printing, typesetting, design and layout consultation, and binding services.

Kinko's Copy Centers, (800) 2KINKOS, offer round-the-clock service, with most outlets open 24 hours a day, seven days a week. Kinko's has more than 800 locations in the United States, Canada, Japan and Korea.

PIP Printing, (800) 894-7498, has more than 650 independently owned outlets in 42 states and 18 outlets in the United Kingdom. With PIP's Desktop Publishing program, you can bring your typed book or newsletter on disk, or the outlet can provide typesetting for you. Prices will vary from market to market, depending on the services you require.

PIP's PIPLink software program enables you to transfer files electronically, via modem, to your local outlet. A manuscript from a few pages up to 1,000 pages can be printed and then delivered to your home or picked up at any local outlet. "Digital technology is more cost-effective and faster for both color and black-and-white work in many cases," says Susan Falck, PIP's public relations director.

Kinko's also provides its customers with software for digital document transmission. This Kinkonet option enables customers to proofread the final document by fax before the pages are printed, bound and delivered. Kinkonet is designed for businesses needing multiple-point distribution of documents such as training manuals and reports, but a writer who gives seminars and needs numerous softcover handouts could contract for this service.

National quick print companies offer toll-free numbers for customers needing to know the nearest location; however, a quick glance in the yellow pages will give you that information. Locally owned printers in your own town can also provide a wide range of services.

Talk with printers before you rush into a contract. Find out what services each outlet offers, and then decide which one can best meet your book's needs.

Your working relationship with a printer can begin at various stages depending on how much of the work you have already completed. Some printers will accept handwritten material, but you can decrease your printing costs by providing typed material or, better yet, material on a disk.

A manuscript typed on even the most inexpensive IBM-compatible or Macintosh-compatible word processor will save you significant typesetting charges. And if you plan to write on a long-term basis, the word processing capabilities alone will pay for themselves. For each extra step a printer must complete, there will be a charge.

Quick printers are a good outlet for writers who need fast short-run printing and in-house binding. Some printers will even store negatives and mechanicals at no charge. Again, you'll want to compare stores and their services.

One drawback of quick printers is that they don't print trade books as frequently as book manufacturers or commercial printers. Most quick printers do not have the facilities to bind a book with a spine, although some will arrange to have the bindery work done elsewhere.

To get a list of book manufacturers and printers, consult *Literary Market Place* or the *Directory of Printers.*

Because printing/manufacturing costs can be two to six times different in price, you'll want to get estimates from numerous companies. Next, request a price quote from two to three vendors whose prices and policies seem to best fit your project. An experienced printer/manufacturer can sometimes suggest ways for you to stretch your printing budget.

Most self-publishers produce pages on their laser printers or pay a service bureau to produce resin-coated pages. A printer then will produce negatives of those pages, which in turn will produce the printing plates. You can save additional money by requesting that your service bureau produce negatives instead of the resin pages. This is a frequent approach for advertising agencies and graphic designers, but rare among self-publishers.

If you try this approach, however, make sure your service bureau and printer compare specifications for the pages and negatives. Reshooting or restripping the negatives could be more expensive than resin-coated pages.

Carefully investigate and compare printers. Their work will make your work look more professional or brand it as an amateur product. Also realize that if you cut costs on paper, ink or binding, your printer is not at fault. "In the printing industry, the final quality that you get is the result of what you want to put into it, what you need out of it, what your readers expect, what your readers will demand, and what you *perceive* your readers to demand," points out Clifford Weiss.

One problem self-publishers often encounter is the lack of clout with printers. Printers will sometimes delay the work on a onetime book project to accommodate regular customers or print brokers representing self-publishers. Build in extra time in your publishing schedule to allow for possible printing delays.

Overruns by printers can also alter your careful plans—and budget—depending on the company's overrun policy. Most printers cannot guarantee an exact number of books and impose on you a 5% to 10% overrun range. You will be billed for extra books (within the company's specified range) or receive a credit for the books not printed. This is a standard practice among printers; allow for a higher printing bill or fewer books within the range.

Whether you contract with a quick printer, commercial printer or book manufacturer, consider that firm a partner in your creative process.

The printer gets to do the final polish, and then your book or newsletter is ready. Finally. Now you can really pamper your project: Promote, advertise, market and enjoy what you've worked so hard to accomplish.

## LISTINGS

### Kinko's Service Corp.
*255 W. Stanley Ave., P.O. Box 8000*
*Ventura, CA 93003-8000*
*(800) 2KINKOS*

### Minuteman Press International Inc.
*1640 New Highway*
*Farmingdale, NY 11735*
*(800) 645-9840*
*New York: (516) 249-1370*

### PIP Printing
*27001 Agoura Rd., P.O. Box 3007*
*Agoura Hills, CA 91376*
*(800) 894-7498*

# CHAPTER 5

# SELLING IT

# NEWSPAPERS

## THE DAILIES

Newspapers use freelance writers to a greater or lesser degree depending on the size, budget, locale and preference of the particular newspaper, as well as a host of other factors worth investigating on a case-by-case basis. Unlike magazines, just about every city has a newspaper—sometimes more than one—and they usually look for local writers if they need to supplement their staffs, so it's wise to focus close to home in making inquiries. (Sunday newspaper magazines may be the exception to this rule; see "Weekly Magazine Sections" later in this chapter.)

While newspapers may buy an occasional local news story from a freelancer, the biggest need for freelance material is in a paper's feature sections. These sections include food, lifestyles, travel, arts and entertainment, gardening, science, business and a variety of special interest topics. Many newspapers are now publishing zoned supplements aimed at particular neighborhoods or specific audiences, such as children or seniors. These special sections or supplements are a way to attract more local advertisers by targeting specific markets.

"We have a whole group of sections called our special town sections, which feature stories about people or businesses in different suburban towns or urban areas," says Janet Franz, associate managing editor for features at the *Chicago Tribune*. "We also have special employment and education sections. These are written almost entirely by freelancers, so they're not a bad place for someone to get a start."

To make the initial contact, target the editor of a particular feature section. Newspapers usually assign their editors to different "beats"; at smaller papers, one editor may cover several beats, but they still are charged with writing, assigning or gathering the material for those areas—entertainment, business, science, health and so on. Newspapers divide these sections up in the manner that works best for them. You can find a list of newspapers according to geographic location in the *Gale*

*Directory of Publications* (see "Daily Newspaper Listings" at the end of this section).

Query the section editor by phone or by letter. At larger newspapers, it's less likely an editor will want to talk extensively on the phone, but you can at least introduce yourself. If you freelance for other markets in the area and can drop the name of a colleague or mutual acquaintance, so much the better. With this call, you are basically inquiring about the editor's need or interest in using freelance in general. You can offer to follow up with a letter detailing your credentials and perhaps suggesting some story ideas—unless the editor asks you to elaborate on the spot. The editor is more likely to be interested in your writing credentials than your story ideas, so be prepared to supplement your interest with evidence of previous writing credentials. Clips from other newspapers or those on similar topics will carry the most weight.

If you can't get initial telephone time, don't pursue it. Begin with a query letter that includes your credentials and references—a few clips are a big plus—and perhaps a story idea, if it's something you are in a unique position to write about.

All things being equal, an editor would rather assign a story to a writer he knows, if not someone on staff. Newspaper editors tend to keep fairly tight editorial reins on the ideas that form the content of the newspaper. They're not as hungry for ideas as they are for reliable and talented journalists who will come through when they're in a time or staff crunch. So concentrate more on making initial contact and on proving your reliability than on inundating section editors with endless story ideas. That's not to say that once you're in your ideas won't be appreciated—they will, and may even be used—but to think that you will break into the market on a story idea alone is probably a waste of time and energy.

Franz says it's important for freelancers to understand how a big newspaper works. She's often pitched ideas from freelancers, although she is not the one who makes assignments. "Section editors make their own assignments. I think knowing how a paper works is almost as important as knowing what kinds of things go into a paper. It's also very unusual for us to accept a story over the transom [an unsolicited story]. Our editors want to shape a story with the writer. The only exceptions to this are the travel section and the Womanews section, which takes essays."

Freelancers should be aware of which editor is in charge of a specific section and target their queries to that editor, says Franz. At the *Chicago Tribune*, for instance, there are 15 different feature and special sections.

It's best, she says, not to try to query editors on the phone there. Instead, send a brief letter with writing samples.

On smaller papers such as the Louisville *Courier Journal*, a local writer might have a better shot at making personal contact with an editor because networking is always easier in a medium to small city.

"We publish freelance stories with some regularity," says features editor Greg Johnson. Writers who live in the area come in and describe what they're interested in, usually bringing samples of their work. (It's always wise to call before going in to see an editor, so you can schedule a time that won't interfere with deadlines.) Though Johnson rarely will give a definite assignment to a first-time freelancer, he often looks at stories on speculation.

When an editor promises to look at a story on speculation, you've succeeded in arousing some degree of interest. The editor can't make any promises, but can at least assure you of a fair read, and you have a better than even shot at getting published. After one or two on-spec successes, you're more likely to get called with an assignment the next time.

An on-spec assignment is definitely a step in a positive direction, though it still requires a gamble on your part. It means you are being asked to complete the story without any formal assignment or guarantee that it will be used. This means no kill fee (a percentage of the full fee guaranteed a writer on assignment if the story ends up not being used).

Newspaper editors don't give even on-spec assignments lightly; it means they believe your story—and you—are worth the chance. They just want the odds to be in *their* favor so if it turns out to be a bad gamble, they haven't lost anything. Of course, for your part, you will have lost both time and money, so you have to decide if the possible payoff of a new client is worth the investment of time on your part.

Johnson has some additional advice for would-be newspaper freelancers: If you're trying to interest an editor in a freelance feature story, "see what the newspaper is investing a lot of effort in and [therefore] probably wouldn't need your help in," then see if you can offer them something not likely to be covered by someone on staff.

A few subjects in particular surface as areas in which many newspapers are long on interest level but short on talent. Freelancers are used, if at all, more heavily in travel sections in many papers. In larger cities, opportunities may be more widely available on the entertainment beat. In cities with an active nightlife, even a large newspaper doesn't always have the staff to cover everything going on.

Editors are always on the lookout for freelancers with expertise in computer technology. More and more newspapers are developing their own home pages on the Internet and are looking for freelancers who can write about online communication. John Lux, who was associate features editor for the *Chicago Tribune* for several years, is now that paper's online editor.

"A lot of papers are developing their own Internet pages and some are carried over commercial online networks. Our Internet page is called Digital Coffee, and it's a great area for freelancers, especially those who can write about technical issues from a consumer point of view. We also like to see stories about the Internet itself. We are now buying a couple of freelance articles every week."

In addition to technology stories, Lux has also bought freelance material for a Chicago hotel guide and a shopping area guide. Right now, he says people look to the online section to provide information specifically about Chicago, and this localized material is still the key, but he sees his audience expanding in the future as the Internet allows access to a national and even international readership.

Writers who have some knowledge about the technology and variety of home entertainment products and services are in an area still short of good writers, some editors say. Other specialties include gardening, art and antiques, and food. And the area of health and fitness remains a never-ending source of interest. If you can spot and document a trend early, you're at a distinct advantage.

Once you've made a successful contact for newspaper freelancing, editors will tend to call you repeatedly when the need arises. In the newspaper business, the need for reliability usually outweighs the desire for "new blood." Newspaper feature writing follows a more standard, more established style than magazine writing and must serve a mass audience. For the most part, newspaper editors come up with the ideas— that's what they're hired to do—but if you can write well in appropriate newspaper style, and you prove to be both available and dependable, it's possible to become part of a "stable" of freelance writers the newspaper calls on with some regularity.

That's the good news. The bad news is the pay is not great, so you better be doing this for supplemental income only—or as one freelance outlet among many if you're trying to make a full-time living as a freelancer. The most you'll be paid for a single article is about $400—$150 to $250 is the norm in most cities, with some assignments such as a record or movie review running in the $25 to $75 range.

Newspapers don't always have the staff they need, but development of syndicated services and wire services has led to a decline in the use of freelancers. A wire service is a cooperative news service that has the right to reprint any local news stories or photographs that originate with member papers. Most newspapers are paying members of Associated Press (AP) or clients of United Press International (UPI), the two major such services—but there are many others. What it means in practical terms is that the daily newspaper in your city has access to hundreds of stories every day that are written for other newspapers around the country.

Gary Kiefer, managing editor of the features department for the *Columbus Dispatch*, agrees wire and syndicate stories are an inexpensive way to fill space. "It's true, and the sad fact of the matter is many newspapers have shrunk as the cost of newsprint rises, so there's less space to fill. Much of the space is now filled by breaking news and regular columns."

On the other hand, *Denver Post* travel editor Mary Ellen Botter says, "If you use [wire service material] as a steady diet, then you just regurgitate what everyone else is doing, and there's no originality, no surprise."

The travel beat can be an exception. Travel stories are widely available to editors through the wire services, but they're not always the stories local papers want. Catherine Watson, travel editor of the *Minneapolis Star-Tribune*, points out, "Every freelancer ever born wants to write about Paris, but they don't want to write about Wisconsin." Half of her paper's readership travels internationally, and half does not. It's the half that doesn't for whom she seeks articles about places to go on a two- or three-day weekend and what to do there.

"It's almost impossible to get good regional travel writing," states Watson, "and that's true throughout the Midwest."

So for freelancers living in almost any area of the country between the two coasts, exploring out-of-the way vacation spots or day trips may be a good way to get a foot in the door of the travel section of your local paper.

At the same time, editors tend to be very careful in assigning travel pieces to freelancers, and even more so in accepting unsolicited travel articles from people whose names are not familiar to them. This area has a large potential for abuse. Some people claim to be travel writers, expecting perks either from a restaurant, hotel or travel agent hoping to lure customers with the expected "free advertising"—or they naively hope that they can get a newspaper to pay them to go somewhere and write about it.

The reality is that few papers have the budgets to send freelance writers on location for a story, and even fewer writers have the resources to take on this kind of expense on their own. Editors are understandably wary that writers who have been treated to a trip will write less than objective articles. Most newspapers, underbudgeted for travel, also must make do with wire stories even when they'd like to expand their regional travel focus.

This is where an enterprising freelance writer can step in. You may be able to submit a travel piece on spec—for example, say you're an avid camper and you submit the definitive piece on off-the-beaten-track campsites in your area. If you can suggest a piece that interests a fair number of the paper's readers and doesn't strain the travel editor's budget, there's a good chance of getting published and paid, perhaps with a modest budget to cover expenses as well.

In any case, the key to successfully freelancing for newspaper dailies in your area involves narrowing your focus. Cultivating a personal relationship with an editor is recommended often by editors at daily newspapers.

The other piece of advice offered almost as often is "find a speciality." Perhaps better than "find" would be "have"—that is, concentrate on an area you know well. Often an editor will look at a writer's background, because most writers freelancing for newspapers are doing other things as well. It may be a full-time job in business or another profession (some people in law and medicine, for example, just like to write and publish) or it may be devotion to an art or volunteer community work. That other interest or field of expertise can easily be the hinge that swings you into an editor's field of vision. A classic example of this would be the drama professor at a local college who freelances reviews of local theater productions, mainly for the free tickets and the satisfaction of publication. If you're a generalist, it's going to be difficult to compete for space in the entertainment section with someone in the community who's got the credentials for this particular area. You may be just as able and willing to cover theater, but you're probably going to have more success if you capitalize on your *own* expertise.

This kind of thing—"serendipity publication"—probably happens more often in newspaper writing than any other freelance market. There are many stories of the right people and subject coming together with the right editor at the right time. Sometimes people cross over from another medium (having a radio show or teaching a cooking class that's very popular) or expand another role (say, as a management consultant with a strong reputation in the business community).

You've read about the unofficial expert in thrift shops who "just for fun" or "to try her hand at writing" completes the definitive story on this subject, writes it well and gets published. The editor thinks of her for another consumer-oriented piece; she completes the assignment on time with a minimum of rewriting necessary. Before too long, she's a regular freelancer for the paper. I don't know if this particular woman exists, but there are stories about people like her. Sometimes, if the writer has a little bit of savvy, some guidance from someone with more experience or just a healthy dose of ambition, she may end up self-syndicating, especially if she is able to generate several stories on the subject.

If you're good, you *can* be "discovered," or more likely, you can take pains to *get* yourself discovered. It is worth bearing the following caveat in mind while pursuing freelance opportunities in the newspaper business: In some areas—for example, television writing or book publishing—the odds may be long, but the rewards are great. In newspapers, however, there *is* a point of diminishing returns because the monetary rewards are limited. So if you're not having any luck at a particular daily paper, or with newspapers in general, turn your attention elsewhere— there are plenty of other writing opportunities out there.

## DAILY NEWSPAPER LISTINGS

### Editor & Publisher
*11 W. Nineteenth St.*
*New York, NY 10011*
*(212) 675-4380*

This publisher of a weekly trade magazine for the newspaper industry also has annual directories of newspapers and syndicates.

### Gale Directory of Publications, Volumes I and II
*Gale Research Inc.*
*Book Tower*
*Detroit, MI 48226*
*(313) 961-2242*

This directory is available in the reference section of most libraries and must remain in the library. Volume I (Catalogue of Publications) supplies information on newspapers, including the name, address and phone number; date of establishment; frequency of publication; printing method; physical description; (number of columns per page, column width and depth); circulation; and a few names—generally the publisher and business manager or circulation manager. Volume II (Indexes and Maps) lists the section editors by name and telephone number, cataloged geographically.

Selected national and regional newspapers:

**Atlanta Journal-Constitution**
*P.O. Box 4689*
*Atlanta, GA 30302*
*(404) 526-5151*

**The Boston Globe**
*P.O. Box 2378*
*Boston, MA 02107-2378*
*(617) 929-2000*

**Chicago Tribune**
*435 N. Michigan Ave.*
*Chicago, IL 60611*
*(312) 222-3232*
*Digital Coffee's World Wide Web site: http://www.chicago.tribune.com/*
  *coffee*

**Cleveland Plain Dealer**
*1801 Superior Ave. NE*
*Cleveland, OH 44114*
*(216) 999-6000*

**Columbus Dispatch**
*34 S. Third St.*
*Columbus, OH 43215*
*(614) 461-5000*

**Denver Post**
*Media News Group*
*1560 Broadway*
*Denver, CO 80202*
*(303) 820-1010*

**Detroit Free Press**
*Knight-Ridder, Inc.*
*321 W. Lafayette Blvd.*
*Detroit, MI 48226*
*(313) 222-6400*

**Houston Chronicle**
*P.O. Box 4260*
*Houston, TX 77210*
*(713) 220-7171*

**Los Angeles Times**
*Times Mirror Square*
*Los Angeles, CA 90053*
*(213) 237-5000*

**Miami Herald**
*One Herald Plaza*
*Miami, FL 33132*
*(305) 350-2111*

**Minneapolis Star-Tribune**
*425 Portland Ave.*
*Minneapolis, MN 55488*
*(612) 673-4000*

**The New York Times**
*229 W. Forty-third St.*
*New York, NY 10036*
*(212) 556-1234*

**The Philadelphia Inquirer**
*P.O. Box 8263*
*Philadelphia, PA 19101*
*(215) 854-2000*

**Pittsburgh Press**
*34 Boulevard of the Allies*
*Pittsburgh, PA 15222*
*(412) 263-1100*

**San Francisco Chronicle**
*901 Mission St.*
*San Francisco, CA 94103*
*(415) 777-1111*

**The Washington Post**
*1150 Fifteenth St. NW*
*Washington, DC 20071*
*(202) 334-6000*

## WEEKLY MAGAZINE SECTIONS

The caveat that there's not much money in freelancing for daily newspapers does have an exception—but there's also a catch. The exception is the Sunday magazine section, which, though technically part of the newspaper editorial hierarchy, is usually run more like an autonomous magazine. The catch is that contributors to those publications are often hustling the magazine freelance market as well as looking to the newspaper for work.

Although the fairly average pay results in some freelance turnover in the dailies, there is more steady competition for the Sunday magazines. The competition can be pretty stiff, too, particularly for the better-quality and better-paying magazines. And even if you do sell a piece, you're not as likely to become a regular as you are on your local daily newspaper.

Magazines in general—and the ones published by newspapers are no exception—tend to vary their writers. They are generally more willing to take a chance on someone they haven't used before—particularly if the writer's credentials and portfolio are solid. This is good if you're the new writer and not so good if you're trying to get steady work. Don't rely on these magazines for steady work—unless it's the magazine published by the newspaper daily you're already writing for. Regard the better-known Sunday newspaper magazines as long shots, something to aim for but not rely on.

The positive side is that these magazines often depend heavily on freelance writing, and they are also more likely to open the door to a writer outside their immediate area. And, as mentioned earlier, payments can reach $1,000 to $2,000.

Some of these weekly magazines have an editor in chief who is responsible for the content of the magazine and may rely on freelancers almost exclusively. That editor may or may not be the same person who runs the features section of the daily. The magazine has a production schedule similar to a monthly magazine but much tighter because it comes out weekly. The magazine staff usually plans several issues ahead and works on numerous issues simultaneously—each at a different stage in production.

Some of the larger magazines do have staff writers, and some may use reporters from the paper, perhaps deciding that a particular story originally slated for a section instead belongs in the magazine.

In evaluating newspapers as a freelance market, here is a useful generalization: At larger national and regional papers, opportunities for freelancers are probably best in the various sections. The magazines usually have staffs of writers, and when they go outside, they tend to look for "name" people who are accomplished in their fields or are magazine writers with a specific focus. For these papers, contact the individual section editors as discussed before. At smaller papers in smaller and midsize cities, freelance opportunities in the daily paper are likely to be more scarce, so you should check out the Sunday magazine, which may be more likely to rely largely on freelancers.

A third group consists of just two magazines, one or the other of which appears in a good many of the Sunday newspapers across the country: *Parade* and *USA Weekend.* Some newspapers rely on one of these magazines alone to be their Sunday magazine, and some include a local publication as well. *Parade* and *USA Weekend,* which consider themselves weekly magazines and not supplements—as they are sometimes referred to—both use freelance writers, are open to writers outside their immediate publication area and pay top-of-the-line fees to their writers.

*Parade*'s headquarters is in New York, but managing editor Larry Smith insists that writers can come from all over the country "because we like those different points of view. We make it a point to look for people without 'contacts,' and we try each year to publish some. Last year we published two or three articles that came in over the transom."

While acknowledging they are very receptive to new writers, Smith admits that "the essence of successful freelancing is contacts." He reiterates the importance of writers becoming familiar with the magazine and recommends that freelancers "try to develop contacts with individual editors at particular magazines."

As important as contacts may sometimes be, "the other key to successful freelancing," says Smith, is still "coming up with good ideas." *Parade*'s audience is the entire country, and so while a subject has to be specific and interest the individual reader, it must at the same time "cover the entire spectrum of the reading audience in America."

*Parade* is included in 320 newspapers with a total circulation of 33 million. They figure their readership is twice that because, on average, there are two readers for each copy of the magazine.

"When you're writing for that many people," Smith says, "it's not like you're writing for the Sunday newspaper." It's more like writing for a magazine, though even most national magazines have a narrow audience that can be considered a subset of the "American reading public."

If you can sell your idea in a two-paragraph query letter, the reward could be a fee in the $1,000 to $2,500 area, as well as probably the largest audience for your writing possible.

When freelancing for these magazines, remember that while your story must have current relevancy, it also must have "a sense of timelessness," because issues are generally planned several months in advance of publication.

*USA Weekend* also uses freelancers—about 70% of the magazine is freelance-written. Managing editor Amy Eisman says they use a lot of writers from Los Angeles because they are heavy on entertainment coverage. Again, contacts *are* important and often "one good freelancer suggests another," she says. Local writers in the Washington, DC, area have an advantage: They are more likely to make the contacts through social events, and they can stop by the office to meet with an editor personally. But Eisman offers some concrete tips for potential contributors: "Write in a magazine style, not a newspaper style," she says. "Look for a high-profile hook on a story; have a sense of humor; be creative and not predictable."

It's also important, she notes, for writers to feel comfortable talking with editors on the telephone, to be able to communicate their ideas and to be willing to take direction and be edited or rewritten to fit the style and tone of the magazine.

Again, a paradox inherent in writing for mass-market publication exists here: While you do need to be distinctive in your style to capture the attention of the editors, you also need to gain access to the widest possible reading audience, which ultimately requires a certain uniformity in style for these publications.

If you can do this, you might make up to $2,500 for a cover story "of broad-based interest to baby boomers."

Eisman says "good credentials and good clips" are key here. For all the difference between these two high-end magazines and the average regional daily newspaper, they do have one thing in common: Once an editor finds a good writer, that writer's name won't be forgotten.

Also considered high-end markets, but in a different class, are the following Sunday magazines: *The New York Times Magazine*; *The Los Angeles Times Magazine*; *The Washington Post Magazine*; *Boston Globe Magazine*; and the *Chicago Tribune Magazine*. Even the typeface on their flags is the same—each a variation on the Old English typeface that connotes authority born of tradition.

These are important Sunday magazines: Their audience may be, to some extent, regional, but also includes a wider geographical focus and perhaps a more sophisticated or more educated reader.

These magazines can be as difficult to break into as any of the more prestigious national monthly magazines. Most of the editors have been in the business for a long time. They know a lot of good writers who are publishing regularly in nationally known magazines, and many of them are competing with one another for space in these Sunday newspaper magazines.

The freelance writer who has the best chance of breaking into a magazine such as *The Los Angeles Times Magazine*, for example, is someone who is an accomplished reporter and has some good clips—perhaps with a glossy city magazine, another major metropolitan newspaper or even a quality trade magazine.

According to the executive editor Kelly Scott, "*The Los Angeles Times Magazine* is looking for distinctive stories propelled by strong reporting and graceful writing. No big secrets there. We consider ourselves a magazine for southern California readers, so we do have an interest in local and regional subjects, but we aren't limited to that. Southern California readers are interested in stories with a national context and impact as well; we want to do those stories, and first, of course. We're looking for writers who either have experience writing magazine stories with depth, resonance and skill, or can demonstrate with other clips that they're capable of taking the next step."

Editors at these magazines often spend a lot of time reading other magazines, and if they see a byline on an article they like, they'll seek out that writer. But it's worth knowing that a good magazine clip can go a long way—and payment for an assigned story can run as high as $3,000.

All of these magazines get a high volume of mail. Linton Weeks, former editor of *The Washington Post Magazine* and a regular contributor, says: "There are so many good ideas and so many good writers with good ideas. . . . I'm of the school that believes the cream rises to the top. If you've got a good story and can tell it well, it'll see print."

*The Washington Post Magazine* tends to look for more of a local angle too. It works in close partnership with the newspaper's feature section, and the magazine enjoys a special relationship with the reporters on the other sections of the newspaper. Despite having a pool of hometown reporters, a staff of writers on board and a stable of freelancers to draw on, Weeks says the paper is "always on the lookout for good writers."

If you're outside the region, you better have a good reason or a good method for contacting one of this group of magazines: An inside connection, a good angle on a story that is tailor-made for that publication and some superhuman persistence and optimism will help.

It may be wiser to look close to home at Sunday newspaper magazines. Many of the dailies publish a strictly regional magazine—though often you have to search through piles of look-alike advertising supplements to locate it. These magazines pay an average fee of about $250, depending on the locale, and vary widely. (Some, such as the *Pittsburgh Press* magazine, pay a top rate of $400, while the *Miami Herald's Tropic* may go as high as $1,000.)

These magazines are tuned in to regional topics, so if you write well and have good ideas, persistence usually *will* pay off in this area.

The writing found in this type of publication varies widely; it can range from mediocre to excellent, depending on the individual magazine editor's ability to attract and pay good writers. You'll have to judge the writing of the magazine in your area for yourself and determine just where you fit in. You may consider it a coup to see print in the magazine, or you may not even want to bother with it at all.

Tom Shroder, executive editor of *Tropic* magazine, says he looks for "superlative writing skills. We're looking for people who can both report excellently and turn it into really excellent writing. There are some people who are great reporters and who can't write, and some people who are great writers who can't report, so when I see that combination of talent, I really go out of my way to nurture that."

Freelancers also may find that many newspapers now include a weekly supplement appearing during a weekday that focuses on community news, people and events in the neighborhoods around town. These are good places to get a foot in the door, particularly if you can alert the editor to newsworthy people in the community.

## ALTERNATIVE WEEKLIES

Another kind of weekly publication in the newspaper field is in a class of its own—the alternative weekly. *Writing A to Z* (Writer's Digest Books) describes these as tabloids distinguished by their urban readership, concern with urban issues and political liberalism. Some are the offspring of the underground papers of the 1960s, but many have grown in size, in budget and in readership, and they are frequently the best place to get in-depth coverage of cultural events in the region, particularly events outside the mainstream ballet, symphony and theater activities.

In fact, at many of these papers, entertainment features and reviews have as big a place in the editorial mix as political commentary and issues reporting. Book and record reviews are a good place to break in on these papers, and some, like the *Village Voice* in New York, have even developed literary supplements and special review sections.

There are also a growing number of specialized local weeklies devoted to the interest of targeted groups, such as senior citizens, women, or children and their parents. Others cover topics such as home-based businesses or environmental concerns. If you have contacts with local experts on these subjects or have developed your own expertise, you'll find many of these newspapers are open to freelance material from new writers.

The *Village Voice* has very specific policies regarding the use of freelancers and staff writers. Many regular freelance writers have a formal contract with the paper—and the *Voice*, therefore, is not an easy place for an outsider to break in. Others, such as the *Chicago Reader*, operate more informally: Editors actually make no assignments. A portion of the paper is staff-written, but editors look at everything that comes in and publish what they like best. Besides the *Reader's* staff of writers and stable of regular contributors, it has also published freelancers on a one-shot basis only and has some once-or-twice-a-year contributors.

Payment at these newspapers varies according to the size and scope of the paper. Some of the newer papers pay $30 to $50 for a review or short feature piece. For larger articles, the range can be from $300 all the way up to $1,000.

Who are the contributors? Generally, people who are freelancing for other publications around town, some of whom have full-time jobs that may or may not be writing related.

Many of the alternative weeklies publish writer's guidelines and will send them to you when you send a self-addressed stamped envelope. Because each of these papers has its own quirky preferences, it's worth reading the particular paper and getting guidelines before querying with your story idea.

## NEIGHBORHOOD WEEKLIES

Suburban papers, city neighborhood and rural weeklies also use free-lancers, but the pay is usually minimal. Many nonstaff contributors are beginners looking for an opportunity to gather published clips for their portfolios. These papers are *excellent* ways to do exactly that, and if you *are* a beginner, you can't find a better way to get published and make contacts for your future endeavors.

Freelancers must make mental notes of the people they meet in all contexts—you never know when a chance meeting in one place can catapult you into a successful meeting or new freelance contact in another. File all this information, whether longhand or on computer disk, and collect business cards. If you are committed to working freelance, develop a long-range plan and then be willing to swerve from it. Build a career out of the best possibilities you have for steady work—and look at the high-end assignments as "gravy." Even more than for people who work in a single office or for a single company, the lines between friends, acquaintances, colleagues and mentors can be quite blurry for the free-lance writer. It's useful to make this work to your advantage—and it begins as early as your first assignment.

## WEEKLY NEWSPAPER AND MAGAZINE LISTINGS

See "Daily Newspaper Listings" for *Editor & Publisher* and *Gale Directory of Publications* information.

**Writer's Market**
*1507 Dana Ave.*
*Cincinnati, OH 45207*

*Writer's Market* has listings by category. You'll find a selection of newspapers and newspaper weekly magazines listed alphabetically by state in the section called "Regional."

Sunday magazines:

**Chicago Tribune Magazine**
*435 N. Michigan Ave.*
*Chicago, IL 60611*
*(312) 222-3232*

**The Los Angeles Times Magazine**
*Los Angeles Times*
*Times Mirror Square*
*Los Angeles, CA 90053*
*(213) 237-5000*

**The New York Times Magazine**
*229 W. Forty-third St.*
*New York, NY 10036*
*(212) 556-1234*

**Parade**
*Parade Publications, Inc.*
*711 Third Ave.*
*New York, NY 10017*
*(212) 450-7000*

**Pittsburgh Press Sunday Magazine**
*The Pittsburgh Press Co.*
*34 Boulevard of the Allies*
*Pittsburgh, PA 15222*
*(412) 263-1100*

**Plain Dealer Magazine**
*1801 Superior Ave.*
*Cleveland, OH 44114*
*(216) 999-5000*

**Tropic Magazine**
*The Miami Herald Publishing Co.*
*One Herald Plaza*
*Miami, FL 33132*
*(305) 350-2111*

**USA Weekend**
*1000 Wilson Blvd.*
*Arlington, VA 22229*
*(703) 276-6445*

**Washington Post Magazine**
*The Washington Post*
*1150 Fifteenth St. NW*
*Washington, DC 20071*
*(202) 334-6000*

Note: The "alternative" weeklies listed below are all members of the Association of Alternative Newsweeklies. That organization publishes a roster that lists all its member papers, but it has no central headquarters, only a rotating governing board that rotates its headquarters as well, depending on which paper's editor is presiding that year. Any of the newsweeklies listed below may be able to send you a roster upon request, or at least direct you to the proper office for additional information.

**Boston Phoenix**
*126 Brookline Ave.*
*Boston, MA 02215*
*(617) 536-5390*

**Chicago Reader**
*11 E. Illinois St.*
*Chicago, IL 60611*
*(312) 828-0350*

**East Bay Express**
*931 Ashby Ave.*
*Berkeley, CA 94710*
*(510) 540-7400*

**L.A. Weekly**
*P.O. Box 4315*
*Los Angeles, CA 90078-9810*
*(213) 465-9909*

**San Francisco Bay Guardian**
*520 Hampshire St.*
*San Francisco, CA 94110*
*(415) 255-3100*

**The Village Voice**
*36 Cooper Square*
*New York, NY 10003*
*(212) 475-3300*

# SYNDICATION

Syndication is a highly competitive field for a writer to enter, and there are no guarantees about how much money you can make. This will depend on whether the syndicated material is sold to a few papers or, in the best-case scenario, to many papers nationwide—and beyond. Examples of successfully syndicated columnists are Abigail van Buren, Dave Barry and Molly Ivins.

A column that is likely to be picked up for syndication must be unique, both in content and in voice, and it must have breadth enough to generate ideas for material on a regular basis.

A syndicate's choices are as unpredictable as the changing and tricky tastes of the American reading public. A column can also work in one part of the country and not in another. Syndicate representatives rely a great deal on their newspaper contacts to steer them in the right direction: They need to know what the newspaper editors see as trends and what the newspapers are looking for to interest their own particular readership. Besides keeping in close touch with newspaper editors at conventions and meetings and through informal networking, syndicate representatives scout newspapers around the country on a regular basis.

"I look for something that our client newspapers can't do without. It also has to be something readers can connect with, otherwise it won't last," says Maria Carmicino, managing editor for King Features Syndicate.

If you are writing a regular column (also called a "continuing feature"), you may want to take a shot at syndication by sending your work to one of the syndicates for review. *Editor & Publisher*'s annual directory of syndicated services lists addresses, telephone numbers and key staff. *Writer's Market* also lists syndicates. Although its listings are not as extensive as *E&P*'s, *Writer's Market* offers more comprehensive information about the 50 or so listed.

Columns should be 500 to 750 words on average, although some are as long as 1,250 words. Send a half-dozen samples with a cover letter; you can submit simultaneously to other syndicates, but be sure and let each organization know what you are doing, as a courtesy. Of course, if you should have the good fortune to come to a working agreement with one syndicate, let the others know of the change in status immediately.

Payment is usually split 50/50 between the writer and the syndicate and can vary in amount, depending on what the newspaper pays for the column. It could be as low as $8 or as high as $100 per piece. While the tradition has been that the syndicate owns the writer's material after the point of sale, more and more syndicates are beginning to follow the example set by the innovative Creators Syndicate in letting the columnist retain copyright.

For a columnist on the staff of a newspaper, syndication is considered by many the zenith because he is reaching the widest possible audience for his work and getting paid over and above his regular salary. If you are freelancing a column for a local newspaper, selling to a syndicate gives you some assurance of steady work, a little measure of security.

Competition is keen at most syndicates. Elizabeth Owens-Schiele of the Chicago Sun-Times Features Syndicate says, "We're among the top ten syndicates but we are not the largest, and we get around 150 submissions a week. I imagine the larger syndicates receive up to 600 a week." At Creators Syndicate, four submissions were accepted one year—out of 7,000 received.

But if you write a column that is really different—or you have the time to market single articles to syndicates as a regularly scheduled part of your work week—you may want to give it a shot. Some syndicates will try to sell unpublished work to newspaper markets, acting as a broker for the writer's material. You have nothing to lose but time and some postage.

"I would advise writers to study newspapers and find a niche in the market. That's what we're looking for," says Owens-Schiele. Those interested in marketing a column should be prepared with several written pieces and ideas for additional columns. "If someone has an idea for a column, we ask them to send a proposal that includes five sample columns, 600 words each, and a list of 20 additional column ideas."

Dan O'Toole, editor of special series for the Los Angeles Times Syndicate, says it's really tough to break into syndication; only one or two new people make it each year. "A syndicate is not the place for a freelance writer to start. Smart freelancers know that if they get that article published somewhere first, so that they get some up-front money, [they can then] look at syndication as icing on the cake . . . a way of squeezing some extra revenue from the piece."

Some writers choose to self-syndicate, contacting newspaper editors on their own and retaining control of their material and a full percentage of the fee. Sometimes writers self-syndicate as part of a long-range plan to interest a larger syndicate, one that can take on wider distribution and marketing of the work. In any case, self-syndicated writers agree it is not easy. According to one now-retired self-syndicator of a column on auto racing, to not only write but also be involved in "the mailing, the advertising, the promotion . . . you've got to be a one-man game."

Fred Flaxman of Flaxman Features is one inspirational success story for those determined to syndicate without the help of the "big guys." Based on his own success, he says, "There are still editors out there who read unsolicited material from people they've never heard of." But he also warns that spending all that time on marketing can be a good way of procrastinating in your writing.

Flaxman had a full-time job as vice-president of a public television station outside of Chicago and started writing "almost as a hobby." He started out as a journalist before succeeding as an executive in the broadcasting field. He regularly stayed late at the office, while his wife took an after-work yoga class, and began writing humorous columns that he thought would fill a void in newspapers. ("When you're writing humor, you don't have to be an expert, you just have to be funny," he notes.) Flaxman tried his writing out on friends, who responded positively.

Then he began the "real test," as he calls it—sending the work out to editors. Though successful in his own field, he had no contacts in the newspaper business, and he sent his work out cold to *The Wall Street Journal* and *The Washington Post*, among others. His theory was "start at the top and work my way down." He also contacted a syndicate, but the syndicate wasn't interested—then, much to his surprise, his pieces were accepted by his first-choice newspapers. Once he had gathered a few impressive clips, he decided to see if anyone would take him on a regular basis. He approached a local newspaper chain in northern Illinois that purchased rights to his self-syndicated column "Unconventional Wisdom."

Before too long, Flaxman had won a prestigious first-place award for his writing from the National Society of Newspaper Columnists. It encouraged him so much he decided to leave his job and accept a full-time newspaper job, leaving Chicago for California. He calls his experience "beginner's luck," but clearly it was the combination of talent and persistence—and yes, luck.

So before you venture into the world of syndication, honestly assess your body of work so far and your willingness to keep plugging away, even in the face of rejection. "No matter how good your things are, you're going to get enough rejections to wallpaper a room," Flaxman says. And, finally, ask yourself the Clint Eastwood question, "Do you feel lucky?"

## *SYNDICATE LISTINGS*

A comprehensive list can be found in the annual *Editor & Publisher Syndicate Directory* (11 W. Ninteenth St., New York, NY 10011).

**Chronicle Features**
*870 Market St.*
*San Francisco, CA 94102*
*(415) 777-7212*

**Creators Syndicate**
*5777 W. Century Blvd., Suite 700*
*Los Angeles, CA 90045*
*(310) 337-7003*

**King Features Syndicate, Inc.**
*235 E. Forty-fifth St.*
*New York, NY 10017*
*(212) 455-4000*

**Los Angeles Times Syndicate**
*218 Spring St.*
*Los Angeles, CA 90012*
*(213) 237-7987*

**New York Times Syndication Sales**
*122 E. Forty-second St., 14th Floor*
*New York, NY 11680*
*(212) 499-3300*

**Tribune Media Services, Inc.**
*435 Michigan Ave., Suite 1500*
*Chicago, IL 60611*
*(800) 245-6536*

**United Features Syndicate**
*200 Madison Ave.*
*New York, NY 10016*
*(212) 293-8500*

# RADIO AND TELEVISION

## RADIO DRAMA AND COMEDY

In the good old days before television, radio was *the* home entertainment venue: It offered a wide variety of drama and comedy programming and was considered a writer's medium. In the last 40 years, television has overtaken radio as an entertainment medium, and the latter has remained strong by emphasizing an alternative identity rather than a competitive one with television. Radio holds its own by programming that consists primarily of music and news.

However, there is still *some* original drama and comedy in radio programming. And while radio relies on staff support almost entirely, freelance writers can sometimes find a home for their writing—creative or commercial—in the small market of radio entertainment.

This is not an area to get into for the money. It is, rather, strictly a labor of love, a creative venture. Most of the money for dramatic projects comes from the same sources that fund other fine arts endeavors—government or state grants (which have only been shrinking in the last decade), corporate or private donations and the like.

Commercial radio has shown almost no interest in radio drama; public radio is the place where just about all radio drama is broadcast—and public radio has its own problems staying financially afloat. What usually happens is a radio production company works in concert with a public radio station, sometimes using the radio's technical facilities gratis, and ultimately finds a home for the work that is produced. If a production company has some funding, an honorarium is paid to the scriptwriter, the actors and the director, and sometimes an attempt is made to compensate the radio station for the use of its facilities. More often, everyone is donating talents and resources toward the cooperative creative effort.

Target the program you want to write for by listening to locally produced programming (check newspaper radio listings to find out what is broadcast, when and where). This is an informal and somewhat esoteric community of writers, so begin networking with people associated with public radio and the drama community in your area. Again, radio drama is more closely aligned with *drama* than with commercial *radio*, so talk to people in local playwriting groups and check out the drama departments of local colleges for people in this field. If you become involved with local theater productions, you also may be instrumental in the evolution of new radio drama production. This is an area ripe for innovators, and strong on creative control, if not exactly high-end moneymaking.

For more information on the art, craft and marketing of radio scripts, see *The Complete Book of Scriptwriting*, by J. Michael Straczynski (Writer's Digest Books).

If radio is still your calling, but you want to concentrate on the more commercial avenues, the short-form comedy market is an area to explore, particularly if you have a comic bent. If you've ever heard those 60-second (or less) parodies of songs and commercials that sometimes appear on commercial radio stations, you are listening to something that a freelance writer may have earned $50 to $200 for writing. There are a few companies that sell these "products"—fake commercials, song parodies, "interactives" (interviews between the disc jockey and a celebrity impersonator) and other features—to radio stations that may not have the time or the resources to produce this material in-house.

Unfortunately, the market for original radio comedy is shrinking rapidly. Due to deregulation in the 1980s, more and more stations are coming under one ownership, staffs have been reduced and material is shared among several stations. Todd Cummings, head writer for the American Comedy Network, says staff reductions have thrown a lot of experienced talent into the freelance pool making it especially tough for newer writers to break in.

Advertising may be the best way to get into writing for commercial radio. "I would suggest if you really want to write for radio, start by getting a job as a copywriter at a station or through ad agencies. Listen to radio and learn the way ads are put together. Know the lingo—what a jingle is, what a wrap around is, etc. Some radio stations offer internships. But be prepared to work for nothing or almost nothing," Cummings says.

Yet, Cummings knows some writers want to write comedy material despite the odds. "Right now I don't know of any syndicated comedy service taking freelance. In comedy right now, the supply of material exceeds the demand. This is not a market for beginners. You need to have a background in comedy writing or in writing radio commercials."

Knowing somebody is the best way to break into comedy writing, says Cummings, and that may not be as hard as it sounds. Find local radio personalities who you think would be a good match for your style of writing. "Call them up, talk to them, ask them about themselves. Then ask them if you could write a little something for them."

This is very much the same advice given by Bill Tooker, who has been writing for radio personalities for years. Tooker worked at a radio station and now writes on a sort of contract basis for a network of radio stations. "Find a disc jockey who's funny and offer them material," he says. "It can't be scattershot though. It has to be someone you know you can work with." He adds that the key to his success has been following two simple tenets of comedy writing: Never get personal and never be mean-spirited.

Getting your name out in comedy circles can really help. Tooker says he now not only writes for specific radio personalities, but he also gets called frequently to write comedy material for roasts, speeches and anything funny the network wants.

The best place to find outlets for short-form radio writing is in the trade magazine *Radio and Records* and its *Radio and Records Program Suppliers Guide*, which is divided by subjects, such as comedy, and lists places providing such material.

## TV NETWORKS

Writing for television is potentially one of the most lucrative areas for a writer—and one of the toughest to break into.

In this section, we divide the television broadcast market into four sections for ease of discussion—though there is certainly some overlap in all of the areas: the "big four" network stations, independent (local) television stations, cable broadcast stations and public access.

The most important thing to understand about writing for network television shows is that the networks rarely deal with writers directly. Unless your Uncle Ralph is a major executive (and even then you still have to go through the usual channels), there are no doors to bang on at NBC, CBS, ABC or Fox where you won't be immediately directed elsewhere. That "elsewhere" is the production companies. Network executives work with producers in a relationship that mimics that between the producer and the writer: unstable, unpredictable, erratic and market- and ratings-driven. Furthermore, the television industry is extremely collegial, and the work itself is not as singular as writing in other media normally is—rather, it is very collaborative in nature, some might argue to a fault. If you're serious about succeeding as a writer in this business, you must be sociable and probably hyperconfident—but not falsely so. Finally, you will probably have to relocate to California where the television center of gravity is.

But if you are a beginning scriptwriter, you can do all your groundwork wherever you are. And if most scriptwriters live in California, certainly they were not all born and raised there. In fact, it would be foolish to move to California in the hope of writing for television with no contacts, no interest shown in your work and no experience dealing with the people who run this show. Years of preparation in the craft itself are necessary before you need begin to think about the practical aspects of competing in the marketplace. That means your work is to learn how to write a perfect television script—whether it is for an episodic half-hour or one-hour television series or movie-of-the-week (known as MOW).

You will need to have at least two scrupulously honed scripts to send out to an agent or a producer, and you may have to write a half-dozen drafts or separate scripts before your sample scripts are ready. You prepare by watching and studying television, particularly the show you want to write for, by reading and taking workshops in your area and by writing. And writing. And writing.

When you're pretty sure you've got a really solid MOW script or a great episode of, say, *Friends*, you can send your script out to a production company or an agent. An agent is the better bet and is highly recommended by people in the business. You don't *have* to have an agent, but it frequently works to your advantage. Besides the obvious—the contacts that an agent has in the industry—there is another reason producers are wary of unsolicited, unagented material. The networks are extremely cautious—some people use the word paranoid. Lawsuits occur frequently in which a writer claims a network used an idea without giving due credit or monetary compensation. The networks claim that similarities in ideas, even in scripts themselves, are very common; producers concur, and thus go to great lengths to protect themselves against litigation. Most production companies won't even read an unsolicited script unless it is accompanied by a release form (which can be obtained from the company in question) that protects them against a lawsuit should they reject your work and end up developing a project that, in your opinion, has similarities. Producers, therefore, prefer to work with agents who are known quantities to them.

If you have talent, and if you've been working hard to develop that talent, you should be able to get an agent with a little persistence. The Writers Guild, with headquarters on both the East and West Coasts, will send you a list of its signatories for a small fee. Agents on this list indicate if they will consider new writers, if they will consider writers only as a result of references or if they will take letters of inquiry only.

You can send out a lot of queries or send your script to a lot of agents, but if you can get a personal recommendation, you will probably have better luck, says Kerry Cox, publisher of the *Hollywood Scriptwriter* newsletter.

"If it's a family friend, an aunt twice removed, fine. Search your family tree and find somebody [who] knows somebody, so you can say 'take a look at the first three pages. . . . If you think there's some promise there, read it,' " advises Cox.

It is *not* necessary to be a member of the Writers Guild to sell a script to a producer. A producer can hire any writer he likes, but if that writer is *not* a member of the Guild, he or she is required to become a member immediately after selling that script. Usually the writer's contract will stipulate this, and frequently the terms of the contract include payment of Writers Guild dues as well.

Once you have an agent, you're a step closer to breaking in—but you still have a long way to go.

Producer Alan Wagner, who recently produced movies for Lifetime and ABC based on Robert J. Parker's "Spenser" novels, says even when a script sparks a producer's interest, it's rarely bought outright. Usually it's used as a sample script—something representative of the writer's potential.

"It's rare in television anywhere that any of the end users is going to buy a finished product. The only time they buy a finished product is in a very, very, very few instances where a major 'name' writer has 'spec'd' something, or [when a new writer] has so caught the spirit and tone of the characters in a series that their spec script is 100% right," says Wagner, president of Boardwalk Entertainment, a joint venture with the Rainbow Group.

"The usual procedure is that the end user looks at the script and will decide if this writer either understands the program and can write episodes for it, or he or she is a terrific writer and maybe we ought to get some other ideas and explore them."

Kerry Cox sheds some additional light on this from the perspective of the writer. He begins by stressing that the writer should have at least two of those "first" scripts.

"What happens—and this happened to me in the early going—is that you come up with your first [script], and you're inspired, and it's 'great' and you want to get it out there. So you send it out, and the first thing that happens—*if you're lucky*—is you get *the call*. They say, 'This is really good, we like it, you've got a lot of talent. *Can you send us anything else you've done?'* . . . And maybe you've had some other ideas in your head, so you quickly hack something off that's no good whatsoever and send it out and forever destroy your reputation with that particular agent or whatever. [This] happens to a lot of people. You're going to have to be able to say 'Yeah, as a matter of fact, I've got another script, and several ideas I'm working on right now as well. Let me send you the second script and see what you think.' And *it's got to be as good as the first.*"

The ability to "pitch" an idea is a very important part of the game in television as well, so the writer who is great with words on paper but a disaster in face-to-face interaction with people is going to have a very tough time. The importance of this verbal medium—pitching—reflects the role of collegiality in the television business, and, as Cox says, "It helps to have a good personality."

These presentation skills—which include not just a facility with words but an ability to think quickly on your feet—are crucial. Writers must further understand that even when a script is purchased, by the time it is rewritten by an assortment of other writers, producers, directors and actors, they may not recognize the original script. This is to be expected in television writing; projects are not written so much as developed. This is very different from the experience of a book author. Even writers who are grateful and appreciative of the work of a good editor are surprised to hear an editor say, "Great book, but I think we need to rewrite the ending."

"The writing of comedy is the *most* collegial of all forms," asserts Wagner. A comedy is assembled by a complex hierarchy of 8 to 10 writers per show, on average—beginning with the writer-producer who created and wrote the pilot, an executive producer and chief story writer, and a line of writers under that graded on levels of seniority. When a show is fairly new, the scripts are mostly written by staff writers. After a show has been on the air for a while and has established a track record, it's more common for the staff to look at scripts that come in from outside. So when targeting a show to write for, be sure and select one that has been around for a while.

This inevitable system of collaborative creativity has proved to be too much for some writers to handle, so it may be worth reflecting on whether you have the necessary personality characteristics to work in the television business. In addition, writers should decide early on whether to pursue comedy or drama. ("There's a great deal of suspicion of people who cross over—that's a rule of thumb.")

"Many people have themselves removed from the system because of [this] excess of collaboration," says Wagner, citing examples of industry gossip where writers or producers left a project due to "differences in creative control." Those who stay, he said, must be "tenacious" and "hardskinned."

Cox reminds writers who are determined to break in and stay in television writing that "the main thing is to retain flexibility and remember that, as a television writer, you're a hired gun. You have to deliver what the show wants, not necessarily what you want. So when you go in and pitch your idea and they start changing it around, don't be protective and defensive, but rather go with the flow. They're not trying to make the show bad, they're trying to make it good. So go from their viewpoint and help them make the show better."

Of course the assumption here is that the writer has faith in the producer's vision. And here is the crux of the matter: Television is a producer-dominated, not writer-dominated, field. Most television writers, therefore, have as their goal to become writer-producers, giving them much more control over the final product.

*If* you have an agent, have some contact with people in the business and perhaps have your scripts read, *then* you can consider yourself as having a proverbial foot in the door. It's still a long, hard road to getting your work produced, however.

If you are pitching ideas, you may have an idea bought—but there's still no guarantee you will be hired to write the script. Yes, it's certainly nice to make the $5,000 or $10,000 on an option, but if you're a writer, you will not ultimately be satisfied with that. This is where having an agent negotiate deals for you can sometimes be useful in giving you leverage. An agent's advice may vary, depending on the particular circumstances. You will have to decide, though, if the advice is working for or against your best interests.

One New York writer, having interested a producer in her MOW story idea—which amounted to a scene-by-scene treatment—had an agent that, in her words, was "hanging tough." The agent didn't want her to sell the story without a guarantee that she would write the script, since that's where the money is made. The producer finally convinced the writer, in this case, that "you can't hit a home run unless you get up to bat," and the writer decided to sign the contract, overriding her agent's advice. This particular story has a happy ending: The story was optioned, and a few weeks later the writer got the go-ahead to write the script.

There are several lessons illustrated here. One, sometimes it becomes necessary to take a chance. Two, your agent is your *co*pilot; don't abdicate total control of your career. The agent was not trying to hold back the writer's career—he would have had nothing to gain from that. But he knew the industry game: It's not until you sell a *script*, not a *script idea*, that you gain any credibility in the business. He wanted to hold out, but the writer took the chance. It could have turned out differently: A story can be bought, and then the producer can hire another established writer to flesh it out—and get the credit and the money. The writer with the original idea is then back to square one.

Scripts can be written and rewritten, with several writers hired and fired anywhere along the way, and still never get produced. And writers can be "bought off," thrown off the project or offered "step-deals" where the producer can cut them off at any point in the development and bring in other writers. Writers, for the most part, have very little control until they get to be writer-producers—at which point you begin battling with the network for control.

"Every studio has a room filled with turnaround scripts," says Wagner. These are scripts that may not turn out well, or as expected, or aren't needed as the producer's or the network's needs change, or that the studio has difficulty casting. After a certain amount of time, the rights revert back to the producer or the writer or some kind of joint arrangement of ownership. But the point here is that even selling an idea *and* writing the script is no guarantee of a successful production.

However, Wagner says, "Once you've gotten produced and had a small modicum of success, the escalation is very rapid from that point on." But he concedes, "the first years are hellish."

You really have to want it. And you have to be prepared to sweat over a perfect script whose destiny may only be to get you an agent or an invitation to pitch ideas or an assignment to write yet *another* script. The irony is that the first script can end up gathering dust over the years even as your career takes off. You can't get bogged down in sentimental attachments to your writing when writing for television. Writing is more craft than art in this business; you need to be a fountain of ideas, ready to develop or discard them at someone else's whim. Writing and polishing those first scripts for television should probably be considered more of an investment in your future, as writer Lydia Wilen terms it.

Wilen, who works in partnership with her sister Joan Wilen in New York City, displays the kind of tenacity needed to survive and thrive as a writer in the television industry.

"You've got to get the scripts out there. *You* have to get out there. You have to talk to everyone who will listen—you never know where [an opportunity] is going to come from. You have to constantly remind them: I'm a writer, and I'm looking for work. You just have to keep pushing yourself so much."

Asked what she would advise aspiring scriptwriters, Wilen gave a surprising response but with absolute conviction: "Don't let anyone read your script who isn't in a position to really further your career. That's very important. Everyone's a critic—and that's a very dangerous thing. What happens is, you write something, you give it to someone who is 'so bright'—you give it to your English teacher or to someone you really trust, and they start making you crazy. It doesn't *matter* what they say, whether they love it or they hate it—it doesn't matter. What they may not like, a producer may absolutely love."

This is advice worth reflecting on, though not every writer will be able to—or want to—follow it. Feedback is very important to most of us, after all. But Wilen maintains that if your friend or teacher doesn't like the script—and worse, tells you so kindly—"it's very damaging to your soul, and you'll never like that person again." And so what if the person *does* like the script? "It's an ego boost, but it's not worth it." When all is said and done, the fact that the person likes the script has no practical value to you. She maintains a strict rule for her own work: Don't give the script to any person not in a position to buy it.

And what about living in New York? Is it the next best thing to living in California for an aspiring television writer? Wilen says it's tough. The competition is tough because "writers love living in New York," but "it's rough to be in New York and expect the California production companies to use you." Once you're well established, you can live anywhere, she says. But you have to establish yourself in Los Angeles for a couple of years. So the word on living in L.A. seems to be that television writers have to put in some time there. You don't want to go too soon, and you don't need to stay there forever. But you can't avoid it completely. As Wilen points out, L.A. is a company town: Almost *everyone* has a friend or relative or an aunt twice removed who is in "the business."

## INDEPENDENT AND PUBLIC TELEVISION STATIONS

Although NBC, ABC, CBS and Fox—the four major network stations in the United States—dominate the television industry, they are certainly not the only stations on the air. Even before cable TV expanded the broadcast alternatives, there were other independent television stations, particularly in the larger cities. But opportunities for writers are almost nil unless you are hired to be on staff. Programming is created internally most of the time—as in the case of public TV—or purchased as prepackaged material by many independent stations whose lineup consists primarily of reruns from old network shows.

Speaking for a Cincinnati public television station, WCET senior vice-president Jack Dominic said a station such as his might occasionally work with freelance writers in a number of ways, perhaps "to flesh out an idea that is already created and developed" or more likely "to create copy for various campaigns, [such as] on-air fund-raising."

"Most public television stations out of the 200-plus in the country do very little actual production. They serve more as a conduit of materials coming from a national source," said Dominic.

As for locally produced programs in the smaller markets, he added: "These materials are created internally by producers mainly because programming at that level is very, very underfunded, and there just isn't additional funding available to bring in someone else to collaborate."

The other avenue for writing for television is through advertising, discussed in the "Word Markets" section of this chapter. The employer in these cases would normally be the advertising agency hired by a company who has purchased television airtime to advertise a product.

## CABLE TELEVISION

The advent of cable television has provided subscribers with alternatives unheard of just two decades ago: Sixty-four cable channels is standard, and 600 or more is possible if you have a satellite dish. The most popular stations are the movie channels (HBO, Showtime, etc.), music stations (MTV, VH1) and programming for children (Disney Channel, Nickelodeon). The Turner Broadcasting System includes TBS, TNT, Cable News Network (CNN) and CNN Headline News.

Adrienne Bramhall, development coordinator for Turner Original Productions, handles the company's nonfiction and documentary scripts. While they don't insist scripts be registered with the Writers Guild, they do want writers to sign a release form.

Scripts are looked at by a reader within the company who then writes "coverage"—a plot summary plus a subjective assessment of the strengths of the idea. The best scripts are brought to a weekly development meeting where the executives discuss and possibly fight for any of the scripts they feel passionate about. Usually a quarter of the week's submissions makes it to the weekly meeting, and the ones selected out of that grouping go to network president Ted Turner for final approval.

Cathy Wischner-Sola is the manager of development for Turner Broadcasting System. She says movies for cable are different than those written for the broadcast networks. She reviews scripts for two-hour features or miniseries, and many of these are based on books. "There's a real renaissance in material taken from books in the last few years," she says. Often the company will use books that are in the public domain, but they will often need scripts written from these books.

Because of legal constraints, says Wischner-Sola, she almost always works through an agent or attorney, and it is preferable that the writer register the script with the Writers Guild. Writers can obtain and sign a release form from the company and bypass using an agent, but, she says, "considering the glut of submissions we receive, it's very hard for a writer to break in with an unsolicited script." The company now receives some

50 or more submissions each week, and this does not include the tremendous amount of books they receive.

Turner Broadcasting System is a studio, and they are approached all the time by producers with proposals for projects. If they decide to take on a project, the producer may hire the writer or work in concert with the producers to obtain a writer's services. Many scripts are rewritten, too, says Wischner-Sola, offering another opportunity for writers.

Again, she says, an agent can help you get a foot in the door at the production companies. You may have to do several scripts on speculation for the agent first. This is the same way a lot of writers break into script writing for television shows, she says. "Writers interested in writing for shows like *ER* and *Friends* will send an agent a script based on the characters. Playwrights, too, need to get an agent's attention. Try to get an agent to see your work being performed. Some agents specialize in finding new talent."

Another way to break into television script writing, she says, is to write coverage, a synopsis or an analysis of a script for a studio or production company. Many people hired as "readers" or "story analysts" have sold their own scripts once they got inside the production company. Several universities offer courses in story analysis. These jobs don't pay much, but they do help you get inside the studio where you may find a sympathetic ear. Says Wischner-Sola, "It's all about networking. First you have to establish credibility, and then establish relationships with people who can help."

Those writers interested in writing for cable programs should not approach this as a "market" en masse, but should concentrate on each individual program. Watch the program and become very familiar with it; you should probably have a genuine enthusiasm for the kind of programming offered if you intend to be a writer for that program. If you *are* enthusiastic and persistent, and you're good, you may eventually convince those looking for writers for the show that you are the one writer they've been waiting to find.

Writing for television means either relentless dogged pursuit of the high end—writing scripts for television movies or episodic shows—or exploring what might be called piecework for the various cable stations. Movies aside, your method should include focusing closely on the particular show or program that interests you and trying your hardest to be original while still making sure that your writing conforms closely to the style and tone of the show as it exists. This can be a very fine line to walk, but if you think you can walk it, you certainly could be the gold that buyers are mining for.

## PUBLIC ACCESS

Finally, the newest opportunity for writers who want to test and perhaps expand their capabilities in television writing: public access television. In more than 1,000 cities in the United States, public access television is a noncommercial, nonprofit venue for citizen-produced programming of every conceivable kind. Typically, church groups and educational or community organizations have used the airwaves to promote their beliefs or publicize their concerns, but there has also been a growing interest in creative programming by anyone and everyone with a hankering to produce a talk show, a comedy show or their original dramas and documentaries on videotape. Most public access stations offer training in video production—including hands-on experience—either for free or for a nominal fee. Many also have staff to offer assistance as you plan and produce your program.

This is not a commercial venture, but rather a place to learn about writing for television production if you've never had any contact with this medium—and you can learn while offering your services to any worthwhile organization you may want to promote. You may attach yourself to a production already in the works, or you may organize your own crew and plan your program from scratch.

Typical programming on public access may include a videotaped board of education meeting, a panel discussion on issues facing city council, a production of a Cub Scout talent show, minority- or ethnic-oriented programming, video art and a documentary. The programs may be recorded on location or in the public access studios, shot live in one take (for example, if you are shooting a play that you've been rehearsing for weeks), or shot out of sequence and edited for airplay, or any combination of these. You might be working with a crew of four or five people, each responsible for an aspect of production (audio, lighting, cameras, etc.), or you might be the entire crew yourself.

However you decide to proceed, public access television is a marvelous opportunity for the writer who has been working primarily in the print medium but would like to experiment with "air words." Once a show is complete, you are guaranteed a venue for your work—something we wish we could say after completing a written work for print media. In fact, normally each show is aired 6 to 10 times during a month.

You will be asked to sign a contract before training and using public access resources that says you will not profit monetarily from any production done on the premises or through using the station's equipment, but there is no objection to your using the tape or a copy of it as part of your résumé or portfolio for other potential clients.

*RADIO AND TELEVISION LISTINGS*
For a list of literary agencies, send your request plus $1.25 to:

**Writers Guild of America-East**
*555 West Fifty-seventh St., Suite 1230*
*New York, NY 10019-3402*
*(212) 757-4360*

or

**Writers Guild of America-West**
*700 W. Third St.*
*Los Angeles, CA 90048-4329*
*(213) 951-4000*

Good trade publications:

**Hollywood Scriptwriter**
*1626 N. Wilcox #385*
*Hollywood, CA 90028*
*Phone/fax: (805) 495-5447*

(One-year subscription is $44; six months, $25)

**Radio & Records**
*1930 Century Park W, 5th Floor*
*Los Angeles, CA 90067*
*(310) 553-4330*
*Fax: (310) 203-9763*

$299/full year (51 weeks) or $80/3 months (13 weeks) subscription, goes to radio stations, record stores and some bookstores

For nationwide listings of cable TV, consult the *Cable Programming Resource Directory*, available from your local library.

# WORD MARKETS

Words are everywhere we look—and someone has to write them. Freelance writers have an endless number of markets, from the most obvious and conventional, such as magazine writing, to the vast array of businesses and products that require brochures, newsletters, customer letters, catalog copy, advertising, signage, software manuals and contracts, as just a few examples. Even the wording on utility bills and product warranty labels was planned, written, approved and paid for by someone, somewhere.

The magazine market itself extends far beyond the high-end, well-known "glossies," such as *Esquire, Redbook* or *Vanity Fair*. Go into any good bookstore and you will find hundreds of specialty magazines in every field imaginable, many of which rely on freelance writers with regularity. If you're aiming for freelance magazine writing, buy the ones you'd like to read—or write for—and send out query letters to the managing editor (who will route it to the appropriate reader on staff) as often as you have good ideas. Make sure your idea is well thought out and described briefly and energetically in an engaging query letter—and send one or two of your best published clips if you think they will improve your chances of getting an assignment.

Newspaper or other magazine clips are best, if you've done these already. If you're crossing over from another field, rely on the strength of your idea and letter rather than send irrelevant pieces, such as media kits, brochures or technical articles. If you've targeted a couple—or even a half-dozen—magazines that you'd like to publish in, send queries as often as you have ideas, especially if you get any kind of encouragement at all. Some writers draw encouragement from any kind of response at all—even "thanks for sending, but not at this time" on a form postcard. (If an editor specifically requests that you stop sending letters because you're way off base, it's time to look elsewhere.) The point is, persistence and familiarity pay off. Even unsolicited mail is still handled by a person, not a computer. An editor "programmed" to be skeptical of unsolicited ideas can reprogram herself pretty quickly if the right idea crosses her desk.

Also be aware if you're intent on freelancing for magazines that the array of magazines distributed to retail outlets are *not* the only magazines that employ freelance writers. There are thousands of trade and specialty magazines in businesses, nonprofit organizations and professional organizations around the country. Some may use only staff writers or contributions from professionals in the field; some may not pay very well, but any can open doors to other opportunities. You can find these publications listed by subject or by geographical location in the *Gale Directory of Publications, Writer's Market* and *Standard Rate and Data Service* directories.

Again, target specific magazines if you have a good reason or relevant background for contributing to that particular magazine. Sometimes it's worth a phone call to inquire if the magazine publishes writing from freelancers; if you happen to be a professional in a given field, you're a step ahead. Often, for example, professional journals publish book reviews—and if you have the credentials and the idea, you may tap into something steady. In addition to book reviews and article writing, some publications need copywriters and editors for various departments.

## CORPORATE WRITING

More than ever, the kinds of assignments a company is likely to farm out to a freelance writer can be unpredictable and varied in category and scope. Manufacturing companies, health care and other service industries, nonprofit organizations of every type and retail businesses are finding that hiring freelancers cuts overhead costs, as well as hefty health, unemployment and other benefits. In addition, they can hire freelancers only when needed instead of hiring an employee who may be idle during slow work periods.

Savvy freelancers keep tabs on the local business scene to find out about new businesses in town or changes in existing businesses that may indicate a need for freelance help, such as new ownership or expansion. As in other areas of business, networking is an important tool when looking for corporate writing assignments.

Call all writing-related professional organizations in your area and join the active ones. Women in Communications, the Public Relations Society of America, the International Association of Business Communicators, the Society for Technical Communications, the American Society of Journalists and Authors—all or some of these national organizations may have branches in your area. Most of them publish directories of their members, often listing the member's place of employment. This gives you an automatic contact—especially if you've involved yourself in the social networking system these organizations encourage—with people who may hire freelancers or who can direct you to the person in their company who does.

Take a look at the business community in your area: Who are the 10 or 20 biggest employers? Your local business newspaper can give you this information. Keep your eyes and ears open for listings of all kinds; search them out in business newspapers as well as those provided by the Chamber of Commerce or tourism bureau, and collect directories of every stripe. Brainstorm in your local library where there are directories published for a variety of fields, often indexed geographically, including the *Encyclopedia of Associations* and a directory of directories. (See listings at end of this section, as well as the "Researching It" chapter.)

Heighten your awareness of the social and economic community in which you live. If there's a big university, are there professors or departments frequently struggling to write grant proposals? Some must publish articles or even books regularly in order to compete for a tenured position—and getting their research material into acceptable written form may be the biggest chore in the world for them. But be forewarned when working with independent private clients instead of companies: Get everything in writing. It doesn't have to be formal; a simple letter of agreement will do the trick. Just have in writing your agreement about the nature of the work, deadlines, fee payment and schedule.

If there is a large food industry, think about the needs of related businesses like supermarkets and restaurants—what are *their* communication needs? Almost every city supports a telephone company (AT&T is a virtual city of communication needs, and they *do* use freelancers); insurance, banking and real estate firms; utility and transportation companies of various kinds; computer or other engineering-related manufacturers; department stores and smaller retail businesses; and a host of museums, social service and religious affiliated agencies. All of these organizations communicate, by print media at the very least, to the public and often to other individuals or groups.

The kinds of materials that may require a writer's professional expertise with language form and content include press releases, brochures, newsletters, internal and external magazines, proposals, speeches and catalog copy among the obvious—and new home descriptions, appetizing menu selections, program notes and employee orientation manuals, to name a few that are less obvious.

To get an idea of just how far you can take this game of "who needs writers?" try this exercise: Take a conscious look around you today at written copy, wherever you are, beginning with what's right in front of your eyes—a calendar that has photo captions; an advertisement on the back of a cereal box; a button or T-shirt with a cute slogan on it—and continue throughout the day, wherever you are. Don't overlook the fliers posted on telephone poles by a local theater company, signs on the backs of benches or high up on billboards and your own mail, especially your direct (also called "junk") mail. These were all written by someone, somewhere, who spent hours with pen or keyboard and presumably collected a nice paycheck for his trouble.

Of course not all of these were written by freelancers, but it's safe to assume that any of them *could* have been. There is no communications area left—with the possible exception of top-secret government agencies—that excludes work-for-hire as a possibility. Notice I didn't say that every company hires freelancers; some do not, even as a matter of policy. But policies can change; what is done by a staff person in one company may be done by a freelancer in another.

Once you've located which businesses might need your help, contact them by sending a cover letter with a short bio and a few clips, says Kathleen Heins, who has written for a variety of businesses and specializes in working with health care facilities. "Make sure you have a name and the correct spelling of that name. Contact someone in the corporate communications, public relations or media relations department." Heins also suggests writers get everything in writing. Make sure the assignment, deadline and payment terms are clearly outlined in a contract or letter of agreement.

It's not practical for you as a freelance generalist to be a one-man or one-woman band, hiring yourself out for *any* kind of writing, anytime, anyplace and for anyone. You will cheat yourself and your employer if you attempt to do this. Writers are like doctors; specialization is the key. To get anywhere you need to focus your energies. So the question is who or what do *you* focus on—and how do you get the work?

## ADVERTISING AND PUBLIC RELATIONS

One way to sell your writing is to target the kind of company that depends on writers and may frequently use freelance writers: advertising and public relations firms. These are the experts to whom many companies turn for help in developing their various communications-related projects. In fact, if you go to a company on your own to vie for a freelance assignment, you may compete against agencies for an assignment. But for now, let's look at how to get an assignment *from* such a firm, and what the advantages of selecting this route actually are.

The biggest advantage—once you've made the connection—is that the agency finds the clients; all you have to do is complete the work. This can be attractive if you tire of freelance hustling, especially if you can become a regular in an agency's stable of freelancers. You may assure yourself a steady source of income, and if it's a quality firm, you enhance your own reputation by association.

If you already have some experience with a specific kind of assignment (you've designed and written brochures in your last job) or you're well grounded in a certain area of expertise (you're a volunteer or a past employee in an organization that caters to senior citizens) *sell yourself* as an expert in this area. If you do your job well, the agency can be persuaded not only to see you as someone they can use for a certain kind of assignment or project, but they may also see you as a subtle selling tool to bolster *their* client base in the area of *your* expertise. In other words, if you are well known in the retirement home community and doing work for Agency X (which has been trying to attract clients from a health care industry in your area), you become doubly attractive to the agency. But it's up to you to make sure the agency views you in this way. They won't know if you don't tell them.

"There are two main reasons public relations firms might hire freelance help," says Judy Ganulin, president of Judy Ganulin Public Relations in Fresno, California. "Sometimes expertise is needed, such as in writing about engineering, medicine or accounting. So, it's good to have special knowledge or develop an expertise. Other times, however, we need freelancers to help handle the overload when our staff does not have the time to do it."

The type of assignments can vary widely, she says. "Not everybody uses freelancers for everything, but they may be needed to work on brochures, annual reports, project reports—anything that a client needs." Most importantly, a writer must be flexible. It's not enough that you know how to write well; you must also be able to write in the client's style and understand that particular client's needs.

Do you need to sell your services to big agencies to get work from big companies? Not necessarily. Many companies, because they must produce a large volume of what some call collateral material, still find themselves in need of freelance help when the work load gets heavy. These pieces—from a postcard or brochure to a direct-mail piece—are used to advertise the company to the public, as opposed to an internal publication for employees only. Sometimes a company will be looking for someone who can shepherd a project from conceptualization to production; other times they may only need simple copywriting done—but done immediately.

Ford Motor Company in Dearborn, Michigan, is one of those large companies that has a lot of communications professionals on staff and so doesn't ordinarily need the kind of service an agency would provide, says Harold Sieloff, manager of the creative services department. When hiring freelancers, Sieloff looks for "a proven performer" whose previous work is "of a high level, highly regarded." In addition, he deems "a sense of confidentiality and security" to be crucial, so take note: When showing your portfolio to one company, don't inadvertently betray the confidences of internal communications of another company that are either still in progress or not meant for outside viewing.

The person to contact at some of the larger companies may go by any number of titles. It may be a director of publications, of corporate communications or of public relations. If the company has a sophisticated operation, it may have borrowed the term "creative services director" from the advertising industry, particularly if it uses both print and audiovisual media. Sometimes the word "marketing" will be in the title; other times that word will lead you into the wrong department altogether. It depends on the kind of company. If in doubt—and especially if you're cold calling—a well-placed phone call to the personnel or human resources department will probably get you the name of the appropriate department, staff person and title.

Sieloff, who pursues freelance assignments in addition to working a full-time job, says "There's a lot of freelance writing in corporate America—which is where the money is." He reminds his colleagues that they need not only writing, but marketing skills as well. "In order to get the business, you've got to get out there and chase it hard. It takes tenacity, perseverance and self-confidence."

"One way to learn how public relations and advertising agencies work is to work first in a firm" says freelancer Sherree Geyer, who has worked in a firm but now provides full account executive services on contract to an agency from her home. "I read recently in *PR News International Weekly* that in the next 15 years, 30% of all public relation account work will be outsourced, and this pretty much seems to be the trend." With the fax, computer, phone and e-mail, it saves firms money to contract out work, she says. Freelancers interested in breaking into the market should network as much as possible. "Join professional societies such as the Public Relations Society of America or the International Association of Business Communicators. It's very important to establish your credibility with firms."

To identify new businesses, especially small businesses that may be in need of your services but are not big enough or established enough to hire a full-service agency, call the Chamber of Commerce and ask them to update you or send you material on small businesses. Scout local business newspapers or the business section of daily newspapers to identify companies that have just applied for vendors' licenses. Then send them a personal or form letter to generate interest in what you have to offer. If you can be specific, so much the better.

If high-profile aggressiveness is the key in some businesses, it may not be the appropriate style for every freelancer, and some employers appreciate a lower key. Particularly when networking among social services, arts and educational agencies and the nonprofit sector, generally personal reputation, civic and community connections—along with a reputation for results—may weigh in a little more heavily than they do in businesses, where the bottom line is emphasized. Of course it's sometimes tricky to draw lines between where public relations leaves off and advertising/marketing begins—today more than ever.

Hospitals are a case in point. In the last 12 years, almost all hospitals' public relations departments have become marketing communication departments as federal cutbacks and product line competitiveness have forced hospitals to walk a financial tightrope—while producing more written copy. Hospitals have had to cut costs dramatically, and it's no coincidence that hospitals have increased their use of freelancers to supplement or take the place of in-house employees. It's a simple matter of cost-effectiveness.

Many arts organizations are suffering from a similar fate, but even more so because fund-raising for the arts is lately more of a hard sell than fund-raising for hospitals. Still, the educational and social service functions of many organizations require writers who can write for media (press releases, media kits) and communicate ideas that may often be complex (explanation of a disease, billing instructions) or sensitive (education about care of the mentally ill or aged) to varied consumer audiences. Sometimes harried executives must balance their responsibilities to inform the public (annual reports), keep employees satisfied and informed (internal publications) and please their own top brass (who may delegate a corporate history written consistently with the company's projected image).

Some organizations have a department they call public affairs where much of this kind of work is done. One director of marketing and communications for a major real estate firm also reminds freelancers that "practically every corporation of any size that has senior executives has speechwriters." Executives don't hire speechwriters the way a politician might hire a speechwriter. Someone from public relations is usually assigned to do the job. It may be something *you* can do a few times a year, along with numerous other assignments, so if you find you have a particular knack for it, serve it up as an area of expertise.

The trick in such a case is the confidentiality question. It makes some people uncomfortable to think that their leaders—community or corporate—are speaking words that flow from someone else's pen, even if the words are designed to mirror their thoughts. You may need to clear this with the people for whom you write speeches. Consider the case of Peggy Noonan, former president Ronald Reagan's speechwriter. Even the former president's detractors agreed that his speeches contained some of the most well-turned phrases in American political history. Reagan's term has been over a long time, of course, but not Noonan's career.

The usual methods of networking through individual colleagues as well as professional associations, combined with cold calling, will help you locate the jobs you seek. But whether you are approaching an agency, a company or an individual, it's always wise to use each previous experience as a way of opening doors ahead.

## TECHNICAL WRITING

Even specialties have specialties within them. Technical writing is seen these days as a freelance specialty—so much so that there are not only separate professional organizations for technical communicators, there has also been a proliferation of certificate and degree programs in technical writing. Technical writing can be described as putting complicated information into plain language in an understandable form. Pam Ecker, a technical writing instructor at Cincinnati State College, expands on that definition by calling it "writing that is primarily designed to inform, to instruct and sometimes peripherally to persuade."

By far the biggest area for technical writers is in the computer industry, though writers in the field cite a wide variety of possible technical writing assignments, including preparation of customer letters (an insurance company may have 50 different letters to compose), utility and phone bills, owner and user manuals for cars, insurance benefits packages, contracts (some states have "plain language" legislation that requires contracts and insurance policies to be written in plain language) and franchise documentation (writing the forms needed for franchising a business).

But the biggest market for technical writers is definitely computer software and hardware manuals. Writers who can bridge the gap between technicians and engineers who design the things and the customer who buys and uses them are still in high demand.

Jolene Gustafson, an associate communications specialist in the Information Design Center of the American Institute of Research in Washington, DC, says there are a lot of opportunities for writers coming from the expansion of the World Wide Web. These jobs require writers who can not only write well, but who understand the need for graphics and writing to work together on the Net. A lot of writers with experience in this area work on what is known as help systems, systems that are set up in programs and are designed to help the user along. Writers need to be adept at identifying key words and organizing information on screen in a logical way.

Technical writers themselves often shy away from the term "freelance writer." For some reason, it seems to have negative connotations in their business, as if to be freelance is to be not quite legitimate. (All freelancers usually run into this attitude sooner or later, so it's not only confined to the engineering field.) But for whatever reason, they tend to be known more often as independent contractors or consultants.

Christopher Juillet, an independent contractor from Ann Arbor, Michigan, is a member and founding manager of a special subsection in the Society for Technical Communications designed specifically to meet the needs of the growing number of consultants and independent contractors in the technical field. Juillet says that there are as many ways for writers to enter this particular industry as there are people entering it, but he emphasizes that "you don't need an engineering background." He explains the growth in this area in this manner: "Some engineers can write very well, but more of them are not as practiced in the science and art of writing technical material that nonengineers can understand. They're doing their jobs by being engineers. To describe clearly an engineering process does not necessarily require an engineering degree. It requires the inclination to be able to do it. Maybe it requires the ability to step back and not be so close to the problem. [Maybe] it's better *not* to be an engineer."

Pam Ecker's experience differs somewhat: "The strongest need is for people who have the most advanced knowledge of computer systems. [The people] who combine knowledge of programming language with the knowledge and ability to write about it will demand the highest salaries." She concedes, however, that within the broad field of technical writing, "there are still opportunities for the literate generalist ... the good writer who is a quick study."

There are a number of ways to locate these jobs, besides word of mouth, as you build a reputation for good work. If you're cold calling large companies, you'll want to contact the manager of technical communications or manager of documentation. There are also a number of contracting agencies that act as liaisons between the companies' needs and the people looking for work. These agencies have been around since World War II and they can be found in your local yellow pages under Engineering Consultants. They are also listed in several directory-like periodicals with listings (see "Word Market Listings"). They used to be strictly for technicians and technical professionals. Only recently have they begun to find that technical writers are much in demand by these same companies, and the writers are out there as well, looking for work.

## SETTING FEES

Fees can vary widely for the freelancer exploring word markets. Sometimes a fee will be based on an hourly rate set by you or by your employer. Sometimes it's based on a per-project estimate. Hourly wages can vary—employers and writers alike have quoted a range of $15 through (rarely) $90 an hour, with the average freelancer hovering in the $20 to $40 range. Business or the private sector pays more than the non-profit sector. Experience counts, and so does previous salary history. It's a good idea to set an hourly rate for yourself that you feel comfortable quoting when asked, but be prepared to be flexible. Some employers will tell you what their pay rate is; others may ask what you charge. If they ask, they generally don't like you to be evasive or wishy-washy. It's not very professional to show uncertainty in this area, and often, if they're asking, you can feel free to quote your high-end fee. In the meantime, do some research in your area to find out what the going rate is for different jobs. Colleagues in most cities will be helpful, and you can raise or lower your rate depending on your own experience and comfort level—and how competitive you feel you need to be.

Whether you're writing a videoscript for an employee orientation, writing a grant proposal for a doctor trying to get funding for his latest research or working on just the right 10 words for what retailers call point-of-sale signs, someone has probably done it—or something like it—before. Join associations, contact colleagues and remember that people are usually flattered when you ask for their advice. Feel free to be equally generous with counsel when it's your turn. Remember that the person who solicits or offers advice today may offer you a job lead tomorrow.

## FINDING WORK

So far we've identified three specific methods for locating freelance work: Connect with advertising and public relations agencies that already have client bases and become part of their pool of talent (which can certainly help expand your own personal client base); contact the communications arm of the individual companies on your own; and home in on a specific area. It might be a subject you've written on frequently, or you may have a medium in which you have worked frequently. In either case, you'll make the most headway the fastest if you zero in on your area and stick with it. Nowhere is this technique more necessary and more useful and advantageous than in the word markets. When you write for a magazine or a newspaper, your voice tends to be distinct and you are awarded a byline to distinguish your accomplishment. But in word markets, the *information* is *key*; language is first and foremost utilitarian.

If you know the "hows" of a particular methodology, you can pretty much plug in whatever information is applicable. For example, in writing direct-mail pieces, there is a basic structure that is generally followed. You can't deviate too much from that structure or the piece ceases to function as a direct-mail piece. If you know how to do direct mail, you can do it again and add this expertise to your résumé.

All this talk of utilitarian language and formats for different media doesn't mean there is no place for originality in writing for word markets. On the contrary, a quality initial concept for a campaign or project is probably the only difference between an adequate direct-mail packager who's done it a dozen times and the first-timer who has a creative spark. In fact, one advertising copywriter said, "You don't have to be a really good writer [in this field]. You need to be a good thinker and a good conceptualizer."

Content and form, plus creativity, are the elements that contribute to all communications projects. It's up to you to isolate your own strongest knowledge areas and examine closely your professional accomplishments and experiences, as well as your interests and personal enthusiasms. You can shuffle these elements like cards and come up with endless combinations. Some opportunities will find you, by serendipity. You may go after others in an aggressive or more laid-back style, whichever suits your personality. It's wise to aim high, find a practical middle ground and have a secure fallback position. That is, locate a way to have a secure and regular partial income, at least; set aside a certain amount of time in your work schedule to vigorously pursue new freelance assignments in your domain; and never lose sight of your dream assignment.

## WORD MARKET LISTINGS

In the reference section of your library, look for the following:

### CO Publications, Inc.
*P.O. Box 97000*
*Kirkland, WA 98083*
*(206) 823-2222*

This company publishes a weekly mailing of jobs listed, a periodic magazine and a state-by-state directory that lists companies who use contractors regularly.

### Direct Marketing
*Hoke Communications*
*224 Seventh St.*
*Garden City, NY 11530-2823*
*(516) 746-6700*

### Encyclopedia of Associations

This excellent sourcebook lists by category all kinds of organizations. For example: trade business, commercial; agricultural and commodities; legal, government, public administration and military; scientific, engineering and technical; health and medical; public affairs; fraternal, ethnic, religious; hobby and vocational; patriotic, athletic and sports; labor unions; chamber of commerce; fan clubs. The main volumes do not list geographically, but a separate volume does give a geographical cross-index. It's likely that your local branch will not have this, but the main library may. If the main library doesn't either, inquire about your library's extension services. Perhaps they can get this directory for you on a loan from another institution.

There are a number of "job shopper" directories for technical writers. A good many of the jobs listed are related to military contracts, but more and more commercial jobs of a technical nature are being included.

### Greeting Card Creative Network
*1200 G St. NW*
*Washington, DC 20005-3814*
*(202) 393-1780*

### National Technical Employment Service (NTES)
*P.O. Box 217*
*Scottsboro, AL 35768*
*(205) 259-1828*

This service publishes a weekly newspaper called *Hot Flash*, which gives jobs listings for contract employees nationwide. It includes information like a company's fax number so you can fax your résumé immediately. The $60/year subscription rate also includes a quarterly directory of companies as well as a "shopper index" that will publish summaries of contractors seeking employment in this field.

### Standard Directory of Advertising Agencies

(also called the "Red Book")

# PROMOTING YOURSELF

Suddenly you're an author and if previously your prayers were "If only I could finish this book" or "If only I could get it published," now your cries are "If only it would sell!" or "If only people *knew* about it!" Your friends and colleagues all know, but is your book reaching the wider reading public for which it was intended?

In this section, we focus on some of the things you can do to promote your book and, in some cases, yourself. For some authors, your book and your profession are intertwined: Say you're in the real estate business and you give seminars or teach a class on buying your first house. Now you've distilled the information from your popular local classes into a book you hope to promote nationally. Naturally, good book sales may bring new offers to teach or speak—after all, now that you have a book, your "expertise" is official—and wherever you appear from now on becomes an ideal opportunity to promote your book. Promotion opportunities range from a table of books for sale outside the lecture hall to a bookstore signing (probably only right after the book comes out) and perhaps some local media attention, including newspaper reviews, feature articles and radio interviews.

The scenario I just described includes all the elements for a smooth and comprehensive promotional campaign: a targeted audience, a hardworking author willing to do the advance legwork and make the most of a natural opportunity and the snowball effect of rippling interest. If the entire operation is a success, you'll be armed that much more when you approach book buyers and media contacts in the next city.

But not every author fits the formula so perfectly. Some authors may need to work a little harder or dig a little deeper to unearth their audience and motivate that audience to buy the book. Some books are just harder to sell than others: There may be many other books on the same subject, or the subject itself may be one the public has resistance to.

If it's fiction—especially fiction that is self-published—you will not want to delude yourself about best-seller status. A great many novels by even the major publishers die an early death on the bookstore shelves. There are outlets for specialized fiction—romance, mystery, science fiction—and there is a very focused audience for literary fiction as well (see "Promotion Listings" for some of the organizations that can offer more information in these areas). But for the most part, the reward of writing fiction is frequently the publication of the work itself; the pride that comes with recognition, acceptance and reputation among one's peers; and, finally, whatever sales can be mustered through independent bookstores, local publicity and—if you're thorough, lucky and talented—distribution through one of the small-press distribution networks.

But for nonfiction, almost anything can happen. And it doesn't "just happen." There are countless stories of nonfiction works that are self-published or published by a smaller press on a tiny budget that suddenly seemed to burst through to the public's awareness. Sometimes an author just seems to hit a nerve or be on the first wave of a new trend, but more often it is due to a lot of hard work and creative effort on the author's part. Assess your book realistically—who is it written for? How can you let those people know about it?

"Nonfiction doesn't sell well in bookstores," says Dan Poynter, head of Para Publishing, which specializes in books that help publishers and authors sell more books. Poynter is also an author, having written and marketed a line of his books on skydiving, and he has used the technique of targeted promotion with great success.

"Sky divers and parachute engineers don't go into bookstores," he says. "But I know what magazines they read, what organizations they join, what conventions they go to." Although you may not agree that sky divers avoid bookstores, Poynter's point is well taken. Whatever it is that you're writing about, give it some concerted thought and you'll realize that "you already know where your customers are."

If you are a self-published author, you will have to do *all* your own promotion unless you hire someone to do it for you (see the "Publicists" section). If your publisher is a smaller or "independent" press (which can range from a shoestring operation that publishes one or two books a year to one that publishes a half-dozen or so titles a year), you can do quite a bit to supplement their efforts. These publishers are probably going to take care of distribution and sending the most important review copies quite effectively, but you should work closely with them to make sure they know "where your customers are"; it is very likely that you'll have more information on this subject than the publisher. Finally, if you've published a book with a major publisher, don't make the mistake of thinking that they've got it completely covered. There is still quite a bit you can do, especially after the first few months when the money and time allotted to your book by their publicity department have run out and their attention has turned to newer books.

Probably the most important points to keep in mind are the following:

1. Media attention (print reviews, radio and television appearances) is important, but if the book doesn't have the proper distribution, either through bookstores or through telephone ordering, any efforts you make to put yourself or your book in the public eye will be completely wasted. You must be sure your books are in the stores and/or libraries or can be otherwise easily obtained; if your publisher is not doing this, you can handle it on your own, but there is only so much you can do by yourself. This will be discussed in more detail in the section on distribution.

2. To make the most efficient use of your personal time, energy and financial resources, target your audience whenever possible. There are a number of resources, directories and listings that can help you compile

a list of associations, trade shows and conventions where *your* audience gathers and help you tap into the periodicals, newsletters and other publications they read. You may very well have some information at your fingertips, or at least in your own files, that your publisher didn't think to check out. Again, find out what your publisher is willing to do—and let your contact in the publicity department know what *you* are willing to do. Often, the publicity staff's efforts increase in direct proportion to your demonstrated commitment.

Poynter offers a great deal of advice on penetrating the "nontraditional markets," which he contends are "where all the fun is" in book promotion.

"It's all about going where people congregate. If you're selling a book on scuba diving, you deal with 'dive' shops. If it's a book on parachuting, you deal with parachuting associations, you deal with their members, with catalog houses that sell parachutes, with parachute clubs and parachute schools. There are [parachute] magazines. . . . Concentrate your efforts where you know you can find the people."

Whether you're placing an ad, asking for a review or getting a brief mention in a specialized publication, you're putting into motion the keys for effective word-of-mouth publicity. But don't stop there, especially if your book is on a less esoteric subject, perhaps even of wide general interest.

Poynter believes strongly in sending out review copies. "Most publishers will send out 25 or 30," he says. But "book reviews are the least expensive and the most effective promotions you can do for your book." For those whose commitment to self-promotion includes a certain amount of financial investment, a little can go a long way if you spend it wisely. You may think a full-page ad in a national publication will reach a lot of people, but it's more likely a lot of people will turn the page very quickly and your extravagant shout into the marketplace will fall on deaf ears. Poynter recommends that the author "blast 300 to 500 of the books out to all the appropriate magazines" with a well-written news release, declaring that "a great many are going to get reviewed."

His logic is that at $2.50 per package—the approximate cost of sending out one review copy and accompanying materials—you can send out 400 books and "you've only invested $1,000. How much advertising can you buy for $1,000?"

Reviews are worth much more, he contends, because "people *believe* editorial copy; they don't believe advertising copy." So, "don't spend your money on advertising. Put your creativity [and money and time] into review copies and news releases and trying to achieve editorial copy."

Jeff Herman, a onetime New York book publicist and currently a literary agent, says that "if the author is up front about [his] commitment [to do promotion of his own], the publisher will usually cooperate by giving you all the review copies. They love it, in most cases; they're stupid if they don't."

Poynter reminds authors that a publisher normally budgets a certain amount of money on the book ("and it may not be very much"). He strongly recommends that "you should be there with a program and suggest *where* that money is going to be spent. Otherwise, they'll just go and blow it."

## BOOK REVIEWS AND EDITORIAL COPY

### TRADE PUBLICATIONS

Be sure you communicate clearly with your publisher so you don't duplicate one another's efforts. The in-house publicist probably will send review copies (frequently prepublication galleys) to the major review publications, especially trade publications. *Publishers Weekly* is, of course, the most influential and widely respected, but there are a number of publications like it—smaller, sometimes more specialized, of varying degrees of influence—that are read by bookstore and library buyers. These publications are the first and most important outlet for publicizing your book because they will heavily influence what books become available to the buying public through the largest bookstores in every city.

If you are a self-published author, you must start with these publications, even before you develop your specialty mailing lists. The time to begin thinking about your marketing plan is not *after* your book comes out, but *before*.

If you can send galleys (or, because galleys are expensive, copies of the galleys), you will be perceived as much more thorough and professional. Sending a published book to a book trade publication is a case of doing too little too late.

A very useful guidebook for this task—and a wealth of additional information—is the *Book Publishing Resource Guide*, by Marie Kiefer, author and publisher of Ad-Lib Publications. This guide, and the *Literary Market Place* (R.R. Bowker)—available at libraries—should give you plenty of specific places to send your galleys or review copies.

In Kiefer's book, look under the heading "Magazines for Booksellers, Librarians, and Publishers"; in *LMP*, you'll find listings under "Books and Magazines for the Trade." Some of the best known are *Booklist* and *Kirkus*. Some have a special focus, such as reference books, young adult books, small press or science. Many distributors also publish reviews of the books they carry. It is likely the mainstream trade publications will not be receptive to self-published authors, but you can give it a try if you are convinced you've got something with wide appeal. There are, however, plenty of alternative and small-press trade publications that are geared toward these books, and the buyers who are most interested.

"I feel book reviews are crucial to a book by any writer, with the possible exception of Steel or Clancy," says Sybil Steinberg, the editor of Forecast, the book review section of *Publishers Weekly*. "This is especially true for first novels or first collections of fiction."

While the magazine does not generally review self-published books, simply because authors often lack the distribution and other resources necessary to meet the demand created by a review in a national publication, Steinberg says *Publishers Weekly* has made it a policy to try to review books from many of the smaller presses. "We may be the only place where a smaller press's book might get a review. It's really a mission with us to identify new books from smaller presses."

She advises self-published authors to try to build a following with reviews and features in their local or regional paper. If the book builds a regional interest, it can lead to interviews on radio and television which eventually alert major publishers. When a big publisher picks up a self-published book, it garners attention. Two books come to Steinberg's mind immediately—*The Celestine Prophecy* and *The Christmas Box* both were self-published books picked up by larger publishers. Reviews, even in small local outlets, can lead to big things for a well-written book.

## MAGAZINE AND NEWSPAPER REVIEWS

After the trade publications are taken care of, the next important group is book reviewers in general magazine and newspaper publications. Many of these are also listed in *LMP* and Kiefer's book; you might also check the *Gale Directory of Publications* and the newspaper listings. Call to double-check or find out the name of the book editor so you can send your book directly to that person. (Book review editors will be listed in the *Gale Directory* as well.) Again, be sure you are not duplicating the efforts of your publisher, but by all means make sure these reviewers get a copy of your book.

The *Book Publishing Resource Guide* lists 500 book reviewers of large and small magazines, with information about any special focus—for example, mysteries, science fiction, nursing, music, engineering, books by Pennsylvania authors, careers, psychology, law books and genealogy. The geographical index in the periodical guide will help you locate regional publications in your area, as well as appropriate publications likely to be interested in the subject of your book. Poynter also publishes book promotion mailing lists you can rent. The *Encyclopedia of Associations* is equally useful here (see "Word Market Listings"). Make phone calls to find out who reviews books, and don't neglect your own alumni publications when selecting controlled-circulation publications. If you target closely enough, you can almost guarantee to, in Poynter's words, "achieve editorial copy."

As an example, Galynn Nordstrom, editor of *Recreation Resources*— a magazine that goes to people who manage recreational facilities—says, "We run [reviews] on most of [the books] we get, if they're appropriate."

You can send a copy of the published book to a specialty magazine such as *Recreation Resources* later in the game to pick up extra sales, but when you're contacting trade publications or newspaper reviewers, the earlier you send—preferably galleys before publication—the better your chances are of getting attention. When considering newspapers, emphasize the word "news" in your mind. Book review editors usually get galleys in March to assign to a reviewer with an April deadline and schedule it to appear sometime in May. They prefer that the book not be two months old when their review comes out, so you've got to think ahead, too.

George Myers, Jr., book review editor at the *Columbus Dispatch*, says his paper regularly covers the small and independent presses, particularly when it's an Ohio author. Authors should look at local and regional markets for reviews ("A newspaper has to cover its own backyard first"), he says, and also tap into newsworthiness whenever possible. ("A smart author knows what's newsworthy. And [if it is newsworthy], we'll always take a second look at [a book].")

### FEATURES

Myers also points out that book reviews are not the only way to draw attention to your book: Feature articles are equally, and sometimes more, effective.

"In our Lifestyles pages," he says, "probably 20% of the copy is book-driven. Actually, you're better off getting a feature sometimes than a book review."

Your local paper is a good place to start angling for feature copy. Once you have a local write-up in hand, you can send that, along with a press release, to larger papers.

In *1001 Ways to Market Your Book*, author John Kremer takes this scaffolding strategy one step further: "If you want to get good national publicity from newspapers, one of the most effective ways is working with the major city local newspaper [in your town]. Work with a reporter there to get a good feature article on you and your book, preferably primarily on your book. Once the feature article comes out, encourage [the reporter] to put it over the newswire. If it goes over the AP or UPI newswire, it's not uncommon for 100 or 200 or 300 newspapers to pick it up—and it's one of the most effective and efficient ways to get national publicity. I know people who do it that way all the time. If [the reporter] has done a good story, it is to [his] benefit to get it on the newswire. A good reporter is going to want to see his or her story published nationally—it's good for [his] career."

You can also go directly to your local AP or UPI bureau (it's listed in the phone book) and point out the story. "They may have done it already, but it doesn't hurt to remind them, says Kremer."

Send books not just to book editors, but to the various feature editors at the newspapers, adds Kremer. "If you have a cookbook, send it to the food editor." Travel book, travel editor. Business book, business editor. And so on. Send a news release that is tailored to inspire a feature story.

Kiefer warns writers, however, that it may take awhile before they see results from their efforts. "It's not going to happen overnight. You have to persevere. Even if you don't have good name recognition but you have a good product, you will get reviewed. It may take a year or more, but it will happen. Our company still receives requests for books published years ago, and we know people are getting the information from reviews."

Be sure, however, you have a good product. Self-publishers should do a short run of their book, 2,000—not 10,000—books, she says. "Writing the book is only about a third of the work. You have to make sure you have a salable idea. Do your homework. Check libraries and think about what makes your book unique. Get opinions."

"Come up with an issue," suggests Poynter, "something that is vital to this readership. If that issue is a problem, and you can answer the question or solve the problem, then way down in your release you tell them that more information is available in your book—[this] makes for a very interesting piece." This method will probably get better results than sending a release that announces the publication of your book with all the specifics right up top; editors get dozens of these releases in a day. They need to know right away why they should pay special attention to *your* book.

Keep in mind at all times that attention to distribution is as important as getting those reviews. Don't make it hard for the reader whose interest you have piqued to find your book (see "Distribution" section).

*TELEVISION AND RADIO*

If Jay Leno should happen to mention your book on the *Tonight Show*, you may just have it made. If Oprah invites you as a guest, you may also have hit pay dirt for book sales. Though these are the most oft-mentioned and probably best known of the talk show hosts, they do book authors regularly, and not just famous names. Nor are they the only ones who do so. Frequently you may land a guest spot on a show to talk not about your book per se, but about whatever it is that you are an expert on, whatever it is that you wrote about—because it's timely or relevant or relates to something going on in the news. In such cases, your book will almost always get a plug anyway—if not by the host, you can certainly find a way to mention it ("As I discuss in my book, *Daring Adventures for the Midlife-Bored . . .*").

*Good Morning, America*, for example (and other shows similar in structure), produces numerous interviews and special interest segments. The show has a fashion segment producer, a money segment producer and segment producers for the following additional topics: science, fitness, medicine, consumer news, law, entertainment, gardening, politics, film and music, plus other special projects producers.

Lifetime Cable Network has several talk shows on the air, and many of the other cable television stations do as well. Television is no longer just the "Big Four" networks: The rise of cable has expanded programming needs across the board, and the viewing public's apparent insatiable interest in people and information make it possible—and even likely—that you can find a way to promote yourself, and your book, on television.

The lists of shows and names of people to contact are fairly easy to gather. There are listings in *Literary Market Place* (LMP), and Kiefer's Ad-Lib Publications publishes a report on "The Top 200 National TV News, Talk, and Magazine Shows," which is updated every six months (see "Promotion Listings").

Rather than doing a massive mailing recommended for print—where just a few printed lines are a good bet if you target well, and can go a long way toward boosting sales—it's a good idea to do firsthand research for television promotion to narrow down your selections.

Spend a week watching television. Look in the television guides and locate anything that might possibly be construed as a talk show, or anything that might find a place for you as a guest. If you find a show you want to be on, become familiar with the format and visualize yourself in the hot seat.

"What writers should do," recommends John Akesian, publicist for

The Free Press (Pocket Books), "is watch a week of everything [relevant] on TV and [ask yourself] how would I fit into this?"

Do authors unaccustomed to appearing on television need to prepare in any way? Should they get video coaching from a professional?

"Almost every author needs to be media-trained," says Akesian. "It helps the author focus on the message of the book. It's hard to get a 400-page book into a seven-minute discussion. Media training involves polishing oneself and your message. Some people are naturals, but most people aren't. The reality is the most important interview will be your first one. If the *Today Show* wants you, they go first and you have to be ready."

Most publishers and agents can steer you to a good media trainer, and sessions can take from two to four hours or a couple of days, depending on the situation. Some authors get retrained with each book, says Akesian.

He adds that authors must be realistic and know if their topic is going to be a good bet for an interview. Watch television interviews to see what types of things are discussed and what topics get covered most.

Says Kiefer, if you don't have a media trainer, try practicing locally. "There are often programs on local access television stations eager to interview local authors. Try to polish your performance and get experience first before going on to bigger interviews."

On the phenomenon of "getting on Oprah," Kremer says: "They're looking for somebody who knows what [he] is talking about. They're looking for the expert, or people who have had the actual experience of whatever they're covering. You may send them something and it may be six months or a year before you hear back from them because what they do is hold on to [your material] until they're ready to do a show on that subject. It helps to remind them periodically—even if they didn't respond the first time—after three or four months that 'I'm available anytime.' I know one author who did that for a year—and a year after her initial contact with them got a call on Tuesday saying 'Can you be here Thursday?' They flew her in, put her up in a fancy hotel, [rented] a limo [etc.]."

Radio is, in the words of more than a few "mavens" in the book business, "hungrier" than television—and the chances of being able to promote yourself through this medium are excellent.

The main advantage is radio interviews are frequently done (live or taped) over the telephone, which means you can do it without that wear and tear on your body and you can hit many radio stations without ever leaving your home or office. Ad-Lib Publications also publishes a report that lists 900 radio stations that do book/author programming, including details of time, host, subject interests and so on (see "Promotion Listings").

"People have had wonderful success with our radio report," says Kiefer, "especially if they've included in their letter a note that they are available at any time. Some of these shows are done late at night. Also, some of these shows are repeated, if enough people ask for them. Radio by and large is the easiest medium to get on."

"I know people who have sold thousands and thousands of books through radio interviews," says Kremer, "averaging from 5 to 10 to 25 books every time they do an interview."

John Akesian says that radio in the smaller markets, particularly, is a good vehicle for authors. "We get desperate calls from radio stations all the time, 'We need an author, any author,' " he says. These stations "have a lot of time to fill," but they are usually looking for how-to books.

"You've got to be teaching someone something," says Akesian, cautioning, "A person may know all about their subject but [they have to know] what interests other people."

Controversial call-in talk shows sometimes feature an author interview—generally, 15 or 20 minutes straight with the author. Then the host opens up the phone lines to listeners who call in.

Yancy Deering, executive talk show producer for WLW Radio in Cincinnati, Ohio, says the controversy he looks for is not so much a sensational topic but, instead, someone who has a decidedly different opinion than the host of the talk show. He likes to find authors who take a different angle or opposing viewpoint. "I'm not looking for a belligerent argument, but someone who can stand up for their opinion."

Authors must get Deering's attention in the first two paragraphs of a press release or in the first chapter of a book. If he likes it, he'll take it to the show's host to see what he or she thinks. "What it takes for me is a book I can open up and identify the main subject and some sub-subjects without taking a lot of time and involvement. I like to get a review copy, and a phone call from the author really helps."

Deering says he books about three authors a week, and 80% of his shows are controversial. Occasionally, he likes to book an author with a humorous book just for fun. Noncontroversial books on special topics, such as car care or gardening, can also do well on weekend specialty shows, he adds.

The *Broadcast Yearbook*, published by the National Association of Broadcasters, lists specialty shows. Deering says a new way to find out about these shows is over the Internet as more and more stations get online with their own home pages. Those already up and running profile the radio station's shows and list upcoming guests and topics.

Although radio interviews are generally done on the phone, if you are traveling to another city, it could be advantageous to do a live interview in the studio. While it's not worthwhile to make a special trip for a radio interview, if you're going somewhere anyway—for business or pleasure— certainly a little advance work can go a long way in securing some publicity for your book.

Kremer says most radio stations have a "stable of people that they can call on at almost any time—people they've had on before that they've liked." He recommends, therefore, that if you do a radio interview, "write a follow-up letter saying basically 'I was really happy to do your show, I think it went really well, I'd be happy to do another.' If they liked you, if there was a good response," they're likely to invite you back.

## BOOKSTORES AND DISTRIBUTION

Along with editorial mailings and radio television bookings, you'll want to make sure that copies of your book are available to people after they hear and read about it.

If you're publishing with a major publisher, you can probably rely on their national distribution abilities. They have all the machinery in place to ship books—usually through a major distributor or wholesaler, like Baker & Taylor or Ingram—to the main retail outlets. But it never hurts to double-check specific stores, or outlets in specific locations, in advance of a publicity tour.

"You should not assume the book is in every bookstore," says Jeff Herman. "The bookstore might carry three copies and they'll get sold out—and it will be three weeks before another shipment comes in."

If you're going to do a local radio show, for example, it might be wise to alert the local stores *in advance* so they can stock up. (Bookstores always have the option of returning unsold copies to the publisher, though it creates extra work for them. But they'll order books if they expect to sell them.)

Another option—and this is particularly useful for smaller presses or self-published authors—is to have an address or a toll-free number where people can call or write to order books directly from you—or your distributor/wholesaler depending on what avenue you've chosen for order fulfillment. One advantage to this method is that it taps into impulse buyers—the person who calls immediately after hearing about your book. Not too many people literally rush right out to a store to make a book purchase, but if they can "act now" with a phone call, they may just do so. Make it easy for them.

This is as good a place as any to explain the distinction between what a distributor does and what a wholesaler (also referred to as a "jobber") does. In truth, though there *is* a difference, the terms are sometimes used interchangeably by people in the book business, and there are often areas of overlap, so be sure to get complete and specific information from any company you may deal with about *exactly* what they do and do not do. Never assume anything.

For your purposes, distributors market the books they carry and so they select books based on what they think they can sell. They publish their own catalogs or directories, even including reviews at times. These are, of course, not reviews in the strict sense since they are designed to promote the book, but frequently these capsule reviews can make the difference with an unknown quantity and end up boosting sales for the author. Distributors often specialize: There are library distributors and small-press distributors, as well as distributors that carry New Age titles or other specialty areas.

The wholesaler is strictly there for fulfillment of orders. He is a middleman between the publisher and the stores or customers, and he waits for the publisher to create the demand. You can contract with a local wholesaler, though. If your sales realistically are going to be fairly small, it may be just as easy for a bookstore or individual to order the book directly from you or your publisher. It's always a good idea, for such titles, to include an ordering address in the book itself.

*LMP* gives fairly comprehensive coverage of distributors and wholesalers. You can also find listings in Kremer's book or your local yellow pages. If you are fairly certain you have a book with good sales potential, distribution can make all the difference, especially in conjunction with good self-promotion. (See "Promotion Listings" for names of some distributors and wholesalers.)

You can send a review copy of your book with a letter or flier or news release to a distributor just as you would to a reviewer and ask them to consider distributing your book.

If you're a self-published author it's a good idea to join a marketing association such as Publishers Marketing Association on the West Coast, which will take your book along to "all the important trade shows." Attending trade shows can be a big help, too, especially for locating a distributor that is a good "match." The national trade shows, such as the American Booksellers Association's annual convention, can sometimes be overwhelming, but there are regional shows, too, including the New England Booksellers Association and New York's annual Small Press Book Fair, and these gatherings occur all over the country. *LMP* and Kremer's book both offer listings.

One distributor that deals with several self-published authors is

Quality Books, a library distributor outside Chicago. Michael Huston, manager of vendor relations, says, "Our line is mostly nonfiction—travel, self-help, cooking, business, diet and nutrition, and health. We also handle children's fiction and nonfiction. And now we're carrying an extensive selection of adult and child video and multimedia materials as well. We do carry books from a few small presses and self-publishers. Some have only a few titles, but many small presses have a number of titles."

Quality Books representatives call exclusively on libraries, and the number of books they sell can vary widely. Very specialized publishers may sell as few as 50 of their titles, while other publishers sell thousands. Most are trade paperbacks, even those that go to specialized or academic libraries.

This does not mean, however, that books can be put together without care or concern for professionalism, says Huston. Thanks to technology, "today self-published and small-press books can be very professional-looking pieces. [They] must compete with the book on the shelf next to it that has also been professionally done."

Books distributed by Quality Books must have ISBN numbers, and it's highly desirable for them to also have catalog and CIP information, the information libraries use to classify and properly shelve their books. Huston advises any self-publishers or small-press publishers who do not know about including this information to seek help from one of the professional publishing associations designed for small presses, such as the Publishers Marketing Association or COSMEP.

Authors who contact Quality Books will be sent its basic literature that explains how the company operates, a book information form and a distribution-to-libraries agreement (the contract). Once you fill in the basic information and return the forms, along with your book, a committee reviews it. The selection committee works closely with the sales and marketing teams who know what the libraries are looking for, whether or not it's a title they can expect to do well with and so on. Libraries are generally looking for books that will improve their overall collections.

As far as the logistics of book shipment and fees paid, Quality Books works on a consignment basis. You may be asked to send 50 to 100 books. You'll be paid when your books are sold, minus the percentage taken by the distributor.

Some distributors such as Independent Publishers Group in Chicago usually do not take on one-book publishers or authors as a matter of policy. They will take on small publishers but not individual titles. Like a number of distributors, IPG also requires an exclusive agreement from a publisher.

"We're looking for companies that will supply us with several titles every six months or year," says Mark Suchomel, vice-president of sales and marketing. "There aren't too many [distributors] out there who will deal with one-book publishers," he adds. "There are reasonable whole-salers that will—like Ingram Book Company—but they do not create the demand, though they fill the orders. But it will be up to the publisher [or author] to get [the books] into the bookstore initially."

There is an exception to the no-one-title rule, however. IPG partici-pates in a special program with the Publishers Marketing Association, called "Small Press Selection," designed to highlight books from very small publishers. Before the program, explains Suchomel, IPG spent too much time educating small publishers on the basics of the book business. Now, PMA has taken on the role, and he advises any new publisher who is not a member to consider joining.

Develop your marketing strategy before you publish, advises Huston. Be realistic about the number of books you can distribute, and have your plans all ready to go. He also sees the Internet as soon opening up new avenues for self-publishers and small presses to market their books.

Technology is already beginning to change the way Quality Books markets to libraries. The distributor handles more than 100 CD-ROM titles including Compton's and Grolier's encyclopedias. They even provide library customers with laptop computers for order entry, which allow them to preview CD-ROM titles.

On the local (and less technological) level, you can, of course, walk your book around to the stores in your city, establishing yourself if you're not already known locally. It can't be stressed enough that this may be a case of too little too late; you should begin your promotion before your book is published. But there is still some value in the human touch, especially in the case of a self-published or short print run book. Some bookstores will take books from self-published authors on a consignment basis. Some will also work with you to set up autograph sessions—espe-cially if it can be timed to coincide with a local radio interview, if you've had local press coverage or have done readings. But there is some differ-ence of opinion as to how effective these really are.

John Kremer, on autograph sessions: "It's worthwhile doing it be-cause if it works locally—and it really works well—maybe [you] can talk [your] publisher into doing more somewhere else." On the other hand, he says, "If it doesn't work well locally, it's not going to work anywhere else," so it can be a good testing ground of where to put your energy and resources.

"Obviously, the local people are going to be interested in you if you're a local person and you do it right," says Kremer. Ad-Lib Publications has been compiling an "author signing list" of independent and specialty bookstores that welcome author signing sessions. At the time of this printing, they have 300 on the list.

Dan Poynter, however, on the same subject: "Book signings at bookstores are usually dreadful. You can make it work, but you have to do a little promotion. Running a little ad in the newspaper isn't going to do it. Do a mailing to all your friends and relatives. You've got to turn the bodies out."

## PUBLICISTS

Advice about the use of publicists abounds, even among the publicists themselves. A publicist might be a good idea for authors who really think they have an undiscovered gem, but who really don't want—or are too busy—to get involved in all the planning and legwork necessary to effectively promote even a very worthwhile book.

The main drawback to publicists is that they are quite expensive, and they basically do for you the same things you can do for yourself with proper research and planning—though they frequently have more contacts in the book business and thus may be able to take some shortcuts, get some breaks and do the job more quickly and effectively.

It's not uncommon for a publicist to charge anywhere from $1,000 to $3,000 as a monthly retainer for his or her services—and that will not include expenses such as postage and travel costs. It may take that first month for a publicist to read and become familiar enough with your book to write up all the requisite material—press releases, biography, fact sheet, media kit. So you will have shelled out quite a hefty sum before getting any return for your money.

You can find professional publicists listed in *LMP*, *The Writer's Yellow Pages* and the *Book Publishing Resource Guide*. Some are listed as public relations and advertising agencies that include authors among their clients, and some are specialists who work only with authors.

If you wish to explore this route, however, John Akesian recommends that you "find out what they've done. Have they done [publicity] for a book? Do they know the special rules that apply to doing a book? If they did publicity for a book, did that book sell?"

Agent Jeff Herman recommends the word-of-mouth approach: "Talk to other authors who have retained publicists, and see who *they* recommend. Find out what campaigns the person has done recently, who his or her clients were. Talk to the clients. Look at the person's track record."

What about gimmicks that authors and publishers seem to come up with to grab attention from reviewers and buyers? Can't a publicist come up with gimmicks that will set you and your book apart from the crowd—perhaps like the author in Florida who promoted his novel about a magician by performing a magic act at selected bookstores?

By and large, professionals in the book business are skeptical of the value of such offbeat promotion. A magic act might be fun for the pedestrians in that mall, but it's not likely to sell more books.

"Initially, the idea of having a gimmick with a book was so unique that everyone reacted well to the idea," says Akesian. Now, he says, "gimmicks are increasingly a waste of time." Says one trade publication reviewer about the "gimmick" method of book promoting: "It doesn't get my attention at all."

## PUBLIC SPEAKING

"Once you write a book, you should really think about all the possible profit centers," advises Dan Poynter. "If you like to do public speaking, join the National Speakers Association." This is an educational organization that Poynter says "has tried to elevate the whole speaking field" by running educational workshops, holding conventions and publishing newsletters, a magazine and audiotapes for its members (see "Promotion Listings").

Please note that this organization does *not* do bookings—it is not a speakers bureau. But various speakers bureaus are listed in *LMP* and *BPRG*. These organizations set up paid speaking engagements for you and take a percentage of your fee for their services. They can be useful if you have something of serious interest to say to the business and corporate community—the major clients of speakers bureaus—and if you have some solid professional speaking experience. But most of them don't take amateurs: They won't take you on as a client just because you've written a book. Too many books have been published by this huge industry; being an author does not automatically confer any kind of status to CEOs and corporate heads.

"There is no shortage of speakers," said one representative of a national speakers bureau, claiming that most authors "will be sorely disappointed if they contact speakers bureaus." This assessment, he said, is the result of getting 20 unsolicited packages a day from people who want to speak, primarily so they can sell books.

His advice? "Develop a good presentation," and look for contacts locally—service clubs, community organizations, church and synagogue groups, PTAs, the Chamber of Commerce and so on. You can come up with other more specialized groups the same way you targeted publications to which you sent review copies. Ask yourself two key questions: *Who* are the potential readers (or buyers) of your book, and *where* do they gather?

Make sure you bring or ship plenty of books to display before, during and after your presentation. Arrange to have someone handle sales. Leave plenty of time for questions and answers. Your speaking presentation is bound to improve over time, and you can fine-tune your talk by listening closely to the questions people ask most often. What seemed to spark the most interest in the audience? Next time, *begin* your talk with that focus.

Keep trying the speakers bureaus—not all are so formidable. Carol de Long at the American Program Bureau says authors should put together an information packet including the book, information about yourself and an audio- or videotape, if available. She says, "We'll look at it—and use it as a sales tool [as well]." Some speakers bureaus target several different markets, such as the college market or corporate market.

As one television executive said, "It doesn't matter what the name of the publishing house is. What matters is the title and the content of the book, and the willingness of the author to get out there and support the promotional efforts with dollars and with hard work. Be available, and be willing to give the hours. Be creative!"

## PROMOTION LISTINGS

### PUBLICATIONS
### *Book Publishing Resource Guide*
*by Marie Kiefer*
*Ad-Lib Publications*
*51 W. Adams St.*
*Fairfield, IA 52556-3226*
*(515) 472-6617*
*For ordering: (800) 669-0773*
*Fax: (515) 472-3186*

At $34.95, this book is a little more within reach—and it offers a wealth of information for anyone interested in promoting a book: information on distributors, wholesalers, fulfillment services, bookstore chains and independent booksellers, book clubs including special interest clubs, magazines that feature reviews for the book trade, reviewers at general, special interest, and business trade magazines, book fairs, author associations, and a bibliography of more than 500 additional books on the subject of book publishing.

Ad-Lib also publishes a number of books and special reports on book promotion, including the very useful *1001 Ways to Market Your Book*. Other products and services from Ad-Lib include various data files and newsletters on the subject.

### *Literary Market Place*
*R.R. Bowker*
*245 W. Seventeenth St.*
*New York, NY 10014*

This bible of the book publishing industry is updated every year, but is probably too expensive for most individuals to buy. It's available in library reference sections, however.

### *Para Publishing*
*R.R. 1, Box P*
*Goleta, CA 93117-9700*
*(805) 968-7277*
*For ordering: (800) PARAPUB*
*Fax: (805) 968-1379*

Some very useful *free* information from Para Publishing is worth sending for: newsletters, special reports and so on. Call or write; Dan Poynter will put you on his mailing list and keep you there if you wish. His marketing newsletter has lots of useful news and tips. Probably one of the most useful things he offers is the book promotion mailing lists.

Both John Kremer and Dan Poynter have a wealth of information that can set you on the right track. Both have personable office staff, are very willing to help you isolate what it is that you need or want, and both have plenty of well-produced brochures and sample material that will give you a very good idea of just what they offer before you order anything that costs money. Both are well worth exploring.

### RELATED PUBLICATIONS
### *The Publicity Manual*
*by Kate Kelly*
*Visibility Enterprises*
*11 Rockwood Dr.*
*Larchmont, NY 10538*
*(914) 834-0602*
*(800) 784-0602*

### BOOK PROMOTION AND MARKETING
### *Oxbridge Directory of Newsletters*
*Oxbridge Communications*
*150 Fifth Ave., Suite 302*
*New York, NY 10011*
*(212) 741-0231*

This directory of approximately 20,000 newsletters will help you target those specific to the industry or topic covered by your book.

### Pocket Media Guide
*Media Distribution Services/PRA Group, Dept. P*
*307 W. Thirty-sixth St.*
*New York, NY 10018*
*(212) 279-4800*

This guide lists addresses and phone numbers for more than 700 consumer, trade and technical publications, newspapers, TV and radio stations.

### Success Strategies to Increase Your Sales
*(six hours of tapes with a workbook)*
*Communication Creativity*
*P.O. Box 909*
*Buena Vista, CO 81211*
*(719) 395-8659*

### PUBLISHERS ASSOCIATIONS
### COSMEP
*P.O. Box 420703*
*San Francisco, CA 94142-0703*
*(800) 546-3303*

COSMEP is a 1,500-member international association of small, independent book publishers and self-publishers.

### New Age Publishing and Retailing Alliance
*P.O. Box 9*
*East Sound, WA 98245*
*(360) 376-2702*

This organization has more than 700 members, and they focus on New Age publishers and bookstores. Their magazine, *Napa Review*, is circulated to both mainstream and New Age bookstores. It focuses on book industry trends and music industry news.

### Publishers Marketing Association
*2401 Pacific Coast Hwy., #102*
*Hermosa Beach, CA 90254*
*(310) 372-2732*

This is a 2,500-member national association of book publishers that at least one marketing director of a small press suggests is useful for smaller to medium publishers. Call for information to see if it's appropriate to your needs. Specializes in trade nonfiction.

## TRADE PUBLICATIONS

The following two publications do prepublication reviews for booksellers and librarians.

### Kirkus Reviews
*200 Park Ave. S, 11th Floor*
*New York, NY 10003*
*(212) 777-4554*

### Publishers Weekly
*249 W. Seventeenth St.*
*New York, NY 10011-5501*
*(800) 278-2991*

The following two publications do prepublication reviews of general interest books for librarians only.

### Booklist
*American Library Association*
*50 E. Huron St.*
*Chicago, IL 60611-2795*
*(312) 944-6780*

### Library Journal
*249 W. Seventeenth St.*
*New York, NY 10011-5501*
*(212) 463-6819*

## TV/RADIO
Books on this subject:

### Radio-TV Interview Report
*Bradley Communications Corp.*
*135 E. Plumstead Ave.*
*Landsdowne, PA 19050-1242*
*(610) 259-1070*

The report is used by talk show producers, book reviewers and feature editors. Ads can be placed by those interested in getting a message to these groups.

### The Top 200 National TV News, Talk, and Magazine Shows; Radio Phone Interview Shows: How to Do an Interview Tour From Home
Each of these books is $30 and can be ordered from Ad-Lib Publications, address above.

## WHOLESALERS
Both of these major wholesalers have east and west distribution centers and numerous offices. Be sure to ask for the office closest to your area.

### Baker & Taylor
*652 E. Main St.*
*Bridgewater, NJ 08807-3384*
*(908) 218-0400*
*(800) 233-3657*

### Ingram Book Company
*One Ingram Blvd.*
*LaVergne, TN 37086-3629*
*(615) 793-3845*
*(800) 937-8200*

## OTHERS
*Publishers Weekly* magazine compiles a handy source of wholesalers each year in late October.

### Bookpeople
*7900 Edgewater Dr.*
*Oakland, CA 94621-2004*
*(510) 632-4700*

Focus: wholesalers and small press to bookstores and libraries.

### Inland Book Company
*140 Commerce St., P.O. Box 120261*
*East Haven, CT 06512*
*(203) 467-4257*
*(800) 243-0138*
*Fax: (800) 334-3892*

Focus: general interest; small press; alternative.

### Moving Books
*948 S. Doris St.*
*Seattle, WA 98108-2728*
*(206) 762-1750*

Subjects: health, self-help, addictions, New Age titles. Distributes to bookstores.

### New Leaf Distribution
*401 Thornton*
*Lithia Springs, GA 30057*

*(770) 948-7845*
*(800) 326-2665*

Focus: New Age; holistic health; New Age music.

### Publishers Group West
*4065 Hollis St.*
*Emeryville, CA 94608-3505*
*(510) 658-3453*

Subjects: business, consumer issues, cooking, hobbies, family, health, house, New Age, philosophy, travel, general interest. Distributes to bookstores, schools and libraries.

### SPEAKERS BUREAUS
Extensive lists of speakers bureaus can be found in *Literary Market Place* and *Book Publishing Resource Guide*.

### American Program Bureau
*36 Crafts St.*
*Newton, MA 02158-1250*
*(617) 965-6600*

Focus: general interest.

### Toastmasters International
*23182 Arroyo Vista*
*Rancho Santa Margarita, CA 92688-7052*
*(714) 858-8255*
*Fax: (714) 858-1207*

# CHAPTER 6

# WRITING AND SELLING IN CANADA

The scope of the preceding sections of this book might easily boggle the mind of the average person. But not, we would assume, of any successful writer, nor probably even of most aspiring writers.

Writing is work—that has been made quite clear in the material you have read up to now. But it is the nicest work you can find around—if you are intent on writing. That's probably why there are so many of us writing or wanting to write.

What you have read up to this point is pertinent, in general, to a writer living, working or selling anywhere in the world. We emphasize "in general" because there are regional differences—differences in markets, research resources, laws, restrictions and so on.

In the North American context, some of the greatest differences exist where one might least expect them. After all, the bulk of this continent, at least from the point of view of geography, though not population, rests within two huge countries that sit north of the Rio Grande River and the Gulf of Mexico. The United States (fourth largest country in the world, in terms of geographic size) and Canada (second largest country in the world) share a common heritage, a common language and, in great part, a common network of communications. It should be noted here—in terms of the marketplace—that the population of the United States is 10 times larger than that of Canada—and Canada's population is essentially only two-thirds English speaking; the other third is French speaking.

But the sameness is not totally pervasive. In fact, the differences are sometimes greater than the sameness. And that can be a surprise to a large percentage of Americans—and perhaps a similar proportion of Canadians. For the American writer seeking to sell in the Canadian market, there are as many differences, not quickly perceived on the surface, as there are for the Canadian writer looking to sell in the American market.

And strange as it may seem to some, especially Canadians, this exists in fiction (and by extension, drama) as well as in nonfiction. Poetry, music and other less strictured of the artistic disciplines don't present as many problems for the writer.

It's easy to understand why nonfiction can present differences. If you are writing on a political topic, for example, there could be much to explain to a reader across the border—in either direction—because the two systems of democratic government vary considerably. And if your novel has a political theme, the same problems may well exist. However, what the Canadian writer of fiction discovers quickly is that American publishers will frequently reject work because of a Canadian setting or an essentially Canadian theme. "No one will understand where Moose Jaw, Saskatchewan, is," one American publisher told a highly talented best-selling Canadian novelist not too long ago. "In fact, they won't even be able to pronounce Saskatchewan!" This rarely proves to be a problem for a British novel or one to be translated from a European language, and these novels often have settings far more obscure to the reader than a novel set in Montreal or Toronto, let alone Moose Jaw.

Nonetheless, this cultural bias (if that's what it is) has begun to dissipate for such writers as Robertson Davies, Margaret Atwood, Alice Munro, Mordecai Richler, Carol Shields and countless others. The day seems to be rapidly approaching when a writer in Canada will be able to reach an audience in the United States without any biases other than the dictum that good, entertaining writing finds an audience while clumsy, dull writing doesn't.

What you are provided with in this section are the differences that exist on one side of the border as contrasted to the other, differences that a writer needs to know about. That information is as valuable to the American writer seeking to write for and sell in the Canadian market as the information available in the previous sections is valuable to the Canadian writer seeking to write for the market in the United States.

More important, however, this section is compiled for the writer in Canada or in the United States who is writing for the sizable market available in Canada. The structure of this section follows the structure of the earlier material in the book. It avoids the sometimes complex subject of vocabulary (Canadians call a tract of land set aside for Indians a "reserve," not a "reservation," for example). Nor does it refer to the differences in spelling (Canadians write "cheques" on their bank accounts, not "checks"), but uses the U.S. spelling except in rare instances of proper names.

All prices are in Canadian dollars unless otherwise noted; U.S. authors should check the latest exchange rate before ordering material. And note our style is to run postal codes one space after the province while it's traditional in typing an envelope to have two spaces to avoid confusing the alphanumeric postal code with the province abbreviation.

What you will find here is information specific to the Canadian market and to Canadian source materials—where, and if, information specific to, or concomitant with, what you have already learned is vital or useful to your needs as a writer seeking to sell in the market in Canada.

# LIVING AS A WRITER

## INCOME SOURCES

Opportunities for freelancing in Canada are not as numerous, obviously, as they are south of the border—but they exist in numbers that are just about adequate for those writers who actively seek assignments. Various writers' organizations regularly update listings in their respective newsletters—and some, such as the Canadian Authors Association and the Periodical Writers Association, provide information about regional opportunities as well in the newsletters of their branches and chapters. *Canadian Author* also carries a markets section in each issue.

As for freelance editing, the Editors Association of Canada maintains an up-to-date data bank both of members whose interests and specialties are readily available and of potential clients.

## SETTING UP SHOP

The basic needs for going into business are similiar in Canada to what they are in the United States. You may find that getting a bank willing to help finance you in starting a small business is not easy or even likely. Banking in Canada is carried on by fewer than a dozen national banks and not the many local or statewide banks found in the United States.

While Canadians are comfortably covered by a national health scheme, the need for disability insurance still exists. A number of the national writers' organizations and some of the provincial writers' guilds have signed on with major insurance companies and provide disability protection for their members.

## RECORDS AND ACCOUNTS

Writers with freelance experience who have resided in both Canada and the United States have found that there seems to be more appreciation of the entrepreneurial aspects of freelancing within the IRS than one finds generally within Revenue Canada. In the United States, you are likely to find at least one agent in most large urban centers who knows what a freelance writer does and who can be sympathetic to the trials and tribulations of earning a living at a keyboard that isn't hooked up for musical output.

Nevertheless, if you keep records well—and accurately—you have a better chance of a civil discussion with the civil servant (if that isn't an oxymoron) assigned to your tax audit. The advice given earlier is excellent and, in the main, applies to the writer in Canada. There are retirement plans (with different names and acronyms) and other ways of getting the best break on your tax return—but essentially, with the help of a knowledgeable accountant, you should be able to stretch your dollars to cover most "taxing" contingencies.

A good number of writers who earn a living (or at least the bulk of it) from the sale of their writing have found that setting up a small corporation is worth the expense and the other small requirements of operating a formalized business. For one thing, filing your taxes at the corporate rate is far less expensive than filing as an individual.

In Canada, as in the United States, if you are engaged in earning money from self-employment activities, you have to make a quarterly return on your estimated taxes. This is necessary if all three of the following apply to your situation:

- Your net federal tax for the past year, including surtax, is more than $1,000.
- Your net federal tax for the coming year, including surtax, is more than $1,000.
- You will have income tax deducted at source from less than three-quarters of your net income for the coming year.

These returns are due by March, June, September and December 15. The rules may change in any given year, and there are penalties if you don't file and pay as you go—a very important reason for getting yourself a competent accountant.

## AVOIDING PROBLEMS

Among the things you should consider in full-time freelancing are, of course, saving receipts for purchases and other related paperwork. But the one piece of paper too many writers totally disregard is the cursed rejection slip.

True, some writers like to keep these missives to paper the walls of their workrooms (or bathrooms), others to fill a scrapbook. The wise ones file them carefully against the day that a Revenue Canada auditor wants proof that they're serious writers.

Yes, those rejection slips, along with copies of all the query letters and other correspondence you have had with editors, and records of long-distance phone calls, copies of all manuscripts—as well as the receipts you already have been saving—should be preserved for a reasonable number of years (some accountants suggest six or seven). You'll want these in the event some curious tax department employee decides to ask questions long after you've forgotten the tax return you filed and the hard-earned dollars you sent the government.

It's a good idea to get a date stamp so you can stamp all the undated correspondence (especially memos) that might otherwise look suspicious in an audit.

As far as what receipts to keep, you must realize there are countless items you purchase for daily use in running a freelance business, items you take for granted and probably forget to keep account of.

Do you remember to ask the post office clerk for a receipt when you buy stamps or send a special delivery letter or a package? Do you record, and get receipts for, purchases of books and periodicals you use for research? Do you record your magazine subscription and newspaper delivery payments, as well as payments to the lawyer, researcher, typist, etc.? Do you attend, and keep records of payment for, professional development seminars, fees to writers' associations for memberships, meetings and conferences?

And, of course, if you face a tax audit, have you a solid record of your writing successes? Not only does this entail keeping your portfolio, but you should also save clippings of any articles that refer to your accomplishments. If you've decided to write for some nonpaying periodicals, you can't show that the free copies they sent you added anything to your financial income, but a copy of your writing output in these journals is as impressive to the tax auditor as any for which you did receive payment.

You'll have to keep up with the tax laws if you don't use an accountant. They change almost annually, it seems. The Revenue Canada District Office in your area (it's listed in your phone book) should be able to help you with the most recent bulletins published by the department, which apply to small businesses and the self-employed.

## LAW AND THE WRITER

### BOOK CONTRACTS

The Writers' Union of Canada publishes four pamphlets on basic contract terms: *Help Yourself to a Better Contract*, *Tradebook Contract*, *Writers' Guide to Electronic Publishing Rights* and *Anthology Rates and Contracts*. Prices and ordering information can be found later in this chapter under "Additional Resources." Essentially, the details are similar to the Authors Guild model contract, but there is special emphasis on the Canadian market as separate from the English-language market elsewhere in the world.

It is important for Canadian writers (and other English- and French-language authors) to understand that the market in Canada is sufficiently large to warrant separate publication rather than having the Canadian sales territory granted to a publisher in the United States, United Kingdom or France as a subsidiary source of income. For the writer, this method means more earnings because royalties will be paid to the author by the Canadian publisher rather than shared with the originating publisher. Sales also are usually greater for books published by Canadian publishers than books shipped into Canada and sold on an agency basis.

*MAGAZINE CONTRACTS*

The Periodical Writers Association of Canada also provides a model contract appended to the association's membership directory. Write to PWAC at the address listed in "Additional Resources."

*RESOURCES*

Many of the problems writers face are legal ones—problems with a legal basis or aspect, problems that may have legal solutions. Acquiring legal rights or defending them are survival skills that are costly. To provide assistance to writers—and artists in all disciplines—Artists' Legal Advice Services has been formed in Toronto and Ottawa to offer legal assistance and educational services to artists of all disciplines. The service is free to all artists and writers; funding is provided by the Ontario Legal Aid Plan—at least as of the date of this publication.

The lawyers on duty have expertise in issues that affect the artist's confidentiality. If your problem cannot be dealt with immediately, you will be advised about how to obtain further legal services.

An appointment is essential; do not drop in unannounced. To make an appointment in Toronto, telephone (416) 340-7791 between 9 A.M. and 5 P.M., Monday to Friday. The ALAS office is located at 183 Bathurst St., Toronto, ON M5T 2R7. There is a clinic held every Thursday evening from 5:30-7:30 at that address. In Ottawa, the address is Two Daly Ave., Ottawa, ON K1N 1P1, and the phone number is (613) 567-2690.

Several unique sources of income are available to Canadian writers. These are grants available from various governmental bodies for works in progress and public readings, etc.; payments to writers whose books are held in libraries (Public Lending Right); and payments to writers whose work is photocopied for various purposes (reprographic rights).

A tax that went into effect at the beginning of 1991, known as GST (for Goods and Services Tax), is the equivalent of VAT (Value Added Tax) now current in some countries around the world. Writers are required to add 7% to their invoices to publishers and pay that tax on materials they buy for their own use as writers. Remitting the tax to the government involves a sometimes-complicated formula that will probably prove time-consuming. There has been talk in governmental circles that the tax may be dropped or unified with sales taxes. If that occurs, there is no indication at this writing (in 1996) how writers will be affected. Writers who have not already done so should inquire from their local Revenue Canada Excise Office as to whether, and how, they are involved. Registration forms are available at local post offices.

## GRANTS

A major program of grants is administered by the Canada Council, a body created by the Canadian Parliament in 1957 to promote and foster the arts in Canada. The council's programs provide assistance in all the arts, and its writing and publishing section has a wide variety of support for writing in various genres—fiction, children's literature, poetry, drama and nonfiction (biographies, studies, essays and criticism).

The council supports Canadian writers engaged in writing projects, provides awards and literary prizes, assists Canadian-owned publishing houses and periodicals, supports and collaborates in efforts to promote and improve the distribution of Canadian books, and administers other programs to assist writers.

Four types of grants are available to individual professional writers in literary genres. The largest of these is to a maximum of $31,000. "This program is designed to allow free time for personal artistic activity to writers who have made a nationally or internationally recognized contribution to their discipline through a number of years and who are still active in their profession," says Gordon Platt, head of the writing and publishing section at the council. The grant allows the writer to work on a novel, a collection of short stories or poems, a stage play or a work of children's literature over a period of between 4 and 12 months.

A second grant program provides writers with the opportunity to do personal creative work or improve their skills and provides for living expenses up to a maximum of $17,000, also for the same period of time as the larger grants.

Grants for nonfiction writers cover living expenses, production and travel costs up to $17,000 for periods up to four months. These are for writing projects that include biographies, studies, essays and criticism.

A grant of up to $4,000 is available to help writers pursue creative work or to work on a specific project. This program provides a living allowance if the applicants arrange to devote the major part of their time to their program.

Travel grants not exceeding $2,800 for round-trip airfare plus $100 a day are intended to enable writers to make trips on occasions important to their professional careers.

A fifth program for emerging writers in projects that "venture into new territory in the arts and literature or for collaborative projects to develop Canadian literature," called Literary Arts Development, is available to individuals and groups with "innovative projects that may introduce new approaches to creative expression, cross disciplines, or which fulfill specific needs in the development of the literary arts," says Platt. The maximums available are $10,000 for individuals and $15,000 for collaborative projects. Deadlines for both programs are March 1 and September 1 annually. For further information and/or application forms, contact Silvie Bernier at the Canada Council address in the listings that follow. Bernier's e-mail address is: silvie_bernier%canada_council@mcimail.com.

There is also a program that provides funds for public readings by authors. Organizations may apply to have the Canada Council sponsor readings by "approved" Canadian writers for which the writer gets $200 plus travel expenses to a maximum of $400.

The Canada Council hopes to develop a writer-in-residence program in 1996.

*LISTINGS*

Detailed information on deadlines and program criteria are included in a kit, *Programs in Writing and Publishing*, available from the council, which also accepts collect phone calls from writers.

> **The Canada Council**
> *Writing and Publishing Section*
> *350 Albert St., P.O. Box 1047*
> *Ottawa, ON K1P 5V8*
> *(613) 566-4144*
> *In Canada: (800) 263-5588*
> *Fax: (613) 566-4410*
> *E-mail: lise_rochon%Canada_Council@mcimail.com*

There are grants available from some provinces. For specific information in your province write or call:

**Alberta Community Development Communications Branch**
*10405 Jasper Ave., 7th Floor*
*Edmonton, AB T5J 4R7*
*(403) 427-6315*

**British Columbia Department of Tourism and Culture**
*Cultural Services Bureau*
*800 Johnson St., 5th Floor*
*Victoria, BC V8V 1X4*
*(604) 356-1718*
*Fax: (604) 387-4099*
*In British Columbia: (800) 663-7867*

**Manitoba Arts Council**
*525 - 93 Lombard Ave.*
*Winnipeg, MB R3B 3B1*
*(204) 945-2237*

**Newfoundland and Labrador Arts Council**
*P.O. Box 98*
*St. John's, NF A1C 5H5*
*(709) 726-2212*

**New Bruswick Department of Culture**
*Arts Branch*
*P.O. Box 6000*
*Fredericton, NB E3B 5H1*
*(506) 453-2555*
*Fax: (506) 453-2416*

**Nova Scotia Department of Education and Culture**
*Cultural Affairs Division*
*P.O. Box 578*
*Halifax, NS B3J 2S9*
*(902) 424-6389*
*Fax: (902) 424-0710*

**Ontario Arts Council**
*500 - 151 Bloor St. W*
*Toronto, ON M5S 1T6*
*(416) 961-1660*
*(800) 387-0058*
*Fax: (416) 961-7796*
*E-mail: oac@gov.on.ca*

**Ontario Ministry of Citizenship, Culture and Recreation**
*Arts Branch*
*77 Bloor St. W, 3rd Floor*
*Toronto, ON M7A 2R9*
*(416) 325-6200*
*Fax: (416) 314-7313*

**PEI Council of the Arts**
*115 Richmond St.*
*Charlottetown, PEI C1A 1H7*
*(902) 368-4410*
*Fax: (902) 368-4418*

**Québec aide à la création**
*Ministère des affaires culturelles*
*225 est Grande Allée*
*Québec, PQ G1R 5R5*
*(418) 643-2110*

**Saskatchewan Arts Board**
*3745 Albert St.*
*Regina, SK S45 6X6*
*(306) 787-4056*
*In Saskatchewan: (800) 667-7526*
*Fax: (306) 787-4199*

**Yukon Arts Council**
*P.O. Box 5120*
*Whitehorse, YT Y1A 4S3*
*(403) 668-6284*

**Yukon Tourism**
*Government of Yukon Arts Branch*
*P.O. Box 2703*
*Whitehorse, YT Y1A 2C6*
*(403) 667-5264*
*In Yukon: (800) 661-0408*
*Fax: (403) 667-4656*
*World Wide Web site: http://www.arts@yknet.yk.ca*

A number of municipal governments also maintain grants programs. Call your local city hall's information desk for the appropriate department to learn if such programs exist and what they are.

## PUBLIC LENDING RIGHT

The Public Lending Right Commission, which consists of authors, librarians and publishers, was established in 1986—after decades of lobbying by writers' groups, starting with the Canadian Authors Association in 1946 and continued in more recent years by The Writers' Union. The commission administers a program of payments to Canadian authors for books of theirs that are eligible for the program and are cataloged in libraries across the country.

Payments are determined by sampling the holdings of a representative number of libraries. The more libraries in which an eligible title is found, the larger the PLR payment. The number of copies found in a library is not important; it is the title's presence in a library's catalog that determines the payment.

The available budget determines both the dollar value of each title held in a sampled library as well as the maximum that an author can earn. Compensation has been ranging in the $30 to $40 area for each title found in each of the libraries checked. The maximum an author can earn is 100 times the per-title payment—no matter how many titles are registered in an author's name or in how many libraries his or her books are found. Checks are sent to eligible authors each spring.

An author who has not registered in the program has to apply for an Author Registration Sheet. These are obtainable from the Public Lending Right Commission at P.O. Box 1047, 350 Albert St., Ottawa, ON K1P 5V8. If you wish to phone the commission, the number is (613) 566-4378, and the PLR fax number is (613) 566-4332. The PLR office does *not* accept collect calls. Along with the registration sheet, you will receive a Title Data Sheet. You will need to submit one Title Data Sheet for each book you seek to register, so make photocopies of that form for as many books as you intend to register. It is important to complete the sheets in every respect. "It is shocking to learn that writers sometimes can't read and don't follow instructions," says Gwen Hoover, executive secretary of the commission. "This causes delays and can result in the loss of your payments for a year." The only question that need not be answered is that of a pseudonym, but only if that happens not to be applicable. For each title registered, you must send a photocopy of both the title page and the table of contents page. If the work does not have a contents page (as is usually the case with fiction), you must make this fact known to the commission.

The PLR program is applicable if you are a Canadian citizen (whether living in Canada or abroad) or are a permanent resident in the country. Your name must appear on the title page or, for contributors to an anthology, in the table of contents. However, you are not eligible if your work was created for an employer in the course of your employment, that is, a work-for-hire.

It should be noted, too, that "a claim cannot be made on behalf of a deceased author by the estate or survivors," warns Hoover. Nor do the shares of ineligible or deceased authors accrue to the eligible or surviving authors, or to contributors in the case of anthologies, or to books that qualify for payments to editors, translators and illustrators or photographers; you may only claim your own percentage share in such cases.

Every time you register a new title, you must also submit a photocopy of the title page and the table of contents as you did the first time you registered.

What isn't eligible for PLR?

A title is not eligible if it is:

- wholly or mainly a musical score
- a newspaper, magazine or periodical
- a calendar, agenda, coloring book or game
- a directory, index, compilation, bibliography, dictionary, atlas, encyclopedia or genealogy
- the catalog of an exhibition or the published proceedings of a conference, seminar or symposium
- a work containing fewer than 48 pages, or a children's work containing fewer than 24 pages
- a report, study, survey, analysis or program evaluation prepared for or published by a governmental or paragovernmental organization, institution or corporation
- an instructional or self-help book or manual (including books that describe "how-to" techniques, skills or games, travel guides and cookbooks)
- an unpublished work (e.g., dissertations or theses in manuscript form, etc.)
- a textbook or book designed primarily for an educational market
- a second or subsequent edition of a previously registered book (however, if at least 50% of this edition constitutes material that did not appear in the previous edition, the subsequent edition will be considered eligible as a new title)

Translations are considered individual works and should be applied for separately.

For specific eligibility criteria regarding authors, editors, translators, contributors to anthologies, illustrators and photographers, write to the commission and ask for its pamphlet *What Is PLR?*

## COPYRIGHT LICENSING AGENCY

The Canadian Copyright Licensing Agency—known popularly as CanCopy—represents the interests of writers when their published works are photocopied by individuals or organizations for various purposes. The collective, established in 1988, "negotiates contracts with various governmental bodies, businesses and library systems so that records can be kept of photocopying," says Lucy White, the collective's associate director. Writers who register with the collective are eligible for payments when their works are photocopied.

***Canadian Copyright Licensing Agency***
*6 Adelaide St. E, Suite 900*
*Toronto, ON M5C 1H6*
*(416) 868-1620*
*In Canada: (800) 893-5777*
*E-mail: admin@cancopy.com*

# A COMMUNITY OF WRITERS

## AUTHOR ASSOCIATIONS

In addition to a number of major national groups in various disciplines, there are writers' clubs in almost every community in the country. To find one in your community, ask your local bookshop or library for help. You also might find notices of meetings published in the "What's On" column of your local newspaper.

The largest and oldest major group in the country is the Canadian Authors Association. Founded in 1921, the CAA currently has branches in 15 centers from the Atlantic to the Pacific. Dedicated to the concept of "Writers Helping Writers," its membership consists of professional (published) writers and associates, who either have insufficient published material to meet the criteria to be full members or are still in the process of learning about the craft. The principal programs in the branches involve workshop groups in various writing disciplines. At the national level, the CAA publishes a variety of publications in print and cassette tape formats for the benefit of writers and beginners, and maintains an active awards program that is highly regarded by the arts and publishing communities. In the last quarter-century, it has sired a variety of other writers' groups that have specialized interests.

### Association des écrivains Acadiens

*140 rue Botsford*
*Moncton, NB E1C 4X4*
*(506) 856-9693*

### CAN:BAIA

*(Black Artists in Action)*
*45 Wolseley St.*
*Toronto, ON M5T 1A5*
*(416) 369-9040*

### Canadian Association of Journalists

*Carleton University*
*316-B St. Patrick's Bldg.*
*Ottawa, ON K1S 5B6*
*(613) 788-7424*

### Canadian Authors Association

*27 Doxsee Ave.*
*Campbellford, ON K0L 1L0*
*(705) 653-0323*

### Canadian Farm Writers Federation

*% Hugh Maynard*
*P.O. Box 80*
*Ste-Anne-de-Bellevue, PQ H9X 3L4*

### Canadian Science Writers Association

*1111 - 40 Alexander St.*
*Toronto, ON M4Y 1B5*
*(416) 928-9624*
*Fax: (416) 960-0528*
*World Wide Web site: http://www.interlog.com/~cfwa*
*E-mail: cfwa@interlog.com*

### CANSCAIP

*(Canadian Society of Children's Authors, Illustrators and Performers)*
*35 Spadina Rd.*
*Toronto, ON M5R 2S9*
*(416) 515-1559*
*Fax: (416) 515-7022*

### Crime Writers of Canada

*3007 Kingston Rd., P.O. Box 113*
*Toronto, ON M1M 1P1*

### Federation of British Columbia Writers
*P.O. Box 2206, Main Post Office*
*Vancouver, BC V6B 3W2*
*(604) 683-2057*
*In British Columbia: (800) 663-0796*
*Fax: (604) 683-8269*

### Federation of English Language Writers of Quebec
*3 - 1200 Atwater Ave.*
*Montreal, PQ H3Z 1X4*
*(514) 934-2485*

### The League of Canadian Poets
*54 Wolseley St.*
*Toronto, ON M5T 1A5*
*(416) 504-1657*
*Fax: (416) 703-0059*
*World Wide Web site: http://www.swifty.com/lc/*
*E-mail: league@io.org*

### Manitoba Writers' Guild
*206 - 100 Arthur St.*
*Winnipeg, MB R3B 1H3*
*(204) 942-6134*
*Fax: (204) 942-1555*

### PEI Writers' Guild
*P.O. Box 2234*
*Charlottetown, PE C1A 8B9*
*(902) 894-9933*

### Periodical Writers Association of Canada
*54 Wolseley St.*
*Toronto, ON M5T 1A5*
*(416) 504-1645*
*Fax: (416) 703-0059*
*World Wide Web site: http://www.cycor.ca/PWAC*
*E-mail: pwac@cycor.ca*

### Playwrights Union of Canada
*54 Wolseley St.*
*Toronto, ON M5T 1A5*
*(416) 703-0201*
*Fax: (416) 703-0059*
*E-mail: cdplays@interlog.com*

### Saskatchewan Writers Guild
P.O. Box 3986
Regina, SK S4P 3R9
(306) 757-6310
E-mail: jmayer@unibase.unibase.com

### La Société des écrivains canadiens
1195 rue Sherbrooke ouest
Montreal, PQ H3A 1H9
(514) 733-0754
Fax: (514) 342-3866

### Society of Writers, Researchers and Composers
1229 rue Panet
Montreal, PQ H2L 2Y6
(514) 526-9196

### Union des écrivain(e)s québecois
3492 rue Laval
Montreal, PQ H2X 3C8
(514) 849-8540
Fax: (514) 849-6239

### Writers' Alliance of Newfoundland and Labrador
P.O. Box 2681
St. John's, NF A1C 5M5
(709) 739-5215 (voice and fax)

### Writers' Federation of New Brunswick
P.O. Box 37, Station A
Fredericton, NB E3B 4Y2
(506) 459-7228

### Writers' Federation of Nova Scotia
901 - 1809 Barrington St.
Halifax, NS B3J 3K8
(902) 423-8116
Fax: (902) 422-0881
World Wide Web site: http://www.ccn.cs.dal.ca/culture/writersfed
  /resources/html
E-mail: WRITERS@fox.NSTN.CA

### Writers' Guild of Alberta
111759 Groat Rd.
Edmonton, AB T5M 3K6
(403) 422-8174

### Writers Guild of Canada
*300 - 35 McCaul St.*
*Toronto, ON M5T 1V7*
*(416) 979-7907*
*(800) 567-9974*
*Fax: (416) 979-9273*

### The Writers' Union of Canada
*24 Ryerson Ave.*
*Toronto, ON M5T 2P3*
*(416) 703-8982*
*Fax: (416) 860-0826*
*E-mail: twuc@the-wire.com*

## COLONIES, RESIDENCIES AND RETREATS

There are a few places that writers in Canada can go to get away from the regular routine of daily life—to write, commune with other writers as well as nature, and partake of the opportunities that such retreats provide. Among them are:

### Saskatchewan Writers Colonies
These colonies (which now include retreats for artists in all disciplines) are run by the Saskatchewan Writers' Guild. Subsidies are available for writers from provincial culture departments in Alberta, Manitoba, British Columbia and Ontario, as well as from the Canada Council. Information can be obtained by writing to 1925 Seventh Ave., Regina, SK S4R 1C1, or phoning (306) 757-6310.

### WestWord Retreat for Women
This retreat is run by the Canadian International College in conjunction with its summer school in North Vancouver, British Columbia, and is held for two weeks in August. Information can be obtained from Gloria Greenfield at (604) 872-9014.

## CONFERENCES AND WORKSHOPS

### Ad Astra Convention
*P.O. Box 7276, Station A*
*Toronto, ON M5W 1X9*

Ad Astra, a society of science fiction and fantasy writers, holds a convention every June.

### Banff Writing Workshops
*Banff Centre School of Fine Arts*
*P.O. Box 1020*
*Banff, AB T0L 0C0*

Workshops are held each spring and summer.

### Canadian Authors Association Annual Conference
*27 Doxsee Ave. N*
*Campbellford, ON K0L 1L0*

A four-day program each June is jam-packed with workshops in all genres. The conference is held in a different city each year, generally moving back and forth across the country. Open to nonmembers.

### Canadian Authors Association Manitoba Branch Workshops
*202 - 180 Market Ave. E*
*Winnipeg, MB R3B 0P7*

This CAA Branch runs highly acclaimed and successful workshops and blue-pencil sessions on an ongoing basis. Open to nonmembers.

### Children's Writing Workshops
*CANSCAIP*
*35 Spadina Rd.*
*Toronto, ON M5R 2S9*

CANSCAIP, the Canadian Society of Children's Authors, Illustrators and Performers, a group of professionals in the field of children's culture, is probably the best able to run workshops in writing for this genre. Information is available by telephone at (416) 515-1559.

### Festival of the Written Arts
*P.O. Box 2299*
*Sechelt, BC V0N 3A0*

A four-day program in August features guest speakers representing all genres. Write, or phone (604) 885-9631, for information regarding future events.

### Kingston School of Writing
*P.O. Box 1061*
*Kingston, ON K7L 4Y5*

A summer workshop is open to all writers who desire to improve their craft, regardless of age or experience. Write, or phone Bob Hinderley or Kathryn Morris at (613) 548-1556.

### Ottawa Independent Writers
*School of Continuing Education*
*Carleton University*
*301 Administration Building*
*Ottawa, ON K1S 5B6*

An annual conference is conducted with workshops in various genres.

### Red Deer College
*Creative Writing Workshops*
*56th Ave. and 32nd St., P.O. Box 5005*
*Red Deer, AB T4N 5H5*
*(403) 342-3300*

The creative writing workshops and a "writers on campus" program are available each summer.

### Ryerson Polytechnical University
*350 Victoria St.*
*Toronto, ON M5B 2K3*
*(416) 979-5129*

Workshops, as well as credit courses, are offered in various genres.

### Toronto Trek Convention
*65 Front St. W, P.O. Box 187*
*Toronto, ON M5J 1E6*

A summer program allows writers of science fiction and fantasy to meet and have their work criticized by professionals. Write, or phone (416) 925-6241, for further information.

### University of Toronto Writers' Workshop
*School of Continuing Education*
*158 St. George St.*
*Toronto, ON M56S 2V8*
*(416) 978-2400*

This summer workshop has instructors who are prominent writers.

### Upper Canada Writers Workshop
*St. Lawrence College Saint-Laurent*
*King and Portsmouth Streets*
*Kingston, ON K7L 5A6*

Workshops are open to emerging and experienced writers, with special programs designed for high school students. The workshops are held in July and are designed to stimulate, refine and diversify each participant's writing ability through group instruction and individual consultation.

# RESEARCHING IT

Perhaps the best reference volume for Canadian writers doing research is *Finding Answers: The Essential Guide to Gathering Information in Canada*, by Dean Tudor (McClelland & Stewart). The author is a professor at the School of Journalism of Ryerson Polytechnical University and was formerly director of the Library Branch of the Ontario Department of Revenue. This is an easy-to-read book, written with clarity and wit, that outlines essentials of how to find and use information.

Also useful is *Finding Canadian Facts Fast*, compiled by Stephen Overbury (Methuen). Overbury is a professional researcher who has taught the techniques of his trade to hundreds of would-be researchers in many walks of life.

Among the volumes you will find handy from time to time are such books as *Dictionary of Canadian Biography* (University of Toronto Press) covering, in the first 12 volumes produced to date, the years 1000 (yes, 1000) to 1900; *Canadians All* (Gage) with 8 volumes so far; and *Book of Canadian Winners and Heroes*, by Brenna and Jeremy Brown (Prentice-Hall).

*Canadian News Facts* (MPL Communications); *Canadian News Index*; *Canadian Periodical Index*, dating back to 1938; *Canadian Magazine Index*, which began operations in 1984; and *Canadian Business Index*, listing some 72,000 articles annually carried in more than 200 business periodicals, all provide excellent factual data for the writer.

## LIBRARIES

Virtually all of the more than 3,000 public libraries in Canada are linked, either through formal or informal networks. This means that you can usually manage to get a copy of almost any book you may need for your research. Your librarian can tell you about interlibrary loans and how you can arrange to borrow a book that may not otherwise be available.

And before you go off searching for books that may not exist, or seek to find what books may have been published in a particular discipline, consult *Canadian Books in Print*, published by the University of Toronto Press.

## SPECIAL LIBRARIES

If you've searched the public library system and the academic libraries without success, your librarian may refer you to a special library.

These are private libraries that serve a particular organization's special needs. They prefer to work through a librarian rather than directly with you simply because the special librarian knows what books are held in the public system. They are unable to afford to serve outside sources unless there is no alternative available.

It has been estimated that there are perhaps 2,000 special libraries in Canada, and some of them are treasure troves in that they are more than a century old. The *Canadian Library Handbook* lists the special libraries, and you should look for a copy of that volume in your own library.

## THE NATIONAL LIBRARY OF CANADA

The National Library of Canada has collections and offers services that can be of great benefit to the writer-researcher. Established in 1953, the National Library is in midtown Ottawa, within walking distance of the Parliament Buildings. One of its prime functions is to collect copies of everything published in Canada. The National Archives, discussed below, is housed in the same building.

A gift of some 300,000 titles from the Library of Parliament laid the foundation of the National Library collection. Under the terms of the National Library Act, two copies of each book and serial printed and published in Canada that is priced at less than $50—or one copy if the price is more than $50—must be deposited with the library. In addition to printed materials, sound recordings with a Canadian connection (Canadian content, composer, artists, conductor, etc.) and educational kits are also subject to the deposit provisions.

Along with the deposited material, a completed information form has to be submitted. These forms enable the National Library catalogers to ensure a complete and accurate entry for each title in *Canadiana*, the national bibliography available in your local library.

As well as works published in Canada, the library attempts to acquire one copy of all materials published abroad that are by Canadian authors or are about Canada.

In addition to collecting published materials, the Canadian Acquisitions Division and Legal Deposit Office maintains clipping files on Canadian authors. Newspaper clippings of reviews, book jackets and author information forms requested from publishers are maintained in vertical files. Access is normally restricted to researchers in the National Library and to authors, in accordance with the Privacy Act.

The National Library has a huge union catalog that lists some 15 million books in the social sciences and humanities that are available in about 300 libraries in the country. Similar union listings of social science and science periodicals are kept at the Canada Institute for Scientific and Technical Information in Ottawa.

While the National Library will answer questions directly from the public, it can often tell you which libraries in the country have the book you are looking for. You can then arrange with your own library for an interlibrary loan.

Among the many publications issued by the National Library's own publishing program, you may find especially useful *Research Collections in Canadian Libraries*.

## ARCHIVES

The National Archives of Canada in Ottawa are a virtual treasure trove of material—especially when you may have found gaps in other research sources. This institution is responsible for acquiring from any source all significant archival material of every kind, nature and description relating to all aspects of Canadian life and to the development of the country. It is also responsible for providing suitable research services and facilities to make this material available to the public.

The Archives Branch of the NAC is composed of the Manuscript Division, the Federal Archives Division, the Machine Readable Archives Division, the National Map Collection, the Picture Division, the National Photography Collection, and the National Film, Television and Sound Archives. Other branches include the Conservation and Technical Services Branch, which provides reproductions for the public of all materials held in the NAC.

The NAC is located at 395 Wellington St., Ottawa, ON K1A 0N3, in the same building that houses the National Library. For information about the archives, call (613) 995-5138.

At the provincial level, there are archives in the following places:

**Archives of the Great Canadian Plains**
*P.O. Box 6263, Station D*
*Calgary, AB T2P 2C8*
*(403) 233-1867*

**British Columbia Archives**
*655 Belleville St.*
*Victoria, BC V8V 1X4*
*(604) 387-5885*

**Manitoba Archives**
*200 Vaughan St.*
*Winnipeg, MB R3C 1T5*
*(204) 945-3971*

**New Brunswick Archives**
*P.O. Box 6000*
*Fredericton, NB E3B 5H1*
*(506) 453-2122*

**Newfoundland and Labrador Archives**
*Colonial Building*
*Military Rd.*
*St. John's, NF A1C 2C9*
*(709) 729-3065*

**Nova Scotia Archives**
*6016 Universtiy Ave.*
*Halifax, NS B3H 1W4*
*(902) 424-6060*

**Ontario Archives**
*77 Grenville St.*
*Toronto, ON M7A 1W4*
*(416) 965-4039*

**Prince Edward Island Archives**
*P.O. Box 1000*
*Charlottetown, PE C1A 7M4*
*(902) 368-4290*

**Québec Archives**
*1210 avenue du Séminaire, P.O. Box 10450*
*Ste-Foy PQ G1V 4N1*
*(418) 644-1069*
or
*1945 Rue Mullins*
*Montreal, PQ H3K 1N9*
*(514) 873-3064*

**Saskatchewan Archives**
*3303 Hillsdale St.*
*Regina, SK S4S 6W9*
*(306) 787-4066*

The Association of Canadian Archivists has published a *Directory of Canadian Records and Manuscript Repositories* that might also prove useful.

## DATABASES

While most of the major computer services are American based (and they do offer Canadian material), there are Canadian services available to the writer who has a computer and knows how to tap into the services available online.

You may want to refer to *COIN: A Directory of Computerized Information in Canada*, published by the Alberta Information Retrieval Association. Also useful is *Omni Online Database Directory*, by Mike Edelhart and Owen Davies, an American book published by Macmillan in 1983 and distributed in Canada by Maxwell Macmillan.

Among the many services available, you may find that Info Globe is quite useful for Canadian material in that it offers a list of articles and the full text of stories published in *The Globe and Mail* from November 14, 1977, to the present. For information on accessing the services of Info Globe by modem, there are toll-free lines: In Ontario the number is (800) 268-8043; elsewhere in Canada the number is (800) 268-9128. In the United States callers can use Info Globe's regular phone service at (416) 585-5250.

## GOVERNMENT PUBLICATIONS

The federal government through the Canadian Government Publishing Centre, a department of Supply and Services Canada, Ottawa, ON K1A 0S9, is responsible for the publication of thousands of pamphlets, books and other materials. The only complete catalog available is on microfiche. Printed catalogs are issued quarterly at $15.20 but only cover the previous three months.

To determine if there are government publications you would find useful for your own research, check with your librarian. Most libraries across the country subscribe to the microfiche service, and this will provide constantly updated lists of everything available, including free publications.

All of the provinces have publishing programs as well. The same advice applies inasmuch as each of the 10 provincial governments prepares catalogs in a different fashion and a library check will provide the information you need more quickly and at less expense.

One of the best sources of information in the country on an ongoing basis is Statistics Canada. This federal department (known familiarly as StatsCan) produces more than 400 publications annually in such fields as economics and demographics. As a result, StatsCan interprets and publishes information on Canada's social and economic life that can prove extremely useful to the work of the writer.

In addition to producing the population census, the department prepares a labor force survey that keeps track of the country's employment situation, the consumer price index revealing changes in prices over time, and many business and economic surveys providing details on the country's economy.

Most of the information is available through various publications and through CANSIM, the public computer system. Thus the writer is able to gain information on everything from the census to Canadian culture.

You will probably find StatsCan's *Market Research Handbook* a useful volume.

StatsCan also utilizes a geocartographic system that translates numbers into visual images such as maps and charts. Information is accessible toll-free through regional offices. Going from Atlantic to Pacific, here are the numbers to call—first if you live in the area, and second if you live outside the area and require information from that region:

### Atlantic Region serving Newfoundland and Labrador, New Brunswick, Nova Scotia and Prince Edward Island
*North American Life Centre*
*1770 Market St., 3rd Floor*
*Halifax, NS B3J 3M3*
*(902) 426-5331*
*(800) 565-7192*

### British Columbia Region and Yukon
*Sinclair Centre, Suite 300*
*757 Hastings St.*
*Vancouver, BC V6C 3C9*
*(604) 666-3691*
*In British Columbia: (800) 663-1551*
*In Yukon: Zenith 08913*

### Manitoba Region
*MacDonald Building, Suite 300*
*344 Edmonton St.*
*Winnipeg, MB R3B 3L9*
*(204) 983-4020*
*(800) 661-7828*

### National Capital Region
*R.H. Coats Building Lobby*
*Tunney's Pasture*
*Ottawa, ON K1A 0T6*
*(613) 951-8116*
*(800) 263-1136*

### Northern Alberta Region and Northwest Territories
*Park Square, 9th Floor*
*10001 Bellamy Hill*
*Edmonton, AB T5J 3B6*
*(403) 495-3027*
*In Alberta: (800) 563-7828*
*In Northwest Territories, call collect: (403) 495-3028*

### Ontario Region (except National Capital Region)
*Arthur Meighen Building, 10th Floor*
*25 St. Clair Ave. E*
*Toronto, ON M4T 1M4*
*(416) 973-6586*
*(800) 263-1136*

### Quebec Region (except the National Capital Region)
*Complexe Guy Favreau, Tour est, bureau 412*
*200 boulevard René Lévesque ouest*
*Montreal, PQ H2Z 1X4*
*(514) 283-5725*
*(800) 361-2831*

### Southern Alberta Region
*First St. Plaza, Room 401*
*138 Fourth Ave. SE*
*Calgary, AB T2G 4Z6*
*(403) 292-6717*
*(800) 882-5616*

The major publication available from Statistics Canada is *The Canada Year Book*, a standard reference for more than 120 years. It is available at most bookstores. It can be ordered by mail for $59.95 (shipping, handling and taxes included) going to Canadian addresses. For orders to the United States and other countries, the price is $72 in U.S. funds; this price includes shipping and handling costs. Checks or money orders should be made payable to the Receiver General of Canada and should be mailed to Publications Sales, Statistics Canada, Ottawa, ON K1A 0T6.

## PERMISSIONS AND COPYRIGHT

Getting permission to quote from other writers is, as you read earlier, "a mysterious and muddied area"—that quoted phrase is permissible under the "Fair Use" provisions of the U.S. Copyright Law. In Canada, however, while quoting those few words is also permissible under the equivalent section of the *Copyright Act*, there is less flexibility in the Canadian law regarding the use of other people's words than there is in the U.S. statute.

The pertinent section of the Canadian law that governs the use of material whose copyright is owned by another writer is called "Fair Dealing." The two concepts—Fair Use and Fair Dealing—are vastly different. The Canadian law provides that it is not an infringement of copyright "to deal fairly" with any work provided that use is for one of five enumerated purposes: private study, research, criticism, review or newspaper summary. In contrast to the American law, in the Canadian statute, fair dealing is not an exception under which a user obtains an advance statutory authorization to do things that are exclusively the right of the copyright owner.

When the Canadian Parliament worked through the 1980s on major revisions to the *Copyright Act*, which had been in place since 1924, almost everyone testifying before the government committee studying the problems of copyright agreed that the Fair Dealing section of the 1924 Act had worked well. No change was made. Meanwhile, says Nancy Fleming of the Canadian Copyright Institute, "work continues to revise the old act. Some revisions, with the major impact on the music industry, were introduced in April, 1996. Revisions embodying important changes for writers are due, but there is no clue as to when they will be debated."

Canada has for decades been a signatory to the Berne Convention, which provides copyright protection to the works of Canadian writers in the international field. This explains why for so many years—despite U.S. adherence to the Universal Copyright Convention under which the copyright notice embodied the © symbol—publishers in the United States arranged to have their books "published simultaneously" by a Canadian publisher. Now that the United States has signed the Berne agreements, this protective move is no longer necessary.

One important point that creative artists in the United States gain in having the country belong to the Berne group is that the writer's "moral rights" are protected. This means that no user of copyrighted material can make substantive changes in the original without receiving the copyright holder's permission. An intriguing court case in Canada some years back involved a sculptor who created a flock of Canada geese in flight.

These carved birds were suspended from the top of the atrium in a major shopping mall. At Christmas the following year, the proprietors of the mall decided to "deck" the birds with winter scarves. The sculptor sued, claiming violation of his moral rights. He won the case.

The moral rights clause protects a novelist's work, for example, from being mutilated in a movie, TV or stage adaptation—unless the writer permits the revised version.

In Canada, authors and their heirs have always retained copyright for life plus 50 years—a term introduced into the U.S. law in the late 1970s. Under Canadian law, writers and other artists possess an automatic copyright whether the work is published or not. Canadian copyright law does not require writers to register copyright, only to provide proof that they are owners of the work.

To register copyright in Canada, ask for the appropriate forms from the Canadian Copyright Office, Bureau of Intellectual Property, Industry Canada, Ottawa, ON K1A 0E1.

## TRADEMARKS

Trademarks are not ordinary words. They are proper names that identify products of a business and distinguish them from products of other similar businesses. The life of legal protection for trademarks varies from country to country. That means that a trademark can lose its protection in one country but not in its neighbor.

A classic example is the trademark registered by the Bayer pharmaceutical company of Germany. They marketed pills composed of acetylsalicylic acid under the trademarked name, Aspirin. Eventually, after World War I, other pharmaceutical companies in the United States began to use the name, and the German company was not given adequate protection against the trademark violation. The name came to be used generically so that now in the United States anyone can market aspirin (without the capital A). In Canada, however, the trademark was zealously protected so that only the Bayer brand is Aspirin (with the capital A), and other drug companies market the product as ASA (the acronym for the drug's chemical name).

The list of trademarks still protected is a mile long. It includes words used casually in everyday language—Vaseline, Jell-O, Deepfreeze, Band-Aid, Jeep, Dictaphone, Mixmaster—and so many more that it boggles the mind. As a writer, you should be as careful with a corporation's trademark as you would want them to be with your copyright. Many of the trademark words are identified in dictionaries—so if you want to be sure not to violate another person's property, the least you can do is spell the trademark word with an initial capital letter.

For specific information on trademarks that are registered in Canada, the Canadian government publishes a weekly periodical, *Trade Marks Journal*, that you might find of interest.

## INFORMATION ACCESS

The *Access to Information Act* has been in operation in Canada since July 1983. It allows Canadians to peruse federal documents—with certain exceptions. The exceptions are intended to provide protection for particular kinds of information, the release of which would cause "an identifiable harm" or would be contrary to the law. These exemptions protect, for example, information about national security or trade secrets. Also excluded is material directly connected with the operation of the federal Cabinet—such as Cabinet documents and minutes or records of decision. The act cannot give you access to records that are outside the control of the federal government, such as records maintained by provincial or municipal governments, or by private institutions such as banks or credit bureaus.

To get access to the records you want, you need to refer to a copy of the *Access Register*, which is available in public libraries and government information offices in major population centers as well as in some 2,000 postal stations in rural areas. You will also need to get an Access Request Form at the same location.

The *Register* and Request Form contain detailed instructions on how to identify, as far as possible, the information you are looking for, how to get assistance—if necessary—and how to apply for access. If you are not able to consult an *Access Register* or fill out a form, you may write directly to the appropriate government institution, clearly stating that you are requesting information under the *Access to Information Act*.

If you want to make personal contact with the Access Coordinator in the government institution involved, you will find the name, address and telephone number of all the coordinators in the *Access Register*. The coordinator will assist you to identify the records you wish to see, at no charge. If you ask for assistance by letter, include as much information as you can to identify the records you are looking for, and be sure you provide sufficient information to enable an official to send you a reply.

There is an application fee of $5 that must be submitted with your request. You also have to pay for time in excess of five hours spent in processing your request, as well as for copying and computer processing time. If the costs are considerable, you will be notified before they are incurred, and you may be asked to make a deposit.

The government institution has 30 days to respond to your request. If the request is for a large number of records, or is complicated, the institution can extend the time limit, but it must inform you that it has done so.

If you are not satisfied with the material you get, the government has established the Office of the Information Commissioner, which will deal with your complaint. You have the right to complain to the commissioner if you believe you were wrongly denied access to information or if the response took too long or cost too much. If, after complaining to the Information Commissioner, you are still unable to get access to the information, you may then take the case to the Federal Court.

You should be aware of the fact that the *Access to Information Act* prohibits disclosure of records that contain personal information unless the person to whom it relates has consented to disclosure, or the information is already publicly available, or the disclosure is in accordance with conditions set out in the *Privacy Act*.

## RESOURCES

*OUT-OF-PRINT/RARE BOOKS*

If you can't find an antiquarian bookstore in your area, write to the Antiquarian Booksellers Association of Canada, % D&E Lake Ltd., 239 King St. E, Toronto, ON M5A 1J9, for assistance. But you should first check to see if your library has a copy of the *Canadian Antiquarian Book Sellers Directory* published by Brandon University Press. You will also find local listings in the yellow pages under Book Dealers—Used and Rare. There are also a number of book search operators who track down out-of-print titles. You will usually find small ads for such dealers in many of the book-related periodicals mentioned later in the "Selling It" section.

# PRODUCING AND POLISHING IT

If you are looking for an editor to help you with the final polish on your manuscript, you may want to contact the Editors' Association of Canada at 35 Spadina Rd., Toronto, ON M5R 2T1. They can be reached by phone at (416) 366-1379. Services from this organization of professional editors include a referral hotline, which consists of members who are available to read your work, offer editorial services and give assistance in rewriting manuscripts.

You may also find editors who advertise in the classified sections of the trade magazines listed later. Some literary agents will provide a reading service, but understand that this does not commit the agent to represent you.

The Writers' Union of Canada (24 Ryerson Ave., Toronto, ON M5T 2P3) has established a manuscript evaluation operation to provide a reliable resource for writers seeking assistance with their manuscripts. As with many such services, the Union *does not* guarantee publication, but it will provide a detailed typewritten or computer-generated evaluation for a distinctly reasonable price. Note: This is not an editing service, and therefore a manuscript may be returned without corrections or marginal editorial comments.

The report consists of comments on content (including but not necessarily limited to characterization, dialogue, setting, believability and research); writing technique (including but not necessarily limited to technical ability and style); suggested steps to develop the manuscript; and responses to three specific questions submitted by the author.

Writers who wish to avail themselves of this unique plan are required to do so in the following manner:

1. Submissions must be typewritten or computer generated, double-spaced, using 10- or 12-point type and one-inch margins. Handwritten submissions will not be accepted.

2. An appropriate copyright notice must be placed on the title page.

3. An addressed return envelope of the appropriate size and carrying the correct postage must be included.

4. A check or money order made out to The Writers' Union of Canada must be included. If the submission is a "partial" manuscript of 10 pages or fewer, the fee is $125 plus 7% Goods and Services Tax (GST) for a total of $133.75. If it is a "full" manuscript, the fee is $125 for the first 10 pages and $2 a page thereafter, plus a payment of 7% GST on the total price. For example: The fee for a 200-page manuscript is $125 + $380 (190 pages × $2) + $35.35 (7% of $505) = $540.35.

Request an application form by mail, or phone (416) 703-8982 (Monday to Thursday only). The Union's fax number is (416) 703-0826, and the e-mail address is *twuc@the-wire.com.*

## TRANSLATORS

If you are looking for someone to do a translation of your work, or are yourself a translator looking for employment, contact the Literary Translators Association at 3492 Laval St., Montreal, PQ H2X 3C9, or 214 Clinton St., Toronto, ON M6G 2Y5.

## INDEXING

To market your skills as an indexer, you should contact the Indexing and Abstracting Society of Canada at P.O. Box 744, Station F, Toronto, ON M4Y 2N6 about membership requirements.

## COLLABORATION

One of the most important aspects of making a collaboration agreement in Canada is that of credit—on the title page. Because of the Public Lending Right (PLR) program and the Copyright Licensing Agency (Can-Copy), referred to earlier, writers who are "credited" formally for a work are entitled to income from the use of their books in libraries and for use by photocopying.

## GRAMMAR SERVICES

Are you the type for *who* the bell tolls? Then maybe a grammar hotline is what you need.

While some 60 hotlines are currently available in North America for the writer seeking an answer to a grammatical problem, only two are in Canada. But long-distance tolls may be less expensive to a hotline south of the border than to one of the Canadian services, so you may want to consider getting your help from one of the U.S. operations.

*The Canadian Writer's Guide*, listed in the "Selling It" section, names more than 30 hotlines in the United States that might be geographically less expensive. Or you can send a self-addressed stamped envelope (#10) to Grammar Hotline Directory, Tidewater Community College Writing Center, 1700 College Crescent, Virginia Beach, VA 23456, to receive a copy of their latest directory.

Remember to use a U.S. postage stamp on your return envelope (postage to Canada was $.40 at this writing) or get an International Reply Coupon from your local post office.

### CANADIAN GRAMMAR HOTLINE

**Grant MacEwan Community College**
*Edmonton, AB T5J 4S2*
*(403) 497-5663*

This service is conducted by Karl Homann. The phones are staffed Monday to Friday, from 9 A.M. to 11 A.M. and from 1 P.M. to 3 P.M., Mountain Time.

The states closest to the Canadian border with grammar services are California, Colorado, Kansas, Missouri, Wisconsin, Illinois, Indiana, Michigan, Ohio, Pennsylvania, New York and Massachusetts.

## ARTISTS AND PHOTOGRAPHERS

The prime published source of illustrators and photographers listed in Canada is *Creative Source* published by Wilcord Publications Limited, 194 Merton St., Suite 300, Toronto, ON M4F 1A1. Wilcord can be reached by telephone in Montreal at (514) 849-5812 and in Toronto at (416) 487-7414. The book is distributed in Canada by Firefly Books. Distribution in the United States is handled by Watson Guptill.

The big, oversize volume lists hundreds of illustrators and photographers from coast to coast, shows samples of their work and indicates in which of 16 styles they create—from abstract to technical.

Another source of photographers is the *Canadian Directory of Professional Photography*, an annual published by The Professional Photographers of Canada and distributed by Craig and Associates at 399 Berry St., Suite 17, Winnipeg, MB R3J 1N6. Their phone number is (204) 885-7798.

In addition, the Professional Photographers of Canada Inc., at P.O. Box 337, Gatineau, PQ S8P 6J3, is the parent body of four provincial member associations. The PPC can be reached by phone at (819) 643-5177. The member associations are:

*Alberta Professional Photographers Association*
*16136 - 110B Ave.*
*Edmonton, AB T5P 4E6*
*(403) 483-4275*

*Professional Photographers Association of B.C.*
*1215 Penticton Ave.*
*Penticton, BC V2A 2N3*
*(605) 492-0202*

*Professional Photographers of Ontario Inc.*
*RR 4*
*Kempville, ON K0G 1J0*
*(613) 258-5432*

*La Corporation des maîtres photographs du Québec Inc.*
*645 rte Marie-Victorin*
*Tracy, PQ J3R 1K9*
*(514) 743-7385*

## SELF-PUBLISHING

Since the advent of desktop publishing, more and more Canadian authors are turning to self-publishing—often without an awareness of the problems they have set up for themselves *after* their books are printed and delivered. Of course, there are success stories that one can point to, but inevitably the authors have outgoing personalities and can *sell* those books just as capably—or even more—as they were able to write them. If you are prepared to make the effort to sell your books, here are a few of the elements of getting them into the marketplace that you should know.

Once you have finished books, you have to establish a marketing plan, including self-promotion. You have to be able to get around to bookstores in as far-reaching an area as possible, and you have to beat the drums with radio and TV talk shows (principally at the local level) and try to get yourself interviewed by the print and electronic media.

If the book "takes off," there is always the possibility that a trade publisher will contact you and seek to undertake commercial publication. That will mean broader distribution but, of course, smaller profits. Getting royalties, on a per-book basis, is never as much as getting all the profits—but that's a decision you have to make for yourself.

The first step you take after having written the book, and having it edited, copyedited, set into type and then proofread (even if you did the typesetting yourself with a desktop facility), is to find a printer and, possibly, a binder if the printing house you use doesn't do binding.

*The Book Trade in Canada*, mentioned later in "Word Markets," lists all kinds of services in this area. Having made your deal, you'll want to find sales representatives and/or wholesalers who might be interested in trying to get your book into bookstores. You will find a listing of both in *Canadian Publishers Directory*, published semiannually by *Quill & Quire*. This directory is not likely to be found on the shelves of your local library, but check at the reference desk. Most libraries subscribe to the journal and get the *Directory* free with their subscription.

You will probably want to carry an ISBN (that is, an International Standard Book Number) in your book. To get ISBN information, write to the Canadian ISBN Agency at the National Library of Canada, 395 Wellington St., Ottawa, ON K1A 0N4, or telephone them at (819) 994-6872.

If you intend to approach bookstores to carry your book, you'll want to consult the list available in *The Book Trade in Canada*. They are arranged by province to ease your task.

There are three useful handbooks that give the Canadian angle to self-publishing:

1. *The Canadian Self-Publishing Handbook* was written by Laura M. Gateman (Spinning Wheel Publishing). If your bookstore is unable to get

a copy for you, write the publisher (a self-publishing operation) at RR 1, Chesley, ON N0G 1L0.

2. Marion Crook and Nancy Wise are the authors of *How to Self Publish and Make Money.* It was published by Sandill Book Publishing in Kelowna, British Columbia.

3. *Publish It Yourself: A Writer's Guide to Self-Publishing* was written by G. Randolph Hemingway and is published by Tyro Publishing at 194 Carlbert St., Sault Ste. Marie, ON P6A 5B1.

A Canadian supplement is now available for *The Self-Publishing Manual,* by Dan Poynter, a book that has gone through eight revisions in the 17 years since it first appeared. The supplement, called *Canadian Book Publishing,* was published early in 1996 and is available by fax or via the World Wide Web. It is eight pages that contain the names, numbers and resources for ISBN, copyright, Legal Deposit, bar coding, distributors, associations, magazines and much more.

To get it by fax, Para Publishing in Santa Barbara, California, has set up a fax-on-demand operation. To utilize the f-o-d system, call (805) 968-8947 using the handset of your fax machine. Follow the voice prompts and request Document 628. When you push the start button at the appropriate prompt, the document will immediately be transmitted to you. The first page will be an invoice for $9.95, which you pay by mail.

To retrieve the document from Para Publishing's Web site, log on to http://www.ParaPublishing.com./books/para/305. The document to order is Instant Report 628.

Both services are available 24 hours a day.

There is also available a useful overview of what goes on in the process: *Signposts: A Guide to Self-Publishing,* a 14-page pamphlet that has been issued by the Book and Periodical Council, 35 Spadina Rd., Toronto, ON M5R 2S9. It is available at no charge. The Council can be reached by phone at (416) 975-9333 or by fax at (416) 975-1839.

## ADDITIONAL RESOURCES

(Prices quoted may change, but include postage, handling and GST unless otherwise specified.)

### *From The Canadian Children's Book Centre:*
*35 Spadina Ave.*
*Toronto, ON M5R 2S9*

*Writing for Children Kit*
$20.00

**From The League of Canadian Poets:**
*54 Wolseley St., 3rd Floor*
*Toronto, ON M5T 1A5*

*Poetry Markets for Canadians*
$13.70

*Poets in the Classroom*
$15.85

**From Periodical Writers Association of Canada:**
*54 Wolseley St., 2nd Floor*
*Toronto, ON M5T 1A5*

*Who Owns What*
A basic primer on copyright. $4.17

*Words For Sale*
A how-to book on "breaking in" to the Canadian market. $18.50

*The Write Way*
A discussion of problems writers have with editors. $8.00

*Who Pays What: A Writer's Guide to Canadian Markets*
Editorial requirements and fee schedules for more than 400 Canadian
  periodicals. $18.50

From Saskatchewan Writers Guild:

**P.O. Box 3986**
**Regina, SK S4P 3R9**

*Saskatchewan Literary Arts Handbook*
Useful for Canadian writers from coast to coast. $15
*From Seniors Secretariat:*

Health and Welfare Canada
Ottawa, ON K1A 0K9

*Seniors' Guide to Federal Programs and Services*
A wealth of information for the writer covering the seniors' scene. Free.

**From The Writer's Union of Canada:**
*24 Ryerson Ave.*
*Toronto, ON M5T 2P3*

*Anthology Rates and Contracts*
Discusses contributions and rates and offers a suggested contract. $6

*Author and Editor*
Describes the author-editor relationship, with a list of dos and don'ts. $6

*Author and Literary Agent*
Guidelines concerning the author-agent relationship and a list of Canadian
  agents. $3

*Authors and Archives*
A guide to marketing your archival material. $2

*Authors' Wills*
Why and how writers' wills are different. $2

*Awards, Competitions and Prizes*
A descriptive list of what's available to Canadian writers. $7

*Ghost Writing*
Details to consider and a sample contract. $6

*Help Yourself to a Better Contract*
A checklist of favorable book-contract provisions. $7

*Income Tax Guide for Writers*
The most recent changes in tax law are explored. $6

*Libel: A Handbook for Canadian Publishers, Editors and Writers.* $6

*Model Trade Book Contract*
A list of reasonable minimum terms and a model royalty statement. $4

*Writers' Guide to Canadian Publishers*
A comprehensive list and details on how to seek the right publisher. $7

*Writer's Guide to Electronic Publishing Rights*
How to negotiate electronic rights' contracts. $7

# SELLING IT

## NEWSPAPERS

There are several sources listing newspapers in Canada. All the reference volumes group the newspapers by province, but they vary in what
information they give. Some give only addresses. Others list the names
of specific editors, as well as mailing addresses, telephone numbers and,
more often than not, fax numbers.

Canada's largest newspaper is *The Toronto Star*. It publishes seven
days a week and offers many special sections, especially in the Saturday
or Sunday edition. There are, for example, sections dedicated to home
and gardening, cars, entertainment, travel, sports, business, careers, lifestyles, insights, people and fashion. Each of these sections is open to

material from freelance writers, according to John Honderich, publisher of the *Star*.

*The Globe and Mail* (also published out of Toronto) calls itself "Canada's National Newspaper" and is printed in various cities across the country by satellite transmission every day except Sunday. As a national newspaper, it specifically stresses the business scene and carries a daily section called "Report on Business" that occasionally uses non-staff-written material.

*The Globe and Mail* also publishes a monthly slick magazine called *Report on Business* and has dabbled in other monthlies from time to time that buy material from freelance writers.

The daily edition is also a market for the freelance writer and has a wider scope of interests in that it has several "opinion" pages that frequently take contributions from freelance writers. The Saturday edition is a larger offering with special sections on travel, sports, entertainment and, of course, business.

*The Globe* has just produced a new stylebook, which might prove useful for the writer seeking to sell to that market. It is available for $22.95 (Canadian orders must add $1.60 for Goods and Services Tax). Orders should be sent to Style Book Sales, Marketing Department, 444 Front St. W, Toronto, ON M5V 2S9.

The daily newspapers in Ottawa (the nation's capital), Halifax, Montreal, Winnipeg, Regina, Saskatoon, Calgary, Edmonton, Vancouver and Victoria, serving, as they do, the larger population centers of the country, are also potential freelance markets.

In many respects, the travel article seems to have the broadest appeal—the subject matter can be most eclectic as well as having the widest possibility of serving more than one market. Two national business papers also provide opportunities for the freelance writer. *The Financial Post* publishes daily and has a weekly edition, while the *Financial Times* is published weekly.

## NEWSPAPER LISTINGS

### CARD
*(Canadian Advertising Rates and Data)*
*Maclean Hunter Publications*
*777 Bay St.*
*Toronto, ON M5W 1A7*

Because this monthly is used widely by advertising agencies, there probably isn't a single newspaper or periodical in the country that isn't listed—and they make sure they keep getting listed by returning corrected proof copy of their listing *every month!* That makes *CARD* a very useful publication for the freelance writer to have access to. Your library more than likely subscribes—it costs $495 a year, or $225 for a single issue if you're thinking of buying one for your own reference shelf. It carries lists of business publications, community newspapers, dailies, ethnic newspapers and periodicals, farm periodicals, religious magazines and newspapers, scholarly journals, "shoppers" (the giveaway weeklies that are loaded with advertising but do carry editorial material), weekend newspapers (there are only two English-language ones in Canada) and even university and school papers. Radio and television stations are, of course, listed—and so are the advertising agencies with listings of their personnel. The addresses are complete—and very up to date, considering that they are checked each month.

### *Canadian Almanac & Directory Publishing Co., Ltd.*
*55 St. Clair Ave.*
*Toronto, ON M4V 2Y7*

This old standby has been around 150 years (the first edition was published in 1847), and it improves with age. Each year, dozens of new features are added. While earlier editions carried slim listings of newspapers and periodicals, under its new management the *Almanac* has a very comprehensive listing in this area—as well as in most other areas that a writer who wants to do as much of his research in one place as possible can find. It's available in most, if not all, libraries, but many writers find it a useful volume to keep on their own shelves. For writers with access to the Internet, this reference volume also lists e-mail addresses. The regular price is $209.45, which includes GST and shipping and handling.

### *The Corpus Almanac and Canadian Sourcebook*
*Corpus Information Services*
*Southam Communications Limited*
*1450 Don Mills Rd.*
*Don Mills, ON M3B 2X7*

This directory is also available in most libraries. Its listings are sometimes more comprehensive than those of its older rival, sometimes less. If you intend to buy one or the other, we suggest you first review both directories in your library to determine which will provide you with the kind of information you need. All the newspaper listings are of publications that are issued minimally once a month and consist only of address, phone and fax numbers. The ethnic press listings range across some 41 languages, from Arabic to Vietnamese, and cover the black and native communities as well. The weeklies listed in this volume include only a few of the "alternative" newspapers published in the country. It sells for $186.18, tax and shipping included.

### Matthew's List
*Canadian Corporate News*
*One Financial Place, Suite 500*
*25 Adelaide St.*
*Toronto, ON M5C 3A1*

The basic Matthew's service, *Media*, provides names, contact information and program producers of Canadian radio and television stations and all departmental editors of newspapers. This volume is issued three times a year and is available for a subscription price of $195 (shipping and taxes included). A new service called *CCE* provides the names of editors of community newspapers, consumer magazines and the ethnic press. Subscription to this service is $115 annually. A second new service, *CATV*, covers the cable TV industry in Canada and is available for $115 a year. All three reference books are found in most libraries.

A selected list of Canadian dailies:

### Calgary Herald
*215 Sixteenth St. SE*
*Calgary, AB T2P 0W8*

### Chronicle-Herald
*1650 Argyle St.*
*Halifax, NS B3J 2T2*

### Daily Gleaner
*P.O. Box 3370*
*Fredricton, NS E3B 5A2*

### Edmonton Journal
*10016 101st St.*
*Edmonton, AB T5J 2S6*

### The Gazette
*250 St-Antoine St. W*
*Montreal, PQ H2Y 3R7*

### The Globe and Mail
*444 Front St. W*
*Toronto, ON M5V 2S9*

### Guardian & Patriot
*165 Prince St.*
*Charlottetown, PE C1A 4R7*

**The Hamilton Spectator**
*44 Frid St.*
*Hamilton, ON L8N 3G3*

**The Leader-Post**
*1964 Park St.*
*Regina, SK S4P 3G4*

**The London Free Press**
*369 York St.*
*London, ON N6A 4G1*

**The Ottawa Citizen**
*1101 Baxter Rd.*
*Ottawa, ON K2C 3M4*

**The Star-Phoenix**
*240 Fifth Ave. N*
*Saskatoon, SK S7K 2P1*

**Telegram**
*Columbus Dr.*
*St. John's, NF A1C 5X7*

**Telegraph-Journal**
*210 Crown St.*
*Saint John, NB E2L 3V8*

**The Toronto Star**
*One Yonge St.*
*Toronto, ON M5E 1E6*

**The Vancouver Sun/Province**
*2250 Granville St.*
*Vancouver, BC V6H 3G2*

**The Victoria Times-Colonist**
*2621 Douglas St.*
*Victoria, BC V8T 4M2*

**Winnipeg Free Press**
*1355 Mountain Ave.*
*Winnipeg, MB R2X 3B6*

Among the alternative press offerings is one national paper, *The Independent*, which is interested in news and opinion from all parts of the country. It is published from 15 King St., Elmira, ON N3B 2R1.

Other alternative newspapers exist mainly in Montreal (*Hour* and *The Mirror*) and Toronto (*Eye* and *NOW*), but their contents are very local in interest and seem to stress the entertainment scene in the main. Most of the major Canadian cities, however, have alternative newspapers that come and go—and they, again, tend to be extremely local in their outlook, with an entertainment bent.

There are no longer any weekly magazine sections in the newspapers of the country. However, some of the dailies do occasionally produce a "magazine" section, depending, it seems, on the economy and whether advertising dollars can be found to support such efforts. One of the more recent magazines to close shop had been included with the Saturday edition of *The Toronto Star*. In its place, the Saturday Entertainment section has been enlarged.

Perhaps the best nonfiction markets in Canada are the community newspapers—usually weeklies—that abound from coast to coast. The *Corpus Almanac*, referred to above, lists about 1,000 such papers. And there are more than 150 ethnic newspapers, which may also provide opportunites.

The editor of one such weekly, Christine Endicott, an active freelancer herself, suggests that these weeklies are possibly the most accessible to the freelancer. Writing in *Canadian Author*, Endicott offers good advice about breaking into this market. "The rules of selling to community newspapers are different from those of selling to magazines," she says. Queries accompanied by stamped, addressed reply envelopes are a waste of time and money. The editors have little time to read them or to write replies. A phone call—or a visit—to the editor is best. But, she says, check first as to when the paper goes to press and avoid calling on that busy day—unless you have a page one story!

A careful analysis of a paper over several issues will disclose areas in which its regular coverage may be weak. Concentrate on those. And *always* discuss payment lest the editor assume you are not expecting to be paid.

The *Corpus* listing gives the name of the editor or publisher and phone number.

## SYNDICATES

Syndication in Canada is not a major source of income for the freelance writer looking for new markets. There is only one major syndicate, affiliated with *The Toronto Star*. It is not interested in seeing material over the transom. The second largest syndicate, run by the Southam newspaper chain, is more likely to take a look at ideas from freelance writers.

The others may be worth approaching. Being smaller, they are usually open to the possibility of coming up with the next world-beater.

A great source for the freelance writer is the *Annual Directory of Syndicated Services*, published by *Editor & Publisher* at 11 W. 19th St., New York, NY 10011. This annual not only lists all the U.S. syndicates but also lists a few in the United Kingdom and elsewhere in the world.

*CANADIAN SYNDICATES*

**Canada Wide Feature Service Limited**
*P.O. Box 345, Station A*
*Toronto, ON M5W 1C2*

**Insight News & Features**
*804 - 10 Huntley St.*
*Toronto, ON M4Y 2K7*

**Miller Features Syndicate, Inc.**
*1100 - 180 Bloor St. W*
*Toronto, ON M5S 2V6*

**Southam Syndicate**
*20 York Mills Rd.*
*North York, ON M2P 2C2*

**Toronto Star Syndicate**
*One Front St.*
*Toronto, ON M5E 1E6*

## TELEVISION

With cutbacks in government assistance to the arts continuing unabated, and the economy generally in a tight situation, the high cost of production—especially in the field of television—means that every project is being gone over with the proverbial fine-toothed comb. Nonetheless, new work continues to be produced, and writers continue to find markets—if they are persistent and have something unique to offer.

The Canadian Broadcasting Corporation, the country's largest network in both mediums, has suffered huge budgetary—and staff—cutbacks, but it continues to consider outstanding ideas, particularly in the one-hour and 90-minute TV categories. Global Television Network is prepared to support productions that have been initiated independently—particularly shows with series potential.

Other TV possibilities include the independent CTV network, through its flag station CFTO-TV, as well as CFMT-TV, which may consider short freelance contributions, and CITY-TV, which is prepared to look at series concepts (5 to 20 episodes) and feature-length films.

Another possibility is the education network, TV Ontario, which does programming in various areas such as children's, educational, part-time learning and adult.

*CARD* carries listings for all the networks, regular and cable, as well as all the TV stations in the country.

## *LISTINGS*

### CBC Television Script Services
*P.O. Box 500, Station A*
*Toronto, ON M5W 1E6*

### CFMT-TV
*545 Lakeshore Blvd.*
*Toronto, ON M5V 1A3*

### CFTO-TV Project Development Department
*P.O. Box 9*
*Scarborough, ON M4A 2M9*

### CITY-TV
*99 Queen St. E*
*Toronto, ON M5C 2M1*

### Global Television Network Project Development Department
*81 Barber Greene Rd.*
*Don Mills, ON M3C 2A2*

### TV Ontario
*2180 Yonge St.*
*P.O. Box 200, Station Q*
*Toronto, ON M4T 2T1*

Cable television continues to provide new markets as more services are approved. The most recent include such specialty services as Vision TV, Bravo!, the Discovery Channel, The Sports Network (TSN) and Youth

Television (YTV). It has been estimated that more than 75% of Canadian homes receive cable service, and there are close to 2,000 systems providing such services across the country.

A quick check of the programming on your local cable channel will give you a fair idea of the kind of material your cable distributor might be interested in pursuing. You can get the cable company's address in your local telephone book, and the switchboard operator can probably tell you who's in charge of programming.

## FILMMAKING

The National Film Board of Canada (NFB) was founded in 1939 to produce, promote and distribute films in the national interest. NFB provides assistance to and works with independent filmmakers, encouraging innovative themes or approaches to filmmaking. About 100 original films are produced annually, and more than 4,000 have been produced since the board's inception. NFB has maintained a high profile at international film festivals and has won almost 2,000 awards, including many Oscars.

In recent years, the board has placed increased emphasis on research and development into film and video technology and has established training programs for young filmmakers. They operate a cross-Canada film library service and produce film catalogs.

Operational headquarters of the board is in Montreal, and the mailing address is P.O. Box 6100, Station A, Montreal, PQ H3C 3H5. For general inquiries, the phone number is (514) 283-9000. There are six regional centers and three offices abroad.

*REGIONAL CENTERS*

*5475 Spring Garden Rd., 2nd Floor*
*Halifax, NS B3J 1G2*

*1564 rue St-Denis*
*Montreal, PQ H2X 3K2*

*150 John St.*
*Toronto, ON M5V 3C3*

*245 Main St.*
*Winnipeg, MB R3C 1A7*

*9700 Jasper Ave., #120*
*Edmonton, AB T5J 4C3*

*1045 Howe St., #100*
*Vancouver, BC V6Z 2B1*

*OFFICES ABROAD*

> *1251 Avenue of the Americas, 16th Floor*
> *New York, NY 10020*
>
> *One Grosvenor Square*
> *London, England W1X 0AB*
>
> *15 rue de Berri*
> *Paris 75008 France*

## RADIO

There are some outlets for radio writing, even in the face of industry-wide cutbacks throughout the 1990s. Experienced writer-broadcasters of commentary continue to find markets for their work, as do writers of documentaries. Radio drama has special needs and Canadian Broadcasting Corporation, particularly, has a variety of programs that are always on the lookout for good radio drama. CBC Script Services at the ubiquitous CBC mailing address (P.O. Box 500, Station A, Toronto, ON M5W 1E6) will send guidelines for both radio and TV dramatic scripts. Address your queries for guidelines to Script Services; for contributions to variety programming, direct your inquiries to Radio Variety; and for radio plays, address the query to Radio Drama—all at the above address.

Aside from the listings in *CARD*, other radio markets include

> **CHFI-FM** *(which does occasional lifestyle features)*
> *25 Adelaide St. E, 12th Floor*
> *Toronto, ON M5C 1H3*
>
> **CJRT-FM** *(which welcomes ideas for "Open College")*
> *150 Mutual St.*
> *Toronto, ON M5B 2M1*

# WORD MARKETS

While there are many magazine markets in Canada (more than 1,250 in the latter half of this decade), the sad truth is that in the early part of the 1990s, more than 150 Canadian magazines disappeared and a majority of the rest have seen both circulation and revenues decline.

This doesn't mean to say that new periodicals aren't appearing on the newsstands—especially in the special interest markets. Some of the areas worth exploring are publications for retirees, for new mothers and for computer buffs. It should be added that these special interest magazines are growing both in circulation and revenues.

Corporate markets, unlike magazine markets, continue to thrive, and the freelance writer is well advised to investigate them as new sources for income.

The advice given earlier in this volume with regard to both the magazine and corporate markets is as pertinent to the Canadian market as it is for the United States market.

In the corporate field, the obvious sources of clients are listings in the telephone yellow pages. Looking under Associations, for example, leads to hundreds of organizations that use freelance writers from time to time. And a quick look through the yellow pages—if you've never done so before—will provide you with endless leads: from accountants to zoos, with hundreds of possibilities in between, including such categories as hospitals, advertising agencies, insurance companies, art galleries and photographers.

An excellent volume to check is *Sources* (4 Phipps St., Suite 109, Toronto, ON M4Y 1J5), in which hundreds of businesses as well as associations buy space to list their public relations contacts. The volume is used by the news media and magazines whenever they need a source to quote or have information to gather. But for the freelance writer, that same PR source can prove to be a useful contact to get leads on writing jobs that need to be done for the organization listed.

The Better Business Bureau in your city (or the largest city near you) probably publishes its own *Directory and Consumer Guide*, ranging from accommodations to wreckers. And the telephone company publishes an *800 Service Directory*, which lists companies and organizations across the country, ranging from abattoirs to yogurt manufacturers—and you can telephone any of them toll-free!

In addition, there are reference volumes in most libraries that will open your eyes to the possibilities that exist. A handful include *The Canadian Book of Corporate Management* (Dun & Bradstreet), *The Financial Post Directory of Directors* (Maclean Hunter), *Who's Who in Canadian Business* and *Who's Who in Canadian Finance* (both Trans-Canada Press) and five directories published by the federal department of Industry, Science and Technology—*Directory of Canadian Consulting Engineers*, *Directory of Canadian Trading Houses*, *Directory of Computer Software and Services*, *Directory of Architects* and *Directory of Management Consultants*.

*The Directory of Associations* (MicroMedia) and *The Blue Book of Canadian Business* (Canadian Newspaper Services International Ltd.) are great sources of leads for the writer interested in the lucrative corporate markets.

## BOOK REVIEWS AND EDITORIAL COPY

### *TRADE PUBLICATIONS*

The book trade in Canada is covered by a number of publications, one of them on the national level—*Quill & Quire*—and several on a regional basis. In addition, *Books In Canada*, while mainly a book review monthly, also carries news of the industry.

### *MAGAZINE AND NEWSPAPER BOOK REVIEWS*

There are a number of periodicals that regularly carry book reviews. While they are not specifically identified that way, the long list of periodicals (divided by category) carried in *The Canadian Writer's Guide* (Fitzhenry & Whiteside) is the most useful source of magazines that should be checked as possible users of items relating to books (and possibly even to reviews).

The newspapers referred to earlier in this section are probably the best bets to getting a book reviewed, though depending on the subject matter of your book, you may find many of the newspapers listed in *CARD, Matthew's*, the *Canadian Almanac* or the *Corpus Almanac* will entertain the possibility of reviewing books that fit their audiences. A query letter with a stamped, addressed return postcard will let you know quickly whether it is worth sending them material.

### *TELEVISION AND RADIO*

The one major national television news show in Canada that can have an impact on book sales is CTV's *Canada AM*. It does author interviews fairly frequently, and every publisher's publicity department undoubtedly tries to get each of its authors onto that early morning exposure slot. Also on television are a number of shows in various locales across the country, and if you are not aware of them, you should consult your local TV listings and check out the talk shows that welcome authors as guests.

On radio, CBC's *Morningside* with author/host Peter Gzowski is the one cross-country show that every publisher tries to sell to. But, in this medium there are many talk and phone-in shows on the local level that you should check out yourself—shows that most publishers' PR departments know about. By stressing the local angle, you might be able to interest the program in doing something on your book.

## BOOKSTORES AND DISTRIBUTION

Checking out local bookstores is a worthwhile activity. If you are not entirely aware of all the bookstores in your area, your library should have a copy of *The Book Trade in Canada*. It carries an extensive listing of bookstores across the country.

**The Book Trade in Canada**
*Ampersand Communications Inc.*
*5606 Scobie Crescent*
*Manotick, ON K4M 1B7*

This is the Canadian equivalent (in a small way) of *Literary Market Place* (LMP) in the United States. It is an annual, though publication has not been too regular—yet it does appear with updated material about every 12 to 16 months. If it isn't in your local library, it can be purchased by mail.

Other resources to help writers:

**The Canadian Writer's Guide**
*Fitzhenry & Whiteside*
*195 Allstate Parkway*
*Markham, ON L3R 4T8*

The "official handbook of the Canadian Authors Association," this guide currently consists of more than 100 chapters aimed at helping writers—both professional and emerging—in every possible way on just about every aspect of the writing game. It also has a large markets section that lists details of more than 1,000 magazines published in the country, as well as more than 300 book publishers and their needs. This section will be updated in a new edition slated for publication late in 1996 or in 1997. Like all guides of this kind, it suffers from the vagaries of the publishing business. Almost before it is off press, some publishers have gone out of business, others have changed philosophical direction and still others have moved.

**The Canadian Writer's Market**
*McClelland & Stewart*
*481 University Ave.*
*Toronto, ON M5G 2E9*

This slim volume is mainly a listing of periodical and book publishers. It attempts to give the names of the current editors, but, as with addresses and editorial directions, these change frequently, and you should double-check before sending material.

**Canadian Author**
*1225 Wonderland Rd. N, P.O. Box 8029*
*London, ON N6G 4X1*

This quarterly magazine, known for many years as *Canadian Author & Bookman,* was founded in 1919. In addition to carrying useful craft articles and author interviews (as well as fiction and poetry), it has a regular markets feature that updates the current scene in both the magazine and book fields in Canada. It also reviews books about writing and publishing.

## PUBLISHERS' ASSOCIATIONS

### Association of Book Publishers of British Columbia
*100 W. Pender St., #107*
*Vancouver, BC V6B 1R8*
*(604) 684-0228*

### Association of Canadian Publishers
*Two Gloucester St., #301*
*Toronto, ON M4Y 1L5*
*(416) 413-4929*
*Fax: (416) 413-4920*

### Association of Canadian University Presses
*University of Toronto Press*
*10 St. Mary St., #700*
*Toronto, ON M4Y 2W8*
*(416) 978-5850*

### Association of Manitoba Book Publishers
*100 Arthur St., #406*
*Winnipeg, MB R3B 1H3*
*(204) 947-3335*
*Fax: (204) 942-1555*

### Atlantic Publishers Association
*Lord Nelson Arcade, #202*
*5657 Spring Garden Rd.*
*Halifax, NS B3J 1H1*
*(902) 420-0711*
*Fax: (902) 423-4302*

### Book Publishers Association of Alberta
*10523 One-hundredth Ave., #123*
*Edmonton, AB T5J 0A8*
*(403) 424-5060*
*Fax: (403) 424-7943*

**Canadian Book Publishers' Council**
*250 Merton St., #203*
*Toronto, ON M4S 1B1*
*(416) 322-7011*
*Fax: (416) 322-6999*

**Christian Booksellers Association**
*670 Southgate Dr.*
*Guelph, ON N1G 4S2*
*(519) 766-1683*
*Fax: (519) 763-8184*

**Literary Press Group**
*Two Gloucester St., #301*
*Toronto, ON M4Y 1L5*
*(416) 413-4929*
*Fax: (416) 413-4920*

## TRADE PUBLICATIONS

The following publications carry prepublication reviews and are read by booksellers and librarians:

**Access**
*100 Lombard St., #303*
*Toronto, ON M5C 1M3*
*(416) 363-3388*
*In British Columbia: (800) 387-1181*
*Fax: (416) 941-9581*

**Books In Canada**
*603 - 130 Spadina Ave.*
*Toronto, ON M5V 2L4*
*(416) 601-9880*

**Canadian Author**
*1225 Wonderland Rd. N, P.O. Box 8029*
*London, ON N6G 4X1*

Reviews poetry books in its "Canadian Poetry" section and books on the craft or business of writing.

**Canadian Bookseller**
*Canadian Booksellers Association*
*301 Donlands Ave.*
*Toronto, ON M4J 3R8*

*(416) 467-7883*
*Fax: (416) 467-7886*

**Emergency Librarian**
*810 Broadway W., #284*
*Vancouver, BC V5Z 4C9*
*(604) 925-0266*
*Fax: (604) 925-0566*

**Quill & Quire**
*70 The Esplanade, 4th Floor*
*Toronto, ON M5E 1R2*
*(416) 360-0044*
*Fax: (416) 360-8745*

# Subject Index

# Associations, Organizations and Business Resources

# Books, Periodicals and Directories

# Databases, Online Resources and Vendors

# *More Great Books for Writers!*

**1997 Writer's Market: Where & How to Sell What You Write**—Get your work into the right buyers' hands and save yourself the frustration of getting manuscripts returned in the mail. You'll find 4,000 listings loaded with submission information, as well as real life interviews on scriptwriting, networking, freelancing and more! *#10457/$27.99/1008 pages*

> **Now Available on CD-ROM!**
>
> **1997 Writer's Market Electronic Edition**—Customize your marketing research and speed to the listings that fit your needs using this compact, searchable CD-ROM! *#10492/$39.99*
>
> **1997 Writer's Market Combination Package**—For maximum usability, order both the book and CD-ROM in one convenient package! *#45148/$49.99*

**Writing and Selling Your Novel**—Write publishable fiction from start to finish with expert advice from professional novelist Jack Bickham! You'll learn how to develop effective work habits, refine your fiction writing technique, and revise and tailor your novels for tightly targeted markets. *#10509/$17.99/208 pages*

**The 30-Minute Writer**—Write short, snappy articles that make editors sit up and take notice. Full-time freelancer Connie Emerson reveals the many types of quickly-written articles you can sell—from miniprofiles and one-pagers to personal essays. You'll also learn how to match your work to the market as you explore methods for expanding from short articles to columns, and even books! *#10489/$14.99/256 pages/paperback*

**Writer's Encyclopedia, Third Edition**—Rediscover this popular writer's reference—now with information about electronic resources, plus more than 100 new entries. You'll find facts, figures, definitions and examples designed to answer questions about every discipline connected with writing and help you convey a professional image. *#10464/$22.99/560 pages/62 b&w illus.*

**The Writer's Digest Dictionary of Concise Writing**—Make your work leaner, crisper and clearer! Under the guidance of professional editor Robert Hartwell Fiske, you'll learn how to rid your work of common say-nothing phrases while making it tighter and easier to read and understand. *#10482/$19.99/352 pages*

**The Writer's Legal Guide, Revised Edition**—Now the answer to all your legal questions is right at your fingertips! The updated version of this treasured desktop companion contains essential information on business issues, copyright protection and registration, contract negotiation, income taxation, electronic rights and much, much more. *#10478/$19.95/256 pages/paperback*

**How to Write Attention-Grabbing Query & Cover Letters**—Use the secrets Wood reveals to write queries perfectly tailored, too good to turn down! In this guidebook, you will discover why boldness beats blandness in queries every time, ten basics you *must* have in your article queries, ten query blunders that can destroy publication chances and much more. *#10462/$17.99/208 pages*

**1996 Guide to Literary Agents**—Find everything you need to know about choosing an agent! More than 400 listings of agents for literature, television and motion pictures are included. Plus you'll find valuable information on the agent-author relationship and answers to the most often asked questions. *#10443/$21.99/288 pages/paperback*

**Writing to Sell**—You'll discover high-quality writing and marketing counsel in this classic writing guide from well-known agent Scott Meredith. His timeless advice will guide you along the professional writing path as you get help with creating characters, plotting a novel, placing your work, formatting a manuscript, deciphering a publishing contract—even combating a slump! *#10476/$17.99/240 pages*

**Discovering the Writer Within: 40 Days to More Imaginative Writing**—Uncover the creative individual inside who will, with encouragement, turn secret thoughts and special moments into enduring words. You'll learn how to find something exciting in unremarkable places, write punchy first sentences for imaginary stories, give a voice to inanimate objects and much more! *#10472/$14.99/192 pages/paperback*

**The Writer's Digest Sourcebook for Building Believable Characters**—Create unforgettable characters as you "attend" a roundtable where six novelists reveal their approaches to characterization. You'll probe your characters' backgrounds, beliefs and desires with a fill-in-the-blanks questionnaire. And a thesaurus of characteristics will help you develop the many other features no character should be without. *#10463/$17.99/288 pages*

**The Writer's Ultimate Research Guide**—Save research time and frustration with the help of this guide. Three hundred fifty-two information-packed pages will point you straight to the information you need to create better, more accurate fiction and nonfiction. With hundreds of listings of books and databases, each entry reveals how current the information is, what the content and organization is like and much more! *#10447/$19.99/352 pages*

**How to Write Like an Expert About Anything**—Find out how to use new technology and traditional research methods to get the information you need, envision new markets and write proposals that sell, find and interview experts on any topic and much more! *#10449/$17.99/224 pages*

**How to Write Fast (While Writing Well)**—Discover what makes a story and what it takes to research and write one. Then, learn step by step how to cut wasted time and effort by planning interviews for maximum results, beating writer's block with effective plotting, getting the most information from traditional library research and online computer databases and much more! Plus, a complete chapter loaded with tricks and tips for faster writing. *#10473/$15.99/208 pages/paperback*

**Make Your Words Work**—Loaded with samples and laced with exercises, this guide will help you clean up your prose, refine your style, strengthen your descriptive powers, bring music to your words and much more! *#10399/$14.99/304 pages/paperback*

**The Writer's Digest Handbook of Magazine Article Writing**—This handbook is a valuable guide to every type of magazine article writing, featuring more than 35 chapters of writing and marketing instruction. Practical instructions are included to guide you through the development, proposal and manuscript preparation process. *#10171/$12.99/248 pages/paperback*

**Queries and Submissions**—Looking for proven strategies for writing attention-grabbing query letters? This guide has an abundance of ideas, covering topics from formatting and targeting letters to deciding when a query letter is unnecessary. *#10426/$15.99/176 pages*

**Freeing Your Creativity: A Writer's Guide**—Discover how to escape the traps that stifle your creativity. You'll tackle techniques for banishing fears and nourishing ideas so you can get your juices flowing again. *#10430/$14.99/176 pages/paperback*

**Writing the Blockbuster Novel**—Let a top-flight agent show you how to weave the essential elements of a blockbuster into your own novels with memorable characters, exotic settings, clashing conflicts and more! *#10393/$18.99/224 pages*